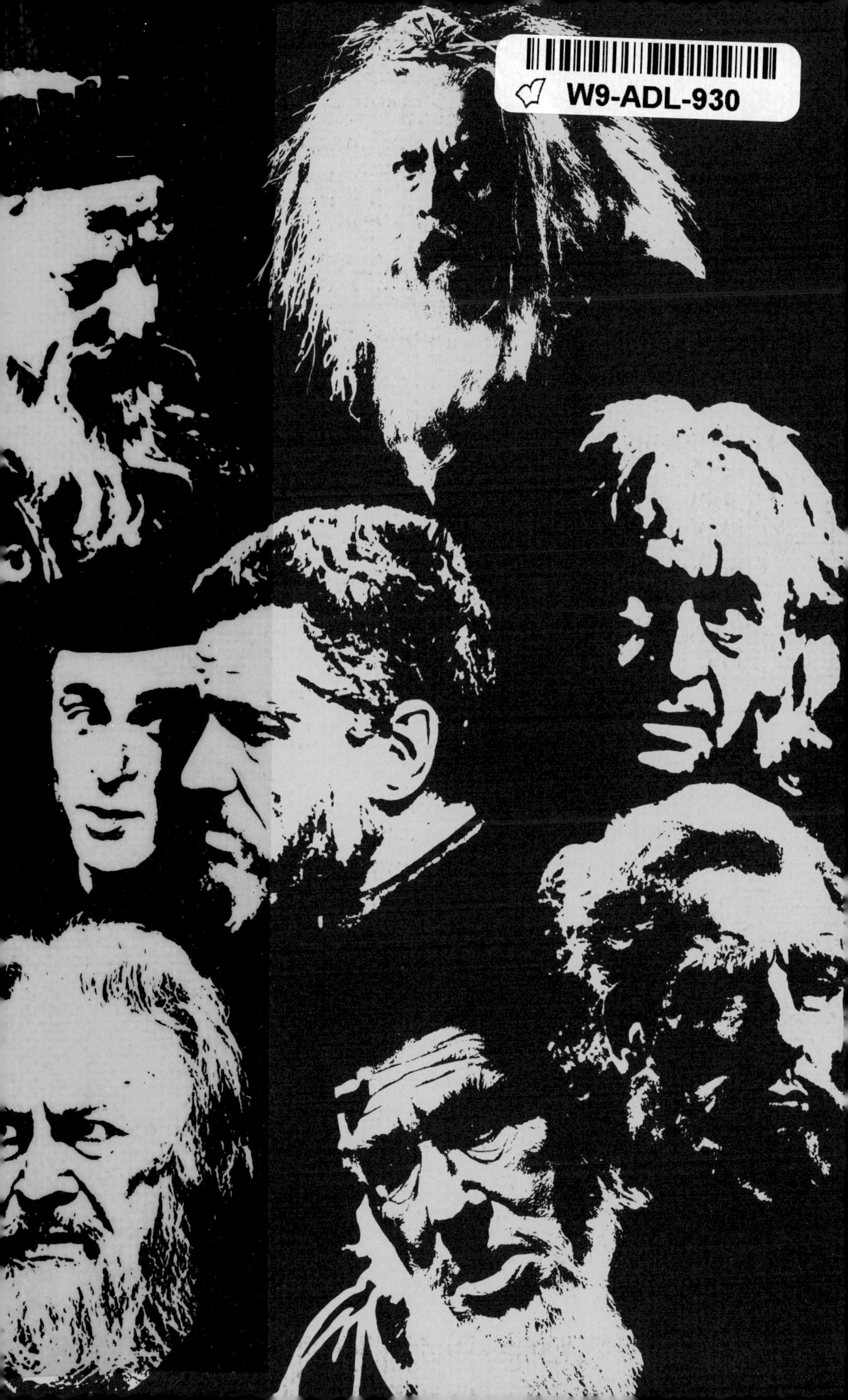

THE MASKS OF KING LEAR

THE MASKS OF
KING LEAR

BY MARVIN ROSENBERG

UNIVERSITY OF CALIFORNIA PRESS

BERKELEY, LOS ANGELES, LONDON

University of California Press
Berkeley and Los Angeles, California

University of California Press, Ltd.
London, England

Copyright © 1972, by
The Regents of the University of California
Second Printing, 1974

Library of Congress Catalog Card Number: 74-115492
ISBN: 0-520-01718-8
Printed in the United States of America

Cover and jacket emblems by Lloyd Hoff

Endpaper photographs: Harvard University Library,
Birmingham (England) Public Library

To Dorothy

Contents

Preface

King Lear was written for the stage, to stimulate sense, feeling, and mind in a massive theatrical experience. Any evaluation must consider the artist's use of all his arousal materials. First, the written language—its texture and imagery, the raw stuff of the verbal poetry; then, the visual and aural imagery—the theatre's poetry of sight and sound. Accordingly, as in *The Masks of Othello*, I will juxtapose the major interpretations of *Lear* by critics experienced in the mysteries of the written words and the major theatrical conceptions of the artists most sensitive to Shakespeare's gestural language—the distinguished actors of England, the Continent, the United States, and Asia. The various stagings of important scenes will be recreated in detail, against a background of the critical visualizations. My own interpretation, based on my experience of the tragedy, organizes the study.

The history of the play in theatre and criticism was pieced from hundreds of books, essays, periodical reports, memoirs, and acting versions consulted, as well as from my notes on performances and rehearsals attended and actors interviewed. To manage all this material I have used a simple reference technique: the bibliography lists all sources; the notes to each chapter list sources (with page numbers) consulted for that chapter.

I assume a general accuracy in the reviews of performances, though sometimes they disagree among each other, or with the comments actors themselves have provided. What is important is how much illumination the synthesized image may lend to our understanding of the play.

1

Actors are identified by nationality and dates of performance in the bibliography. The text assumes some acquaintance with the distinguished American and British actors; where relevant they are placed chronologically. The non-English actors and productions are sometimes identified as such, since cultural contexts may affect interpretation, as in Grigori Kozintsev's staged and filmed Russian *Lears*. Often, however, nationality, or even period, is not significant; German, French, or Italian stage business may be indistinguishable from British. Some actors are not named because, like some critics, they add nothing to earlier illuminations of the play. So repetitive are many of the actors' patterns that the examples of each must be restricted, and only those are reported that contribute to the synthesis. A production may be cited for its director or its decor or conception or a single role in it. Inevitably my selection will leave out bits of interpretation that individual readers will miss; I would like to hear from such readers, from anyone who has anything to teach me.

Where the historical background is important—for example, when the Jacobean cultural context illuminates *Lear*'s meaning—I refer to it. I do this with some reservation. We must be assiduous to discover the denotations of Shakespeare's words, hence my search through the dictionaries and other references; but evidence from outside the play as to the relevance of contemporary thought to Shakespeare's writing must be used with care. The playwright was not primarily reflecting establishment *mores*; he dealt in the fantasy life that often functions precisely to counteract society's superego. Some people in the first *Lear* audience may have judged Cordelia by those stern Elizabethan admonitions that children should obey parents, but the play obviously challenges this, as do such other Shakespearean fantasies as *Romeo and Juliet* and *Othello*. The thrust of the *Lear* art work is clear from the language as we know it. Audiences then as now could be relied on to be generally on the side of Lear, Cordelia, Fool, Kent, Gloster, Edgar, and Albany, and against their enemies. The complex shadings that modify and discolor these sympathies and antipathies likewise declare themselves almost always in unmistakable verbal and visual images.

My own sense of *Lear* was enhanced by the privilege of sitting in on some two months of rehearsals as directed in Berkeley by Robert Goldsby and designed by Henry May. Apart from the value of this experience, it provided me with clues to the play's language that justified putting the text through a computer (with the indispensable help of Paul B. Augst) with results that will appear in the book; and also made possible two experimental approaches: one, a psychological examination—in association with Frank Barron—of the roles, and the actors, as they developed during the rehearsal process (see appendix); two (because, alas, critics can never again come fresh to *Lear* for the first time, and so we miss some of the primary excitements), a study of how spectators (designated in the text as "naive"), unfamiliar with the play, invited to see it, responded to the expectations designed in the characters and action.

Without the help of many actors, designers, scholars, critics, librarians, and students throughout the world, without the patient readings in the manuscript by colleagues, I would not have been able to make this study what it is. Thank you, Paul Scofield, John Gielgud, Maurice Carnovsky, Eric Porter, Jack MacGowran, Alan Howard, Michael Williams, Brian Murray, Ian Richardson, Donald Wolfit, Josef Svoboda, Fred Harris, Jean-Bernard Bucky, Douglas Johnson, Nevill Coghill, Mary Bell, Louis Mackay, Norman Rabkin, Stephen Booth, Elizabeth Key, Terence Lamb, Dana McDermott, Charles Shattuck, Jerzy Got Spiegel, Bretislav Hodek, Elemer Hankiss, Grigori Kozintsev, Inna Levidova, Peter Milward, Jean Georgakopoulos, Manfred Boetzkes, Terence Spencer, Waveney Frederick, Paul Myers, Alexander Anikst, Gunnar Sorelius, Joseph Kerman, Marco Mincoff, Nigel Rollison, Ingrid Dahl, William Schrixx, Attilio Favorini, Valentina Komarova, Alan Badel, Thomas Tolmasoff, Edgar Reynolds, and thank you, Max Knight, my editor. Thanks to Lloyd Hoff for the beautiful cover and jacket drawings. Thanks to the University of California Research Committee; and to the University's Humanities Institute, for help one summer. A boundless thanks to Mary Rosenberg for seeing the book through with me.

No critical method, no amount of line-by-line para-
phrase or interpretation, will ever envelop the whole experience of this work. The nature of great dramatic art is
dynamic: there can be no single, absolute image of Lear,
or Cordelia—or of Shakespeare's other characters—because
the final shaping depends on the virtuosity that the actor—
or visualizing critic—brings to the image. In an open-
ended creation such as *Lear*, there is always something
more. But the attempt to encompass the work, on stage
and in print, will go on; and we must try every useful approach that promises insight.

> If more thou dost perceive,
> Let me know more.

M.R.

The Design

The design of *King Lear* resists definition. The play insists on communicating on multiple levels, in multiple styles, to the senses, the feelings, the intellect. Theme, action, language, spectacle, and character are sustained by paradox and contradiction, but these are only elementary clues to the whole. Paradox and contradiction imply polarities, pairs of conflicting terms; in the *Lear* dialectic, many voices confront each other.

Any critic of the play willing to find a unifying thematic assertion in it—that men learn through suffering, that they do not, that the gods are just, or unjust, or heedless, or random, or absent, or imaginary, or anything else—can find a counterassertion, if he will look for it. Similarly, the actor of Lear, tempted by a clear, bold character pattern—the titan brought low, the father driven mad by ingratitude, the bumbling fool-king learning wisdom, the wise monarch descending to madness, the tough autocrat ground down by an absurd universe—thins the design by simplification. There is always more, and always flux.

What holds the play together, then? Nothing, its detractors say: it is a crudely told fairy tale, unmotivated in character, its personae black and white; it is a patchwork of incongruities, of uncontrolled dramatic devices; Shakespeare tried to do too much, he couldn't manage his material; the play is formless.

No. The restless dialectic shapes the design. A firm artistic control makes of the ambiguities and paradoxes a system of reciprocating tensions. The counterpointing of motifs that sustains this dynamic keeps the ultimate mystery of art. Attempts at defining it always reveal further depths. "Mirroring," one aspect of the counterpoint technique has been called—when an action or character obliquely reflects that of another action or character—but this stops at the looking glass; the confronting image may be beyond the mirror, in an antiworld: a man sometimes stares at the reflection of an animal. The metaphorical web that unites the play's polar opposites is never fixed; it changes and develops as the characters and action do.

The highly charged visual and verbal imagery—the raw stuff of the *Lear* dialectic—has the same restless ambiguity. Sometimes the two imageries complement each other: as when seen, physical blindness echoes the language of unseeing. Sometimes word and sight-sound ram head-on: the language of love is spoken by those who hate. Or the words themselves strain with contradictory meanings. A nuclear word like "nature" may fission into multiple significances, including antimeanings: a "natural" son is "unnatural"; Lear calls on nature to destroy nature. The language of gesture likewise echoes and denies: a royal fist shaken in kingly robes is mocked by the same gesture in a beggar's rags; on the chain of being a king's command is at another extreme from a fool's cry, but in a looping world where opposites seek each other out, it is also closest to it.

The words are the primary clue to the Lear system of world and anti-world. Not only the large words, so full of reverberant meanings (I include some variant forms): *heart,* 44; *nature,* 46; *poor,* 48; *eye,* 50; *life,* 54; *love,* 60, *father,* 70. Their energies and the energies in their evoked opposites contribute to the play's turbulence; but they are themselves activated by a verbal structure of simpler, smaller language units. Listen to continuous rehearsals of *Lear,* and small skeletal words begin to assert themselves, to announce substructure, the bone and connective tissue in the threshing about of the great body. Run the whole vocabulary mass through the computer, and these words, in their frequency, come clear, words that the old concordance makers did not report, because they are so small. It is a small word, at the center of the *Lear* world, that best reflects the whole dynamic—almost the smallest of words: *if.* *

Well over a hundred times the word sounds, more than twice as often as the substantive words. If . . . if . . . if . . . The word is symptomatic. The *Lear* world is a world of uncertainties. Even the eternal basic values Shakespeare affirms—love, kindness, loyalty—have corrupting shadow sides. Nothing is sure in this world, not bonds, power, cunning, wisdom, service, disguise, gold, the gods, men, animals—if they are a different thing; not hate—or even love itself; not family, or friends, nothing on this side of the grave—and there may be no other.**

*When Marvin Spevack's concordance came out, I checked my computerization against it. I not only confirmed the word patterns discussed here in *Lear;* I found that Shakespeare uses variations of these patterns throughout his plays; and going on from there, I discovered that his contemporaries, and even modern playwrights, have exploited some of the values of this language structure. (This will be the subject of another discussion.) But no other writer has mastered it as Shakespeare did; and in no other of his plays is the verbal machinery so fused with the dialectic of character and action as in Lear.

**Other words of expectation (*rather, whether*) serve the same purpose as *if;* and *if* itself may be swallowed into subjunctive forms: *had I, could I, would I,* and so on.

More small words such as *if*, that help shape the design of the play, will be observed in action later; but note now that in this *if* world where fulfillment of expectation is tenuous, *but* occurs even more often (122 times), *yet* about half as much—appearing either as intensifiers or in their more common role as interrupters, casting doubt on what has gone before, complicating expectation, equivocating. Number words (*one*, 42, *two*, 19, etc.) impart additional energy with their implications of differences. The proliferation of alternatives, the uncertain balancing, are similarly evident in the many appearances of *or* (61) and *nor* (35), and in the multitude of adjectives of measure, in simple, comparative, and superlative form (*little, any, much, more, most, well, better, best*, etc).* Criticism is familiar with the force of the *nothings*; at the other extreme are almost four times as many *alls* (95)—aptly, for much in the design strains between all or nothing.

The play stretches toward extremes, beyond extremes, where words ultimately fail, where language abdicates before the unspeakable, and only gesture or silence function. The love Cordelia cannot bear to say comes to *nothing*; the pain that Lear will feel cannot be said, only howled. Roles reverse sharply: men move from base to top, from throne to mire; values zigzag: all offend, none offend. Men should not treat animals as they treat each other in this play; but men are animals, too, and make animal sounds. The words and sounds reflect the nervous equilibrium of the whole system: the conditional mood permeates it, unsettles it, infects it with the whipsaw of choice. There is, accordingly, much interrogation, a wondering of which? who? why?—a multitude of question marks, asking, asking, from Fool's insistent riddling to Lear's cosmic puzzlement:

> Who is it that can tell me what I am? (I, iv, 238.) Is man no more than this? (III, iv, 105.) Why should a dog, a horse, a rat have life. . . ? (V, iii, 306)**

Aptly, in this impossible search for understanding, the word *know* in various forms, and in various degrees of certainty, occurs over a hundred times.

The totality of the *Lear* maze is formidable; sometimes criticism, unable to penetrate the whole depth, has settled for discerning limited dimensions. In particular, the visual imagery has been scanted, the mean-

---

*For convenience, I will sometimes lump comparatives and superlatives together as "comparatives." Other frequent tension words include adjectives like (I note one form of each here): *great, dear, long, short, low, common*, and intensifiers like *very, ever, even, every, each*.

**Line references follow, generally, the Arden edition, edited by Kenneth Muir.

ing of the play as it must be seen and heard in the theatre ignored; and the next step has sometimes been to deny that the play, written for the theatre, even belongs there. This is the stance of critics who, under the guise of admiring Shakespeare's poetry, are damning him as a failed playwright. First among these was Charles Lamb who, safe in his study, imagined a Lear whose whole suffering was conveniently of the mind—and thus spared himself confrontation with the brutal details of the body's experience that Shakespeare nailed into the portrait. That poor Lamb should stray so far from engagement with the art object is perhaps understandable: during much of his critical lifetime there was no *Lear* at all in the theatre, in deference to the "madness"* of George III; and when a so-called *Lear* was played, it was Nahum Tate's hideous corruption from the Restoration.

Nahum Tate drained the realistic from the *Lear* dialectic: his kingly king stereotype did not weep, had no unseemly Fool, had the regal grace not to die at the end, but live happily forever after, along with Cordelia and her beloved, an Edgar fully as noble as any parchment hero of melodrama. Tate subverted Shakespeare's form by taking out of the *Lear* world the *if*, the ambiguity, the antiworld. Sensitive critics have similarly retreated from the tragedy's complexity, to seek a gestalt more comfortably comprehensible. Thus A. C. Bradley saw within it a kind of morality minuet: the good confronting the bad; and more recently Maynard Mack, alert to some aspects of the play's dialectic, but determined to find a homiletic structure in it, and skeptical of its theatricality, discerned "characters who are pure states of being, unmixedly good and bad." This means ignoring insistent moldings in the roles. Typically it was with some dismay that Bradley admitted in Oswald the "good" quality of loyalty while he resolutely missed the darkling sides of Edgar, Kent, and Lear—and, ultimately, the shadow side of their world. Decorum has in this way persistently tried to deny Shakespeare the theatrical as well as poetic multiplicity of his art. The physicist's hypothesis of "complementarity"—mutually contradictory elements coexisting—may apply to Shakespeare's work, Norman Rabkin has observed; nowhere more than in this play.

King Lear must be staged in a mode that explores the full dimensions of its dialectic, if the whole of Shakespeare's design is to be perceived. The universal in *Lear* has meaning as it reciprocates with the harsh details of living that are meant to be forced deliberately, often brutally, on the senses of audiences. The throned, ritual king must unbutton on the

---

*Medical science now suggests it was a biological abnormality.

straw of a hovel; through the ritual furred gown, later torn, a half-naked aging body must appear. Implicit in Lamb is the assumption that only the gestures of written language can bear the universal implications of art. But visual language came first; its symbols stir deep responses partly because they are rooted in the flesh that responds. So Shakespeare made the tissue and function of the physical body omnipresent in *Lear*, in name and action: arm, leg, hand, skin, hair, face, eyes, nose, cheeks, tears, blood; the body suffering, or being made to suffer, by blinding, tripping, striking, biting, bleeding, wounding—itself or another—and killing. I stipulate here not only the verbal imagery of tortured bodies that Carolyn Spurgeon recognized, but the bruised flesh, the very thing itself, as a central symbol in the design. The sight of Gloster's bloody eyes, of Lear holding the "challenge" up before them for Gloster to read, are as integral to the whole as the line

Bless thy sweet eyes, they bleed (IV, i, 53).

As well take from the drama of crucifixion the nails in the flesh, the vinegar in the parched mouth, as the physical details of this tragedy. Shakespeare did not make the smell of mortality a remote platonic image: he designated the reek of a man's hand, sweet, sour, made of sweat and skin, a nose reacting to it, offending flesh rubbed vainly against rags, wiping at what can never be wiped off, and a voice crying out against it. The mingled stench and perfume of transient flesh is, insistently, an integral part of the dialectic of Lear's world. This world is made of sight, sound, and word, and it cannot be comprehended unless the three components are perceived in a single gestalt.

The characters inhabiting this dialectical world are, appropriately, never fixed entities, but dynamics, sustained by the tension among their conflicting values and impulses. Each character will have to be seen as a spectrum of possibilities and be identified in terms of movement between the poles of the spectrum, for example between loving and hating, approaching and withdrawing. Lear will be the prime example; but such other "good" characters as Kent and Edgar, such "bad" characters as Goneril and Oswald, will also be mobile within the more limited spectrums of their designs.

The characters cannot be analyzed as "real people"; they are designs made of heightened, controlled words, sound, and movement to fit the artist's larger intent, and I will speak of them as designs. But in their making went selected materials of instantly recognizable humanity; and as each design is validated partly by the authenticity of these materials, so I will search them out as the actor must who seeks the human centers of the roles. The characters need not be found to have the "consistency" of living persons—who have little enough "consistency." In fact, the more complex and ambiguous *Lear*'s characters, and the more (like Lear and Edgar) they range turbulently, even erratically, between the poles of their dialectics, so much more—despite the distancing of the language and incident—are they "lifelike" for audiences.

The dialectic design of *Lear*'s action may be apprehended best by musical analogy. The first movement with Gloster, Kent, and Edmund, the calmest opening of the major tragedies, swells with apparent serenity to Lear's entrance, and his announcement of the love auction. A seemingly secure, majestic tonic chord is established: Lear is safe on his throne, his loving family surrounds him, a future of great harmony, free of strife, is projected.

But even in these first moments, the tonic, as in music, implies its undermining dominant forces: Lear's own insecurities, and the tensions between him, his daughters, his subjects, his friends, his state, and the tensions among these elements themselves.

The undertones of the dominant storm and overwhelm the tonic as Lear breaks out against Cordelia, then Kent. But the tonic is not extinguished, and as the play goes on, a return to its relative stability seems, to a naive spectator,* continually possible—even promised. The action develops as a series of tensions between these tentative movements to reestablish the tonic equilibrium and the countering, anarchic dominant strain.

---

*See introduction. "Naive" will refer to some spectators at *Lear* who had never before read or seen the play, and who reported their responses.

Act I, Scene i

The first words and the first visual images of *Lear* awaken the if-but-yet disequilibrium that energizes the play:

Kent: I thought the king had *more* affected the Duke of Albany *than* Cornwall.

Gloster*:   It did *always seem so* to us; *but now* in the *division* of the kingdom, it *appears* not *which* of the Dukes he *values most*; for *equalities* are *so weigh'd* that curiosity in *neither* can make *choice* of *either's moiety* (I, i, 1–7).

The persistent pressure of uncertain alternatives is enforced by the whole texture of the passage, but the italicized words are especially forcing, in this, their first of many appearances. *But* will again and again reverse the flow of thought. *More* will recur in the play some 80 times, *most* 50, in a large company of comparatives and superlatives charged with asymmetry. The insistent divisioning will announce itself by name in the constant, rival measurings, as above, of time, substance, and value, and in the verbs of uncertainty, wonder, appearance, doubt, choice. Intensifiers will enhance the dialectic force of the verbs and adverbs—thus, *so* will recur about 130 times. The *either* and *neither* are pure symptoms of the if-but-yet world. These words, and the conditional intent and structure of many sentences, will play against the recurring pattern of balancing phrases evident in this passage.

The action, similarly, projects at once visual signs of tension and division. The first sight of Gloster, Kent, and Edmund asserts acute cleavage —between age and youth. Two lines later, explicitly and in subtext, the division is dredged deeper with related divisions: between father and son, and between father-and-child-of-nature and father-and-child-by-law. Visually, a contrast in values is immediate: the older noblemen dress and move—now—with the easy power and ornament appropriate to their rank; the young man's dress and behavior belong to his ambiguous station.

With Gloster's first reference to his son, the materials of feeling enter

---

*I will use this spelling for convenience and consistency.

the design. The Gloster image will be made of some of the same strokes as Lear's; but where the tones of sensuality are repressed in Lear for many scenes, for Gloster they are painted in quickly here—and only here. Against his first leering note will be played all the resistances of the later Gloster pattern. Now it sets the atmosphere: the father derides the bastard boy, speaks jovially of the boy's mother, a sportive whore. The father says this before the boy, as if the boy were nothing. The boy hears. I will speak later of the underlying satisfactions of the motif; but note here the clear, if soft, sound of Nemesis. A father who carelessly rouses the image of the primal sexual act to inflict pain on his son in the fantasy life of fiction does so at great peril to himself. This father has blushed to acknowledge the boy; the boy will indeed bring blood to the old man's cheeks: cheeks now *braz'd*—hardened—to the shame of this illegitimacy. *Shame*—this is to be a central motif of the play.

The dialectic within Gloster is still muted now. "Good," Bradley would classify him; but he is too subtly made for that, even when he will seem the most "good"; a denying struggle will go on inside. His assurance in private with Kent and Edmund will diminish to public subservience before his superiors and his gods, until he turns—and turns again. He would have all well, yet will endure torture rather than be traitor. Courage will wait upon timidity; servility will swallow the assaults of arrogance until decency will, momentarily, be roused; self-reproach will ambush licentiousness, impulse will betray prudence, despair will play at seesaw with hope. The complex dynamic is sometimes oversimplified in the theatre as well as in criticism. One stage Gloster *manqué* missed the lecher part, seemed, at the outset, "hardly the man to get 'sport' out of Edmund's making, let alone boast about it." Gloster has been played, too, a Polonius, "an ineffectual dodderer" from the start; but this undercuts the later, intense countersurges.

As a small-scale mirroring of Lear, a distorted and sometimes reversed reflection, his conflicting urgencies are always implicit, but in this opening scene, once Lear enters, Gloster's part in the design is diminished almost to nothing verbally, and his self-revelation will be almost solely in the visual imagery of face and physical movement. Shakespeare will use Gloster's body later for some of his most eloquent visual gestures; here it is constrained by subordination: in the theatre the character design now shows in "complacency . . . concern . . . fear of disagreeing . . . obsequious bustling." We will learn later how outraged he is by what Lear does—but whatever his body may signal, never a word of objection will he speak before the court.

Kent, of the first trio, is by contrast outspoken; and since he seems in broad outline drawn so firmly on the side of Lear, he too is often labeled "good"—"loyal, sturdy, faithful to the end; courageous; steady, sensible, Stoic." Put down the trouble he causes Lear to over zealous devotion, and he may be seen—and on the stage and in criticism has been seen—an archetype of the simple, loyal friend who will follow a hero to any end. So he was as Perillus in the old *Leir* play; so Tate remade him. But Kent is a native of the cross-grained if-but-yet world, will swing erratically along the man-beast axis. His "goodness," his frankness, even his loyalty, are crossed with a dark savagery. His public and private faces will be largely the same, even when he is in rustic disguise.

Now his body, like Gloster's, is in the disguise of civilization; later, like Gloster's, though less violently, his flesh will be seen to endure the loss of mask, change of mask, bodily insult, decay, and submission to death. Kent's age is important visually: he is Lear's old friend and associate; he will, when disguised in I, iv, say he is forty-eight—perhaps understating in order to be taken on as an attendant. *Greybeard . . . old fellow,* Cornwall will call him. He will age with Lear, and be ready to die when Lear does: *I have a journey shortly to go . . .*

Kent will choose his second disguise and will wear it when next he meets and crosses swords with Gloster's bastard boy. Now, as they measure each other:

I must love you . . .
I shall study deserving . . . (I, i, 30–31).

they wear the masks of men, of social personality, the visual and verbal design is all surfaces; furred gowns and smiling faces seem to hide all. The hidden demons, unspeaking except by implication, must be known by the actors' silent projection.

Edmund's young outside is smoothest of all, unmarked except for the passing lash of his father's affectionate contempt. We need to remember that the Quarto's directions invariably, and the Folio's almost so, designated him simply as the *Bastard.** Later editors have ordinarily censored this; but it is a name as well as a role. The angry Albany will remember to call Edmund, in his glory, *half-blooded fellow.* Now Edmund's private winces are his own; he is used to presenting bland surfaces. He is surely the most physically attractive of Shakespeare's villains. Where Richard and Iago lament their comparative ugliness, where Aaron is

*I will also use this designation occasionally.

beautiful in some beholders' eyes, Edmund is admired by all who know him—or who, until very late, actually do not know him, but his mask. He will wear his surfaces shining until the end. Edmund aims high, highest, and moves on a steep ascent.

Lear's fall to unaccommodated man, to the very base, is intersected by the Bastard's rise, up past Gloster's falling star to within a hand's grasp of the throne itself. Edmund will rise as the old men do fall; and so in the theatre the first scene sometimes begins with him alone on the stage—eyeing the throne? trying it?—and then the old men chaffering around him, the meaning of what they say reflected in his beautiful face. The temptation is to make his clothes as beautiful; and one production began simply with a single light on Edmund, in a "magnificent red cloak," center stage. But magnificence is a garment he has yet to wear, that will depend, as the *Lear* world does, on *ifs*:

> if this letter speed,
> And my invention thrive ... (I, i, 19–20).

The chief role Edmund will play is the playing of roles; here his part is the modest, diffident outsider, suffered to be at court with his father for the briefest of interludes—unless he can quickly find some reason not to be sent immediately away again. In his subordination there may be the touch of a menial: he may carry the map for Gloster, serve quickly at a gestured command. Kent, casually or in condescension may, however politely, snub Edmund's offer to study deserving, turn his back; alternatively, he may offer Edmund a warm greeting to repair his humiliation. In the Peter Brook-Paul Scofield *Lear*, Edmund developed the business of polishing Gloster's boots, until Gloster thrust him away. Edmund here may perhaps even be seen living in the shadow of his brother. Edgar is not named in the stage directions; but assume he has become—as Regan and Edmund will say he has—one of Lear's attendant knights, and is now on stage helping prepare for the king's entrance. He might, then, exchange nods with Gloster, as in Grigori Kozintsev's (b. 1905) Russian film; this would cue the old man's

> But I have a son, Sir, by order of law, some
> year elder than this ... (I, i, 19–20).

For a moment the nobly attired legal son may cross smiles with his bastard brother. Edgar's loyal service to Lear could lend an additional irony to the later relationships of the two madmen, on heath and in hovel, specifically where Lear names him—renames him?—an attendant. But this is a speculation in visual imagery; and Edmund is our subject now. Since he is so much masked in this brief scene, the range of his possibilities is masked—and misleading. The archetypal undertones of his relationship to his father remain ambiguous: he is the younger, the underprivileged, the exiled, called Bastard. The conditions are often signs of a triumphant hero's beginnings, and indeed will almost reflect, in the antimirror, Cordelia's fate. Such underdogs often give us joy by topping the "legitimate." A naive spectator begins to expect here that Edmund will end in glory.

Another visual impression of Edmund is possible: if, at Gloster's command, he does courteous service at the entrance of Lear's company, he may attract briefly, almost unnoticeably, the attention of Regan and Goneril. Sometime their glances must first meet.

Lear enters and announces almost immediately the love auction, a major challenge to equilibrium, the forcing of choice against balance, the tonic evoking a subversive dominant. This scene is often a great one in the theatre; but it has given critics a good deal of trouble.

A legend has gone about that Goethe called the scene "absurd"—in the sense of ludicrous, incompetent—and so is sometimes cited by critics. Goethe did not call the scene absurd. He was commenting on the acting version by Friedrich Ludwig Schroeder (1714–1816), a distinguished German actor who, like Tate, was a bloody butcher of dramatic poetry. Schroeder had cut *Lear's* first scene entirely. Goethe wrote:

> in this scene Lear seems so absurd that we are not able, in what follows, to place all blame on the daughters. We are sorry for the old man, but we do not feel real pity for him; it is pity that Schroeder wishes to arouse, as well as abhorrence for the daughters, who are indeed unnatural, but not wholly blameworthy.

Cutting the scene suited Schroeder's purposes but, Goethe observed, it "annulled" the play.

Schroeder's butchery is a sample of the insults that *Lear* has suffered from both theatre and criticism. The theatre has sometimes gutted the art work of its essential ambiguity in order to exact sentimental audience response; criticism has sometimes abetted this misdemeanor, or pointed to the stage experience as a warning against trying at all to dramatize unplayable archetypal, mythic, inward elements.

Does the scene play? Can its full range and complexity be realized by the instrument for which Shakespeare designed it—the theatre? Or is it an artistic failure?

Begin with a sense of what the range and complexity is. The first

Gloster-Kent-Edmund lines have murmurs of doubt, alternatives, disequilibrium, but not yet awe or mystery. Kent and Gloster are puzzled, may even be troubled, by uncertainty over how the kingdom will be divided; but the fact of the division they accept. They may calmly go about lining up attendants, soldiers and courtiers for the king's entrance—Gloster assigning the least tasks to Edmund. All is remarkably serene for the opening of a major Shakespearean tragedy: no darkness, nothing uncanny or supernatural, no ominous conspiracy, no insistent ambivalence. There is no felt storm in the air.

Then the royal sennet is heard, and the court prepares for Lear's entrance. He may break in, followed by his entourage; his coming may be signaled by the growing expectation, even apprehension, of the assembled court. The unseen Lear, as in Kozintsev's film, may tease and tense court and audience with his chuckles at Fool—or with other sounds —as he approaches. Then, preceded by one bearing a coronet, he enters. He may pause as he moves past Gloster: the order to attend France and Burgundy offers a chance for the two old men to be caught together in an intimate moment that may be echoed in the mad interchange in IV, vi. But Lear presses on, impelled by his *darker purpose*.

Lear

Lear's immediate insistence on choice will enforce unbalance on himself and others; so that each will move toward intensifying disequilibrium, driving the pendulum further off rest. Lear's overt actions are the love test, his repudiation of Cordelia, his frenzied division of the kingdom and his exile of Kent. The problem of his motivation has been insistent for most critics: where does it fit into the design? Irrelevant, say the archetypalists: Shakespeare is working out a morality or a mythery, and was above "the psychological processes that ordinarily precede or determine human action" (Maynard Mack). Incompetent, say some others, like Leo Tolstoy: simply a bad job. The second stance is at least fairer to the craftsman: Shakespeare's source of artistic data was human behavior, and in his designs he used—for good or ill—its logic, heightened and distanced. But behavioral logic, in life or art, is not simple cause and effect: motives are cloudy, action emerges from a matrix of obscure impulses and counterimpulses residual in the character and his experience. Generally the more fertile the matrix, the more ambiguous and reverberant the issue. The design of Lear's motivation is as complex as any in drama; when it is narrowed to simplified "correlatives," the character is savagely diminished. Yet a synthesis of all major critical and theatrical interpretations begins to match the dimensions of the role. Here, simplified, are the main ones:

Lear is a barbarian, with primitive, untamed impulses.

Lear is senile.

He is old—with all the frailties, physical and mental, of age.

He is mad from the first.

He is not mad—but capricious: angry, impetuous, spoiled, wilful, unnatural, revengeful, proud, stubborn, tyrannical, implacable, lacking imagination, etc.

He is a slave of passion (wrath); though the very greatness of his passion reveals the greatness of his soul.

He is wise, loving, magnanimous, a tender father upset by ingratitude.

He is conditioned to rule, he cannot adjust to the rule by others, especially others whom he once dominated.

17

He is an archetypal king figure, living out its inevitable fate.

He is a troubled Everyman in the robes of a king.

He is selfish, narcissistic—needs love desperately, but cannot himself give love.

He is masochistic, self-hurting (moved even by a death wish), self-pitying.

He has a repressed incestuous attachment to his daughters, particularly Cordelia or Goneril.

He is regressive, mainly in the direction of a return to the womb, the shelter of the mother (here, too, the element of death wish).

His motivation is mysterious. (Sometimes an alternative for: Shakespeare failed.)

Some of these "motivations" seem mutually exclusive; and yet perhaps only one does not apply: that Lear acted the barbarian, out of a primitive world. This excuse for Lear's folly was a particularly welcome notion to nineteenth-century critics hunting for a simple logic for the character. He could be seen as a typical hot-headed, uncivilized Celt. Contemporary actors did not accept this rationale, but they did provide a context for it, for this was the time of the theatre "archaeologists," who, as we will see, sometimes recreated the imagined *Lear* epoch by hanging massive sets with the skins and furs of animals, dressing soldiers in rough leather and huge, horned helmets, and mounting their acting against painted drops brooding of ancient time.

But the play disclaims primitivism, except, in an ironical dialectic, the savage primitivism of sophisticated man—an irony Shakespeare seems constantly to have intended. The *Lear* world suffers the pains of civilization, with robed and furred gowns of wool and silk, women gorgeously dressed and perfumed, a court fool, an elegant nobility at home visited by princely courtiers from abroad, with justice advanced enough to be perverted, and a lavish monarchical economy so sophisticated it casually spawns the bedlam beggars and poor naked wretches of the audience's experience. The first stage of Lear's journey is from sophistication back to the primeval "thing itself."

At the outset, Lear asserts his distance from—and civilized kinship with—the primitive, when he casts off Cordelia; he is as likely now to neighbor, pity, or relieve her as

> the barbarous Scythian,
> Or he that makes his generation messes
> To gorge his appetite (116–18).

In our own century Australian mothers and fathers in the outback have routinely eaten their infants. As far as this from our world seemed the barbarian to Lear and his brilliant court, its dukes and earls, its knightly troops, its clever fool. There was violence in this world—though no more, surely, than colored Shakespeare's histories about Britain's recent yesterdays; and certainly it was not as primitive and barbarian as some of the excesses of the twentieth century, or its drama. The violence was deliberate, touched with atavism to link the characters with the clawed, fanged animals of their imagery. A sophisticated courtier tore out eyes: a touch of animal lurked behind the most elegant of robes, the most furred of gowns. A central theme of Lear's diatribe in IV, vi was that the surfaces were so glossy: the gold-plated men, the mincing women indulged the utmost pretensions of social polish, while being within so far down the scale of sensuality and lust as to be at the bottom —where hell is. On this axis—from the lowest lust-ridden insect, to the most tender and loving of mortals, from a vision of the diabolical to the divine—the characters of *Lear* move, and he himself moves with them.

On this axis, there is room for all the suggested motivations noted above. They do not together, any more than separately, provide a correlative for the tragic action: again, an essential of the play's form—as in most great tragedy—is disbalance between cause and effect. But the motivations do reflect the representational materials Shakespeare used to make the complex Lear image and the remarkable range of these materials. Some sense of that range is suggested by descriptives for Lear, very roughly divided into positive and negative, used by scholars and critics.*

Positive descriptives: absolute, acustomed to the chase, active, affectionate, alert, amiable, amused easily, athletic, austere, benevolent, brave, charming, cheery, civilized, contrite, deep-rooted, dignified, eager, eager in appetite, energetic, feeling, fierce, fiery, firm, fond, forgiving, frank, generous, genial, genius, good, good-natured, grand, great, grieved, hale, handsome, hearty, honest, hot-blooded, human, humble, humorous, imaginative, imperious, impetuous, impressive, impulsive, inclined to softness, inclined to tears, indignant, infantile, intelligent, jolly, jovial, kindly, kingly, large-hearted, like an oak, lovable, loving, lusty, magnificent, majestic, masterful, merry, mighty, monumental, moving, naïve, normal, old, outraged, passionate, patriarchal, pensive, piteous, pitiful, poetic, polite, powerful, proud, rapt, realistic, reflective, regal, religious, robust, roguish, roistering, romantic, rosy-cheeked, rugged, sagacious, sensitive, shrewd, sinewy, soft-hearted, sombre, stately, stout-trunked, straight-forward, strong, strong-willed, sturdy, sublime, suffering, swift, sympathetic, tenacious, tender, thoughtful, titanic, tough, trusting, understanding, unyielding, vehement, venerable, vigorous, virile, vital, warm, well-intentioned, well-preserved.

Negative descriptives: abject, abrupt, absolute, abstracted, absurd, afflicted, aged, angry, anxious, arrogant, autocratic, baffled, bent, beside himself, blasphemous,

The significance of the footnote terms lies not alone in their variety, but in the dialectic they express. Lear's design can never be caught in single terms—gentle, or violent, etc.—nor even in a succession of terms—gentle, then violent, etc.—but only, always, in a compound of terms: gentle-violent, strong-weak, etc. Nor is the design even this limited: within a single speech, many qualities may converge, Lear will move among a multitude—gentleness, violence, love, hate, anger, pity . . . Lear is not only never twice the same; he is almost never once the same. The character is a dynamic equation, the terms of which are constantly changing, new terms drawn in, vanished ones reengaged. The other characters are more or less similarly designed tension systems, but none touches the complexity of Lear: he is the primary if-but-yet character of his if-but-yet world.

In fact, Lear shares some characteristics of every other character, the "good" and the "bad." I resist, however, the gambit of seeing the other characters in the *Lear* world as making up Lear. All the characters have individual dialectics; Lear's design is only most complex, embraces the most human qualities.

To express the role's variety, Michael Redgrave (b. 1908), the British actor, found a metaphor from astronomy: Lear is not a single star, but a whole constellation. Solomon Mikhoels (1890–1948) the distinguished Russian Lear—Gordon Craig had never seen a better—drew his image from music:

---

blind, blind to his own fault, broken, brutal, capricious, careless, childish, choleric, churlish, complacent, confused, contemptuous, cranky, crass, craving to be loved, credulous, cruel, crumbling, curt, dazed, decrepit, deficient in judgement, degraded, deluded easily, demanding, desolate, despairing, despised, despotic, devious, devoid of passionate feeling, dictatorial, difficult, discarded, distrustful, doddering, eccentric, egotistical, escapist, explosive, fatuous, feeble, foolish, forbidding, forlorn, frail, fretful, frivolous, frustrated, furious, fussy, glum, gnarled, gray, grim, gruff, half-crazed, hard, harsh, haughty, headstrong, heartbroken, heart-weary, helpless, high-tempered, hysterical, idiotic, ill-balanced, imbecilic, impatient, implacable, incautious, infirm, inflexible, infuriating, injured, insane, insecure, intellectually isolated, intractable, irascible, irrational, irresolute, irresponsible, irritable, irritating, jealous, lonely, lost, mad, malignant, mastered by passion, megalomaniac, miserable, moody, muddled, naked, nerve-drawn, noisy, not wise, obsessed by his royalty, obstinate, opulent, pale, passive, pathetic, petulant, pitiful, pompous, pomp-spoiled, poor, possessed, primitive, querulous, raddled, rash, rasping, raucous, revengeful, rigid, rough, sadistic, sardonic, savage, self-deceived, self-involved, selfish, self-pitying, self-righteous, semi-barbaric, senile, sexually obsessed, shaggy, short-sighted, sick, silly, simpering, smug, snapping, snarling, spoiled, stern, stooping, storming, strange, stubborn, stupid, tearful, tempestuous, testy, tetchy, tired, tortured, tottering, tyrannical, unable to give love, uncertain, uncontrollable, undignified, ungovernable, unhappy, unjust, unpoised, unpredictable, unreasoning, unteachable, vain, vindictive, violent, weak, weakly fond, weak-willed, weary, whining, wilful, wrathful, wretched, wrong-headed.

[Shakespeare's art] is never a monody, and it is the actor's task to hear the separate notes making the character... They may be separated by quite an interval; on the other hand, contrasting and diametrically opposed notes may coincide in time.

To think of the Lear design as a series of chords is useful. Multiple tones are often sounded simultaneously as well as successively. Dominant resists tonic. Strength and weakness will pair in Lear: physical strength and psychic fatigue; spiritual force and bodily exhaustion. Similarly wisdom and folly will coexist, alternate, reciprocate; as will madness and sanity, age and vigor, love and hate, anger and kindness, authority and submission, conditioning and impulse. Lear will need to be absolute, alone; and dependent, nourished. These are the overt manifestations of the motivations noted above. On subtler levels, the Lear design suggests masked motives to which the names narcissism, regression, repression, incest wish, or death wish may apply. These are more elusive symbolic structures; I will examine them later in terms of the total aesthetic response the play evokes.

Since the Lear design, compounded of so many dialectics, was drawn to be perceived through eye and ear in the theatre, it had to be made recognizable to audiences, and so there are various familiar archtetypal gestalts assembled and opposed in it: king, father, man (old, wise, foolish, childish), child, lover, fool, madman. Thus the German actor of Lear, Eugen Klöpfer (1886–1950), described as half self-willed child, half violent-tempered old man, portrayed one of the role's dialectics. The playwright experimented elsewhere with combinations of similar archetypes; but never with so much friction among them, and within each one. Shakespeare restructured and distorted the familiar gestalts, sometimes blurred the boundaries among them. Never a king with so absolute —and apparently earned—authority so undermined by qualities and experiences deadly to his role. The image of kingly power leans on the archetype of wise old age, then collapses in a whirlpool of counter-images of decay, folly, and madness. King-father, man-father, mad-father, mad-man, man-child, man-animal, man-fool—they all clinch and coalesce. In Lear—as in the characters that surround him—the normal expectations of linear drama are established, and then often frustrated by a turbulence drawn from impulses that lie deep in human consciousness. The tragic sequence of events has a logic, but it is a psychic logic, as we will see.

Lear Enters

Such is the impulse to creativity and individuality that no major interpretation of Lear has been exactly like any other; and even when the distinguished actors and critics I cite discerned somewhat similar shapes in the design, they expressed these shapes differently, never in stereotype.

The moment the actor—or critic, in his mind—decides on his arrangement of the Lear character materials for the first entrance, he initiates a design that develops its own dramatic logic, and that logic enforces inexorable consequences in action and character. When a powerful, clearly sane, titanic figure comes striding across the stage—or the stage of imagination—he sets up expectations that often lead in a recognizable sequential cycle toward an end. An old, short, slightly mad figure that crawls hesitantly up the throne steps will point another way. In terms of first appearances, then, I will follow, with their variations, four general patterns found in the characterization: the archetypal titan; the hard, practicing monarch; the madman king; and the everyman-king. None of these designs is "pure"; each partakes of the qualities of the others; in some phases of the action all may fuse. They represent, for our purposes, different emphases on various elements in the Lear design; if we can observe how these emphases interact with the other character designs, we may be led toward a deeper experience of the work of art.

The archetype of the archetypal titan was Tommaso Salvini (1829–1915). A giant of a man, looking every foot a king, he entered on his court with a firm and heavy step, old but not aged, towering over his attendants, who gave way before him in awed respect. Salvini seemed at first invulnerable as he moved vigorously, cheerfully through the court, paused to inspect his kingdom, then regally mounted his throne. When a knight offered an arm to help him, he shook it off, with an instant, almost petulant rejection of any suggestion of weakness. The denial was itself the only whisper of weakness he now allowed.

This first image of Lear clothed in majesty just short of divinity, of power and grandeur never assailed and seeming almost unassailable, has

been a popular one in criticism, and it informed the acting of the role
in many countries and times: Edwin Forrest (1806–1872) in the United
States, Werner Krauss (1884–1959) in Germany in his earlier performances,* and Boleslaw Ladnoswski (1841–1911) in Poland. It suited best
the big men, like Salvini himself, or the men who could seem big, like
John Gielgud (b. 1904) in his 1940 interpretation, which followed
Harley Granville-Barker's dictum that Lear entered "more a magnificent
portent than a man." Gielgud's sudden advent was almost like a revelation, the great tall figure, the noble face with its patriarchal white hair
and beard—not wild, the beard carefully curled, civilized—in lavish
satin and rich furs, a great king proud in person and mind, in his hand a
giant staff that he wielded rather than leaned on. His entrance was like
an advance, until he reached stage center. There he suddenly stopped,
and with lordly impatience, struck the earth with his staff. His first
words to Gloster were rapped out, a command; then he handed the staff
to an attendant, and proudly mounted the throne. But under the power
was the human tremor, the little satisfaction: Gielgud remembered to
note that he felt pleased, happy. To such a king all courtiers will kneel
—and by so diminishing their stature, visually accentuate his.
    In Redgrave's Lear, an archetype of oldness, of almost timeless, nerve-
less age, was integrated with the image of authority. Redgrave used his
commanding height to show what time could do to immense stature: he
entered, an Ancient of Days, stooping and frail, the great bent back
barely carrying its burden as far as the throne, where he sat frozen,
immobilized, so old he seemed to smell old, isolated within the walls of
his age and the absolute power and grandeur of royalty. Salvini and
Gielgud, a half-century apart, were compared to blasted oaks; Redgrave suggested a great elm, that had survived the winds so long it was
decaying. So old, and still sane; the hidden fires almost dead: but dissonance persisted in the very rigid exertion of control needed to hold
age erect in the kingly robes, and in the incessantly working lower jaw
that suggested a narrow margin of self-control.
    The archetypal sense of a Lear who saw beyond this world—and
even in his gestures communed with it—was suggested by the German
Klöpfer. A giant to begin with, he would later be a wounded giant,
stumbling and groping in an ambiance that had become a void; then
a despairing, clumsy old father, every inch a man.
    Sustaining the unrest of Lear's inner dialectic presents a major prob-

---

*Later, Krauss would put more emphasis on the age and suffering. Krauss said:
"When you have the strength to play it, you lack the wisdom; when you have the
wisdom, you no longer have the strength."

lem to the titan image at the entrance. Much more than a facade must crack in the storm that will assault this image; it will yield, too, to counterforces alive within. The titan is flawed; the flaw authenticates the image as a work of art.

On the archetypal level, the authority of Lear is simply given; in the second mode of the power image, the authority seems earned as well as held: Lear is king by grace of toughness, arrogance, unrelaxed command. Such a power image was projected by Paul Scofield. The austere marble of the Salvini titan had been softened by an inner, Jove-like warmth, an inglow of kindness, even joviality. Scofield emphasized a practicing monarch at work: a hardbitten, despot-king used to ordering people about, getting things done, no nonsense, customarily feeding on flattery and fear. A thorny figure of rigid, cold arrogance, weary, old —but rock hard, grizzled grey, ramrod straight—very real, very deliberate, entering without ceremony, stalking straight to his hard wooden chair of a throne and holding himself stiffly in it. This Lear will look at each speaker, listen, the thoughts will slowly form, he will answer in a harsh, weary voice. This is a hard man to live with: he humiliates his family, makes enemies of his children, wades into folly with a deliberation that must evoke quite a different retribution than that of the titan who stoops to error. This Lear charges at the scales to unbalance them. A critical theory affected Scofield's director: Peter Brook took a cue from Jan Kott's vision of *Lear* as an *Endgame* world. But there was nothing in Scofield's Lear of the clown, the grotesque, that Kott saw; and Scofield said he never considered the Kott conception in his interpretation. His Lear was as immediate as life: a king who had known conflict, suffering, pain, and had few illusions. In the *Lear* film produced by Lord Birkett and directed by Peter Brook, there are lapses from Shakespeare's text and action, but Scofield's face, made large on the screen, is as beautifully complex as in the theatre. Lamb, to demonstrate the impossibility of producing *Lear*, had said that you might as well try to put one of Michelangelo's figures on the stage. Scofield's grave image, luminous as if graven from Michelangelo's warm marble, might be another vision of the sculptor's Moses. Scofield himself saw Lear as a characteristically hyperenergetic Elizabethan hero, rising to fits of intense feeling and activity that get out of control. Lear's toughness, Scofield felt, was balanced by his tenderness toward Fool, Gloster, and Cordelia. Audiences, Mary Bell has observed, responded sympathetically to the intensity of this Lear's feeling, and the inhibitions that kept it compressed behind his stony surface. Scofield suggested, among other images, a Teutonic grimness, reminiscent of a leather-jacketed, booted Prussian fieldmarshal. An earlier, somewhat kindred interpretation was that of the German, Ludwig Barnay (1842–1924), who conceived of a Lear of Prussian hauteur. He strode on proudly, head stiffly erect, turned his back on his court and treated his courtiers with arrogance and contempt. The stage Lear directed by Kozintsev in Russia was in this tough pattern; he began the scene at a chess table with Fool, ignoring his courtiers until he was ready to mount his throne and matter-of-factly announce his abdication* It has not been a popular conception, either in theatre or criticism: it may provoke a harsh, logical Nemesis almost frighteningly desentimentalized, and it risks suppressing the inner dialectic as much as the more sentimental Lears have done.

At a far extreme has been a third Lear, one from the beginning slightly mad, or senile. He usually projects an image of nobleness decayed, not quite responsible, driven to mistakes, helpless before the hardheaded. A critical theory prompted the first stage interpretation of this Lear. A. W. Schlegel had suggested that Lear began senile, and moved beyond childish imbecility toward the wildest insanity. Ludwig Max Devrient (1784–1832), probably the greatest German Lear, took Schlegel's cue, and played the role for the pathos in madness. He diminished the majestic, commanding side of Lear, and emphasized early helplessness in mind and body. He came in bowed down by the weight of his years, leaning on a crutch, crawling toward death, already a dotard: a cheerful, kindly old man, with no trace of melancholy, or ill humor, or despotic character. He exuded friendliness, even gaiety.

This conception was supported by some of the motive-hunting nineteenth-century critics who felt madness amply explained Lear's initial folly: some actors embraced it for this reason, and because it demanded pity from the audience, though their stage treatment varied in details from Devrient's. At one extreme was Ernesto Rossi (1829–1896), so detailed, so "physical" in his insistent madness that he generally offended his English audiences, though the French and Germans applauded his insane niceties. Rossi was certain that Lear began mad: the king's dispossessing himself of the kingdom, his acceptance of Regan's and Goneril's flattery, his rejection of Cordelia—these were to Rossi clearly the acts of a dotard. His hands trembling, his head wagging from age and uncertainity, Rossi came on first in a kind of chuckleheaded jig, danced around

*For his film Kozintsev wanted a Lear with the face of Voltaire. Juri Jarvet, his choice, played the role beardless, had a frank, naive quality, combined the curiosity of an old wise man with an almost childlike spontaneity.

his courtiers and dropped on the throne. The German Albert Basser-mann (1967–1952), playing an old, "touched" Lear, was less active, a slumbering volcano. Something of the confusion of a daydream seemed to infect the noble old Lear of August Lindberg, a Swedish actor-director (1846–1916): as if he could no longer sharply measure pro-portion, no longer distinguish between truth and falsehood, and yet sensed this deficiency enough to try to cover it in large words, to force himself to noblemindedness or contempt, rather than beg for the affec-tion he so intensely, and touchingly, wanted to give and get.

But this early madness could have dignity. Or be masked by dignity. So Edwin Booth (1833–1893) played it, as if the remainders of con-sciousness tried to shelter the inward disarray. The inner whipsaw was thus conveyed from another angle. The signs of senility were hidden—and made evident—in Booth's too carefully staunch gait: his voice steered narrowly over an undercurrent of quavers. There was a studied quiet and repose; this near-mad king would be noble in spite of all.

This was the mood of most of the mad Lears of the nineteenth cen-tury. They appealed to audiences accustomed to a play drastically di-luted of its violence—Gloster's blinding was almost invariably cut—and drastically refined: the allusions to sex were laundered or removed. Fool, if used at all, was often a kindly accomplice in rendering Lear a pitiable image—often of Gothic splendor: "a gentle glamor cast over a wreck." The most glamorous wreck of all was Henry Irving (1838–1905), whose mad Lear was a model of the mode. After much inward debate over the character, Irving decided the old king must have been mad—for a concrete reason: a sane British ruler would not have considered giving the largest part of England over to French rule. But a mad Lear, even an old, feeble, mad Lear, did not mean to Irving a first appearance dod-dering or dithering. Irving's wreck still had the outlines of a mighty titan in him, and echoes of the archetype of terrible authority mingled with the tones of pathos. Irving dressed his play in the fierce garments of a prehistoric time, and his first theatrical appearance, to the cry "The King is coming!" was at the head of a flight of stairs, where, furred and gaunt, he leaned on a huge scabbarded sword. He raised it in a wild cry in answer to the shouted greeting of his horn-helmeted guards, and strode down to his court. A rhythmic, repeated animal cry, accompanied by the staccato of spear butts on the floor, intensified the primitivistic ritual of this kind of entrance in James C. Dunn's production.

Copeau had the impression that Irving prepared for the unsteadiness of his unbalanced Lear by drinking; a Swedish Lear, Rune Turesson, play-ing the barbarian king (1970), a self-indulgent autocrat who thrashed

about in all directions with his whip, seemed tipsy enough that there
was ambiguity as to whether he was sane, insane, or drunk. His director,
Anita Blom, had at first engineered a great fanfaronnade for his entrance; but as she became convinced that Lear must be closer to normality, very human, she had him enter a rather coarse, foolish, jolly old
man, his arms around Goneril and Cordelia; as he passed Gloster and
Kent, he embraced them. His Fool, who had been enjoying sitting on
the high throne, caressing it, made way for him, and he looked down
on his court, purring.

The mingling of the madman-king archetypes so early in the play
would point to particular dramatic inevitabilities. Lear could not *become* mad; the storm madness would be another stage in a path that
would cross the fall of the titan.

A fourth general stream of Lear interpretation, very wide, moves
amorphously between the august king archetype and the very human
father driven to madness. It generally avoids the nearly allegorical extreme of either archetype, and insists on the human qualities staining
the imperial marble.

At one sentimental extreme, that was particularly popular in the
nineteenth century, Lear was simply the grieved father, kind, gentle,
good, murdered by filial ingratitude. This interpretation took at face
value Lear's self-assessment:

> A poor, infirm, weak, and despised old man* (III, ii, 20).
> old, kind father whose frank heart gave all ... (III, iv, 20).

In this version, the archetype of ruler, and even of man, was subordinated to that of old good father, much put upon. David Garrick
(1717–1799)—I hesitate to soil a serious discussion of how *Lear* was
acted by mentioning a performance of the Tate version, but Garrick did
lend his art to it, like a Stradivarius used for a fiddler's jig—Garrick set
a pattern for this conception. Garrick had to resist Tate's stereotype—
sometimes, as we will see, by providing Shakespeare's subtextual physical imagery for the lines Tate cut or mangled—and he used his genius
largely to bring life to the more intimate qualities of the role: "When
we see the little, old, white-haired man enter, with spindle shanks, a
tottering gait, and great shoes upon little feet, we fancy a Gomez, or a
Fondlewife." (The pantalones from Dryden's *Spanish Fryer* and Con-
greve's *The Old Bachlor*.) He spoke like a king; but he was a Good Old

---

*Support for this aspect of the character survives in a simplification in the elegy
to Burbage: he played "kind Leer." *Shakespeare Allusion Book*, 1, 272.

King, Tate's wronged parent, generally so well-behaved he could with
perfect poetic justice survive and live happily forever after with Cordelia and her Edgar, evoking from the audience "those gushing tears,
which are swelled and ennobled by a virtuous joy." To Garrick, Lear
was a "weak man ... old and weakly fond of his daughters ... an Old
Fool." Garrick's wish to differ from the current pattern set for the
Tate Lear (Barton Booth's [1681–1733] stately, regal ranter) may have
been an influence, but the evoking of response from audiences seemed
primary. To his contemporary rival, the statuesque Spranger Barry
(1719–1777), in the words of the rhyme, they gave huzzas; to Garrick
"only tears."

When William Charles Macready (1793–1873), in 1839—to his ever-
lasting credit—staged *Lear* with Fool* and much of the original text, the
first reasonably authentic production of which we have any record, he
inherited the tradition of the grieved father, long gone in age. Macready
tried—not always successfully in the eyes of reviewers—to restore the
image of strength. Macready:

> Lear's was in truth a "lusty winter;" his language never betrays in-
> becility of mind or body ... there is still [energy] to ride, to hunt, to
> run wildly through the fury of the storm, to slay the ruffian who mur-
> dered his Cordelia, and to bear about her dead body in his arms. There
> is, moreover, a heartiness, and even a jollity, in his blither moments no
> way akin to the helplessness of senility.

Actually, too hearty, too energetic, Macready seemed at first; he
learned to shade down the sturdiness, and as he grew older played Lear
older. He was not an actor of ultimate power, in his weakness he seemed
sometimes too weak, not Jovian enough; he countered this with a magnificent visual display of royal power, the trappings of grandeur: his
first entrance was preceded by

> twenty-four guards—twelve with spears, twelve with shields. Following
> them come twenty knights, Locrine [Macready gave this identity to a
> speaking knight] being one, then Lear's Physician bearing Lear's sword,
> an Officer carrying a map showing the division of the kingdom, then the
> Herald with Lear's crown. Then come six Ladies, followed by Cordelia,
> Cornwall and Regan, and Albany and Goneril. Lear then enters, fol-
> lowed by two Lords and four Attendants.

---

*I hope readers will not mind my naming Fool as others address him: simply
"Fool," not "the" Fool. Fool is not only his role, it is also his name. Edmund, on
the other hand, I call *the* Bastard because, though Shakespeare gives him the name,
he is not called by it.

Macready remained, primarily, the old, failing, failed father: as Alan
Downer puts it, he "contrived to remind the audience that it was wit-
nessing the sorrows of a person like themselves, to make them feel
emotionally for Lear as they did for Joe Gargery or Little Nell."

The "good old father" image, supported as it was by some critical
favor, became a pattern for many of the nineteenth century Lears. Since
the complex equation of emotional materials in the Lear design demanded some cross-graining even in this image, if it was to have any
validity, there were some notes of irritability, irascibility, anger. But
the symbols of kindness and love were dominant, and the darker tones
were strained through them. Typically, in Charles Kean's (1811–1868)
mild Lear, "tenderness [was] a channel through which phrensy finally
rushed upon the king and overwhelms him . . . not a particle of malice in
him." Kean, one of the new "archaeologists," staged the tragedy in a
prehistoric period, but there was nothing barbaric about his Lear: he
was of no time, a pleasant and pathetic old man from the moment the
curtain rose on his domestic tableau: old Lear discovered seated on his
throne, his two elder daughters at his knee, kneeling, Cordelia at his
feet.

Models of the grieved father driven mad by ingratitude were frequent in Germany. There, where theatre and criticism both reflected a
primary disturbance over Cordelia's filial disobedience, perhaps the
most extreme example was Heinrich Anschütz (1785–1865), well named
a "weeping Lear": a dear old man, emphasizing "the child in the king,
the helpless child, who gives and demands love and stretches out trembling hands for the pardon of a fellow feeling heart." This Lear entered
to divide his kingdom with an absolutely rosy optimism, with little of
the aura of majesty and mystery. The problem in such a design was how
to move from this toward tragedy. Anschutz, at his fiercest, would remain a farmer king, a bourgeois. This would be the fate of some Lears
with the highest ambitions, notably in France, where André Antoine
(1858–1943), who bravely produced in 1904 what was probably the
first uncut Lear since Shakespeare's century, could not bring enough
stature to his own performance, seemed more Pere Goriot than king,
more querulous than furious; or where, four decades later, Charles Dullin (1885–1949) in an equally ambitious try—at an absurdist interpretation—failed similarly to realize Lear's stature.

That it is possible to project, in this mode, a man-king of complexity and admirable contrapuntal dissonance has been demonstrated
by many distinguished Lears. One such was the Russian Mikhoels. His
entrance was almost an affront to the mighty archetypal image. Into

his lavish court, already assembled, he came dressed royally enough, in black and gold, his long cloak studded with crowns, like a dark sky with stars; but the image of royalty seemed to end here. Mikhoels was, like Garrick, short—so short he had been urged not to try Lear—and he felt this ruled out the pretentiousness of a beard, or the kingly grandeur of a proudly raised hand and other monumental gestures. But his size only partly determined his interpretation: he wanted also to suggest a quality of withered age, age holding to the past, and challenged to let go. He had passed beyond being wise to believing in his wisdom, in his power and authority; folly was close by.

When he entered, the ritual music that had marched the courtiers in, in slow balletic movements, stopped dead. The silence was for a little king who, except for his cloak, was any old, hunched figure, almost sexless. What he saw first was Fool on his throne. Lear would become Fool in midplay; Mikhoels seemed almost to have gone the whole way already. He went to Fool, took him by the ear, gently led him down, and at last turned to look at the court. Here Mikhoels introduced the first of several important, repetitive, thematic gestures. As he described it:

> ... as his daughters stand before him, their heads bowed, Lear slowly counts them with his finger ... Goneril and the husband, Regan and the husband—he sees that the fifth, Cordelia, is missing. Again he counts them all, and makes a querying gesture: Where's Cordelia? They point at Cordelia, the spoilt child who has hid behind the throne for fun, and this is the point where the first sound is heard—a feeble chuckle of the king. The chuckling Lear shakes his finger at Cordelia and, teasing her [giving an extra nudge to the line about her suitors], pronounces, "Attend the Lords of France and Burgundy, Gloster."

This chuckle was one of the echoing notes of aural and visual imagery we will observe Mikhoels using throughout the play to hint at Lear's inner dimensions, and to orchestrate the flight from his initial foolish wisdom. Now he chuckled his way to the throne, and sat where the other Fool had been.

The comic note, to be continued as theme and variation to the very end of Mikhoel's Lear, has often been made part of the character's polyphony. The Polish actor Jan Kreszmar (b. 1908) projected at first a mixture of powerful king and fool; he would later shed royalty to be fool literally, before his final stage of wondering man. Charles Kean sounded the comic note, but with little of the darker, savage counterpoint of more modern Lears. Sir Laurence Olivier (b. 1907) projected a kindred spirit: he came on informally, threading his way through his court, his snowy hair and flowing beard suggesting physically a wild,

Blakean figure, or an Old Testament prophet; but he seemed, at first, a slightly fussy, almost roguish, and very lovable, if at times irritating, old man. On the way to the throne he stopped to whisper to Cordelia, as though enjoying a private joke with her; he eyed one of his soldiers quizzically from top to toe and back again; he was bursting with an overflow of vital forces: from his brain at any moment might spring some plan, some scheme, half joke, half earnest which might, in a sudden change of mood, have serious consequences.

This quality of enormous, if often muffled energy, on a nervous trigger—a characteristic of all Shakespeare's tragic heroes—lay, in Charles Laughton's (1899–1962) Lear, deeply concealed under layers of fat, of age, of indolence. Laughton's was another "crowned fool", large, round, padded about the middle, a chubby Father Christmas—his face framed in soft, white hair and beard, looking like a cross between Falstaff and Moses. He came on ponderously, cheerfully, without crown, in a long, billowing, glistening gown that suggested variously a priest's robe, a nightgown, and a tent. Without any great effort at dignity he slowly climbed, an old fat Everyman, up the steps of his throne, and sat down comfortably to get on with his business. He seemed at first more an old Party leader than a king; only faint rumbles of the concealed counter-forces, the majestic anguish later to appear were hinted now.* In Lee J. Cobb (b. 1911) the energy was even more muted; he came in calmly, yawned, nibbled at food. A Lear directed by William Ball had already lost his power: in the hubbub of courtiers, an old man wandered from group to group, seeking attention, only to be ignored. Then his first lines, and his mood, exuded his frustration, loneliness, anger. Timothy West (b. 1934) suggested a historic image of transient power: his stocky body, bowed shoulders, the head thrust forward, the incipient decay, were reminiscent of the failing Winston Churchill.

In Maurice Carnovsky's (b. 1898) ritual entrance, on the other hand,

---

*The strategy of this characterization was observed by Harold Hobson: " . . . this absurdity of appearance is made the foundation of an extraordinary pathos later on. There is something overwhelmingly touching in the thought that the universe should pour so many sorrows, such a multitude of griefs upon a head that seems, deliberately seems, so undistinguished as this Lear's. Even a sort of magnificence develops from the gigantic disproportion between the punished and the punishment. That the universe should single out so small a figure for its wrath gives a lurid splendour to the performance; it is as if an ordinary man were called to crucifixion.

"That is the effect of this production; and it is an effect wrought with the most careful art. He would be a naive theatregoer indeed who supposed that Mr. Laughton's Lear is really small and ordinary. It is small and ordinary with an intensity far greater than the intensity of Lears who look grander but who weary us" (*Sunday Times*, August 23, 1959).

the leashed power made the air tremble. In the first of his series of performances he was a tired old man; but in the second, he led the royal procession up from a pit entrance like a kind of old demigod rising out of the earth, the power of age proclaiming itself in his proudly held shoulders, his broad back, his majestic rhythm. Lear, Carnovsky said, was "doom eager"; energy lay waiting to explode within him, as he sat on his low, fur-covered throne and peered about him. His eyes narrowed with his effort, he listened, hard, as if he was not satisfied with his sight, as if he needed to pierce beyond what he saw.

However powerful any one note in the first appearances of the distinguished actors of Lear, some contrapuntal tones sound in all of them, and in the greatest actors the full range begins to be heard. The most powerful Lear needs help as he enters, or will deny that he does; the weakest has a reservoir of strength that will fire his anguish; the most secure needs assurances of his security; the mad Lear will have a flash of lucidity, the foolish Lear a moment when wisdom seems possible; the sanest Lear a tremor of doubt of his soundness. As Lear enters to take his royal stance—usually to sit on some kind of throne—his inner dialectic must mainly be expressed visually, subtextually. Then he begins to ask for love.

The Scene

To discuss the set after the actors have entered it is logical here because the Lear symbol is so dominant a figure that the ground across which it moves must be subordinate. The restless oppositions of character, spectacle, and action by themselves provide almost all the eye-arousing spectacle Shakespeare intended: his physical stage, as Granville-Barker has noted, might well have been bare except for Lear's "state." The play's dialectic is partly visualized in the sharp juxtaposition of crowded scenes of bold pageantry and action with quick cuts to quieter moments of men alone, or in pairs. So the calm, prefatory opening with Gloster, Kent, and Edmund gives way to the massive interaction of Lear's abdication, which is followed by the tight dialogue of the daughters and then Edmund in soliloquy. Again, the developments to such big scenes as Lear's confrontations with Goneril (I, iv) and with Regan and Goneril (II, iv) are modulated by preceding intense, but lower-keyed, private encounters. Scenes move from within to without, from night to day, from field to camp. On Shakespeare's fluent space stage, the opposition and reciprocation of these elements made by themselves a dynamic tapestry.

As the theatre developed, stage designers, sensitive to the implications of the tragedy, have been impelled to use new techniques to make visual statements about it. I am not concerned with a history of these statements, but rather with the range—from the utmost realism of the early productions to the frequent modern efforts to escape actuality—as it illuminates the play.

Realism is not now in fashion in Shakespearean production; but given the eighteenth- and nineteenth-century devotion to romantic detail as a support to the drama, the impressive artistry of some of it deserves admiration, if not acceptance. It was often highly imaginative, the painters' symbolic means seeking to match the playwright's. Act I, i might involve not only the panoply of royal ritual, as in Macready's elaborate entrance (see "Lear Enters"), but also enormous set pieces, particularly as the "archeological" impulse developed. Thus, Charles Kean's first scene:

> The room of state is a long chamber, with an open roof like Westminster Hall.... The walls are decorated with the heads and horns of wild bulls, deer, and other animals of chase. Around and about are instruments of warfare, and instruments of the chase. In the center of the apartment, against the wall, is the throne of the aged monarch.

These solid furnishings to the imagination were the first to be dispensed with in modern production, partly because scene changes took so long, but also because a new artistic spirit demanded some of the same ambiguity and symbolic asymmetry in the ground as in the tortured figures that moved across it. Ground and figures tended to merge: places and things became related architectural forms, or free forms, extensions of the experiences of the actors. Meanwhile, another spur to the imagination was coming into primary use: the easy electrical control of light and dark, and in association, of sound.

A stripped stage, such as Antoine's, was the first modern imaginative stride toward—back toward—Shakespeare's *Lear*. The theatre became an impersonal platform again, to be furnished mainly with language and costumed action. But in the modern, enclosed theatre, even a bare undecorated multilevel stage made a statement about the play; and if a statement was to be made, the artists of the theatre wanted to articulate it. A designedly empty stage, an insistently empty stage, could be a shout of placelessness.

So the first scene of the Brook-Scofield staging emphasized the meaninglessness of the *Lear* world by beating down on a bare platform a hard, blazing white light. There was no comfort in this world, not even a curtain to shut the actors off: they entered while the house lights were on, into a flat, open stage, nearly emptied to emphasize its vastness. The fierce illumination banished any shadows of divinity, mystery, or superstition. The few objects in this world were themselves bare: Kent and Gloster went to a simple table for their preparatory talk; Lear sat on a rough wooden throne, the wood of which had been broken down to simulate wear, as had been the plain leather costumes. From above hung beaten metal thundersheets. This was a worn world; even Lear's map seemed to be little more than a faded scroll. Men seemed small on the bare stage—in a vast, heartless world. The bareness of Brook's stage was metaphysical, as well as actual, and carried over to his characters, who were muted in outward color, as the stage was.

Another statement of bareness has been social: that the old, patriarchal society has been stripped by the new men, the new, hard materialists. A further implication of this world, reflected by Shakespeare through the poverty images in the heath scenes, would emphasize its economic bareness: to assert the outer world of beggary not only, as in Kozintsev's Russian *Lear*, in the emphasized contrasts of lavish castle and bedraggled heath and hovel, but also by bringing the poverty close to the palace: lurking paupers on the fringe of the courtly rituals.*

A further distancing of representation has been attempted by minimizing the identity of *things* on the *Lear* stage, by using timeless, archetypal furnishings. Most commonly, these are monolithic Stonehenge-like shapes, often varying levels and stepways, that serve both as atmosphere and variable properties. For Gloster's castle in Act II, Appia designed a corridor of sloping pyramid-sided walls leading to the doors at the rear that Lear never entered; but for Act III, Appia used his favorite bare stage, with two series of steps and a veil as of cloud looming over it. Norman Bel Geddes formed massive rectangular pillars that towered over a stage empty except for steps; the columns made a well of the stage, but did not wall out space. For a Hungarian *Lear* (1960), Josef Svoboda suspended from the flies similar rectangular columns, their bottom surfaces giving off light that helped illuminate the stage. As the action became more oppressive for Lear, some of the pillars, moving lower, bore down on him. In a 1967 Japanese *Lear*, the opening darkness gave way, in swirling light, to a central ziggurat, spiraling upward with steplike levels for acting areas. Similar abstract forms were used in the Laughton, Donald Wolfit (1902–1968), William Devlin (b. 1911) and Redgrave *Lear*s: in the latter production, a central twisted, vaguely phallic pylon served as throne and, later, ironically, hovel in the storm and sickbed. Behind the throne, in the first scene, an abstract drop strove to reflect inarticulate images of the collective unconscious; but as the old man lived his anguish, against this background of *if*, he would be fronted on either side of the stage by the hard faces of the castles of Gloster and Albany.

The tension between the timeless and the now, the world of imagination and the real, has been suggested even when clearly representational decor has been used. Olivier's madcap Lear entered on a royal interior that opened, through an arch, on a view of crazy-colored roofs that seemed almost fairy-tale in their unreality. In Orson Welles' (b. 1915)

*Kozintsev, regarding his staged *Lear*: "Outside the palace is a landscape of . . . less well-fortified strongholds of feudal robbers. They are surrounded by emptiness and the rotting thatch of huts." In his film, the climate of poverty, waste, war is insistent. The opening scenes focus on human feet trudging along in shabby boots and ragged puttees. Then Lear moves through the poor homeless wretches whom he will soon be seen to join.

Lear, the castle that filled to the top a proscenium arch soaring almost beyond vision seemed to be a solid front of red and grey stone; and then at scene end it would, before the eyes of the audience, be lifted, limp canvas, lightly into the flies, as transient as Lear's pretensions. In the Mikhoels' version, time was dissolved in a design materialized out of Ur-time, of impressions Hebraic and Druidic; huge carved wooden figures, vaguely medieval, suggestive, Kozintsev thought, of the "folk-theatre . . . with its passion for bright colors and its synthesis of the real and fantastic," supported an upper acting area. Goneril and Regan moved halfway up the stairs to offer their love to the enthroned Lear looking down on them. For the Robert Goldsby production, Henry May flung a massive shelf across his broad, uncurtained stage, on buttresses of enormous, mythic logs; and created a world of cave and ledge from which the action flowed onto a raked apron that was anywhere. Kozintsev stood huge faceless statues of iron knights at the edges of his stage, figures hostile and uncanny, antihuman, seeming human. The intent was to suggest the "myth of civilization"—man trapped by the iron age he had made, imposing in its material beauty and splendor, but now hostile and dangerous to human society. Armed men in knightly armor projected this atmosphere live in the 1971 Norwegian *Lear*: they stood in cold, impersonal ranks, or moved in drill patterns, men of stone, in conical helmets and robes, enclosing or channeling the action, forming backdrops, corridors, courtyards, walls. The curtain for this *Lear* seemed made of old iron, rusted, smudged, gutted with black holes, seeming to decay almost before the spectator's eyes. Deep backstage the chief actors sat on benches when not in the play: they could be seen to come forward for entrances.* The intention, as Jan Bull, the director, explained, was to suggest that we are all dispassionate, detached spectators to the sufferings of others; the effect, some reviewers and spectators felt, was that the whole house seemed part of the play, anyone in the audience might be called on to participate. Sound accompaniments were mainly human—a choir voiced chants, laments, laughter, over music and drums and effects of outside action: barking, galloping, and so on.

In the Carnovsky *Lear* at Stratford, Connecticut, men sometimes rose from the deep forestage pit; when they exited downstage, they disappeared in shifting shadows that seemed to go on forever. (Carnovsky saw Lear's hubris as a compulsion to match himself against nature; in California, in an outdoor theatre backed by a huge dark mountain that

---

*Something similar was seen in the Colorado Shakespeare Festival the same year: all the actors, when not "on," sat muffled in red mantles, from under which they provided choric sound effects.

brooded over the lights thrust up from the stage, nature indeed seemed to play the role of antagonist.)

The golden opulence of Lear's beginning that tarnishes as the play proceeds has also influenced the play's design. So, in the Eric Porter (b. 1928) *Lear*, directed by Trevor Nunn, gold robes gave way to black. In Warsaw, in 1962, heavy golden streamers were wreathed about a four-tiered stage, with Lear at the top, in regal magnificence. Scene by scene, the gold was stripped away, the action descended, until, in the second half, only the empty stage remained. The elevation of Lear's throne offers a visual symbol of the early eminence from which he must fall; it has been as steep as in Sweden (1929) where an unsteady Lear had to climb ten feet high stairs that seemed to go almost straight up to his throne under a giant rock. There was a sense of real hazard as he stepped down to the level of his people.

Max Reinhardt used light and dark to suggest the mystery that he felt was at the heart of *Lear*. In Vienna, he projected a sense of an uncanny, otherworld, "superworld." His curtain went up on darkness, as if the stage were an abyss. Then the foreground blazed with a slash of harsh, cold light; the abyss remained. A few rough blocks made the throne, set under a rough dome. The shield bearers on either side of the throne could have been hewn statues as much as men (Reinhardt took his clue from Lear's dying line, *Oh, ye are men of stones*; he designed metallic rubber garments that seemed hewn from serpentine). Reinhardt's king in this performance, Klöpfer, came storming up the stairs to this throne, standard bearers running before him. With Basserman as Lear, in a production in Germany, the same sense of mystery was preserved: Bassermann, soft, already half-insane, bald, with a long white beard, was carried on in a sedan chair, like an Asiatic king, in faint light, to music that sounded as if it came out of the beginning of time, past dim groupings of shadowed draperies with the loom of the castle high above.

Theodore Komisarjevsky began by distancing his *Lear* in space as well as time. The proscenium was covered by a scrim, that seemed a solid black curtain during the brief Kent-Gloster-Edmund scene. As the three moved up toward it, sudden bright spots lit the red and gold, ten-tiered inner set—a system of levels and steps, with the tableaux of the court spread out across it. The light seemed to paint this tableau like a tapestry on the scrim gauze; then suddenly the scrim flew away, and the world of the court came alive. At the back, in an inner block, was a bare, massive arcade of ancient stone, roughly shaped: here was Lear's first appearance, here the later inner scenes. Komisarjevsky used lighting to change his scenes: the light that led up the golden stairs to a bright blue cyclorama would change in color and shape, pick out and form locales in multiple levels of the set.

This was essentially romantic mystery—gothic, made of the haunting darkness that revives old dreads. The archetypal sources were still representational, the uncertainties of this world recognizable. Further steps toward antirealism, toward enunciating a visual "but yet" to the little world of men who inhabit *King Lear*, have led to a purer expressionism. David Tyndall, in a university production (1969), projected against his backdrop a fluid design in dark and light, the moving lines forming patterns that often suggested one of *Lear*'s central images: an eye, opening, closing, suffering, vanishing. Something of the same effect was described in Brook's film script (1970) for his opening:

> On a blank screen, dots and blotches slowly materialize. What are they? ... the disconnected patches are tantalizingly enigmatic ... then suddenly from the chaos a coherent shape emerges. A pair of eyes.... For a moment they are sharp and clear ... then they dissolve away again.... Now faces, old and young, men and women: characters we do not know yet, but will identify later. Slight sounds and voices fade in and die away. Always, the very first or the very last shapes to resolve into sense are the eyes.

A German effort in 1924 made a kind of *Dr. Caligari's Cabinet* of a *Lear* stage: strange cubistic forms, violent colors, unearthly costumes, dissonant lighting assaults suggested that the play's world was a nightmare of Lear's mind. In Gielgud's 1955 *Lear*, the artist Noguchi designed a world made timeless not with the familiar archetypes of age and eternity, but with shapes of time unknown—although, in fact, the forms finally used were recognizable from the vocabulary of futurism, and even of science fiction. An arch overhead encompassed the *Lear* world, a looming black finger would knife down promising doom; a floating wall represented time, or history, and two smaller screens, moving about, evil elements of human will. A special shape accompanied Lear's first scene: a blue diamond, to signify the king's dominion, but also the link with France, and the distance of Cordelia's banishment. The costumes defied identity: cloaks with shaped holes designed into them, concentric rings that suggested garments of rubber tires, strange, halo-like hats and net jerkins for the men, swathes of drapery for the women. Gielgud enjoyed the venture, but was disappointed with the results: he felt Noguchi, with ballet experience, had designed for a balletic movement "which of course we do not use"; and had gone off before the costumes could be tested and adapted in the theatre. The effort was generally regarded a failure.

Dullin, in his 1945 Paris *Lear*, sought a stylized absurdist continuity: there were no fixed sets, panels dropped from the flies to mark the play's dissolves. The decor was meant to project an archaic, barbarian Saxon atmosphere, but suggested to critics a wild confusion of exotic backgrounds—among others African, Viking, Manchu, Tibetan, Samurai—but no coherent image related to the play. An attempt in Frankfurt (1970) to suggest a circus background for *Lear*, with Oswald doubling as ringmaster, succeeded mainly in irritating.

No designs that interrupted, filtered, or shaped the drama have worked; some by their explicit statements—even of the inexplicable, of the resistances, and contradictions—some by their very beauty, have constricted the play's imaginative reach. Exact realism in costumes has diminished the universality of the human confrontation, but surreal costumes, however symbolic, that denied Shakespeare's insistence on rank and disguise, have left unstated important stipulations of the tragedy. The play remains the thing: it will not submit to any concept impressed from the outside, any limitation to its freedom of movement between styles and between the poles of its dialectic.

Lear Begins

One quick line to Gloster, and Lear plunges into the action:

> Meantime, we shall express our darker purpose (36).

He is on his throne, his world seems safe, and yet the tonic mood of this transient moment of rest is infected with hints of conflicting tonalities. *Darker*—unlighted, secret, covert, not known. One movement of the play will be the journey to uncover the source of darkness; now the word stirs apprehension, starts verbal patterns that will jolt the balance farther and farther out of true. Sustaining the disequilibrium is the continuing play of comparatives: *darker, younger, largest, most*; the explicit statement of division; the urgency of choice; the posing of force against force; and also, now, a series of surprises, sharp dramatic shocks. A split of the kingdom between Albany and Cornwall has been anticipated by Kent and Gloster. But what else, what darker?

> . . . we have divided
> In three our kingdom (37–38).

In *three*. Cordelia will be in on it too.

In this first speech, the dynamic qualities of the Lear image are tested: his gesture of generosity is shadowed by inner darkness. Selfishness, self-pity, insecurity? Fear of loneliness, of insanity, of unspoken impulses toward his daughters, of his sons-in-law, his friends, himself? Unless this is a fairy-tale ritual, centering on a hollow old man victimized by allegory, the design of the character, with its grandeur as well as its flaws compels the movement to disaster.

One historical consideration must be confronted here. The play has been seen as dominated by the consequences of unnatural action, and Lear, a prisoner to this theme, as initiating unnaturalness with his abdication.* This would presumably shock and alienate a Jacobean audience,

---

*In this context, we can ask: given that Lear is designed to be already mad or senile, or susceptible to madness as he will turn out to be (the character may be shaped to fear this even at first), how wise and "natural" would he in fact be to go on ruling? Would a king do any better to wait until he died—or lost his mind—and so

trained to regard the act as improper, even blasphemous, a violation of
the laws of God and the chain of being.

The counter to this is not primarily to be found in further reasoning
outside the logic of the play—although a political scientist, Harry Jaffa,
has argued plausibly that Lear begins, in fact, as a very successful king
who has ruled well, and whose plan for division is wise and practical. But
the proper response is to the work of art: in its design, is the intent of
Lear's act made to seem natural or not? The wiser men in Lear's court,
Gloster and Kent, have spoken calmly of the expected division, and will
only object when Cordelia is disenfranchised. There are no implied directions to make what he does now seem unnatural in the theatre.

If history is to be cited to explain art, and this is always a risky thing,
we may notice, as a suggestion that in Shakespeare's world abdication
was not regarded as horrible or unnatural, the case of Emperor Charles
V. In this same era, he had resigned his empire, forsaking the cares and
business of the state, for a quiet retreat where—nature imitating art?—he
wanted to rest in his human identity: "The name of Charles is enough
for me, for henceforth I am nothing."

Nobody seems to have noticed that Montaigne, that bright stimulus
of the age, used some of Shakespeare's own imagery to describe Charles'
abdication as the emperor's "worthiest action," an

> imitation of some ancients of his quality, that he had the discretion to
> know, that reason commended us to strip or shift ourselves when our
> clothes trouble and are too heavy for us... He resigned his means, his
> greatness and kingdom to his son, when he found his former resolution
> decay... (*Essays*, Book II, 8).

To call merely "ritual" Lear's act of stripping himself of the royal
clothes, now too troublesome and heavy for him, ignores the energy of
the character's development and of the dialectic in the speech. Lear does
want to prevent future strife, but he also pits his daughters against each
other as his lovers. Presumably this is a test to see where nature doth with
merit challenge—but in fact, the partition is already planned. The language of division is now supplemented by the first of a tide of negative
comparatives: *our no less loving son*. Like its counter, *no more*, this
phrase will affect the balance of the language throughout the play and
especially now: soon Goneril will give it back to him,

---

leave the kingdom to what he anticipates correctly would be *future strife* between
the dukedoms? In fact, there will quickly be division between the dukes; would it
be otherwise if Lear died without assigning powers to these sons-in-law?

No less than life ... (58)

and he will return it to Regan,

No less in space, validity, and pleasure ... (81)

and Cordelia will pair the opposites.

According to my bond, no more nor less (93).

The energy of Lear's words, and the intent of the act, belie the ostensibly statesmanlike purpose: to prevent future strife. Lear will still want to bear the title and all the addition of a king, though he proposes to

unburthened crawl toward death (41).

This is one of many obliquely prophetic lines of the play, instinct with subverbal echoes of infant and animal; its importance to the character design lies in the difference between statement and act: he will say this of himself, full of rich self-pity and dramatized weakness, but his actions will betray his words—he means to hunt, carouse merrily with his knights, seek physical joys. But yet . . .

Actors of Lear have integrated the implications of the abdication into their individual characterizations. To the titan Lear, Salvini, the event was his show, he sat back on his throne, a great image of authority, looking much too strong to start upon a crawl toward the grave. He was all power and lofty grace, but as he invited his older daughters to speak, a kingly smile warmed his face; and he chuckled with pleasure at their protestations. Some critics were troubled at so commanding a representation of royalty and fatherhood, as distracting from "the petulance and unreason which also characterizes Lear" . . . "we lose all sight of Lear's defects."

Gielgud (1940 production) turned this sense of strength and power to dramatic use: his virile monarch was clearly dividing his kingdom and abdicating before he was, in physique and temper, ready to relinquish authority. This was an older Lear than Gielgud's first (1931), but not so old as in the 1955 interpretation; he "left room for aging." It was this Lear who was "pleased and happy" at the effect of his magnificent entrance. He enjoyed the power the love-auction gave him.*

The mad Lears at once added their own imbalance to the asymmetry of the action. Irving, pursuing his vision of "violent weakness," spoke with a "feverish haste," as if the very naming of the royal powers fa-

---

*Unless otherwise noted, observations on Gielgud's interpretation will refer to the 1940 production.

tigued him, as if they were wasps he held in his hand. Randle Ayrton (1869–1940) was a dictatorial old tyrant, cranky, snarling, the edge of senility showing in his easy delusions, his quick shifts of attention. Devrient was childish, mild, cheerful, inattentive; glad, when his mind was on it, to get rid of his burden.

To the good-father Lears, the love auction was an opportunity to show their tenderheartedness, their generosity, their vulnerability. It was a game they played. Charles Kean's simple king began the game without a shadow, and all conspired with him. Laughton's genial, hearty old Lear made the trial seem the "silly trick" Samuel Taylor Coleridge thought it was; he did not realize that all about him were shocked. Olivier, playing the surface here for comedy, suggested a Lear of restless intellectual energy ready to break out in any direction, who suddenly chose this way to show his affection for his daughters. Similarly, to Klöpfer's Lear the test seemed a sudden vagary, a whim that he went about with utmost cheerfulness. Mikhoels laughed away his kingdom. Scofield, on the other hand, was all business: he spoke without gentleness or kindness, deliberately, precisely, giving away the first princedoms with an abrupt, formal dismissiveness, arrogantly; the manner of his announcement of the competition for his favor shocked and almost affronted his daughters.

Now the daughters had to respond.

The Family

If only we could see *Lear* for the first time, as the naive spectator does!

We know it too well; we know, after the fact, that the evil daughters deceive Lear; and knowing their wickedness, we may assume they are embodiments of Evil. So critics and producers are occasionally ready to see the play as a morality: Lear as Everyman symmetrically flanked by personified forces of good and evil—characters "unmixedly good or bad" —as he moves beyond temptation to redemption.

Both the meaning of the play and its artistic premise deny this allegory. The sisters are a controlling factor in the persistent ambiguity of the *Lear* equation. If they are at the beginning mythic harpies, allegories of evil, Cinderella sisters, Lear's character is fixed and static: he is too simply the abstract man, put upon. Now the equation is awry; for Lear not to perceive the duplicity of such mythic figures, he must be either an absolute fool, or himself a mythic figure of such shallowness that the quantum of mortal folly Shakespeare puts into his design is without meaning. The terms of the equation are self-correcting. If Lear is "the great image of authority, inviolable, charismatic," he cannot easily stoop to folly; if he is too foolish, his deception is trivial; if too strong, he makes suspect such residual self-pity as his wish to "unburdened crawl toward death"; if too weak, his capacity must fall short of the power built into his outbreaks. If he is unshakably sane, he is not Lear; if he is quite mad, he makes ridiculous the respect in which he is held by the sane people about him. The art of the scene obliges the older daughters to deceive him without making him too foolish, to pursue a common, masked purpose, but differently, individually, with personae that are both contrasting and alike.

The spoken words only hint at the complexity of the equation. A familiar critical exercise is to seek in the verbal imagery of Lear's opening the polarities that will be developed symphonically later: of age–youth, natural–unnatural, parent–child, sight–blindness, sanity–madness, love–hate, man–animal, clothes–nakedness, ruler–follower, appearance–reality, loyalty–treachery, order–disorder, good–evil, justice–injustice, fate–chance. The first signs of the interlaced visual imagery deserve as

44

careful tracing, and perhaps even more scrutiny because they are so elusive, screened. Shakespeare had always to decide for his characters how much of their fifth act possibilities might be concealed, hinted at, or proclaimed in their first entrances; in *Lear*, the bold animal shapes in his personae are first subtly camouflaged. If the molding and shadowing were at once stripped away, as in mythic staging or criticism, the design of surprise and peripety, of the pervasive dialectic, would be dissipated. The tension at first grows from the very existence of the masks, the interplay between the layers of social disguise and the shifting centers of identity that are glimpsed beyond. This tension depends largely on how body and voice are used—or imagined—to sustain the ambiguity of the design.

As in other aspects of the play, similarity and difference reciprocate. Shakespeare centers his cast largely on the families Lear and Gloster: he asserts both the separate identities of the family members, and their likenesses. The language subsumes this dialectic; eye and ear are meant to be struck by it immediately.

A familial note is sounded when Gloster jests about the son he blushes for: Edmund will have in some ways more resemblances to his father than Edgar will. Both sons voice and act aspects of their father's sensuality, and his accommodating role-playing as well as his other qualities: if only in direct mockery, as when Edmund pretends astronomy; or in oblique irony, as when he protests piety or fidelity; or in echoes, as when Poor Tom imagines adultery. In the mockery Edmund may also, visually, parody Gloster's gestures; in the piety he may practice them; other moments he may reveal, by unstudied movement, remote, unconscious copying—mirroring; and this may also be true of Edgar.

A similar resemblance runs in the verbal and visual design of the Lear family. Lear and his daughters share fierce, terrible angers that erupt suddenly and possess the possessors. All four are designed with linked prides, jealousies, dreams, and compulsions to love and resist. The gestures of the daughters will all be individualized, perhaps deliberately so, because among all three antipathies are active; but even so, arrested or controlled, subtextual patterns of movement, however feminized and in far removes from Lear's, will echo what the three have learned by living with this parent. Goneril, mocking the father so skilled at mockery; Regan, banishing Gloster from her sight; Cordelia, at the head of her French army, are his flesh, his blood, his daughters.

Much depends, in the family equation, on the simple chronological ages of the personae. Not only Lear's age (where, as already observed, variations from vigor to senility can initiate striking variations in expectation and in feeling response); how old are the daughters? And their husbands? And Gloster's sons? (And then Kent? And Fool?)

The "children" are all relatively young: the critic may say so and stop there, leaving the impression indeterminate. But in the theatre, the physical presence enforces more precision. If Goneril and Regan are seen to be thirtyish matrons—as they often are—they confront Lear with the strength and independence of early maturity. If they are older, in their forties, still relatively young, their stance has the bitterness of ambition for power and ultimate wealth frustrated by long waiting, hope deferred. Then, to cut across families, their late passion for the young Bastard would have a further tension—by discoloration. Thus, to make this visual, one actress of Regan, in a solitary fourth act moment during the Edmund intrigue, sat at a mirror scrutinizing her beauty, before a black backdrop lighted with branch candlesticks, dropped belladonna into her eyes with a sigh for vanished youth and a frivolous gurgle of laughter. Regan's place on this age level fits if she is approximately contemporary with her husband, who acts as from another generation toward Edmund after the boy has piously betrayed his father:

> Cornwall: ... thou shalt find a dearer father in my love (III, v, 24).

Goneril, older than Regan, has no child yet; if childbearing is almost past her, a special edge sharpens Lear's curse,

> If she must teem ... (I, iv, 290).

But what if Goneril, like Cordelia, is also "so young, and so untender." Suppose they all are, the five children of the two families, a very young younger generation in rebellion, impatient of restraint? The more rebellious of them are out for anything they can get, contemptuous of their elders; the others, apparently more docile, still resist their parents under a less perfidious mask of love. Certainly youth's opposition to age reverberates through the verbal and visual imagery of the play. When old Lear calls a daughter "so young," when he commands the taking air to strike his eldest's "young bones," he speaks from a great height of age. How young should they seem to best suit Shakespeare's purposes?

When Edgar says, at the end (in Folio)

> we that are young ... (v, iii, 325)

he speaks for himself and Albany (Albany himself says this in Quarto). Edmund was "some year" younger even than Edgar; Kent calls him *goodman boy*; and he appeals as a lover to both Regan and Goneril. If they are September matrons looking back to May, the design for Edmund, who is frank with himself about his conquests, would seem to have included a soliloquized notice of this. Arguments from history, again, are hazardous, but it is a fact that Jacobeans took for granted that daughters of the nobility would marry very early—in their teens, even before. "The lawful age to contract matrimony by the laws ecclesiastical," wrote an Elizabethan lawyer, "is when the man is of the full age of 14 years and the woman of 12." Twelve or thirteen was the so-called age of consent. (Juliet's early marriage may be remembered here.) Among the mass of people, marriage usually came in the twenties, when the men could better afford it; but among the titled classes, wedlock was an important social and economic transaction, binding estates, wealth, and even political power, and the sooner concluded the better. Otherwise, the Crown, under its power of wardship, might arrange weddings to its own satisfaction. Heirs were wanted quickly, though a growing concern about the physiological consequences to young parents and their offspring sometimes resulted in token consummations, the youthful spouses living apart (however, failure of the husband to consummate after 18 could be grounds for a nullity suit). Marriage by women of all classes generally took place no later than the early twenties, and children were expected promptly.

That Goneril, the oldest of the "young," has not yet borne a child seems an indication of youth. One suggestion (unlikely) is that she may be obviously pregnant at the outset. Whatever her age, this would certainly add a special tension to her relations with Lear, Albany, and Edmund. Pregnancy would add a dimension of terror to the passion in her *young bones*, and compound her suicide with infanticide. But this inferred condition rests on a doubtful deduction from Lear's

> ... dear Goddess, hear!
> Suspend thy purpose, if thou didst intend
> To make this creature fruitful! (I, iv, 284.)

There is no direct hint, in verbal or visual gesture, of pregnancy; and again, if it existed, the Bastard, who so shrewdly casts his balances in soliloquy, might be expected to weigh this item: an unborn son of Goneril's would certainly complicate his lovemaking, and once born would stand between him and his ultimate ambition—the throne.

If all three daughters are very young, their husbands need not be so. Shakespeare's mirroring, as noted, is often antimirroring: two characters in parallel roles may often be antiparallels. Age will perhaps be one of the differences between Burgundy and France, the rivals for Cordelia; it seems explicit as between Albany, whom Edgar may regard as a young contemporary, and Cornwall, old enough to see himself a father to Edmund. A very young Albany, married to the dominating Goneril, would fit the design of a naive character slow to comprehend evil and intrigue, at first hesitant to counteraction and never fully committed. Cornwall might, as a young and pretentious duke, be taking a good deal on himself, and offset Albany another way; but an older Cornwall would further manipulate the age-youth dialectic, would intensify the asymmetry, would give a dimension to the early exchange of oeillades between his younger wife and Edmund, and would perhaps explain visually Lear's care in the first scene always to address Cornwall first, though (Kent thought) he more affected Albany.

Extreme youth in Lear's daughters would mean a (dead) mother who was much younger than Lear. Shakespeare conveniently leaves the mother a barely mentioned question mark in the design of both family groups. (Gloster only mentions the Bastard's mother, a partner in his own adultery; Lear says he would have to think of Regan's mother as an adulteress, if Regan were not glad to see him—as of course she is not.) With an eighty-year old sire, the older daughters could be visualized as old as sixty; but to make any sense of the Edmund intrigue, Goneril and Regan must still be young enough for a passion that is taken for granted: Shakespeare's design includes no focus on disparate ages. A kind of vague early maturity in the children satisfies the conventional concept; but a character pattern coloring the children toward the younger—even very young—end of the spectrum could offer powerful support to the pervasive thematic contrasts of age versus youth, parent versus child, order versus revolt.

The likeness-unlikeness in the Lear family as a group is echoed in each character. The complexities of the sons-in-law may be discussed first, because most easily. These men may be superficially distinguished by differences in physique and dress, and by the banners and livery of their attendants. The character differences go much deeper. Albany will rise to a kind of heroism; but the pervasive dialectic form alerts us to his anti-heroic qualities. In the first scene, except for the one line he shares with Cornwall, what he is must be manifest solely through physical imagery. Clues to his first appearance come from what will be said about him: *high, illustrious prince* (V, iii, 135), Edgar will call him; but Edmund and Oswald will speak of his indecision, and Goneril will gibe at his cowishness, will call him unmanly in comparison with the Bastard. The difference will lie partly in Edmund's panache, but a physical inferiority in Albany would also fit into the design. Slender? Boyish? Short? Fat? The

living Duke of Albany, when Lear was first performed, was King James'
son, succeeding James himself; Albany's ultimate courage and decency
may have been a compliment to James, but giving him an unimpressive
stature in imitation of the monarch perhaps not. Big men can be as frustrating to aggressive, erotic women as little men; size would be only one
element in Albany's asymmetry, and, in Shakespeare's acting company,
it might have been partly determined by the size and age of Cornwall.

The physical image most tempting to visualize unchanged from the
beginning is Cornwall's. He will be known later as the *hot* and *fiery*
duke, but he will turn out to be a figure of curiously shallow strength,
who needs to repeat his orders, and the design of I, i allows very little
space to express his complexity. In the theatre he has on occasion been
represented as a sour and snarling man, even though almost mute: an
abrupt, dark-browed, shoulderer-aside whose power forces a certain
priority of respect—fear?—from Lear. This makes a comment on Lear in
I, i, as must any clues from the Albany-Cornwall masks that come
through their modulated responses to Lear's comparative generosity to
their wives, to his disinheritance of Cordelia, his investiture of them with
all his power, and his violence toward Kent.

The relationship of his daughters to Lear most powerfully conditions
the initial dramatic equation. At the one extreme, they must surely not
be immediately so monstrous as to make Lear's trust seem merely stupid;
but how disguised, even from themselves, can their eventual evil be?
Naive spectators have been deceived by them, as Lear was. They lean to
the appearance of innocence, in the tradition of Shakespeare's best villains, drawn so plausibly in public that even audiences might believe in
them: Goneril and Regan lean so far in this direction that they seem not
at first to have discovered their own villainy, for at the end of Act I, i,
when they are alone, they will appear at most hardheaded, curiously human: the iron hands will be felt, but not, as yet, the iron claws. Certainly
Kent and Gloster had nothing to say against them in the opening beat.

As Lear first turns to them, and offers them opulence for love, he sees
surfaces that have been pleasing to him. Shakespeare requires that—in
Lear's eyes, at least—they be gorgeously dressed, in fine (revealing?)
clothes that scarcely keep them warm; that Goneril be beautiful, and
aware of her beauty—*vanity the puppet* (II, ii, 39); that they are passionate women, with some humor, social grace, and the physical strength
to ride long hours through the night and preside at battles. They will
not be mere appendages to Lear's story—they will help energize the action by moving forward to tragic destinies of their own. Indeed, if they

were not thought of only as Lear's daughters, the play might be their tragedy.

As the *Lear* design partly depends on how they are made, so they are dependent on his force in the equation. At one extreme, against a tough Lear such as Scofield, who played the love auction as a piece of state business to be got through, Lear's harshness conferred some sympathy on Goneril and Regan—although, in that antisympathetic world, they were proper citizens, and unglamorous too. At another extreme is the Lear like Bassermann's—so old or apathetic that he dozes through their speeches—or a Lear like Mikhoels, thinking only of getting along to Cordelia's response—and then the daughters respond mechanically, or ritually, or impatiently, or to make a public effect, or with desperate effort to communicate. The Lear of Devlin, who felt a love for Cordelia so strong it was touched with incest, cared nothing for the older daughters here, and their speeches were the half-bored, half-scornful recitations of women who knew they were only appetizers to a feast. So with the visual distance preserved between father and children: do the daughters come close, almost cheek to cheek, to whisper their love, or stand formally apart? All such felt extremes, which play with or against the language of love in Lear's speeches, must affect the changing equation later, when Lear will woo these daughters in earnest.

The conventional equation in the theatre—and in most criticism—has been a Lear pleased with any warm words he can get, though he does look forward most to Cordelia's; and Goneril and Regan have sustained their parts best by seeming to love Lear as much as they say they do, in voice and manner earnest enough so that Lear is not diminished by his evident belief in what they say. In this equation, their most successful surfaces in the theatre have been either a sweetness or a serious concern toward Lear that could even convince the audience—up to the moments when they turn on Lear. This would reflect, if not sincerity, a strategy that persuaded Lear, at eighty, that they deserved two-thirds of his kingdom. Regan has been more often the sweet one—"honey turned rancid" in one description—while Goneril, as the strong, elder daughter, has more often projected at first the almost maternal concern for her father that ends in her treating him indeed like a bad child.* Her "exultant brutality," as in Irving's Goneril, waits to emerge.

It has been said that Goneril's first speech shows her to be a quantifier,

---

*Brook's filmscript note: Goneril is the more authoritative, Regan the more feminine—deep down both are stone and both are metal, but in outward form one pushes, the other yields—hard and soft intermingle in different degrees.

a measurer, answering with calculation her father's request for a show of love. A suggested secondary meaning of *love*, from a root to "appraise, price, value" (Hawkes), perhaps distends Lear's conscious and unconscious meaning when he asks the daughters to bid against each other for him with love. The irony is, as always, reciprocal: the king and his daughters put prices on each other, they all misapprise; there will be most love where the material price has fallen. But the invitation to quantify is initiated by Lear himself; and if Goneril weighs carefully later, moving between calculation and passion, she certainly does not do so here. Unless the auction is seen as a kind of mechanical ritual, Goneril may have—must certainly seem to have, as she says—trouble finding good enough words, must be almost out of breath thinking of her filial love—love beyond measure, beyond anything rich and rare; and significantly the things she says she values—only second to Lear's love—are themselves unmeasurable, the verities upon which the play will revolve—eyesight, space, liberty; life, grace, health, beauty (she feels she has it), honor. Her language is intensified with the pervasive *Lear* comparatives and superlatives: *more, dearer, no less, beyond*. She sustains by triple reference the climate of the auction, with words like *loving . . . amorous . . . love . . .*

Those who take for granted that Goneril's speech—or that of Regan—is, on its face, impossibly sugared, may read what an English princess—King James's own daughter—wrote to her father not many years after *King Lear*:

Sire, I now feel the sad effects of separation and distance from your majesty. My heart, which was pressed and astounded at my departure, now permits my eyes to weep their privation of the sight of the most precious object, which they could have beheld in this world. I shall perhaps, never see again the flower of princes, the king of fathers, the best and most amiable father, that the sun will ever see. But the very humble respect and devotion, with which I ceaselessly honour him, your majesty, can never efface from the memory of her, who awaits in this place a favourable wind, and who would return again to kiss the hands of your majesty, if the state of affairs, or her condition could allow it, to show to your majesty with what ardent affection she is and will be, even to death.

Your majesty's very affectionate, very humble, and very obedient daughter and servant

                                                                    Elizabeth

From Canterbury, April 16, 1613.

Elizabeth, like Goneril, was married when she wrote this. The formally worshipful tenor of her letter, published by Mrs. Everett Green,* is repeated in French letters Elizabeth wrote to James.

An actress, entering the role, may well be aware of Goneril's imagined history: Lear knew her first, loved her first, then she was replaced, by a second daughter, then a third, the baby, the favorite. Goneril's involvement in sibling rivalry will partly impel the action of the play; that she genuinely meant her care for Lear here, that she has been moved by grief as well as resentment for his lost love, was movingly suggested by Irene Worth (in the Scofield *Lear*), particularly in her later dialogue with Regan: *he always lov'd our sister most* (I, i, 290) said wistfully, sadly, jealously, and so giving an extra dimension to her later differences with her father. Goneril's own tragic history, as well as Lear's, must not be diminished by visualizing her as only a witch. Reducing her—and Regan—at once to wicked stereotypes destroys both the dialectic and the suspense of character and action.

Note that what Goneril says here is exactly the right thing. She pleases her father. His court, knowing this, if it is not cynical, may indicate appreciation, even applaud. Lear rewards her—often with a show of love as well as land. Lears have usually made it clear they have heard from her what they wanted: from the Olympians like Salvini, with their august chuckles of pleasure, to the good old fathers delighted with the child showing off for company. The Lears who needed more than verbal assurance of her love embraced her, or kissed her as Gielgud did. Carnovsky, who hesitated before speaking the words that gave away his lands, as loath to surrender anything, yet giving, kissed Goneril full on the mouth.

The image of the map of England, of Lear's world given away, is an important visual adjunct here. Daughters and sons-in-law, the whole court, may strain forward at each dispensation to see how much was given, how much left—and so intensify the sense of Lear's importance now. In the shrunken universe of Scofield's Lear, the map was a little scroll, an item of state business. More often it is as grand as the farthest possibility of its symbol: a massive parchment, or leather sheet, on which Lear traces, with staff, sword, or sceptre the outlines of his dispensations. For a Reinhardt Lear, the dome over his head held the painted map: Klöpfer stood on his dais, as it were between heaven and hell, and pointed out boundaries with his staff. The map may be paper, the divisions

*Editor, under her maiden name (M.A.E. Wood) of Public Record Office documents.

torn off and given away. Welles' Lear marked divisions on a map large enough for a man to walk through—and when he was angered, he walked through it.

To Regan, Lear offers more loving language:

> ... our dearest Regan (68).

What is most important in her answer is the new relationship that emerges: hers with Goneril. Regan loves like her sister, *but more*, she tells Lear:

> ... she names my very deed of love;
> Only she comes too short (71–2).

It is a higher bid, a bold comparative, an assertion that she can love better. Aside from any visual imagery the sisters may use in the ritual entrance, this is the first clue to a relationship that will lead them to catastrophe. Regan would be better than Goneril. The second sister would top the eldest. If Regan does not look at Goneril as she says this, she feels Goneril's eyes on her. So do we. Regan knows and may fear the will of her older sister—it will kill her, in the end—and she may speak haltingly, even need prompting from Cornwall; but she too gets out what Lear wants to hear.

The imagery of comparatives Regan uses has curious male and female sexual connotations, if not intentions: *my very deed of love; only she comes too short; the most precious square of sense*. The sexuality of the latter is not explicit, it is not glossed to match the *forfended place* (V, i, 11) Regan will mention later, but a similar reverberation is not beyond Regan's design. She offers everything, leaves herself naked; where Goneril in wooing Lear has not denied her bond to husband or anyone else (though Cordelia will suggest this), Regan's courtship is absolute, beyond comparative: she is only happy in her father's love. A physical bid may enhance the verbal gesture: thus, Gielgud's Regan, kneeling, embraced her father's knees. Kozintsev's Cornwall, toadying gratitude—in contrast to his later show of arrogance—rushed to kneel and kiss Lear's hand.

However Cornwall takes Regan's warm offer, Lear is usually again pleased, and the pleasure may show as it did with Goneril: smile, laugh, embrace, kiss. There is perhaps a higher reach of pleasure, in response to the higher bid, and to suit the design of mounting toward a third, largest, best. An alternative way to satisfy this design is the inverse, as with Mikhoels: manifesting the growing impatience to get to Cordelia. The movement by threes is ready now to reach its apogee, as, before long, in another movement of threes, the fearful descent must be made. Here is the moment for which the whole game has been played: when Lear will receive the special accolade of love from Cordelia, and offer to her the large center of his kingdom, and more, himself.

Cordelia

Lear, as we have seen, has often taken some special notice of Cordelia at his entrance; or has reached out with looks toward her during the first speeches; or has studiously avoided her, as pretending to conceal his scheme. She usually stands or sits apart—unless Fool is with her. Kozintsev's Cordelia sat quietly playing a guitar. Sometimes, conventionally, she has worn white; this is dangerous, if it suggests that she is merely ✳ "purity" or "charity" or some such bloodless image.

From the moment Lear announced a division of *three*, throughout the court awareness has spread that everything was planned to lead up to the moment when he will show favoritism. All know, and now Lear declares, her special dearness—asks her to speak. The language of paradox stretches between superlatives—the last and least will get the best and most.

Gielgud, discussing Granville-Barker's conception, reports that two possibilities were considered:

> The map is already marked and the division of the kingdom announced ...Are we to suppose that Goneril and Regan, though taken aback, are quickly ready with their flattering speeches, but that Cordelia, taken utterly by surprise and outraged by her father's vanity, is choked to silence? Or is her inarticulate obstinacy and the glib answers of her sisters the result of some days, or hours, of deliberation?

The lines were rehearsed both ways, and it was decided that the effect on the audience would be much the same either way. In fact, the possibilities extend beyond these alternatives, are limited only by the special relationships established in the Lear family, and particularly between Lear and Cordelia. His temptation of his favorite daughter is defined by the roles each had learned to play in relation to the other. Thus a Lear who announces proudly that France and Burgundy court Cordelia is different from one who betrays jealousy; and Cordelia must reflect the difference. So with other qualities.

Salvini, the image of authority, would sit majestic on his throne, and from that height offer the richest plum. Where the element of father (and father-lover) was stronger, Lear commonly approached Cordelia, and drew her aside, sometimes with great warmth and intimacy, the formal voice becoming loving and melodious, as with Forrest. Macready, who had austerely given away two-thirds of his kingdom from the throne—at whose foot his elder daughters had knelt—walked feebly down the steps to woo his youngest, caressing her lovingly, expressing "the fondness of a heart beating loud and quick with excess of expectation." Charles Kean, Forrest, Irving, likewise went to Cordelia. Reinhardt's Lear, Bassermann, all father now, took Cordelia to him on the throne, in his arms, caressed her face, rocked her tenderly. (A terrible prefiguring of the end.)

> ... what can you say to draw
> A third more opulent than your sisters? (85–86).

This is the ultimate primary statement of the tonic. Cordelia's troubled asides have been minor dissonances in Lear's swelling, triumphant mood. He clearly expects a sigh, a laugh, a tear, a gush of love. Instead, a shock of silence warns of a threatening dominant.

Cordelia's first answer, in the theatre, is no answer at all. True, she sometimes answers at once, with fire or shyness; but silence seems best. We know what she will say, and knowledge kills expectation; as critics, we may not hear her pause. But that first-day Globe audience probably heard it, for it belongs to the character and scene design, the moment to which all else, including her asides, has led. What can she say? Lear looks into her silent face, the seconds pass, he commands, requests, jests, pleads:

> Speak (86).

Carnovsky, after a pause long enough to hurt, spoke out of hurt. Mikhoels—and Goldsby's Lear—tempted Cordelia by removing his crown, and holding it out to her to take. Dunn's Fool brought the crown to her. Lear is, of course, offering her his heart as well. The court is hushed, concentrated on the puzzling delay. At last she breaks her vow of silence.

> Nothing, my lord (87).

Cordelia alone, of the characters, reveals something of a range of her qualities at once. Only Gloster, thus far, has displayed a shadow side at first meeting; his strengths will emerge only slowly. Edmund and Kent are quite masked; the variety of Lear's qualities is hinted, but nothing of the range. Goneril and Regan wear faces that, like sides of a coin, imply other faces, but give no clue yet to how savage these daughters may be. Cordelia is the first to reveal her private self, her inner conflicts, and to expose publicly, much more than she is allowed to be consciously aware

of, the underside of her nature. "Cordelia is a most difficult part," Ellen
Terry said. "So little to say, so much to feel. Rarely does an actress
fathom those still waters." Certainly the actress must feel Cordelia tensed
for her loved father's disposition of her—to a husband. Wish and counter-
wish work in both father and daughter.

Each polar extreme of Cordelia's possibility has sometimes been seized
by critics and actors as her identity. At one end she is the ultimate Christ
figure, or, close by, "enskyed and sainted" by the powers vested in Bradley. At the nadir, she is sour and egotistic, self-willed, obstinate, sulky,
proud, or a "sweet milksop." In fact she moves between extremes, one
somewhat short of Bradley's canonization and the other touching the
arrogance and ego-aggrandizement of her father. Schlegel, idolizing her,
compared her to Antigone, as to a dream of woman; she is made closer
to the actual Antigone Schlegel did not know, with noble aims but with
a countering compulsion to exalt and destroy the self. The Russian director Alexander Blok saw more realistically an "obstinacy [that] gives
the external push to [the] whole tangled ball of misfortunes." He compared her to the Antigone "whose will is almost a man's lodged in a
woman's shape." Granville-Barker perceived the touch of Cordelia's
father in her; the actress Lena Ashwell saw this expressed in her quick,
fierce judgements, typical of idealistic youth intolerant of foolish age.
William Poel was so troubled by Cordelia's severe tone that he wanted it
softened by a voice choking with emotion.

Cordelia's first aside—the monologues come conveniently as she
watches Lear show map and affection to her rival siblings—indicates that
she feels she really loves her father; but she cannot readily speak her
feelings. She thinks this, and it raises in her the self-pitying, self-
dramatizing impulse that also colors Lear's self-awareness:

> Then poor Cordelia! (76.)

An exclamation of pure sympathy—for herself. Then the peripateic *yet*
as she remembers her nobility:

> And yet not so; since I am sure my love's
> More ponderous than tongue (77–78).

When Lear insists on a response from her, the complexity of their relationships is tested. We will learn in a moment that Lear is thinking of
living with her—and with her husband? Are husbands themselves a
threat to him—will his anger at Cordelia partly be fired by her reminder
that the sisters are married? Later, he will want to steal upon and kill
these sons-in-law.

His reference to the rivals for Cordelia's love who, long in his court have made their amorous sojourn, adds a minor note to the sexual imagery of the scene, but ambiguously: the line might be a proud father's acknowledgement of his daughter's marriageability, or a father's teasing of his daughter, as Mikhoels teased; but it has been read, too, as a scornful allusion, as from a father who would as soon have his daughter for himself. His *darker purpose?* That Lear has such an impulse will be seen when his subconscious more boldly emerges; at this confrontation, the timbre of his voice, of his caresses, overt and latent, begins an equation Cordelia must complete. She will also meet pride with pride, ego with ego, passion with passion. She may sense something darker. To use Redgrave's image, two constellations meet—or better, collide.

The critics who found Christ in Cordelia pass over her first mute response, and her next two answers, and explain her concession that she loves "according to her bond" as a noble transaction: "The expression of love is rational: it recognizes the laws of God and society, duty to father and husband." But the first answers are insistently there; the searcher out of religious parallels should perhaps observe that they are outright denials; and that altogether she denies Lear thrice. No amount of explanation can make anything kind, charitable, or loving of an answer, to the offer of love, of *Nothing.*

Various constructive impulses have been seen in Cordelia: she is instructing the father, forcing on him a shock of recognition, making him see his folly, awakening him from a spell, resisting a *darker* love; but if they exist, they are not realized in her own explication of her one-word text. It is cold-blooded; as the adoring Bradley had to observe, love is certainly not halved between father and husband. As a matter of duty, in fact, the marriage ritual claims all for the husband; but for those with a capacity to love, love is indivisible. One of Cordelia's ironies is that she virtually offers Lear the marriage pledge: to

> Obey you, love you, and most honour you (98).

She offers it, then halves it. The quantifier is Cordelia; she is the one who measures out, so much here, so much there. And as she does, she regresses to self-pity:

> Unhappy that I am . . . (91).

First, then, she says nothing; and then she says *Nothing.* She has nothing to give, except these quibbling words about halves; and even these halves are not offered freely, but only after urging. She never uses a kindness, never an endearment. Only in IV, vii, when Lear is asleep, will she be able freely to express her love in his presence. Essential to the design of this youngest, who must become the heroine, is the prominence now of her shadow side, that matches, on a smaller scale, her father's. In her, "honesty" is folly—she acts indeed his poor fool, if instructing him. She will be consciously the pattern of all patience—until her resentment finds its way out. She is mirror and anti-mirror for Lear.

The effect on him of the first *nothing* must vary with the whole dramatic equation. (Of the philosophical implications of the word, I will speak in a moment.) Generally, the more imperious the Lear, the more committed to an image of authority, the more shocked he must be. Salvini, sitting confidently on his throne, playing the god before his court, leaned backward with the blow and gazed at Cordelia in blank amazement. Gielgud, in his titan role, stared at her, stunned, uncomprehending—"the first sign of danger," he noted. Forrest, who had come down to her from the throne, stood in quiet astonishment. A long pause then, as with Carnovsky, of profound embarrassment—Lear's court embarrassed with him, for him. Of the responses crowding in on the absolute ruler after astonishment, humiliation was one of the first. The court was watching Lear's favorite daughter discipline him at the very moment he was bridling in anticipation of her warmly voiced love. A visual pattern begins: three more times a daughter will diminish him; Goneril, before his whole train, Regan before Kent and Fool, and finally Cordelia to whom he will kneel in abject humility at last. A father fathered. A king— a man—*shamed*. To be thus, to be a fool, made a fool of, to be laughed at, mocked, this will be almost the worst blow this man can suffer. Up to now, Lear has rested secure in his public image; even if the love auction is seen as beginning in an informal, familial rather than courtly ritual, the court has been present to confirm Lear in his intent. The court may laugh, as if sharing a joke; but this will be no comfort to Lear. Now, suddenly, the private world of his humiliation is exposed. This was accented in the Norwegian staging where the knights had stood frozen since Lear's entrance, more decor than personae; at Cordelia's *Nothing* all the still faces looked up, as at some fearful violation. This Cordelia did nothing to soften the blow: she spoke stubbornly, unyieldingly, with a cold will—a proper daughter of the angry, obstinate Lear, and also believably a sister to Goneril and Regan.

An absolute image of authority cannot concede superior wisdom, cannot yield to revolt; less than absolute, it must begin to crumble. If there is an inner insecurity, as in Lear there is, crumbling starts there, inward. Salvini, the most august of Lears, kept the face of authority, but the first wound had been made: he said the primary response was hurt

pride, shame, secondarily disillusion (thus Bradley: "open shame"). A
terrible challenge to pride, Carnovsky said; when Cordelia reached for
his hand, he snatched it back. The fiery Norwegian Lear strode fiercely
up to Cordelia, towered above, almost touching her, his fists knotted
hard, as if to strike her. The *Nothing* shattered Redgrave's old Lear:
where everything had been immovable and rocklike, "the very founda-
tions seemed to dissolve, and he was left looking into a black void."

For the Lears of gentler design, Cordelia's first rebuff was rebuffed.
They could not allow their love to be rejected; or they were afraid to.
Laughton greeted her *Nothing* as a kind of naughty, endearing old-
fashioned answer from a beloved niece. But under his robe, his knees began to move, restlessly. Bassermann, who had pulled Cordelia up on his
lap, now reproved her, still, like an indulgent father, playfully boxing
her ears, and when she started to pull away, drawing her back again to
his breast, and laughing. He was determined to keep his dreamworld.
Mikhoels also resisted Cordelia's meaning. He would have the *Nothing*
a joke—though, as the actor observed, he would say the word later with
a grim irony. But still he suspended his intelligence; he wanted to believe
her. Klöpfer, in the same mode, was hesitant, bewildered, hoped it was
all a misunderstanding, tried for better answers, only at last conceived
the inconceivable. The shock almost felled a Czech Lear, Jaroslav Prucha (1893–1963); he had offered himself to Cordelia with the delight of
a child bringing out the prize Christmas gift; her *Nothing* surprised him
into immobility, he stood petrified, hardly human, like a mortally
wounded animal just before it falls. Like Redgrave, his eyes suddenly
seemed to see only blackness. Irving's Lear tried persuasion. As they
stood apart, where he had drawn her into a privacy that isolated them
from the court, he moved closer, stole his arm around her, spoke lovingly, coaxingly.

Mend your speech a little ... (94).

Another "mad" Lear, Rossi, trusting mindlessly in Cordelia, was confused, glazed: ". . . the vacant stare, the half-opened mouth, the hesitating voice." Scofield, at the other extreme, yielded nothing. He rapped
his lines at Cordelia, with nothing of astonishment or persuasion, building in fury when she gave him her short answers.

But goes thy heart with this? (104.)

Lear's first *but*, flung out to resist the tide, gives her another chance,
and, when she still resists, another:

So young, and so untender? (106.)

As if tenderness were the badge of youth, of the green shoot, as in the play it definitely will not be—or not until youth is damaged, and learns tenderness from needing it. Cordelia does not yet know her damage, or the damage she has done; her thoughts still focus on herself, and when France comes, her sole pleas will be for self-vindication. If she softens toward her father, she will never—when he is awake—do so in words; she will never, even in IV, vi, apologize; if she relents now, it is only in visual language, of the sort that has been used by the soft-design Cordelias in the theatre: she may kneel, approach, touch, lift her arm in appeal, offer to embrace. Whatever the cue, the design of Lear forces him, out of the pride that he shares with her, to resort to the infantile absolutism that will recur until he dies:

> Hence, and avoid my sight! (124.)

"I will not look at what I do not like."

In the complex of emotional material in the Cordelia design, then, the feelings of love, kindness, sympathy, all the virtues that later will seem her special property, now hide in her shell of self-involvement. In the theatre, the range of her expression—leaving out the saccharine fronts of most nineteenth century Cordelias—has been from shyness to impudence, from a neurotic anxiety as to what to say to almost arrogant, exhibitionist assurance, depending usually on the total equation. The Cordelia to Scofield's tough Lear was prim, assertive, prideful, seemed by comparison to her practical, put-upon sisters rather immature and overidealistic, while Redgrave's Cordelia was shy with her old, loving, terrible father—and was appalled and shocked at the effect of her words on him.

Cordelia's large speech, when her heart finally comes into her mouth, offers in its words logic to her father and strong antipathy to her sisters. A soft Cordelia in the theatre puts feeling into the whole design. Ellen Terry's "exquisitely tender" Cordelia clung to Irving; Carnovsky had to pull back from his appealing youngest. But whatever the prompting, Cordelia turns from him to herself, and to the thought of her role vis-a-vis Regan and Goneril. The comparatives and divisions sustain her bitter tone: she has offered logical halves, why have her flattering sisters husbands

> if they say
> They love you all? (99–100.)

If they say—her first if. Goneril did not so say; the if is Cordelia's condition, her push on the pendulum. Then, further, insisting on her righteousness,

> Sure I shall never marry like my sisters,
> To love my father all (102–103).

The last line, with its second *all*, is only in the Quarto. If it is to be included, it is significant: only this one time does Cordelia allow herself a familiar word of relationship. *Father*. If the Quarto line is left out, the speech has a loaded sting aimed at sisters and brothers-in-law:

> I shall never marry like my sisters.

It could be aimed at marriage itself; it could be a cue of love for Lear— *I shall never marry*—that he misses. In any case, without that lone *Father*, Cordelia's language is bare indeed, in comparison with Regan's and Goneril's warmly painted affection of child for parent. But in sarcasm Cordelia's language is gorgeous: her hostility erupts, as it will later in the play. In the theatre she has graced *all* with a little laugh. Abstract Cordelia's lines from the text, and see how often this angry note sounds: *my sisters . . . these sisters.*

The moment of Lear's rejection of Cordelia is pivotal. Whatever combination of qualities dominates Lear, Cordelia will have provided the exact stimulus to his anger; what she calls truth becomes, in the event, the gad that maddens him before his court. Being a Lear against a Lear, her clash with her father must come to seem inevitable; but beyond this, she is prisoner of a pattern that Lear himself sets. From now on, Lear's every encounter—with Goneril, Regan, Kent, Oswald, Fool, Edgar, Gloster, up to the moment when he meets Cordelia again, and then after—he will counter everybody, challenge everybody, the energy boiling in him will find polemic outlet. Lear will not be angry only because, as Coleridge suggests, a "silly trick" has misfired; Lear has violence in him. Because Cordelia has, too, there is warrant for a stage *agon* that pits her young intense force forthrightly against his old and angry power, a force that, even in her voice—however soft—matches him tone for tone to his climatic forswearing of her. She offered nothing; he must have all.

He overbears her. The Lear design is explosive; he is created to destroy himself. If this compulsion is presented from the first through the image of king already mad, or senile, the court's role in the equation has been a sense of expectancy, of a residual embarrassment awaiting with anticipation, even apprehension, the misdirection of his energy. More often, in the theatre, the stichomythia moves slowly toward a climax, and the explosion, first evidence of Lear's latent violence, comes as a terrible surprise, dismaying a court already made awkward by—even, with

Devlin, turning politely away from—the strain between king and daughter. Either way, some terrible event is apprehended, the tense dominant tones must suddenly erupt.

In all of Shakespeare's tragedy, a constant for actors is the design in the chief characters of violent peripety, when, with new temptations or revelations, multiple impulses converge and excite feeling beyond reason. So it is now with Lear. His angry thoughts for the first time may seem unfinished, erratic. The characterization, acted or imagined, must be fired with the full complexity of Lear's motives. To narrow the range is tempting, but it leaves out contributory tensions.

Devlin, feeling as he did the dark undertone of incest in Lear's love for Cordelia, chose a special stimulus to flash out against. He let the *nothings* go by as excusable gaffes; he was quiet until

Happily, when I shall wed . . . (100).

This the father-lover could not stand, he was driven to an almost maniacal rage that was clearly hysterical jealousy.

The appalling rage of Scofield's Lear proceeded logically from the character; the explosions of the older, milder Lears—Devrient was a prime example—have had a startling pyrotechnic effect because what went before was, by contrast, so much gentler. Rossi here tried strenuously to pull himself out of his senile stupor; even old Bassermann, who had been dozing not long before, then cradling Cordelia, came to frantic life, broke out wildly, as if strength and life were coming back to a trembling ghost.

The complex of feeling in the outburst, its place in the action, was deeply sensed by Mikhoels. He, too, had been slow to admit anger, happy to play the fool with Cordelia, as he had played hide and seek with her; but now the jest was over, and his deep feelings erupted—but (in his image) polyphonically. "It is difficult," Mikhoels said, "to tell what prevails in this monologue: anger or the joy of anger." And a new element began to temper the character: where the titan Lears would now begin to make felt their residual weakness, the old soft men and the crowned fools would begin to discover forgotten strength. In a few minutes Mikhoels' Lear changed, the chuckling old man had become someone new, altogether dominated by passion and purpose: wrath against Cordelia, and the wish to hurt her.

As with all of Lear's assaults on others, this act bruises him as well. Salvini, intent on preserving his titan image, kept his place on the throne, and, with iron control, renounced Cordelia in low, deliberate tones, seeming absolutely sure of his absolutism; but his voice was mottled with pain, the deeply concealed weakness glanced out—even so, some observers felt a lack of that dimension of unreason that would begin to undermine Lear's authority. Gielgud let a touch of the coming instability show in his angry outbreaks; Fool, from holding Cordelia's hand, covered his ears as in pain to shut out the oaths. When Macready came to

> And as a stranger to my heart and me (115)

(the first *heart*, a word mingled with psychic and physical overtones that would function as an index to Lear's endurance, and is often, in the theatre, accompanied by gesture), and

> Hold thee from this forever (116)

his voice trembled and broke.

Lear is accustomed to dealing in these absolutes: *all or none! out! away! forever! never!*, but each such regression to infantilism is also a self-punishment. The giant's oath to forswear Cordelia takes a giant's strength; between the shaken titans and the mad Lears were those old and fatherly Lears who, nerved to voice it, were unnerved. Klöpfer, after a determined effort, collapsed sobbing; Redgrave sat in a dreadful quiet, not so much in rage as in unendurable pain, as if inwardly he were banishing every reminder of Cordelia. The Lear who had come from the throne to coax Cordelia often stood over her to pour out his anger; but one might, like the Swede Lars Hanson, intensify the ritual of his oath by returning first to his throne. The angriest of Lears have struck Cordelia: their later anxiety will be in some proportion to the violence they show here.

In the design of the action the banishment of Cordelia starts a rhythmic pattern. Twice more, in sanity, Lear will confront and attack his daughters, and will do it once—in imagination—while he is mad, before he is reconciled to his youngest. These conflicts must have different tonal values, but they will be rich in echoes of this scene's language, gesture, feeling. If the daughters kneel to the king here, he will kneel to the daughters later, in mockery, in remorse. In the first sequence of three, he will each time appeal to the gods against his daughters, but each time differently, in different tones. Each time there will be movements of approach and withdrawal; each time the power will shift from king to daughters, until at the end, in his most powerful curse, he will be powerless. The *fortissimo* of Cordelia's banishment must be leashed, built toward the mounting climaxes to come.

The intent of Lear's oath is to put Cordelia as far from him as possible, and again the imagery is structured comparatively: the barbarous Scythian and he who makes his generation messes will be

> *as well* neighbor'd, pitied, and reliev'd . . .

The imagery is visceral; the note of the animal intrudes: not merely that the barbarian eats his children, but that he gorges his appetite. On this theme, Lear's own imagination is engorged; as in the inspired madness of IV, vi he will tell Gloster of lascivious women:

> The fitchew nor the soiled horse goes to't
> With a more riotous appetite (IV, vi, 124–125).

The man trembles inside the king—Macready's voice broke here—and inside the man, the animal. Lear's next line proclaims it.

> Come not between the Dragon and his wrath (122).

The great animal, the mighty, terrible beast. And then, in instant peripety, the cry of man, lover, child yearning for the breast, voiced in superlative:

> I lov'd her most, and thought to set my rest
> On her kind nursery (123–124).

The spoken line usually follows the peripety of the passion: anger, changing to pathos, both underlined by self-pity. Scofield spoke it grudgingly, Carnovsky plaintively, Macready hardening to inflexibility, Forrest slowly, reflectively, introspectively, as if saying goodbye to tenderness.

Challenged, Lear will initiate visually as well as verbally a motif involved with seeing that is to pervade the play. His *out of my sight* posture, so often to be repeated, prepares for its own mockery when the maddened king will say, as the very mark of his royalty:

> Ay, every inch a king:
> When I do stare, see how the subject quakes (IV, vi, 110–111).

In sanity, Lear will stare intensely, angrily, at Cordelia, Kent, Oswald, Goneril, Albany, Regan, Cornwall; the ultimate shivers of intimidation will not come. Only when Lear is mad, and parodies in rags the royal, banishing frown, may the one man truly submissive to him, Gloster, indeed tremble at the frightening sight.

The order to Cordelia (or Kent?) to leave Lear's presence has sometimes been cued in the theatre by Cordelia's supplicating gesture, but it can as easily spring from the inner design of Lear; a recurrent wash of anger, that overpowers the vision of the denied dreamed-of nursery and provokes a furious megalomanic demand for its opposite. He will ignore rebuff—perhaps even an attempt at reconciliation—by refusing to see.

Lear's rage here has sometimes been described as "ungovernable"; however expressed, the design seems certainly to imply incompetence to govern in one who wants only his own way, who will not look at what displeases him.

A curious subtextual note occurs here. He does not get his way. Cordelia does not disappear (nor does Kent) at his wish. She remains to fill his vision, whether in silent appeal or silent stubborn refusal. The erosion of obedience is visual. Hence his next outcry, to Kent, to the court, to the world:

> So be my grave my peace, as here I give
> Her father's heart from her! (125–126.)

His heart, again. Undermining the most mighty of Lears, even Salvini, will be the simple mortality of the body; Lear will die of a heart that gives out, that will no longer support his breath. His hand will go more often to his heart, to his failing breast; now the thought of death again, of lonely death, has wrung from him the kind of oath that to the absolute mind is the worst of all: "I won't love you any more"—as if nothing else could hurt the other person so terribly. Of course the great hurt is to the swearer, the one who denies, to Lear. This oath, too, will be broken; but now it seems an ultimate step toward finality, on a road beyond return: the heart itself is given from her.

Macready's bewildered pause here—for the awareness of his extremity, of the latent shadow of madness, of his hidden hope for a change in Cordelia—suggests the visual expectancies in the design. We know Lear's decision is final; but a naive spectator does not; he sees in the scene many unexpressed possibilities of reconciliation. Only a gesture is needed . . . Neither side makes it. Lear orders France to be called, but the court is stunned. He must shake it to life.

> Who stirs? (126.)

There is a stir, then; but again a visual pattern begins—servants will not automatically stir for this king. His absolute orders will be ignored, and thrown back at him, until he stops ordering.

Now, without pause, driven by all the motives that converge on him, Lear will redivide the kingdom. Scofield's Lear, chewing on his bitterness, ground out his plans with methodical anger, a king so conditioned to rule that the motions come almost automatically from him. Macready, after his momentary confusion, hurried through the business, his impatience barely under control, but in the context of his Lear, pathetic. Carnovsky slowed to troubled, hesitant speech, working the details out, trying to manage; his note on his promptbook: "This has to be thought out, but it's the best I can do at the moment." Certainly the stipulation of the hundred knights is worth a pause, perhaps long enough to exact a nod of agreement from the daughters and their husbands—for this will be a sore often rubbed.

Mikhoels rushed on unrelentingly: he would show Cordelia, the whole thing was for her hurt: "all the time he is on the move, rushing along the stage, he bows to Goneril and Regan in deep curtseys, spreading his arms in a broad gesture of welcome." He would glance at Cordelia to see the effect on her; there was a touch of malicious buffoonery in it. Gielgud was more ready to put her behind him; his planning out the conditions, the hundred knights, pleased him; he sat back in his throne as if all was well. Other Lears rose to a violent ending that linked visual with verbal imagery; the recurrent canker, which broke out in the middle of the planning, with

Let pride, which she calls plainness, marry her (129).

seized them as they held out to the sons-in-law the coronet. The coronet may symbolize kingship, but in Shakespeare's usage it is normally less than a royal crown. In one critical view (John Dove), Lear would use it to make Cordelia duchess of Middle England if she will stay with him, refuse a French marriage. The option is never clear. Lear does seem to be saving the coronet for Cordelia; whether royal or lesser, it now serves as a focus for his resentment. Olivier flung it to the floor in rage. Powerful Lears have torn it in two in an excess of anger, less powerful ones have tried to break it, and failed. Mikhoels split it with one blow of his sword—and we know, he said, that it is Cordelia he strikes with that violent blow. Barnay hurled the map of his kingdom at Cordelia's feet. Welles, who had been holding high his giant map to tempt Cordelia, strode right through it, "splitting Britain open like a paper hoop," and slashed at Cordelia with the shards. Division is made visual.

Among the patterns in the Lear design, many will shift as the play wears on; among them, Lear's instantaneous appeal to the supernatural to aid or witness his acts and anguish. His first oath, taken in the name of the pagan and natural gods, of the powers of day and night—light and darkness—will be broken like the rest; but now Lear speaks with confidence that the gods are his endorsements. They are the powers *From*

whom we do exist and cease to be (112). The *we* may be royal: "I am
the creation of the gods." How Shakespeare's audience was theolog-
ically prepared for his invocation has been considered by W. R. Elton
in a magnificently thorough study. He concludes that the Jacobeans
represented a spread of thought from orthodoxy to atheism, that Lear's
movement toward an apparent final defiance of the gods was perhaps
dressed in pagan theology to absolve Shakespeare himself from any
charge of irreligion.

But Elton does not insist on this, and wisely, because the impact of the
tragedy does not depend only on theological issues. Shakespeare is not
necessarily committed to Lear's or any other's journey of discovery; the
ambiguity of the play's attitude toward the gods is perhaps most evident
in the intense arguments made by various critics, to be considered later,
over whether the playwright was—or wasn't—working out a motif of
Christian redemption. The various postures toward the gods in the play
—the differences between, say, Albany's opportunist belief and Lear's
developing skepticism—is a component of form that adds one more ambiguity to Lear's uncertain world, one more tension to the turbulent
dialectic of the play.

The story of this king figure brought low is a reprise of the archetypal
fantasy of assault on the most high. Lear's invocations are, dramatically,
not a test of the gods, but of Lear the invoker. His assumption of
semidivinity, of a comradeship with deity, is undercut by his humanity,
and his animal heritage. However assertive or impudent Cordelia may
appear in this I, i equation, nothing royal or sacred can be felt to be vio-
lated; it is Lear's self, not his royal person, that hides behind the oath, a
self that is aiming at its own hurt, its own destruction. The more austere
and authoritative the oath—as with, say, Salvini—the more Lear wears
the mask of a god, the more he is doing an ungodlike thing, a giant mis-
using a giant's power, and in the subtext he knows it, and shows it in the
aftermath—whether in more assertiveness or in collapse. It needs no god,
or nongod, to make Lear's destiny what it is. His hubris is not Faustian;
it does not bring him into confrontation with a god, or even the idea of
god, but with himself. Lear knows, Scofield said, that he has done something unbearable on his own terms, and the thought, that will soon be
voiced, impels him to his catastrophe.

That Lear was asking for retribution with his heresy has been suggested because of his earlier

Nothing will come of nothing . . . (19).

In the sensitive Jacobean society, Elton observes, this might have been perceived as a sceptical denial of the Christian God's creation; the speech—and Lear's purely pagan prayer that followed—could also have been taken as another mask for pursuing a current, forbidden, intellectual fashion—questioning dogma. This, again, is an argument not from the play, but an inference from what seems one element of very many in the cultural climate, and again, perceptively, Elton leaves it problematical.* There is no insistence in the play that Lear may or may not suffer for crossing any god, or gods: he is their determined votary until he can no longer trust them.

Nothing has multiple valences independent of theology; it is another small word symptomatic of the verbal substructure of the play. Nothing comes of nothing but so does everything, spiritual wholeness seems possible from material nothing, man is all and nothing, nothing is nothing. What needs further to be noticed, in the critical attention to the word, is that, while it evokes continuous tension, it is itself part of a larger, pervasive pattern of denial in the *Lear* tapestry. Linked negative words spread through the language like a dark shadow: besides the thirty-odd *nothings*, *no* sounds one hundred fifty times, *not* almost three hundred times, *neither*, *nor*, *none*, *ne'er* and *never* another hundred. Against this, the rare affirmatives—*yes* less than ten times, *yea* and *aye* some twenty-five times—cast only a faint light and some of these are functionally negations:

> *Fool*: Yes, forsooth, I will hold my tongue (I, vi, 203).
> *Lear*: Yea, is't come to this? (I, iv, 313).

To the audience, the accumulated burden of the negatives is not yet obvious. Lear's *things*, his bulwarks against *nothing*, seem not yet seriously threatened; but the undermining has begun.

---

*Such was the multiplicity of contemporary thought that Elton was moved to note: "Any apparent confusion in [my] account should, I trust, be attributed to the confusion in the multiple vision of the Elizabethan age, to its illogical syncretism, and to its mingling of disparate and divided worlds" (188).

Lear and Kent

With the disposition of his lands, the dialectic between Lear and Cordelia goes momentarily underground. Their responses are visual, subtextual, until France and Burgundy enter: but the design requires on each side an afterwash of feeling, ranging from stubborn immovability to a despair for a terrible mistake made. With Lear, a further uncertainty: even if clearly sane now, he is, as Scofield said, a man who knows he can go mad. Sane Lears have, in the theatre, betrayed here, and in their agon with Kent, the dread of instability; this has sometimes been joined with a painful consciousness of the injustice to Cordelia.

Visually, Lear begins now to diminish himself. His conventional taking off of his crown begins the undressing that will go on down to the flesh. The royal headpiece is the chief garment of his kingship: one of the recurrent visual images Mikhoels provided was Lear's habit, in moments of crisis, of reaching up to the crown that was not there and knowing bewilderment. With his crown off, Lear is already part naked; the visual imagery of his formal abdication might well involve disposing of other accessories of royalty. Gielgud's Lear entered with the sword of state before him; his giving up this weapon disrobed him further.

The coronation of James I suggests the possible use Shakespeare might have intended of other ritual garments that dress a king on his assumption of power. James was stripped to his undergarments, and then attired in tunic, hose, and sandals, and adorned one by one with various royal emblems: spurs, sword, "armill," mantle, crown, ring, gloves, sceptre with cross (for the king's right hand) and rod with the dove (left hand). A Lear divesting himself of his royalty in the theatre might well divest himself of some such symbols, in his reverse coronation. Shakespeare knew how to use this kind of royal ritual, as in the *Henry VIII* coronation. The first undressing of Lear here can provide visual preparation for a later clothes incident in the scene.

Once Lear gives the coronet away, Kent begins to strip Lear metaphorically. Not in his first speech, which begins with elaborately polite flourishes of protocol, but next, after Lear has interrupted him. Between these two men, both hot-tempered, a curious, persistent conflict will recur to the very end of the play: on any issue that grows between them, they may differ almost to the point of violence. Kent plays a kind of rebuking Fool to some of his betters, but especially—except in the storm —to Lear. Lear, knowing this, may even at first turn quietly away from Kent's accusing look; Kent is characteristically roused to two brutal attacks:

> ... be Kent unmannerly,
> When Lear is mad. What would'st thou do, old man? (145–146).

When Lear is *mad.* . . . The word is out, for the first time, and is a wound. Even conventionally, as Kent may use it, it stirs fear, starts ripples. The very "thou" is an affront to majesty. Kent follows immediately with almost blasphemous impudence: *old man.* It is a calculated shock for Lear, and, if Lear treasures his image of authority, it electrifies those who hear (Kent may, here, be trying to take Lear aside, to spare him shame). Thus there was a gasp, a hissing intake of breath from Carnovsky's court. Kent goes on to verbalize, for the first time, the king-fool image that has such archetypal roots:

> When majesty falls to folly (149).

He goes on, forcing on Lear a flood of advice about Cordelia that the king cannot tolerate—partly, perhaps, because he knows it is good—sustaining the language tension with comparatives *best, least.*

The aesthetic problem, here, is the build in the next nine speeches to Lear's second act of banishment. A normal rhythm would raise Lear to a pitch higher than his excitement over Cordelia, to give him the outlet for physical violence with his sword which Nicholas Rowe's first stage direction proposed, and which most actors accept. The pitch of fury of even the most outraged Lears needs some tempering at the outset. Gielgud's first rebuff,

> Kent, on thy life, no more (154)

was dead quiet. Lear merely turned, and stared at him.

Kent, as intransigent as he will later be with those less worthy, does not quake, pours on, and Lear's repeated royal infantilism—

> Out of my sight! (157)

is answered obliquely, invoking the whole complex of seeing-blindness-insight, with Kent's wry comparative:

> See better, Lear ... (158).

Lear's vision is figuratively obscure, but Shakespeare may have intended poor physical eyesight too, especially in the later incidents of recognition. Carnovsky's business of seeming to peer into people, and beyond, his very strain at trying to see, reflected this. Krauss dropped from his titan's role sometimes for this kind of effect: a frightened listening, looking, as if his vision were inadequate, as if he were looking into another world. Klöpfer, too, seemed often to be peering, searching, into the distance. From this, the hallucinations of madness followed easily. The visual and verbal imagery of unseeing sight, insightful blindness will converge later; these moments are omens.

Lear turns to his gods again, this time Apollo, aptly enough god of light, wisdom, medicining; and Kent, in a fury, answers prophetically, in the name of the same god, who may infect as well as cure:

> Thou swear'st thy Gods in vain (161).

Now Lear "lays hand upon his sword"—by the direction of Rowe, who probably saw such a business; certainly some violence is on Lear, for Albany and Cornwall, in the Quarto, jointly urge him to forbear. In some productions, they hold him back. This outburst further sketches into the old king's image a kind of physical release for passion that Goneril and Regan will say is frequent; and it also provides a powerful theatrical suspense. A naive spectator does not know Lear will stop, or be stopped, and this advance of the furious king on his sacrilegious vassal is expected to end in blood or death. Lear counts on his kingly stare, but he is also a man who can kill, who can think kill, who will kill Cordelia's hangman. Charles Kean seized a battle axe from an attendant for the attack, but the weapon is usually the royal sword. Dunn's Lear held a knife at Kent's throat. Salvini swept down from his throne, his sword half-drawn, and the intercession of the courtiers, moving in to him, could hardly have stopped this giant figure, towering over all. He could have cleaved his man to the girdle; it was only his own self control that finally stopped him, for Salvini was intent on maintaining the early titan's image, and he stood silent for what seemed a full minute, tempering himself. This self-check is customary in productions that do not use the Quarto's direction to Cornwall and Albany to intercede. At the other extreme, the weak Lears have had their weakness emphasized by their handling of the sword: Samuel Phelps (1804–1878) was stayed so gently by his sons-in-law that it seemed he needed no staying; and Redgrave's old, old Lear, in his fury, could only fumble his great broadsword half out of its sheath. Rage galled by impotency bred humiliation;

in the frantic working of Lear's lower jaw, something more terrible was foreshadowed.

Still Kent cannot leave him alone. *Whilst [he] can vent clamor from [his] throat* (165)—an apt self-description of his angry mode of speech to the man he would help—he publicly accuses Lear of *evil*. The word itself is a shock. Here the background chorus in the Norwegian staging emitted a sudden cry, a kind of doomsday lament. Then, as Kent was made to kneel, on Lear's reminder of his allegiance, the whole court rose, dwarfing the bent, isolated figure.

Lear's banishment of Kent comes as a new shock to disturb the court. Its motive is a recurrent dominant note: Lear's royal self-image when faced with frustration, which

> nor our nature nor our place can bear ... (171).

It is the absolute, infantile "I won't have what I do not like." The language is borne up by divisions, by the sequence of numbers, and the design of intensification to the climactic word *death*. Lear calls again on a god to assert something that has not been questioned:

> By Jupiter,
> This shall not be revok'd (178-179).

The visual cue can be an attempt of intercession from Kent, or from the court. Any imagery of sympathy from Gloster or Albany must be visual here, as it was in the banishment of Cordelia: it may be more of Gloster's "obsequious bustling," but the role's genuine feeling will show through. Cordelia can only speak here, too, by gesture. Lear's last line is an assertion, in any case, that seems to look back, that implies the self-doubt made explicit in some performances: can—should—anything be revoked?

The suspense is not quenched here; Kent might still resist. But he does not. Gielgud's Kent knelt and kissed the brandished sword; Goldsby's Lear brought the flat of the sword down on Kent's shoulder, forcing him to his knees for the banishment. If already in Kent's mind some scheme of a disguised return begins, it must be a felt expression; he takes a conventional leave, his language sustained by formal oppositions, comparatives, and rhymes. Surely Goneril, Regan, and Cornwall are glad to see him go; in the usual first scene equation, the loyal remainder of the court is visually dismayed. He consigns Cordelia to the gods' dear shelter—one of the many pleas to divinity that will be denied—as shelter itself will so often be denied. Kent may be allowed to take his own leave, but if he is marched out between guards, the motif of forced flight is better sustained.

Shakespeare shatters the silence with his flourish of horns, announcing France and Burgundy; and Gloster, eager to smooth over a nasty situation, introduces them. Their attendants follow—a fine opportunity for visual display of the excitement of color and rank. These nobles put their stamp on the sophistication of the court: they are elegant men, who know how to speak the language of diplomacy and love.

A twice-shaken Lear greets them. He may not show his strain: Scofield ground crisply on, seemingly as tough as ever; and Salvini, who delivered the sentence of banishment with measured, majestic quietness, made himself seem still the titan. Gielgud wiped away his anger, and changed back to the mask of his kingly front: smooth, courtly, charming. Carnovsky buckled; at the end of the Kent banishment, he threw down his sword, and fell back on his throne, his hand on his face, oblivious; Gloster had to bring him to himself with the insistent mention of France and Burgundy, and he looked at them at first unseeing. Kozintsev's film Lear seized Cordelia's hand, and jerked her like a refractory child toward the two Frenchmen. Redgrave's Lear had to summon all his strength to speak at all.

When Lear looks from Cordelia to Burgundy, he strikes again the conditional "if" note, here linked with the adjectives of size and value—*aught, little, nothing, all*—that both qualify his character and sustain the suspense of this second auction:

> If aught within that little-seeming substance,
> Or all of it, with our displeasure piec'd,
> And nothing more, may fitly like your grace,
> She's there, and she is yours (198-201).

The language of king and suitors now will continue the pattern of value and comparatives: *more, less, least, worthier, dearer, most, best, dearest, richer*. A price falls, but what is unpriz'd is precious. Disequilibrium is visual too: Burgundy will seem of a different kind from France. The easy asymmetry makes Burgundy older, shrewder, more practical; yet he is something more than a stalking horse, he cares enough for Cordelia to try to make a deal, when it seems none is possible. France is easily seen as the young hero, dressed in a differently gorgeous color and presence. (Kozintsev set him apart by giving him an interpreter, who muttered in French what was said by Lear and Cordelia.) A more subtle asymmetry might reverse the surface patterns; but Burgundy cannot be separated from his shrewdness, and France must have the quality of passion below the surface that all the play's heroes have: not for nothing are we told that he parts in choler from Lear, or—later by Lear himself—

that he is hot-blooded. The pity in the theatre often is that, because the part is so little, the actor is among the least. Cordelia's importance needs to be bulwarked by the worth of her lover. His feeling gives a fillip to what is a second, doubt-edged love auction: who loves Cordelia most? Who will take her for the lowest price? This time practice loses to passion.

The dialogue has criss-cross tensions. Mikhoels observed that his Lear was still acting a painful play to hurt Cordelia. "His fury has not dwindled, but it has settled down, it has condensed, it has hidden at the bottom of his heart." Devlin, from his own love of Cordelia, had no kindness for the Frenchmen; Carnovsky's anger at Cordelia spilled over in snarls at them—"color of contempt," his notes say. Scofield spoke from a settled bitterness; Gielgud's brilliant, sophisticated Lear was ironic, smooth, cruel about Cordelia, a schoolmaster showing up a dunce, with withering sarcasm.

The visual imagery of Cordelia, now usually isolated on the stage, all others—except Fool, if he is there—withdrawn from the poverty of her *infirmities . . . unfriended, new-adopted to our hate* (202–5), but rich in her person, is both a confirmation and contradiction of the language. Lear, offering choice to Burgundy, echoes the whole system of alternatives:

> Take her, or leave her? (205).

Pause. Burgundy would like Cordelia. Will he take her? Diplomat struggles with lover. No, of course; the *no* is fated. Lear swears now *by the power that made me* (208)—as if this was a special making—that she has *nothing*, and turns to France. Gielgud's Lear was short with Burgundy, for even to Cordelia's father-enemy the man is not admirable; Gielgud's Lear liked France, had respect for him and turned his back upon Cordelia to save France from her.

Now a master note is sounded again. Trying to find words enough to demean his daughter—*where I hate*—Lear urges France

> T'avert your liking a more worthier way
> Than on a wretch whom Nature is asham'd
> Almost t'acknowledge hers (211–213).

Nature. Again and again the word will be a private prism through which various characters view the world; by looking back through the prism we will be able to see more clearly the designs of the characters. There is a great temptation to simplify the nature of nature in the play; John Danby, in particular, has written a fascinating and charming book on the "two" forms of nature: Edmund's, to which we shall soon come, as a manifestation of the hard-headed empiricism of Thomas Hobbes (when Hobbes, years later, would get around to enunciating it), and the kindlier nature of the "good" characters, a reflection of the Hooker hypothesis of an ordered, God-descending pattern in which all creatures found —at least, should find—a fruitful place. Hooker dreamed that men could fit themselves into a reasonable order; Shakespeare knew they could not.

Historically, the dream of hierarchical order was the aristocrats' justification for holding their own places and keeping the bottom people on the bottom. In *Lear*, in fact, almost all men touch bottom, and their views of Nature, as we will see, are many more than two—are as many as Nature can hold in this play. *Lear* is not a debate: the views of nature are functions of individual characterizations, and not vice versa.

The convenience of Danby's dichotomy has made it, in some quarters, a critical fashion; but like other over-simplified generalizations on Shakespeare's thought based on non-dramatic evidence, it needs to be examined against what actually happens as the play develops. The word's meaning changes as the personae change. Danby says admiringly,

> Lear's . . . Nature takes for granted that parents
> are to be honored and human decencies observed.

In fact, Lear's Nature takes it for granted that Lear is to be honored whether he deserves to be or not. Lear will invoke Nature, with absolute selfishness, to *destroy*; until his madness, every one of his invocations will be a characteristic "unnatural" outrage of any normal concept of human decency. As Gloster will say, Lear in fact *falls from bias of nature* (I, ii, 116). Surely Danby cannot find anything worthy in Lear's egotistic— later megalomanic—use of the concept, as in calling Cordelia a *shame of nature* here. That phrase (which will be echoed later by his flesh, his blood, his daughter Cordelia herself) tells us, as it first comes from his mouth, nothing about Nature except that Lear is a special manifestation of it; but it tells us a great deal about Lear. This will be true of all characters using the word or reflecting it. They who will seem to their parents most "natural" will be most "unnatural," and vice versa. Yet all will be, in their "natural" or "unnatural" behavior, *natural*—that is, inevitably part of the wide spectrum of nature dramatized in the play.

"How "unnatural" Lear is, France's response tells us. Knowing Lear's favoritism, he is bewildered, startled that Cordelia could have committed a thing to be *asham'd* of: the word, a nerve-center in the *Lear* design, calls up unspeakable images of degradation:

> Sure, her offence
> Must be of such unnatural degree
> That monsters it... (218–220).

or—a crucial *or*—Lear's own love for her (here I think Edmund Malone's interpretation just) must itself be unnatural. It is an aroused speech (for France is hot-blooded), though it is not always acted so. France frankly chooses between Lear and Cordelia, and sides with her. Short of a miracle, the taint must be Lear's.

The note of the strange, the monstrous, the animal, with latent sexual connotations, is sounded again, and Cordelia responds sturdily to it:

> It is no vicious blot, murther or foulness,
> No unchaste action, or dishonour'd step... (227–228).

But she gets her own back too. The whole trouble is, she says, her want of

> that glib and oily art
> To speak and purpose not... (224–225).
> But even for want of that for which I am richer,
> A still-soliciting eye, and such a tongue
> That I am glad I have not, though not to have it
> Hath lost me in your liking (230–233).

This is, again, a persistent attack on her sisters, and an affirmation of her own virtue; she equates the easy expression of love with glibness, oiliness, and ends by affirming that she is glad she doesn't have it, even though Lear hates her for it.

It is a feeling speech, not a wise one, with powerful vectors radiating to France, whose love she wants, to her sisters, to Lear. Lear answers with feeling, a marvelous one-line prose compound of comparatives and negatives that precisely defines his now sulky absolutism:

> Better thou
> Hadst not been born than not t' have pleased me better (233–234).

No "image of authority" could speak this line untarnished; it is the voice of the basic primitive, the infant wish for *all*. Regan and Goneril, tense with visions of greater wealth, abet him now. When France recognizes in Cordelia but

> ... a tardiness in nature... (235)

and gives another chance to Burgundy, the latter pauses, undecided— suspense, again—and asks Lear only for the dowry. Lear's richly echoing answer, sometimes snarled, or muttered in pain, or as a boast that may lack assurance,

> Nothing: I have sworn; I am firm (245)

is glossed by an illuminating note from Gielgud's record: "Real, sulky. Big Ben striking."

Burgundy's pompous refusal of Cordelia, and her proud, tart rejection of him, is always a moment of joy. This is the shadow side of Cordelia at her best.

France takes her in a rich dramatic love speech that deserves eloquent speaking. It is elaborate with the opposing, back-and-forth patterns of sentence structure that accompany, in *Lear's* set pieces, the oppositions and comparatives of the words:

> Fairest Cordelia, that art most rich, being poor;
> Most choice, forsaken; and most lov'd, despis'd (250-251).

There is lofty anger, as well as love in it:

> Not all the dukes of wat'rish Burgundy
> Can buy this unpriz'd precious maid of me (258-259).

He may hold out his crown, for Cordelia to take hold of, for crowns are important to the scene's visual imagery. Lear feels the affront totally. The coming parting in choler with France is foreshadowed in the abruptness and rudeness of this goodbye; Lear's childish *no more* comes pat:

> ... let her be thine, for we
> Have no such daughter, nor shall ever see
> That face of hers again (262-264).

Again, he is a false prophet. This may show in his voice, or face: Robert Mantell thundered the speech, but his voice broke; Scofield locked eyes with Cordelia, trying to overbear her with his king's stare; she returned his gaze, and in the end it was he who gave way, turned to words again:

> ... therefore be gone
> Without our grace, our love, our benison (264-265).

Get out, in fact, he says; another version of "out of my sight."

Lear can put up a hand to block her from view, and to add insult, turn politely to Burgundy, whom he may well despise, and—as in Mikhoels' conception, playing the play out to the end for Cordelia's hurt—say with elaborate geniality,

> Come, noble Burgundy (266)

and lead his court out.

In terms of the aesthetic design, the Lear-Cordelia-Burgundy-France interchange has built swellingly to the pageantry exit—Forrest's Gloster backed out obsequiously before him—grand as the entrance, properly adorned with the flourish directed by the Folio and even more by the tensions among those who stay.

Visually, Lear's exit sets a pattern that is one with a central action-image in the play: flight. Lear seems to take his leave, but in fact he flees, perhaps in such a rush that the flourish is late catching up. France and Cordelia stand their ground; Lear's *begone* does not banish them from his sight. To have his way, he must be the one to go. Now he goes clothed in grandeur, but again and again he will leave in exactly the same mood, denying his paternity of his daughters, swearing oaths he will not keep, each time degraded in power, until he is helpless. What seems withdrawal will always more clearly be flight from what he cannot allow himself to look at; until at last, powerless, he will be in actual flight for his life from those who would destroy him for the symbol of power that remains to him. Flight—and pursuit—will weave through the whole play now, its effect will be as pervasive as the conditionals of the language.

The complex of emotions in Lear as he departs is reflected almost more in his visual imagery than the words. One old piece of business was to have Cordelia, as Helen Faucit (1817–1898) did to Macready's Lear, kneel as he leaves, to try to touch, or kiss his robe.* Macready swept on, the hurt father. Gielgud, who had continued to sulk as France accepted Cordelia, and refused to look at her, deliberately cut her dead as he left. Carnovsky, whose fierce, angry voice had broken to a treble of aged bitterness on

> ... shall never see
> That face of hers again (263–264).

rose abruptly, afraid to be emotional, rapped out the denial of grace and farewell, and marched out, his hand on his heart. Klöpfer made his exit, like his entrance, at a run—a different run. Laughton's Lear, the un-steadied, loving father, moved from disappointment to rage to obstinate pride, hurried out, self-absorbed, giving the impression of a heart and mind at furious odds, as if his awakening intelligence was resisting the knowledge that he had been wrong. In Mikhoels, this same beginning touch of awareness showed in his awakened, passionate parade of indif-ference before Cordelia. A proud Cordelia, armed with France's hand in hers, may give Lear his own back, refuse even to bow.

*Fool, if present, parts grieving from Cordelia. Then he too, like Lear, becomes involved in the series of three flights from the daughters.

Granville-Barker suggests that Lear must leave this scene "as he entered it, more a magnificent portent than a man." But he is unmistakably man now: any mask of the portent has cracked, such human impulses as petulance, self-will, cruelty, jealousy unsteady the image of authority. Lear could not do what he has done and still personate that image. He is the more man when he tries to hold the mask intact in front of him. At the other extreme, the simple, the foolish, the overloving fathers are moving in another direction, as it were upward, toward the endurance of a poverty and pain they had never expected to know. The near-mad, half-mad Lears are being nudged from the safer shelter of mild unbalance into the black storm of passionate insanity.

The Daughters

Goneril and Regan remain behind—Goneril may stay Regan from leaving. The brief beat conveys their cooler judgment of Lear; but there is much more—a developing tension among siblings readying for war. Cordelia sounds the first challenge.

France has asked her, tersely, to bid them farewell. She will not leave it at that. First, sarcasm: You *jewels** of our father—away from him, she can call him *father* now. Then: Look at me; I weep: *with wash'd eyes / Cordelia leaves you* (268–269). She knows them for what they are, and *like a sister am most loth to call / Your faults as they are named* (270–271). Like a sister, that is, she will only remind them that she knows they have unspeakable faults. She will leave her father to these wouldbe mothers and their *professed bosoms* (272); but she would prefer to leave him in a better place. Where? On her better breast, that was not offered? As she weeps, the thought may make her weep afresh. She says good-bye.

In this last glimpse of Cordelia for three acts, the dialectic of her character intensifies. Her design includes an intent love for her father, but also, now, impulses of hostility that only harm him, as they harmed him when he asked for love. She may speak softly to her sisters, even kneel to them, as a gentle Japanese Cordelia did; but a daughter concerned for this father could hardly manage a less effective way of appealing to her sisters to care for him. And as she scorns them, she pities herself—*poor Cordelia* again; but she does weep, and not only for herself. For Lear, too. In her, love and anti-love resist and coalesce.

Regan answers shortly; she has business on her mind. Goneril's hostility to Cordelia needs outlet: you have nothing, are worth nothing. Nothing.

Again Cordelia responds not as the loving daughter, but as the angry sister:

> Time shall unfold what plighted cunning hides;
> Who covers faults, at last with shame derides (280–281).

Jewels-eyes will reverberate.

The imagery of disguise, of concealment, is secondary to a major early motif: wrongdoers, the faulty, will be *shamed*. This is prophecy: we shall see, Cordelia says, you will treat our father badly, everyone will know it. And she returns to sarcasm—or sweetness?

> Well may you prosper! (282).

France has had enough of this and takes her away.

If Cordelia appears here at her least good, Regan and Goneril now seem least evil. They face a practical problem, taking care of an old father, and they discuss this practically. Nothing of the beast shows yet; Shakespeare bides his time. "How finely is the brief of Lear's character sketched," Keats noted; for the daughters see him realistically. Goneril observes that Lear's very banishment of Cordelia is an example of his poor judgment, they agree that his habitual rashness, intensified by age, will make him a difficult ward. If no love is expressed for him, neither is hate: they are concerned with their own convenience. Later, they discover evil; they will become victims, as Walter Kerr says, of a pervasive "progressive mania." William Watson wrote of two at Edinburgh who moved toward wickedness as if it were their own discovery and secret. But even when most evil, they will not be without some grace—flowers of evil. Goneril indeed reflects the older daughters' hurt—motive for revenge?—that their father came to love a younger child better.

Major motifs inform their speech: the polarities of age and youth, of what appears and what is—most wonderfully synthesized in

> yet he hath ever but slenderly known himself (293).

The comparatives continue to sustain the tension: *not little* (twice), *most, poor, too, grossly, slenderly, best, soundest, last, further.*

Behind the prosaic, rather terse exchanges, a powerful, challenging dominant tonality emerges, ominous of the fierce rivalry that will destroy the two sisters. Now that Cordelia, whom Lear loved most, is gone, they compete against each other. Goneril forces the issue. She speaks about three times as many lines as Regan; Regan seems only to agree. But she resists; when Goneril broaches the matter of Lear's care,

> I think our father will hence to-night (284–285),

Regan quickly puts the initial burden on Goneril:

> That's most certain, and with you... (286).

Lear had not stipulated this; had, in fact, named Cornwall first, in proposing to the dukes his alternation of monthly visits. Now Goneril, who has heard her love for Lear described as coming short of Regan's, is burdened with the first trial of his care. Her felt response to this will be visual; in words, she takes care to stipulate how much trouble the old man is likely to be. Regan contents herself with echoes; this is not now an urgent problem for her; their mounting difference is evident in the last two lines, when Regan, in answer to Goneril's *Pray you, let us hit together* says, casually,

> We shall further think of it (307).

and Goneril, with the problem on her hands, retorts forcefully, sometimes with a passion that suits her later action, with an image of compulsion that has sexual reverberations,

> We must do something, and i' th' heat (308).

There was wisdom in a recent Hungarian staging, where Regan walked casually off, leaving Goneril to look after and show, in her face, the intense planning for what lay ahead. Goneril will never be quite sure of Regan; when she lets Lear flee from Albany's palace, in I, iv, she will wonder if Regan will support her.

An accompanying visual imagery may intensify the note of rivalry. If Lear has stripped himself of his royal accoutrements in his abdication, and they remain on the stage, it is left to the two daughters to carry them off—perhaps even partly dress themselves in these borrowed robes. The torn map, or the coronet parted between the two houses—does one sister reach for it, and the second, as she answers in apparent agreement, grasp at her half, and more? Each is going to want all, and now they can lay hands on the symbols of allness. If their words screen a visual tug of war—however covert—for the ornaments of power, this second stage in the rivalry between them is intensified.

Act I, Scene ii

Enter the Bastard *with a letter.*

No place direction is mentioned by Shakespeare for Scene ii. "Gloucester's castle" was an eighteenth-century editorial afterthought; in fact, when Gloster comes on, he will speak as if he is grieving over what has only this moment happened:

> Kent banish'd thus! And France in choler parted!
> And the King gone to-night! (23–24).

No time allowance is stipulated—as it otherwise so often is in this play—for movement from one locale to a new place; the stage direction might as well read "another part of the palace." The matter is not important, except for one interesting possibility: that, with Shakespeare's swift intercutting of scenes, Edmund might have come on at the end of I, i even as Regan and Goneril were leaving, might even bow them out (as, I suggested earlier, he might have bowed them in). He might assist them with any royal accessories they carry—and so finger, for a moment, as he will more confidently later, the stuff of kingship. From the first point of contact among these fated three to their interwoven death, Shakespeare has designed an action line that may be started as early as here, if only with a brief and almost unnoticeable exchange of oeillades.

Edmund's impudent opening address to his goddess has tempted nature classifiers to lump him with the rest of the "bad" characters; but if he shares some of their attitudes, he is not identical with any of them, as none of them is identical with any other and as none speaks of nature in quite the same way. Shakespeare was not creating characters in groups. Here he was making a new kind of villain out of some old materials, some fresh ones, using finely the polarity of evil and charm. The first fifteen lines of the Bastard's soliloquy could as easily be spoken by Faulconbridge, Shakespeare's brilliant, humorous bastard-hero in *King John* who jovially ridicules the pretensions of his legitimate brother, makes his mother confess that she bore him illicitly, and then acts with sardonic heroism to counterbalance the villainy of John. Faulconbridge, too, pro-

84

fesses the virility of nature: better be the bastard of Richard Lion-
hearted than be begot in the dull, stale, tired bed of his father. Edmund
could be Faulconbridge except that Shakespeare builds into this later
design the materials of villainy. These show not so much now in the evil
of his aims as in the planning of them. Faulconbridge, as hero, is open
about his objectives, blunt, cynical, straightforward; his strength is
strength. Publicly Edmund seems a similar material for heroism—and so,
as noted, a naive spectator would see him—until Shakespeare secludes
him for a soliloquy; and at once a mask is shed, a private face shows, a
mind schemes; his strength is his wit, his charm, his capacity for disguise.
Edmund has been called a "new" man, the hard-headed product of Renaissance individualism, mercantilism, scepticism; in these qualities he
repeats the pattern of the practical schemers—the Ulysses—who have always been set against the passionate heroes of the world of artistic fantasy. The innocents are always in danger from the schemers; but in a
work of art as subtle as *Lear*, the edges blur: the passionate innocents
and the schemers share qualities that cousin them, both fail in cleverness,
both succumb to feeling. The character who will speak most as Bastard
does here, about the plague of custom, the corrupt conformity of the
world, the meaninglessness of birth, will be Lear in his mad prescience
in IV, vi. (Regan and Goneril are content to manage the plague of custom.) This was the world Lear once serenely, securely, looked down on;
it is this world, in I, ii, that Edmund plans to mount. With Edmund, particularly, we must beware seeing the character as a fixed pattern spread
out on a tapestry: his character is designed to be perceived as a growing
organism, taking on new garments, new assurances, new ambitions, new
attitudes in face and body, as it moves upward toward the now un-
thought-of apex Lear leaves vacant.

The Bastard's design is frighteningly dynamic, open-ended, of un-
limited possibility. Significant of the energy released by the character
are the eleven *if*'s in this relatively short scene; all but one are Edmund's.
They are all *if*'s of his own expectation, or of expectations— and uncertainties—he projects on to others:

Well, my legitimate, if this letter speed . . . (19).
. . . If our father would sleep till I wak'd him . . . (53).
If the matter were good, my Lord, I durst swear it were his . . . (64–65).
If it shall please you to suspend your indignation . . . (80–81).
. . . where, if you violently proceed against him, mistaking his purpose
. . . (84–85).
If your honour judge it meet, I will place you where you shall hear us
. . . (92–93).

as if we were villains on necessity, fools by heavenly compulsion...
(127-128).
If you do stir abroad, go arm'd...(176–177).
I am no honest man if there be any good meaning toward you...(179–
180).
Let me, if not by birth, have lands by wit...(190).

Only in an *if* world, where structures can change, will the Bastard
find any dignity; so in his first soliloquy he subscribes to a Nature where
all men are created with equal possibility, and do not need the consent
of social fixture—birth—to achieve fortune. This egalitarian doctrine has
disturbed some Shakespearean critics, who oppose to it, for instance,
Lear's "decent" Nature. How decent that is, we have seen, and will see
better in a moment. What signifies here is that Edmund's "nature,"
again, is not a comment on nature, but on Edmund; it lends energy to
his impact on the action, and, with its strong scent of sex and touch of
humor arouses an audience warmly. This is his father's son of the first
scene, talking of sport in a bed, playing with words—and Shakespeare
has given him good ones to play with (*base, legitimate*)—and laying out
the line of his behavior, from base to top (though still he does not dream
of how far "topping" may lead him). Edmund he nothing is; but he will
be something.

Even in this revealing first soliloquy Shakespeare still delays—as if
tempting an expectation of heroism for Edmund—the full revelation of
the character. The very virtuosity of the speech, its bright language, its
dazzling turns and runs, are admirable. He came saucily into the world,
his father said in his presence; he will go saucily through it. He will not
wait to be sent for. But assertive as Edmund is, he is not yet seen to be
evil, what is to happen remains ambiguous, he only says—

if this letter speed...(19).

Not until the Bastard's "wit" is translated into action imagery, and he
actually sets his traps, will his full capacities begin to show. In this first
speech he is interesting, anticonformist, very much aware of how attractive he is: the continuing comparatives here are all in concrete terms,
brother matched against brother; and Edmund, telling us something of
their physical quality and likeness, gives himself full marks:

When my dimensions are as well compact,
My mind as generous, and my shape as true
As honest madam's issue? (7–9.)

Not least, the Bastard is sometimes happily humorous, and his final apostrophe, with its sexual undertones, its joy in the forbidden—

> I grow, I prosper;
> Now, gods, stand up for bastards! (21–22)

teaches the audience it can laugh. In Kozintsev's film, he ended his attack on the stars by throwing a rock at the heavens.

There is danger here. Edmund can draw laughs easily, almost too easily: in the theatre he has been shrunk to a cheerful rascal, carrying the audience lightly with him over even the darker moments. At the other extreme, he has been saturnine, scowling, fierce, weighting the play down rather than lifting it along. He has also seemed to be only a put-upon young man, motivated only by the wrongs and deprivation done him; conversely as if acting only out of his own *panache*, or with a paranoid compulsion. The delicacy of movement in this scene between extremes, the brilliant histrionics—from the clever first introspection through the plausibly earnest confrontations with father and brother, and then the mockery of both, to the final, firm declaration of sinister purpose—demands a very strong, very supple dramatic identity, as supple as Edgar's. Somewhere in the Bastard's flamboyance lurks the generosity to make him, dying, *do some good*; and also the vision that he will realize of absolute power. In the Brook film, his face at first has something of Edgar's softness in it. Then it hardens as his schemes progress until, at death, the softer face momentarily returns. This man, sometimes laughing, sometimes fretful, sometimes terribly earnest, always fitting his environment, might, when he is finished wading through blood and intrigue, be king. If he disguises himself to others, he is very honest to himself. He moves with purpose, as the play does, between light and shadow.

Now enter Gloster, who was first seen in a mood to chaff bastardy, but no more. How swept up he was in Lear's folly in I, i had to be left then to his physical imagery; he dared not speak. Now it comes out, in an anxious, superstitious flood as he stalks in brooding about Lear:

> ...prescrib'd his power!
> Confin'd to exhibition! All this done
> Upon the gad! (24–26.)

So much in this play is *done upon the gad*! Gloster himself is about to act so—like an animal pricked, that lunges irrationally, out of fear or anger. In *Lear*, the goaded animal always breathes close by.

Gloster is deeply absorbed—in the Brook version, he carried and studied an astrologer's board, from which he would draw his dire predictions. Edmund has to get his attention with an overt concealment of the letter, so that Gloster can ask about it. There is the play on *nothing* and the capacity of men to see:

> The quality of nothing hath not such
> need to hide itself. Let's see: come: if it be
> nothing, I shall not need spectacles (33-35).

This is Gloster's last joke, and there is anger in it, for he is already sensitive, and the gad is beginning to prick: he *will* see. The forged letter is a lesson in irony: it says word for word what the Bastard thinks, and much of what the Bastard will say is true: foolish old men are in danger from ambitious sons, and not without some justice; fathers may indeed be so declin'd that sons at perfect age should be their guardians. Gloster will indeed need a son-guardian; and Edgar (the guardian) will indeed be his death.

The youth-age opposition is here both verbally and visually insisted upon: the baffled, frustrated old man, instantly on the gad, the concerned, earnest, superbly controlled young one. Gloster's rage is a reprise of Lear's anger over Cordelia, as is apparent in the theatre in sight, sound, and verbal motifs. Gloster will later say that no father loved his son dearer than he Edgar; but now, in his panic, there comes at once the residual image concealed under so many garments in this play, of the animal: . . . *brutish* . . . *worse than brutish* . . . *monster*. . . . Edgar's heart is suspect: heart as opposed to brain, as opposed to hand, the heart of his obedience.

The dramatic manipulation is carefully handled. Edmund offers in language and implication—echoing Iago—to arrange for Gloster to hear Edgar's treachery:

> . . . and by an auricular
> assurance have your satisfaction (93-94).

This is one of the various promises Edmund will not keep.

Gloster cannot bear ambiguity; he would *unstate* himself—be the outcast he will indeed become—to know the truth. He urges Edmund to resolve his terrible doubts at once; Edmund agrees to go, and then waits to watch his father's anguish—as will Edgar, much later.

Gloster's analysis of the times—visually this may be a reading of his astrologer's board—his rhythmical series, and the antitheses of his language reflect a kind of microcosm of the play.

Love cools, friendship falls off, brothers divide: in cities, mutinies; in countries, discord; in palaces, treason; and the bond crack'd 'twixt son and father. This villain of mine comes under the prediction; there's son against father: the King falls from bias of nature; there's father against child (110–117).

This, and his first remark about Lear, are Gloster's only criticisms of the king. This is a very important one, because it throws a meaningful side-light on Lear's "Nature"—and Shakespeare's use of a focal term. Gloster is saying that Lear, who invoked Nature against Cordelia, was in fact being unnatural. But Gloster will not see into the mirror. He becomes aware of Edmund again, offers him a material reward for finding out this "villain"—he is now, to avoid uncertainty, self-convinced—and before he goes allows himself again the sorrow and indignation he dared not speak in court, about the banishment of Kent.

We have seen the best of our time... (117).

The Bastard's immediate mockery of Gloster's superstitious astrology —he may use his father's astral tablet as a prop—raises interesting problems in audience response. Shakespeare's design of Gloster makes him often foolish and superstitious; yet his point of view, of a world where shocks among the stars, in a shaken universe, affect the lives of men, had some currency in the playwright's time. Similarly, Edmund is designed to be untrustworthy, but he, too, speaks for a contemporary current of thought when he mocks his father's stargazing. Neither character speaks for Shakespeare; each reflects an ambiguity of the design. As for the spectators, Elton's study indicates that they might respond to the treatment of astrology as part of "a continuing Renaissance—as well as Shake-spearean—debate," with Edmund's side getting, if anything, the better of it, not only on rationalistic grounds, but also because the separation of natural catastrophe from supernatural power had some theological support. (R. A. Fraser notes that Calvin despised astrologers, as would his more thoughtful contemporaries; Elton observes that one of James' tutors attacked the superstition of blaming stars for mens' follies.) Shakespeare uses the debate for its dramatic values; if there was probably no monolithic audience response to the issue, certainly there was character involvement, to the design of Gloster as a superstitious, now muddled old man, in some danger, and to that of Edmund as far cleverer, more sensible—and dangerous.

Edmund's second of his three neatly spaced soliloquies in this scene re-emphasizes the Bastard's hidden qualities with the sharp contrast in tone and behavior once Gloster is gone. His sudden, almost savagely humorous attack on his father saves him from too much charm, yet preserves enough panache, enough intellect, to sustain involvement with him. Shakespeare endows him with a dazzling rhetorical brilliance: not only in the pyrotechnic language, but also in the power demanded in sheer breath control over the slippery words that run so far along before a full stop. Again, there is a resemblance between Edmund's awareness of the lusts and follies of man and Lear's comments three acts later. The speech is realistic, accepting man for what the Bastard sees as basic:

> ... we make guilty of our disasters the sun, the moon, and the stars; as if we were villains on necessity, fools by heavenly compulsion, knaves, thieves, and treachers by spherical predominance, drunkards, liars, and adulterers by an enforc'd obedience of planetary influence; and all that we are evil in, by a divine thrusting on. An admirable evasion of whoremaster man, to lay his goatish disposition to the charge of a star! (126–134).

Now the ubiquitous animal note is sounded:

> My father compounded with my mother under the dragon's tail, and my nativity was under *Ursa major*; so that it follows I am rough and lecherous. Fut! I should have been that I am had the maidenliest star in the firmament twinkled on my bastardizing (135–140).

"He means," Danby writes, "that his nature is given and unalterable and separate and his own." Thus Danby fits him into a Danby scheme. But Edmund does not say this at all: he simply says the stars had nothing to do with his being born the strong, virile man he regards himself.

Edmund's abrupt change of manner from solitude to interaction with others provides a powerful theatrical shock. His histrionic talent and enjoyment of it have been evident; he adds a dimension now, as Edgar approaches, by letting the audience share his deliberate assumption of a brooding role—perhaps as he again contemplates Gloster's astrological chart:

> ... my cue is villainous melancholy, with a sigh like Tom o'Bedlam. O! these eclipses do portend these divisions. *Fa, sol, la, mi* . . . (142–144).

The musical notes carry a little joke of their own: they are the *diabolus musica*, the forbidden interval, because of the irregularity of their upward breaks. Closer to the heart is the Tom o'Bedlam reference, since

Edgar will so soon play this role so much more intensely. How much these brothers will resemble each other in their chameleon-like masquerades, one momentary, one painfully long, is a matter for visual imagery. Edmund has, as noted above, described their likeness; but they appear in anti-mirrors: when Edgar enters it is clear—as it would have been earlier if Edgar has made a silent appearance in I, i—that they are also, in their surfaces, different.

They are first of all visually different in rank. Edmund is the outcast bastard, home on sufferance; Edgar is the heir to an earldom. This difference was emphasized in the Brook stage production; a reviewer in Hungary was impressed at the way Brook's Edmund—who lounged on the scene's central chair during his soliloquies—was up and busily dusting about when Edgar came in to take his ease.

What Edgar is, this legitimate son of an earl, may not yet be fully seen. Again Shakespeare pieces out the clues sparingly, in jagged bits, so ambiguously that he has provoked a critical notion that Edgar is not at all a character with any psychological or "mimetic" unity, but simply a dramatic device, made into whatever shape the action requires at the time. A character design does in fact unfold; Shakespeare often delays till the end the full revelation of his intent, but never so much as with Edgar.

The clues in this very brief first appearance are limited; the apparent sophistication with which he questions Edmund's astrology, and his credulity in accepting Edmund's intrigue. Regan, a doubtful witness, will say Edgar has been one of Lear's riotous knights. He will claim knighthood, in challenging Edmund at the end, citing "My oath and my profession." Edmund says he was of Lear's company and even more reliably, because in soliloquy, describes him as *noble*—with a touch of sneer, an implication of foolish honesty. Edgar has been acted here—to emphasize what he will change from—as: naive, dreamily bookish, bewildered, submissive, uncertain, drunk, wenching, a fop.

Pat he comes, like the catastrophe of the old comedy (141), Edmund says. In such a part Edgar will indeed, at the end, appear to destroy Edmund; even now some hint of the familial readiness to play roles may color his appearance. As noted, the likeness to his brother may be striking. These possibilities are meaningful as they contrast with what Edgar will become. Of all the characters, he will change most subtly.

Edmund's style toward Edgar is curious, in the formality of his speech, and in his close approximation—in the long Quarto prophecy on eclipses—to Gloster's manner and message:

... unnaturalness between the child and the parent; death, dearth, dis-
solutions of ancient amities; divisions in state ... nuptial breaches, and I
know not what (151–156).

In this last item, he is going Gloster's prophecy one better: almost as if
he has prescience—or a plan—for Goneril. In one of the ironies of this
scene, both the foolish old man and the clever young one speak true.
Shakespeare may demean astrology by sketching the folly of its proph-
esying, but here as elsewhere he multiplies tension by letting its proph-
ecies sometimes be realized.

By Edmund's last soliloquy, the possibilities of his character, though
not their full extent, are revealed. He is exultant, things have gone entirely as he wanted, he has only gulls to deal with:

> A credulous father, and a brother noble ... (186)

and he uses an animal image that recalls Gloster's earlier one:

> ... on whose foolish honesty
> My practices ride easy! (188–189).

He will bestride honesty, and goad it on to his purposes. Edmund is in a
hurry, he will make things happen in *time*—a word that will be frequently on his lips.

> All with me's meet that I can fashion fit (191).

He is insatiable: he will use anything that comes to hand—the whole
Lear world is in danger from him. The subversive, dominant tonality
sounds clearly.

Act I, Scene iii

A moment later Goneril commands the stage again. The editors locate this scene at the Duke of Albany's palace; but it is now unmistakably Goneril's, she asserts her mastery, her ownership, in tones that pick up where her last speech to Regan left off. In elegance, the place will rival Lear's. She regards it as a royal palace, as we will see, and will use the royal plural in speaking to her father. Now, to Oswald, her intimate, her speech is full of *I*:

> Did my father strike my gentleman for chiding of his Fool? (1–2).

My . . . my . . . But there is more than mastery. Her relationship with Oswald, of a peculiar strength, will endure to Oswald's death. The visual imagery the theatre has contributed to this relationship can be significant. Is Oswald Goneril's "gentleman?" Regan will call him so in II, ii, 149. Does he now bear the mark of Lear's angry blow? And so make tangible the friction in the house? Does Goneril's hand go out to Oswald's wound? Or his bandage? With tenderness? Sexuality? In this play so full of echoes, Goneril's gesture here, welcomed by Oswald, has been a minor motif to be repeated when Goneril "serves" Edmund, and when Regan attempts to seduce Oswald in IV, v. If it is Oswald who suffered Lear's blow, this scene is more tightly bound to the next one.

The Goneril-Oswald equation rests half on the Oswald design. Criticism and the theatre are tempted to see him as a hollow, comic-evil pawn in the greater scheme. The morality seekers begrudge him his absolute loyalty to his mistress—it is easier to see him merely bad. On the stage he has sometimes been made an easy joke: a fop, a less-than-Osric, good for a laugh when he is tripped up by Kent in the next scene, and a laughable, cowardly foil to Kent's anger in II, ii. But he is more. Inevitably he is a loser, and there is comedy in his discomfiture; but unless he has dignity to go with his loyalty, he diminishes the two with whom he has the strongest relationships: Kent and Goneril.

Oswald is subtly involved in the male-female and master-follower dialectics. He generally appears as one of the young enemies of the aged —he is Goneril's age, and even younger than she when she is represented as a matron yearning back toward youth. Before her strength, he is supple and compliant, as he also retreats before Kent's masculinity; but he has learned to look down on Albany's submissiveness—hence will be surprised by the Duke's strength in IV. His loyalty is a curious mirroring of that of Kent, his first antagonist, and that of Edgar, his last. Oswald thinks well of himself and—if Kent's II, ii insults mean anything—he takes care to dress himself well. His mistress confides in him her wounded and angry feelings, commissions him to carry intimate messages, even to her lover. Her confidence in him is well placed; he tries to serve her even beyond death. The mixture in his role of his relative masculinity and his serving role take shape in the loyalty of his relationship, erotic or otherwise, with Goneril. The synthesis was introduced visually in an interesting way in the Kozintsev production, where Oswald was discovered combing the long copper-colored hair of his mistress, as she lay on a red couch beneath an archaic gilt Virgin. Irene Worth's Goneril, an intense, smoldering figure, clearly kept a sensual hold on Oswald. Edgar's Puritan claim that he knows Oswald to be as duteous to the vices of his mistress as badness would desire (IV, vi, 254) can refer to something more than his carrying of messages.

Goneril, in I, iii, has been seen—on the stage and in criticism—as ranging from the wicked daughter immediately scheming her father's downfall to a harassed housewife embarrassed by an old guest's bad manners. She can be visualized as simply, or meanly, angry; more subtly, as with Irene Worth's neurotic, she may seem upset by her father's irrational behavior, nervous about diminishing his authority. The design of the action requires that she remain dynamic, not yet fixed in evil. By still delaying the revelation of her possibilities, Shakespeare maintains suspense. Lear had called on the powers of day and night: *by day and night, he wrongs me* (4), Goneril complains. Her bitter attack on Lear's *gross crimes*, and on his riotous knights, however ill-founded it may turn out, must still in I, iii be possibly true, or the design of expectation falls. The whole scene works toward this expectation: there is trouble in the house, Goneril wants a showdown:

I'd have it come to question (14).

She will—in the only kind of reproduction allowed her—*breed occasion.* Her means are devious, but socially familiar: Oswald must tell for her a social lie—a lie Lear will become painfully familiar with, and, in II, iv, almost be afraid to disbelieve:

say I am sick (9).

Goneril will control other appearances:

> Put on what weary negligence you please (13).
> ... let his knights have colder looks among you (23).

In the Scofield film, she said this not only to Oswald, but to her whole servant staff. In the Brook staging, Oswald began promptly to make *negligence* visual: he tasted one bottle of wine, found it too good for Lear's knights, put it aside, tried a poorer bottle, spat out its vile stuff, and handed this bottle to Kent in the transition between the scenes.

The most energetic verbal motif that emerges in Goneril's lines reverses the child-parent roles:

> Old fools are babes again, and must be us'd
> With checks as flatteries (20–21).

She sees Lear, as Fool will, with his breeches down, and she with the rod in her hand to check him. She ends by confiding in Oswald that she will write to Regan to support her. She is sure her sister will agree—and yet there has been a hint of something darker that supports the rumor that we must soon hear of war between the dukes:

> ... let him to my sister,
> Whose mind and mine, I know, in that are one (15–16).

In *that*—but not much else—does the voice say? With an awareness, or a prescience, of the many other differences that will grow into hatred?

Act I, Scene iv

The immediate visual and verbal image opening this scene is of flight. In the *Lear* world, men are hunted down and killed if they offend authority. Kent, marked for death, now inserts himself into the heart of hazard, Goneril's castle. The very real physical danger to the refugees in this world is repeatedly stipulated: Kent to be executed if he is found in the kingdom, Edgar and any who hide him to suffer the same fate. Later Lear and Gloster are to be killed on sight. But the text specifies visually only the pursuit of Gloster (by Oswald); subtextual action must stipulate the continuous atmosphere of this world of men being hunted down. It is a cold, night world outside; Fool will sensibly want to stay in from it. Some sense of its dark ambience was suggested in the Kozintsev stage production, where, before Lear's entrance to I, iv, a procession of convicts was driven by halbardiers, as in a scene from Breughel, out of the mist of the heath across the stage into a deeper mist. Then Lear's hunting party streamed across, fierce bloodhounds dragging the hunters behind them.

In such a world, Kent's disguise must be seen as a dangerous gamble; recognition means death, and he is in the home of enemies. The pursuit he has evaded may be seen to be going on: men in the shadows search for outlaws. If he has been escorted, he may be seen to escape from his guards, or turn upon them and kill them. A practical problem, for the theatre and the visualizer: the changed Kent must be known to the audience, in spite of his *raz'd likeness* and *defused* speech; or spectators unfamiliar may sit—have sat—through a good part of the play before knowing who this stranger is. The words go by quickly: *Now, banished Kent*; so the visual clues must be unmistakable—a recognizable Kent finishing his disguise on the spot, trying out his new accent (usually a rustic brogue): this goes with the name he will take: Caius, an anybody name.

Kent's danger is tangible when Lear enters—often preceded by the sounds of hunt and horn, of horses and men, sometimes by knights carrying game on line or pole. They have been cold, they blow on chilled hands, slap themselves warm. Lear shouts his command for dinner—*Let me not stay a jot* (9)—and finds Kent in his way. Kent may do him a service to force his attention; or, as in a Japanese performance, Kent is arrested by the knights and hauled before him. Lear's

How now! what art thou? (10)

has reverberations, sets a pattern for his meetings with strangers. His catechism of Edgar will show the same searching curiosity; in each case, he will be questioning a mask that covers a hidden identity—and in each case, there arises (for the naive spectator) the suspense of possible unmasking, and beyond this, the ambiguity that Lear may indeed unmask his man and not reveal his knowing.

Kent does not give himself away, but his answers are characteristic, even to the provocative *as poor as the King* (20) that must draw a special glance from Lear, and perhaps suspicion and hostility from Lear's knights. But Kent's other lines are bluff and hearty, the kind to please hunting and fighting men, down to the church-sex joke, *eat no fish* (18).

Lear's persistent prose questioning, an aspect of the "seeing into" motif, was again visualized by Carnovsky in an intense peering, a searching into the disguised face. The questions were not tossed out casually; Lear wanted to know; he seemed at the point of penetrating Kent's identity.

Does Lear recognize in the half-hidden face his old friend and enemy? Whose death he had commanded for being in the kingdom? Has he any doubts? Conscious or subconscious? This must remain a subtextual ambiguity, and will depend on the Lear design.

The range of Lear's possibility is extended by his ambiguous role as a guest. He still acts King, does not merely wear the additions; his entourage is royal. A hundred knights—the round figure is bland, not so the sight in a theatre of a mass of accoutred men drifting in sweaty after a hunt. They need not be as riotous as Goneril claims, need not be riotous at all, to represent visually a mighty problem for their hostess.

Visual understatement, as in a Krauss production, where a few quiet knights ornamented the stage, makes a mockery of Lear's self-image. Scofield's substantial stage entourage seemed to approach the whole number because in noise and energy it was almost as turbulent as Goneril claimed. Probably no performance has had its full hundred, except in a film; but producers have made impressive efforts to suggest as many, by flooding the stage, as in the Laughton *Lear*, with gouts of active men, and feeding them off and on. The knights often carry the materials of the hunt, weapons, killed game—Mantell's managed a buck and led dogs in. Welles' Lear held a hooded falcon on his arm, Edmund Kean held a boar spear, a common business. Porter's knights rollicked on in a mock hunt circling a man with a boar's mask, hemming him in for Lear to finish off with a pretended, ritual thrust. The mime incarnated the flight-pursuit imagery that would end with the hunter, become quarry, hounded to death. Lear's catechism of Kent allows time for this background activity, before the settling down to Fool and Goneril.

But what chiefly conditions the Lear image is the quality and mood embodied by Lear himself as he enters. He now carries a past with him: his rejection of Cordelia. Does it weigh on him? Later in this scene, and in the next, the sense of it will beat at him—indeed make him beat at himself. How much it may show now, in evident or latent anxiety, depends on the strength of the characterization at this point. Salvini's august, stalwart Lear, still feeling very much the monarch, came on hardly tired from the chase, fresh and laughing, as if he had put entirely aside the memory of Cordelia. Gielgud was in this tradition, following the Granville-Barker dictum that Lear should seem robust, jolly, full of energy; he entered in a swirl of cloak and scarf, enjoying the sparring with Kent and his knights, throwing his accoutrements to attendants, boots off, shoes on. . . . But there would be just a touch of the hectic, of hyper-energy in all this that would run down at the first check. The cracks in his spiritual armor could be felt.

Dunn's Lear, a tough old man who had realistically threatened Kent in I, i, challenged the disguised man here to a fierce duel with staves. Carnovsky was burly and gruff, "a compensation for something he has lost," his notes suggest, and to cover a quality of absentmindedness. Scofield's tough, hard-handed Lear strode stiffly in from the obviously strenuous chase, tired, sweaty, angry, with the repressed memory of his wrong to Cordelia, crashed his whip down with a snarled request for dinner, dominated by the force of his person the gang of rowdy knights that swarmed around him.

At the other extreme, the frankly old men came in slowed and weighted with their age. The mid-nineteenth-century Lears, intent on establishing the pathetic, good father, seemed harmless old gentlemen. Charles Kean was eager, rapid, called for his dinner like a hearty country squire; Phelps seemed only a cheerful, hungry old man—no rumble in either of the autocratic force, the impatient majesty, the cankerous memory. Irving infused these into his characterization, and endowed his pathetic Lear with a dimension of anguish even here. Weary as he was, his passion, touched already with latent madness, energized him. Ayrton's Lear was already dark and moody, shadowed by his memory.

This Lear scene is—as are most of his scenes—a series of challenges;

and the verbal substructure of the challenge may be found in the punctuation. Lear's first scene was a series of declarative, imperative, and exclamatory sentences; in this second, up to the very moment of the "curse," the chief mode will be the question. Almost exactly half the sentences will be questions, mainly from Lear and Fool, and largely related to the puzzle of Lear's identity. In I, i, Lear fought off, overtly, the threats to his security; he declared who and what he was. Now he will ask others to tell him.

His commands have begun to lose their force. This will be evident enough in the larger movements of the scene; it may also emerge in subtler visual dissonances. Lear orders his dinner to come at once. His order is not obeyed; the usual (*Exit an attendant*) was an editor's guess. Time passes. Lear must repeat his order—and there is no textual evidence that he ever gets food, ever has anything to eat in the long night of his madness. The first order may have been conspicuously ignored: Lear is perhaps already getting from Goneril's servants the colder looks she decreed. Everyone seems asleep to Lear, perhaps because they refuse to hear him. They do not acknowledge his existence, his commands dissipate in the air. He is humiliated before he is willing to admit it: there is a curious ambiguity in his later admission to the knight:

> I have perceived a most faint neglect of late; which I have rather blamed as mine own jealous curiosity than as a very pretence and purpose of unkindness... (71–74).

Pretence is a double-edged word here, implying not only the intention of unkindness, but also a calculated show of it. Lear's sense of this may be part of the subtextual design; his loud demands for service may be designed to reflect not only his painful memories, but also a sense of his growing present insecurity—he has preferred to blame himself rather than risk acknowledging reality. After his confession to the knight, he drops the loud demand for dinner, instead turns suddenly again to thoughts of his Fool.

A series of questions marks Lear's growing uncertainty. The first was to Kent, who asked to serve him:

> Dost thou know me, fellow? (28).

Does the subject know his king? Does Lear have his royal identity? Kent said "*No sir*;" Lear is anybody, nobody. The semi-colon after Kent's words may well indicate a sustained pause, time for Lear to react to this denial of his significance. Time for Kent to respond to the shock, for he follows it quickly with an assurance for Lear's ego: something in his face worth serving. What? Lear needs to know, Kent tells him: *Authority*.

In the theatre, this has been the chance for a "point"—Lear is seen flattered, he softens. Macready's Kent took his hat off and bowed, here; and Macready, as Lear, went on comfortably chuckling through the rest of the employment interview. Scofield looked shrewdly into Kent's eyes, with a hint of mockery; he was learning better. Forrest seemed so childishly tickled by this tribute from a nameless stranger that his Lear dissipated his dignity. Something deeper, more complex than simple vanity stirs in Lear; authority was his stay, but it emptied his life, and he is losing it. The response is multiple; Lear has learned something about flattery, if he is not altogether a fool. If there is a touch of pleasure, there is also something of Laughton's response (Byrne):

> no change of expression in the heavy, impassive countenance, a slow, slight quarter-turn of the head, a momentary hooding and lifting of the lids, the shrewd, appraising eyes of Henry VIII looked out...

Thou shalt serve me (43), Lear tells Kent, and this reminds him of failed service: no dinner. Again he calls for it; again no stage or textual direction indicates accommodation. As if to emphasize its denial, Oswald moves unconcernedly past him. This king, usually promptly and even unctuously served in I, i, is now ignored—and he knows it, has felt it, has wanted not to admit it. The design of the action requires that the unspoken ignoring of Lear's commands reaches its climax now in Oswald's deliberate casualness.

Traditionally, in the eighteenth century Oswald passed "in a careless, disengaged manner, humming a tune, as if on purpose" to anger Lear. The tradition survives: so Gielgud's Oswald dawdled by with elaborate insolence. Scofield's Oswald, allowed more dignity, less comedy, suggested a workmanlike aloofness. The provocation must be somehow proportionate to Lear's answering rage: Oswald's impertinence may be seen as partly the excuse for Lear's pouring out a sense of heaped-up wrong, but even so the extent of Lear's fury is delicately dependent on how much Oswald is worthy of a king's anger, and the kind of motivation—from plain anger to desperation—that energizes it. A Lear who storms at a petty comic figure is different from a Lear who snarls at a sullen servant. Salvini's Lear was hardly troubled by Oswald's insult; to Gielgud's, it was a sharp check that punctured his carefully forced afflatus. Scofield said his excess of anger, here and later in the scene, reflected the gnawing memory of how wrong he had been to Cordelia.

The Oswald incident must fit into a larger design: the series of ego confrontations that develop wavelike to the climactic "curses."

That something inward is already eating at Lear is made explicit when Lear calls for his Fool, and the knight reminds him that since Cordelia's exile the Fool has much pined away. Lear's

> No more of that; I have noted it well (79)

is a cry of pain, however muted. Charles Kean's voicing admitted frankly a "world of sorrow and remorse"; more customary was Macready's almost angry, half-impatient, half-ill-repressed outburst that revealed feeling by trying to mask it. Carnovsky let it show with a kind of unconscious anxiety reflex—his arm jerked. Devlin's taut face recalled his blank shock at Cordelia's first *nothing*. Gielgud carefully tossed the thought away, as if it did not touch him. A silence from the assembled knights perhaps best reveals the implications of Lear's outburst.

Most significant about the gentle knight's speech is its courtesy and knightliness. It cannot easily be made the speech of a debauched, riotous hoodlum, of the sort Goneril describes. It could hardly be more thoughtful, more sensitive to the feelings of Lear—and of Fool. In the theatre this knight is usually recognized from the I, i court scene as a particular personal attendant on Lear; he may play the role of Gentleman in the storm, and also rejoin Lear in his brief resurgence at the end: in none of these appearances has he an opportunity for anything but respectful discipline, unless of a non-textual kind enforced by a production idea. Unless played as politely drunk, he will not be representative of a company committed to epicurism and lust. Only Kent of Lear's speaking attendants overtly projects in the text the quality of *boldness* of which Goneril complains.

Lear's confrontation with Oswald marks Lear's second testing of his ego.

> Who am I, sir? (83)

he asks, pursuing his interrogatory mood. Kent-Caius professed not to know him; Oswald professes to know him an appurtenance to a daughter—as a child may be known as the son of his mother. Nothing in himself. Lear's explosion, manifestly fired by a sense of past wrong as much as present provocation, does no harm to Oswald, who stands his ground in a show of considerable courage. He does not quake at the ex-king's stare. When Lear counters, in a kingly charge—or an old man's wonder—

> Do you bandy looks with me, you rascal? (89)

it is in fact Lear bandying looks with a man who no longer fears his anger. In the earlier play, Leir was made to accept mistreatment with Christian patience; Shakespeare made a different, much more difficult design of man, quick to feel shame, and furious at his shaming. Before the company of knights, Lear must assert his role, call Oswald animal, threaten a blow, perhaps give one—Gielgud snatched up a cloth from the table and struck Oswald back and forth across the face, then eyed him with contempt. Oswald has been slapped and hit with the riding whip. But neither contempt nor a blow banishes him; he refuses to be "*strucken*"—*strucken* again, if he bears the mark of an earlier blow. Oswald's own courage, considering his timidity before Kent later (II, ii) may be accounted for visually by an escort of Goneril's men—who would then have to be neutralized before Oswald could be tripped and hustled out.

Oswald's boldness is an ultimate challenge to the dignity of the once all-powerful king: must he try physically to subdue a servant? Use the whip on him? The deadlock—perhaps a dead pause—is broken only when Kent, the first to react, trips Oswald, and shoves him away—often, in the theatre, to the laughter of Lear and his knights, who—if they are the bullies Goneril will describe—may handle Oswald very roughly, toss him up, throw him out. Lear gives Kent money for his service; he will not offer anyone pay again until he goes mad.

The touch of the comic in Oswald's fall is shadowed—as is Lear's anger—by the incessant dialectic of the play. Kent acts as a friend, but as bully too. Lear's vicarious triumph is a cheap one. How cheap, Fool makes clear when he enters—perhaps in time to see how Oswald is treated—and offers Kent or Lear the coxcomb, that symbol of folly, barbed laughter, sexuality.

Three things we know about Fool, before he comes on—unless he has been seen or (by the critic) imagined at Lear's abdication. First, that Lear struck Goneril's gentleman for chiding Fool—a kind of last straw that determined Goneril to the coming showdown. Second, that Lear needs the Fool, depends on him, misses him. Third, that Fool has pined away.

Fool is a professional entertainer, conscious of effect, and the visual imagery of his entrance will be calculated. Lear's strange, grotesque comedy, so interwoven with the anguish of the play—the laughter is "old" laughter, not young, Blok observed—centers on the role of folly in man-animal; Fool personifies both the assumption of folly and the exposure of it. However, he comes on—bouncing, dancing, crawling, strolling, singing, glooming—he must have a sense of the impact on his audience on stage—mainly Lear to whom he is playing. How he does this, how the others respond, make this one of the most dense, complex moments of confrontation in the play.

Fool, Kent and Lear all wear costumes, that separate them from core identities. Kent wears his disguise and knows it; Lear wears the image of a king, resists the consciousness that it is a slipping garment about to fall and leave him naked. Fool wears his professional costume and manner, and would escape them, but they have penetrated and absorbed his being.

Fool bears a cockscomb*—the cock a powerful symbol of the sexual energy traditionally permitted outlet in the jester's erotic images. But the cock was only one of the ornaments that linked fools to the animal kingdom: fools might wear the comb not on a cap but on a monk's hood, that also held ass' ears; they might be ornamented with fox-tails, calf skins, feathers. Madmen, as we will see (III, iv), were likened to beasts; the fool occupied a way station between sanity and madness.

Fools carried "baubles," short sticks topped with some ornament: a puppet's head, the fool's own head or some other figure (in a modern production, a death's head). Fools might well talk to these (or other inanimate objects) ventriloquially; so Lear's Fool might chance some of his impudences by voicing them through his bauble, or conversing with it. The bauble could also serve as a mock sceptre; as it developed, it sometimes took on unmistakably the form of a phallus, and so became a parody of a double power image.

Fools' codpieces might be highly exaggerated. The bells they wore might be sacral mimics, but as bright, tinkling toys came handy to professional entertainers. Lear's Fool could use them for dramatic accents, as he might the inflated bladders jesters sometimes swung at the butts of their jests.

Fool would have been an immediate signal to Shakespeare's audience of one of various customarily sheltered outsiders. He was related to the kind of family retainer who lived by his wits—or by his half-wits, depending on how much of either he had.** Whether "permitted" (artificial) or natural, whether retained for his value as entertainer and friend or fostered as a paid-for, low-intelligence ward, he had a recognizable place in all levels of society.

---

*Fools once had the sides of their heads so shaved that the cock's comb seemed to grow in the middle, Douce reported.

**Enid Welsford believes Fool was "evidently half-witted" (256). Would all whole-wits were as wise.

The town knew such "fools" as the London natural, Blue John, personated by Robert Armin in *The Two Maids of More-Clacke* (written 1590). Foolery was very familiar in James' court, some of it the very bawdy fooling of titled gentlemen. Sir John Millisert, according to Sir Anthony Weldon, was the "best extemporary fool of them all"; but the great professional was a fool James had brought with him from Scotland, Archy Armstrong. Archy deserves some space here because his role and some of his jests resonate with those of Lear's Fool.

Archy boldly made jokes at the expense of court figures, his particular enemy being Archbishop Laud. Archy once volunteered to say this grace at a dinner with the Archbishop: "Great praise be to God, and little *laud* to the devil." The Archbishop was angry, but had to delay his revenge.

Archy lived well as a king's favorite. State papers tell how, on the occasion of Princess Elizabeth's wedding, James ordered for his fool a lavish crimson velvet cloak, lined with gold lace. James might be displeased with Archy for arrogantly forwarding a knight's petition to the king's attention, but the king kept his fool about him, or let him go journeying on state business.

Sent to Spain with Buckingham and Prince Charles, Archy wrote to James: "To let your Majesty know, never a fool was better accepted on by the king of Spain, except his own fool . . . secretly, I am better accepted on than he is . . . I am sent for by this King when none of your own or your sons men can come near him . . . I shall think myself better and more fool than all the fools here . . . whoever could think that your Majesty kept a gull and an ass of me—he is a gull and an ass himself."

Archy could be a bitter fool: once, when James and Prince Charles parted after watching sports, and most of the courtiers followed Charles, Archy made a joke of James's comparative unpopularity that moved the king to tears. Archy could be butt, too, and even plaything—he was tossed in a blanket by Charles' resentful friends when they could catch him.

Laud finally brought Archy down when the fool scoffed at the Archbishop for a diplomatic failure: "Wheas feule now?"* The enraged Laud drove the Council to rule that Archy should "have his coat pulled over his head, and [be] banished the Court." The practical Archy had taken care to become a rich man by then, much to the envy of another fool, Belon, who wrote, comparing himself with the favorite: "I have fallen beneath the degree of a dog, I can petition no more for fear I fall a-howling . . ." But concern for wealth seemed not to bother Muckle

*Who's fool now?

John, the fool who took Archy's place; a letter to Lord Strafford observed, "he will ne'er be so rich [as Archy] for he cannot abide money." After Laud went to the Tower, Archy got his revenge by publishing *Archy's Dream*, which imagined Laud deservedly in hell.

Some conventions deepened Fool's stage role, conventions so immediately accepted over the centuries that they seem archetypal: the "wise fool," the "wise child," the "wise madman"; the mascot; the scapegoat; the Vice, or Folly; the mad clairvoyant; the voice of a possessing spirit; the amusing lunatic; the compulsion of a fool—and a madman and a child —to speak uncomfortable truth; the magic and mystery of the unnatural; permitted vituperation as an amulet against bad luck; the instruction of the lofty king by his lowly jester; the voice of the king's unconscious; the mock king; the interchangability of king and jester (Fool has worn a mock crown as his cockscomb); the choric voice.

Fool shares some qualities found by Olive Mary Busby in many fools: cowardice, a love of creature comforts, a hatred of discomfort—travel, work, hunger, thirst. Fool's genius is partly that he transcends these "knavish" impulses. On *Lear*'s great stage of fools, Fool represents the kind of visionary folly Erasmus celebrated, that in its non-reason sees beyond self to deeper realities. There is a touch of the magical—and the demonic—in his charm-like rhymes, his ritual, didactic utterances. He seems to command mysteries: as simple as his riddles and jokes, whose secrets must wait on his comic revelations, or as subtle as his semi-oracular pronouncements.

Lear's fool is much more than his traditional materials. He is unique to this play; he is himself a kind of microcosm of the play's turbulent dialectic. He is made of contraries, as his language is. He has been projected, by actors and critics, as very hurtful to Lear, a bitter fool; by others as sweet Fool, tender and loving, paining Lear only unintentionally. Because he preaches practicality to Lear, he has been seen as without ennobling weakness and compassion; because he clings impractically to Lear, his idealism has been named his distinction. He has been called "childlike, unsophisticated, uninhibited"; he has been seen as a very symbol of sexuality—the codpiece; as really mad, or idiotic, or as deeply sane. In fact, he is all: and so, in his ambiguity, he has seemed on stage (to Speaight) to guard incommunicable secrets; a mask moving us to a hundred guesses. He is bitter and sweet—bittersweet, to match the play. He is naive and world-weary, practical and idealistic, sensible and foolish, mad and sane, conformist and rebel, dependent and independent, privileged and underprivileged, jesting and melancholy, hurtful and lov-

ing. In Erasmian terms, he is the Folly that both condemns and justifies
the human convention. He clings to life; but like the Death in the Dance
of Death who wore cap and bells, his message is man's mortality. He
evokes erotic images, but scolds impractical sexuality; he preaches order,
and stirs chaos. He voices the id-world that Lear must repress—until Lear
himself is ready to voice it. Lear in sanity resists being fool, shuns what
Fool invites—the shame, the ultimate disorder of being laughed at.

The implications of these contradictions extend to Fool's physical
image. He often wore "motley"—which Leslie Hotson—and much earlier Francis Douce—thought might not be the color-patched suit often
linked to jesters, but rather the childish, long, green-mingled-with-
other-colors greatcoat or petticoat of the idiot. Tarleton commonly
wore a buttoned cap, russet jerkin, and hose, carried a bag, a bat or a
pipe and tabor. A court fool might be dressed like other courtiers.
Traditionally, the fool-jester's costume was often divided by color,
especially from the breeches down, suggesting his near-schizophrenic
nature. His "antinaturalness" was reflected in his body—often, conventionally, distorted: crippled, humped, twisted, or dwarfed: in some so-
cieties jester-fools were deliberately malformed for the purpose, since
abnormal mascots were thought to carry protection against the Evil
Eye.* Alternatively—or simultaneously—fools might be hyperactive, acrobatic. In *Lear*, Fool's characteristic strangeness visually makes special
demands on the imagination; he is an interruption in the chain of being
from man to animal.

Because Fool is called *pretty knave*, Bradley was sure he must be a
young boy, timid, delicate, frail; so, too, Poel: a child with the wisdom
of a child—the profoundest wisdom; Agate said he once saw a child
play the part perfectly. But Fool's wisdom seems ancient, as well as
naive, and men have played him with grey hair; in a Czechoslovakian
performance, an old, old Fool died when he went to bed at the noon of
his age. He was a wisp of an old man, cruelly blown about in the storm.
He seemed older than Lear; he had the fool's agility in body and mind,
but with his frailty it had a spectral quality. He watched Lear with the

---

*"The history of the court fool, if we may include the physically abnormal under
that heading, may be said to open with the arrival of a mysterious little pygmy
called the Danga at the court of Dadkeri-Assi, a Pharaoh of the Fifth Dynasty.
Whether the Pharaohs kept real madmen in their courts, I do not know, but it is
evident from their tombstones that they loved to surround themselves with ugly
dwarfs..."

"The Danga was no doubt an agile and amusing little fellow, but his chief attraction was that he was *mysterious*, that he came from the land of shades, that he knew
the dance of an exotic God" (Welsford, 56–7).

expression of an anxious mother who half with fear, half with compunction watches lest her beloved child be killed by too much medicine. One old stage Fool was praised because his awareness of the passage of years so well illustrated Lear's own age; another was discounted because "one must feel the pathos of youth under the wry shafts of the jester, and Lear's care for him in the storm is the care of an old man for a child." We are reminded that Lear calls Fool *boy*: but Fool calls Lear *boy* too— or is this only part of the mocking inversion pervasive in both designs?

This Fool knows what it is to be Fool—and fool. His nameless name is an insult; he knows it. That a tender connotation had recently crept into the language does not take the sting away for him. He would rather be anything than a fool,* and yet he is *something*—when Lear is nothing. His role—his costume—gives him a power over the king, and he uses it.** In language he never gives comfort to Lear, at best only advice to come in out of the rain; he never verbally commiserates with Lear for his suffering. Fool mainly recalls the king's folly, and recalls it, and recalls it. Yet subtextually, in visual imagery, in his own mock kingship, "sceptre" and all, he is a mirrored shadow of his master (a mirror in Fool's hand would multiply ironies. He is Lear's looking-glass. Does Lear himself carry a mirror?). Fool is obviously bound to Lear by an affection that survives their exile and suffering in the storm. Though even here he has been seen as following Lear only because he has no other haven—as evidence, Goneril will soon order him out after his departing master; and in III, vi, he must be told to help the fugitive king; but these, we will see, are ambiguous moments, part of the incessant dialectic in the character design.

That he is a character, and not merely a "dramatic device," a "poetic distraction," as he has been sometimes called, is evident at once in the theatre, even when Fool is played for only a fraction—the bitter or sweet—of his paradoxical design. Sweetness was in the first known portrayal, in Macready's *Lear* of 1838 (no Fool appeared for the hundred fifty-odd years that the Tate version held the stage). Macready envisioned a "fragile, hectic, beautiful-faced, half-idiot looking boy," and

---

*Welsford: ". . . the fool's dress was sometimes imposed on offenders as a peculiarly degrading form of punishment."

**Jack MacGowran, who played Fool to Scofield's Lear in the film, said what he felt most was the power designed into his role. Only Lear was more powerful, this Fool felt. With power went self-concern: much as Fool wanted the best for Lear, he wanted it even more for himself. In this, as in other ways, McGowran sensed his closeness to Lear. Fool was like nobody else in the play, in nature, but he had much in common with the king.

chose a girl to play him. Casting Fool took as much courage as Macready's revolutionary restoration of the bulk of the Shakespearean
text: not for the "indelicacy" of Fool's erotic lines, which were promptly cut to spare audience sensibility, but for the aesthetic indecorum,
Macready fearing that like "many such terrible contrasts," the role
would weary, annoy, or distract the audience.

It did not, indeed it pleased many, and set a pattern for later women
Fools: "(Miss Horton) thrills forth the snatches of song with the mingled archness and pathos of their own exquisite simplicity . . . a happy
mixture of archness and silliness, attachment and fidelity . . ." But the
softness of the performance grieved the judicious, as unfit "for this
looking-glass of the poor King, in which his weakness is shown to him
with so much truthfulness . . . fails to hit the real point of the motley,
deficient in that irresistible rush of the animal spirits . . . to top the dis-
tresses of the scene with an atmosphere of mingled raillery and wisdom."
". . . an arch, simple-witted, sportive boy rather than the shrewd, searching Fool whose peculiarity of mind enabled him to see deeper into men
and motives, because he disregarded their external trappings."

But there were opposite theatre interpretations even then: an actor in
Phelps' *Lear* was scolded in 1845 for making Fool only

> a professed wit and satirist, a profound moral-monger, a censor-general
> of the vices and follies of the King and Court. When we call to mind the
> almost doating fondness of Lear for his "poor fool" . . . and the terrible
> scene in which none of his wit or his satire are permitted to intrude;
> that he is a sort of second Cordelia to the bereaved King . . . we cannot
> consent to admit that the Fool may be fitly represented as a harsh moral
> censor . . .*

This interpretation indicates how far off Maynard Mack was in general-
izing that all nineteenth century Fools in the theatre were sentimentalized.

These extremes have appeared in performances in many countries;
better Fools merged bitter and sweet with the other dialectics of the
role. One quality often projected was simple fear: subject to the shifting, terrible passions of Lear and his whip, bullied by Goneril and her
servants, compelled by nature and role to irritate and anger these powerful forces, driven into a world of night, storm, and madmen that sicken
as well as frighten him, completely dependent on others, with no base
of his own, Fool is seen to live in perpetual—partly self-invoked—uncer-

Court Journal 11, 8, 45.

tainty. The sheer strain of attending on Lear's passion partly explained the disintegration of one stage Fool.

The quality of strangeness that colors Fool's visual as well as verbal imagery is unmistakable in the theatre. Descriptions confirm that he appears not like other men; his voice pitches differently, queerly, echoing child and sage—and madman; his movements, if not at first excessive in their athleticism, then running down like an overwound clock, are extreme in other ways: grotesque, childish, ancient, with jerky animal movements, crouching, clumsy with premature age, sly, worn, desperate, tender, bold, terrified, vulnerable, sinister, weak, a fusion of Greek chorus and Sancho Panza. Granville-Barker at first saw him as agile, athletic, and Fool has sometimes been played a gymnast; but he has also been a halting arthritic. Rarely has Fool taken on conventional motivation: though the German Barnay, before he acted Lear, portrayed Fool as a pale, careworn young man, in simple dark clothes, his suffering face surrounded by long, black hair, his mainspring frustrated, romantic love for Cordelia. The interpretation was effective enough that Joseph Kainz, another noted German actor, adopted it, but it did not survive. Yet some of a fool's hopeless love for a heroine—a theme touched on as early as in Polyphemus' infatuation for Galatea, as lately as in Cyrano and Charlie Chaplin—may add dimension to Fool; he pines for Cordelia, especially if he is seen with her in I, i. Such Fools can only pine; they must remain non-persons, like madmen, outside the world of normal intimate relationship. Some of Fool's strangeness was suggested in a Norwegian *Lear* by a sad, spectral melody, plucked on strings, that accompanied his first entrance, and, in shreds and hints, followed him faintly in the storm.

Fool's primary loyalty is to Lear. Michael Williams, Porter's Fool, saw this loyalty as almost instinctive, animal-like. He decided to choose a monkey for his model, and was studying the monkey house at the zoo, when he saw a familiar figure in front of him—Alex Clunes, Scofield's stage Fool. Clunes pointed to a monkey at the top of the house and said, "That was mine." A Japanese Fool clung so closely to Lear's back that he seemed almost a hump there; Lear had often to look backward to talk to him. Gielgud's Fool, Alan Badel (b. 1923), took his inspiration from a spaniel, was held to Lear by love and whipping. Badel could not accept the "pale-faced boy" image Granville-Barker then wanted; he preferred the concept of the petted dog; following Lear doglike, he wore a dog collar, and Gielgud did use the whip on him. But Fool was a kind of whip to Lear, too, Badel felt—an externalization of Lear's need to punish himself, hurt himself.

Fool and Lear are in an indivisible equation that has a third, implicit term in it: Cordelia. Gielgud feels the actor in Shakespeare's company who played Fool must have doubled in Cordelia. The characters might well present an echoing image, if only because they are small, dependent, torn between genuine love and an impulse to scold and punish. But they are not simple parallels, in this play where mirror images resist each other: where Cordelia urges righteousness, Fool urges practicality; and both have mirror-anti-mirror relationships to Lear. Cordelia's design, like Lear's, includes an all-or-none impulse; she hates compromises. From Fool Lear learns better—not because, George Ian Duthie suggests, Fool is wise, but because he loves. As Lear does learn, he will begin to take on some of the riddling, paradoxical, fey manner and matter of the fool—until he becomes fool, and then Fool will disappear. The forgiving Cordelia will take her turn again at the end; she is his dearer fool; but her death will mingle in Lear's mind with the other.

Fool's mirroring of Lear—and Lear's of Fool—has been made visual: thus, Fool has given his cockscomb to Lear for a crown, has taken Lear's crown for a cockscomb, and pretended regal power. At Colorado, having exchanged headpieces, the two played a mirror game, mimicking each other's gestures.

The primary intimacy of the Lear-Fool relationship in the center of the play enforces a delicate reciprocation between them. Lear carries the remnants of the tonic key; Fool's note counters that key with dissonance. Fool's language, as Wolfgang Clemen and Paul Jorgensen have observed, is reductive, and except for the rhymes, solid prose, made of simple, earthy, domestic detail—a counterforce to Lear's rhetoric, and the gigantism of his passion and thunder. Fool's imagery, in action and language, permits a laughter that saves Lear's own extravagances from seeming comic—until Lear takes over Fool's role. Lear does not want to be laughed at, mocked; but he helps Fool to laugh at him, mock him. The give and take between them is essential not only to the dialectic of the play, but also of the characters. Many elements compose the motley design: that Lear willingly submits to Fool's attacks, knowing they will come; that for a moment we will see that he has enjoyed laughing at jests; that he is patiently familiar with some of the Fool's hoary punch lines—like why the seven stars are seven; that Lear is upset when he has not seen Fool for two whole days—but though he enjoys Fool, even loves him, may threaten him with the whip, and may use it.

If Fool was present in the opening court scene, his entrance in I, iv

can strike a sharp visual blow: the difference between the happier Fool
then and the one who has pined away since. He strikes blows anyway.
Fool, alone of the personae, seems to reveal almost the whole of his dialectic at once. Others have come masked in lechery, kindness, love,
righteousness, honesty, naivete; Fool's clashing qualities are near his surface, and emerge bluntly.

He begins by ignoring Lear, pointedly. He looks straight at Kent;
looks searchingly at him, for Fool is no fool, and may penetrate Kent's
disguise? Pat his shaven cheeks? If Fool was present in I, i, the scrutiny
of Kent's mask is the more meaningful. His possible recognition of Kent
is ambiguous; but the possibility hangs in the pause, and after

> Let me hire him too ... (100)

when he offers Kent the coxcomb.

One theatre Fool's bitterness, that dominated his impersonation, was
visual here—his cockscomb was a death's head. Another gave Kent his
mock crown-cockscomb. Lear's greeting—*How now, my pretty knave*
(101)—Fool ignores. Lear has been seen as demonstrative here, often
reaching out, as Gielgud did, to touch or fondle Fool; and sweet Fools
have nestled near him; a Fool with much bitterness in him, who has obviously—vengefully?—pined in solitude, keeping himself away from
Lear, will more likely bear a grudge, as Carnovsky's did, and break away
from the caress. Fool speaks to his bauble, or to Kent, but to hurt Lear.
Kent is a fool to serve one out of favor, one who, for giving all to his
daughters, should wear the coxcomb himself. In Fool's simple language,
so full of the proverbial, of concern for preservation of property rights,
of self-protection, so articulated in numbers—here *two's* and *three's*—a
touch of the prophetic often emerges. So, a seeker of shelter, afraid of
cold and exclusion, Fool looks forward to his own ordeal:

> ... and thou canst not smile as the wind sits,
> thou'lt catch cold shortly ... (105–106).

He can't. He will.

Finally, after this oblique initial attack, he turns on Lear himself, with
one of his riddling, provocative jests:

> ... Would I had two coxcombs and two daughters!
> *Lear.* Why, my boy? (110–112).

My boy. It would be hard for the meanest Lear to make anything very
mean of the diminutives applied like this to Fool. Lear's gentler mood is
first sharply tested when Fool takes back the coxcomb from Kent, and
offers it to the prime fool, Lear himself.

Lear: Take heed, sirrah; the whip (116).

The whip. Lear's use of it provides a visual symbol of the character designs. Six times in their brief halcyon time Lear mentions it. Empson sees this as evidence that Fool's position is meant to be a miserable one. If Lear flicks Fool with it, in fun, or with a purpose or pretence of unkindness, a statement is made; a much more explicit one, if he hits Fool, hurts him. How much this declares Lear's present condition, how much the burden of repressed memory, how much the dread of the prophesied poverty depends on the visual action. This will be partly conditioned by the range of response of the knights, from frank amusement to embarrassment.

The more august Lears resist giving up their images of power and self-assurance. Salvini remained positively genial, as if Cordelia, and the Oswald encounter, had never happened. Still a laughing Lear:

> With what gusts of affection he greets the jester. His nature expands; broad beams of laughter gleam over the snows of his face. Every gibe adds to his mirth, and the more foolish the jest, the more impertinent the rhyme, the more he relishes it. "Dost thou call me fool, boy?" and he signs to Kent to mark the reply as a piece of infinite humor. He is all sunshine . . . a boy again, and he and his fool are sporting together.

Gielgud, in this mode, was very fond, promptly set Fool by him, was sweet to him, gave him food, showed him off to Kent. Mantell treated him with whimsical kindness, was childishly happy with Fool's jokes.

The old Lears of the mid-nineteenth century let their oldness, softness show. Charles Kean listened to the jokes with the air of one resolved to be pleased, but Fool's words seemed only slowly to penetrate his mind: a foggy man, and one who loved to enjoy himself. Macready asked earnestly, as if caring, wanting to know, "How dost, my pretty knave?" caressing Fool fondly, laughing easily at what he seemed not quite to comprehend, suggesting subtextually that he was clinging uneasily to Fool as the only being who understood him.

Others showed the burden of memory more. Carnovsky only half heard, was preoccupied, his mind on Goneril and beyond. Out of his bitterness, Redgrave's ancient did hit Fool with the whip. Scofield's tough Lear masked his tenderness for Fool and his grief over Cordelia with crisp badinage.

At the threat of the whip, or the use of it, Fool voices the first of his animal similes—*Truth's a dog . . . whipp'd out when the Lady Brach may stand by th' fire and stink* (117–119). Fool may mimic a whipping, and play a dog—as Lear may later—making the animal imagery visual.

The prophetic note again: Fool will be whipped out, and the image of the lady as a stinking bitch, lodged in Lear's mind, will echo in his mad nausea of IV, vi:

> Stench, consumption; fie, fie, fie! pah, pah! (IV, vi, 131).

Lear's response now seems to return bitter for bitter:

> A pestilent gall to me! (120).

If this is not said to the Fool in jest, but is a brooding back on Goneril, it is another signal of a subterranean activity behind Lear's apparently extrovert exterior that, Jorgensen suggests, is characteristic of Lear's mode of thought.

Fool, already laboring to outjest Lear's grief, offers to teach him a speech: *Mark* . . . Again, in IV, vi, when Lear has become fool, the verbal gesture will be echoed—and perhaps a visual one, too, as Lear takes a stance before Gloster, says, *I will preach to thee* (IV, vi, 182), and does, about this stage of fools.

What Fool teaches Lear in voice and gesture that here or elsewhere may mock—mirror—Lear's own, embodies the system of comparatives sustaining the verbal texture of the play: *more, less, less, more, less, more.* Fool's theme of clever practicality, of property, his championship of self-serving disguise—

> Have more than thou showest,
> Speak less than thou knowest . . . (124–125)

if taken at its face value, reflects "an inability to face reality" Dye suggests; but the more earnestly Fool propagandizes for security, the more tensions develop between what he says and what he is. He himself speaks less than he knows.

Pursuing the *more-less* thread, Fool asks Lear what can be made of nothing—perhaps the best justification for including Fool in the first scene, where Lear said nothing comes of it. If Fool is reminding him, it is a bitter reminder; it is a bitter reminder anyway, as Lear finds himself saying almost the same words that launched Cordelia from him. Scofield paused as the sour taste bit him, and his voice sank:

> . . . nothing can be made out of nothing (139).

This, perhaps, more than Fool's harping on Lear's poverty is what provokes the exclamatory,

> A bitter fool! (142.)

Lear is willing to be taught the difference between bitter and sweet fool; but the inner brooding in the design emerges again when Fool, playing now on differences as he did before on *more* and *less*, confronts Lear with his loss of social identity. The little song defines Lear's folly; Fool would be sweet, Lear must stand for the bitter fool. Fool may balance crown and cockscomb in his hands to point his jest. It provokes the next crucial question in Lear's search for himself:

> Dost thou call me fool, boy? (154.)

Fool's insistence that he does, Kent's acknowledgement that Fool is not altogether fool, does not now draw from Lear any retort, or verbal—though perhaps a visual—threat of the whip; Lear absorbs what he has heard, while Fool jests about the courtly monopoly on foolishness. And again he must awaken Lear's attention with the riddle about two crowns (Scofield's Fool accompanied the jest with the business of cracking an egg). The riddle itself may be new; but Lear, used to playing straight man, asks the right question, only to be reminded of—expecting to be reminded of?—his folly, of his cloven crown. Again, the language is of numbers, division, and earthy imagery that is reverberative. Lear's cleaving of his crown is a symbol for the running motif of division into halves that leaves nothing in the center—the phrase itself will echo later as in *I am cut to the brain.* Fool's plain speaking here may evoke a new visual threat of whipping, for he covers himself in the last line with a paradoxical reminder of the ambiguity between his self and his disguise:

> If I speak like myself in this, let him be
> whipp'd that first finds it so (171-172).

The fool speaks, but not foolishness, ergo it is not Fool speaking—hence Lear cannot whip Fool for preaching against folly.

The scene builds, each confrontation raises temperature, tension, as each wave of Fool's remonstrance smashes harder again Lear's unwillingness to acknowledge his mistake, and when Lear asks, distractingly—distractedly?—why Fool suddenly sings so much, Fool, perhaps with a gesture of his bauble gives him the ultimate shame:

> ...since thou mad'st thy daughters thy
> mothers...gav'st them the rod and putt'st
> down thine own breeches... (179-181).

Again, in his last line, Fool interrupts any visual threat from Lear by changing the subject: can he please be taught to lie? Lear threatens the whip again; Fool builds to a climax: he would rather be any kind o' thing than a fool—than himself—and yet he would not be Lear—a fool; for, again, Lear has pared his wit o' both sides—cut himself to the brain—and left nothing in the middle.

Fool's language vibrates with the play's pervasive imagery. He sings his sorrow that Lear should play Fool, marvels what kin Lear and his daughters are (bastards? offspring of madness?), then still once more distracts Lear's response by looking off to see Goneril coming, and to make his joke:

> ... here comes one o' the parings (195–196).

Shakespeare climaxes the scene, as he often does, with a sudden entrance —an entrance prepared for: the incoming character—here Goneril— known to be a threat, a cause for anxiety; then seen coming before the actual entrance, so that all eyes on the stage—and in the audience—must turn, all await her appearance. Many vectors of force are concentrated in the pause while Goneril enters and absorbs the stares of Lear, Fool, Kent, and the knights, and returns her frown. The angry dominant, muted before, now is announced clearly, especially if we see Goneril being provoked. At Colorado, for instance, Fool, aware of her coming, settled Lear's crown on his head, put Lear's cloak over his shoulders, turned his back, and fooled Goneril for a moment into thinking he was Lear. The *prank* infuriated her. She may herself provoke: Kozintsev's Goneril casually ate through Lear's anger, Lear pointedly remaining unfed—unloved.

What Goneril is again depends on the total equation. If Fool's taunts are painful, if the knights have in fact been rowdy, if Lear is a bully, Goneril's complaining has good cause. If, at the other extreme, Lear, Fool, and the knights are all fine, quiet gentlemen, Goneril must seem an arrant liar. But the form of *Lear* denies easy extremes: Goneril has still not revealed, even to herself, her capacity for evil, and a first-time audience would still have no tangible clue to it. Shakespeare delays the revelation both as artist—dealing with complex behavior materials—and as craftsman, keeping his secrets, building suspense.

The tension may be heightened by an emphasis on the visual-verbal imagery of division that will develop intensely from now on. Goneril enters not as a king's daughter but as a queen—as half-a-queen now, but her ambition aims farther. The first words of the next act will rumor war, division between the dukes—meaning, also, between the duchesses. Goneril will speak to Lear in a moment of how his manners offend *our court*. The royal we ... in a *graced palace*. Goneril has rich fantasies: she will speak later of *all the building in my fancy* (IV, ii, 85), and now

she may well be robed to fit her regal self-image—perhaps in gold, for
Albany will call her *gilded serpent*. His daughters dress gorgeously, Lear
will say: Goneril's gorgeous dress may now, to strengthen her new identity, include trappings of the royalty Lear discarded in I, i—including a
crown? This could explain Lear's first challenge:

> ... what makes that frontlet on? (197.)

How dare you wear the crown? Frontlet had such a meaning; if Goneril
will *have it come to question* (I, iii, 14), she will carry all her guns; her
display of symbolic power would occasion in Lear that reflexive, recurrent gesture by Mikhoels of reaching toward his own head for the
crown that is not there. Lear's wish or gesture to deny Goneril any part
of the *name and all th' addition to a king* (I, i, 136), her response, would
motivate the frown he next speaks of.

The frown itself might of course be, as commonly glossed, her *frontlet*, her gesture of royal power, as it was Lear's. *When I do stare* . . .
Other such gestures may include the attendance of ladies of the court,
as in the nineteenth century theatre; might also include men—perhaps
men-at-arms, for Goneril contemplates war, and may have recruited
formidable soldiers—to enter quietly and take strategic positions where
they may control or disarm Lear's knights. The final stripping of Lear
is about to begin, and the next thing stripped off is his entourage. The
text does not enforce a reader to confront the how of this stripping;
Shakespeare counted on some visual imagery on the stage.

The rising tension of the previous beat, ending with Goneril's appearance, is not now allowed to drop. Lear challenges her frown; Fool, bitter, resumes his theme, of Lear as hollow, empty, without identity, losing his shape, a cipher.

> ... now thou art an O without
> a figure. I am better than thou art now; I am
> a Fool, thou art nothing (200–202).

Editors often follow the eighteenth century pattern of ascribing to
Goneril, in a stage direction, the subsequent visual threat to Fool; but
this may be another in the recurrent provocations that Fool offers Lear
and then sidesteps when Lear is angry:

> Yes, forsooth,
> I will hold my tongue; so your face bids me,
> though you say nothing (203–204).

But the moment the danger passes, he is back at it, with his rhyme on Lear's poverty, and his refrain on Lear's hollowness: *a sheal'd peascod* (208).

To the mounting tension of the scene Shakespeare now brings the stimulus of verse. Goneril formally, in iambics that may reflect her assumption of regality, indicts Fool, Lear, and the knights for quarrel and riot. Goneril has an objective motivation, Bransom suggests: she wants to preserve a "wholesome weal," and she genuinely fears that Lear's unruly entourage is a threat to it. Alternatively, from the view that this play poses old idealism against "new man" practicality, she is seen, with a touch of Puritan hypocrisy, sanctimoniously attacking the institution of knighthood.

Again, the form of the play suggests more complexity: the conflict is essentially between dramatic characters—Shakespeare was no defender of unemployed knights, fat or otherwise, and Lear's men, if they melt away in a crisis, are not presented as admirably loyal. The most significant part of the attack is the personal. Goneril holds the rod now and her words hint at it: Lear's fault would not *'scape censure . . .* the alternative to shame for him is obedience.

Lear is speechless. Kent, uncharacteristically, does not speak at all here. Fool twists the knife, introducing a bird imagery that Lear will later embroider:

> The hedge-sparrow fed the cuckoo so long,
> That it's had it head bit off by it young.
> So out went the candle, and we were left darkling (224–226).

Again, the distant rumble of illegitimacy, of filial cannibalism, and the note of prophecy—the darkness waits. Lear finds his tongue:

> Are you our daughter? (227.)

Lear the Titan, as in Salvini's mode, with his gentlemanly knights, was at first dazed, puzzled, spoke more in sorrow than in anger. His would be a steep ascent to the climax. Gielgud, similarly, was at first still Olympian, sheltered Fool with an encircling arm. Carnovsky was half-serious, half-stunned. Mikhoels, evoking the recurrent aural imagery of the laugh he kept for Cordelia, tried to pretend still that this was a joke that could be passed off. The mad Lears—Devrient, Rossi—in their uncertain world, were the more bewildered. Rossi was slack-jawed, humble; Devrient was simply astonished, and only when Goneril took his surprise for a whim did he begin to show his anger. The tough Scofield was tougher still.

Goneril's answer reads reasonably; again it is Fool who responds with sarcasm. Fool has been said to think highly of practicality; but it is characteristic of his dialectic that—not unlike Cordelia—in his affronts to Goneril, his repeated reminders to Lear of Lear's reduced status, he will make both his own and Lear's world intolerable. Now, taunting Goneril, he may be pretending mock love to her, giving her the name of a common whore:

> Whoop, Jug! I love thee (233).

In the theatre, he is an overt challenge to both Goneril and Lear—a Japanese Fool hopped between them, pretend-interpreter—and must take shelter, behind Lear, or under a table; or rely on his agility, for Goneril may pursue him physically, now and later; but he will not stop this provocation, that must end in his being driven out into the darkness he fears. He, too, is compelled.

Lear's search for his own identity now takes on a note of panic, even though he may be visualized—and has been acted—as speaking ironically now. *Are you our daughter?* (227) raised an echo of Oswald's identification of him. Now he pretends not to know—and in fact does not, or only slenderly knows—who he is, if he is dreaming, or waking. He may, as Carnovsky did, pinch himself to make sure. He may look in a mirror. All his questions seem an attempt to verify his existence by objective phenomena, or testimony—but it is worth noting that he himself denies himself, questions his simple functions, most of all the key centers—for this play—of sight and mind:

> Does any here know me? This is not Lear:
> Does Lear walk thus? speak thus? Where are his eyes?
> Either his notion weakens, his discernings
> Are lethargied—Ha! waking? 'tis not so.
> Who is it that can tell me who I am? (234–238.)

Are his discernings lethargied? The line of thought discontinues—the first hint of the broken utterance that will recur as his brain becomes overstrained by the clamor of thought and feeling.

Who can tell Lear who he is? Nobody; only himself. However ironically asked, infantile desperation underlies the line; it is the question of a child who needs others to confirm the very fact that he exists. Lear is losing his mask as king: the German actor Krauss projected the sense of the man falling apart as his loss of position and power suddenly made him dependent entirely on the chance kindness of those who had been dependent on him. Lear is being forced to know this of himself: he is not the familiar image that once commanded all things; that image, like a garment, slips farther from him. Fool, Lear's looking-glass—he may hold a mirror up—cruelly, compassionately, tells him what is left:

Lear's shadow (239).

Lear's response is curious: indeed, he says, he may well doubt that he has children. The answer is beyond logic; the character design is now such that his identity—his substance—relies on his relationship with his daughters. The implications are dense. Illegitimacy again: if these are not his daughters, they must be bastards. It is a thought that touches off terror in him. His mind misgives: the *marks of sovereignty, knowledge, and reason* (240–241) that tell him he has daughters play him false now. The dark irrational, the subconscious, is close by. The being who calls himself Lear may be only a shadow, a nothingness, and yet uncannily more—shapeless, irrational, a distorted, frightening reflection, as in a fool's mirror, of something mighty. Or: only this encroaching shadow can tell Lear what is happening to him, only the dark reflection within can make him know himself. The moment briefly modulates the accelerating tensions toward the great climax.

Lear is now, as always, torn, divided, and in the theatre this has been reflected in the tension between irony and earnestness. Edmund Kean's (1787–1833) "struggle between affection and resentment" reminds us that Lear still felt the need of Goneril's love. Here, for the first time, the titan image begins to crack. Salvini was at first struck with wonder at *Does any here know me?* Then, as his insecurity broke through, the note of pathos sounded. He moved back toward control, irony, and the eventual anger in *Your name, fair gentlewoman?* The Gielgud-Granville-Barker notes for these moments: "Danger—end of careless exterior. Gasps. Feeling. Speech nothing." But, at *Your name* . . . "Bite. During her speech store it up—hold back . . ." Forrest went from breathless astonished quiet to a mock, derisive courtesy, half bowing on the *name* line. Scofield, too, half-bowed in mock courtesy. Kneeling here sustains a motif on which many variations are to be played.

Carnovsky had already moved through shock to anger, and now chucked Goneril sharply, savagely, under the chin, as he peered into her eyes, searching. As this was a pivotal point toward disintegration for the Olympian Lears, it began a different kind of peripety for the weaker ones. Laughton seemed an old, old man, and still reluctant to let go, he shook his fond old head in incomprehension. Rossi's madness was for a moment penetrated; he examined Goneril, from her feet to her head, restlessly, unconsciously, his mouth open, staring as if his daughter, thus transformed in his eyes, must necessarily reveal some outward characteristic of the inward change; or as if there were still some half-formed hope. . . that the whole scene was unreal, and this horrible image (was not) . . . the daughter he had loved too well.

Goneril provokes Lear to explosion. Her speech is calculated for the showdown she wants; she may take pleasure in the signs of his growing anger, as she will with Albany. This may be evoked more by the shadow than the substance of what she says. Her overt complaint is about his knights: debosh'd and bold, they infect *our* court with epicurism and lust . . . make it more like a tavern or brothel than a palace. These are disputable facts. There is worse. The name of this fair gentlewoman seems to be mother, teacher, nurse. Fool has jeered that these daughters will make Lear an *obedient father*, he who has put his pants down for their rod. Goneril acts this out. She calls his irony in asking her name a *"prank"*—as Regan will call his manners *"tricks."* She speaks of *shame* again, and threatens him bluntly with the rod:

> . . . be then desir'd
> By her, that else will take the things she begs . . . (255–256).

She asks only one concrete concession: that he a little . . . *disquantity your train.* But the sting is in the tail; his remainder must be suitable men

> Which know themselves and you (259).

Who knows Lear? These must be men who will take the shadow for the real. And they must be men who will besort his age—be fit for the old man Goneril has decided he is. This is a particularly painful gibe at a Lear playing huntsman, gourmand, bon vivant; but even to an old and trembling Lear it is a painful check, because it is such a reminder that his child sees him crawling toward death. You are old, they will keep telling him. Here, the visualization of uncaring, upstart youth can contribute powerfully to shock: such an effect was made by Mikhoel's Goneril: a heroic hardness that even in her rejection of her father was neither petty nor mean, but only a terrific scorn for old age and failure.

"Two self righteousnesses meet," Brook's filmscript suggests, "two highly emotional people, each one feeling bitterly wronged by the other." But his Goneril, Irene Worth, on stage and screen showed a genuine concern for her father, and so sustained the mood of her wistful reminder to Regan that Lear has loved Cordelia most, and so also strengthened the lines of her own tragic action.

A tremendous gathering of forces concentrates in this moment, mainly expressed in visual and other non-verbal imagery. How Goneril, asking Lear to disquantity, will say her *little*, how the knights will take it, again involves the whole complex equation. *Little* will turn out fifty men; a large *little*. How is *little* sounded, to mask this: honeyed? patient? businesslike? bitter? sarcastic? fierce? There is a magnificence—and a touch of masculinity—in the courage with which Goneril pits her authority as ruler and hostess against men accustomed to Lear's absolute power: Lear himself, struggling past love of her to hate; Fool, who has always despised her; and the knights, whose livelihood is at stake.

Again, how much the knights live up to Goneril's description helps determine the timbre of the scene. If she must herself try to quiet them, stop sullen brutes from rioting or chasing her servant girls, she will be different from a Goneril imagining these things. If many are old, near Lear's age, Goneril's attack on them will have a special implication. Charles Kean made the knights conventional gentlemen; they listened attentively to Goneril; when she called them "debosh'd and bold" looked at each other in intense surprise; when she suggested their discharge indignantly struck their spears on the stage; Goneril was obviously making up their viciousness. Laughton's knights were turbulent and noisy, often joining as a chorus to echo Fool's songs; but they did not deserve Goneril's worst words. Scofield's knights did. In this anti-heroic world, Lear's people were intolerable guests,* and Goneril obviously much put upon—she could be seen as a harassed housewife. For how harassed, read Charles Marowitz, on the scene as rehearsed; after Lear has returned Goneril's speech with a long, hard look:

> The violence was carefully worked for . . . : the dust outdoors, the feel of hard saddle-leather and hunters returning after a long, sweaty ride. . . . Incensed by [Goneril's] words, Lear overturns the dinner table—as if to prove his strength—and storms out. This is the cue for general pandemonium as the knights following their master's example tip chairs, throw plates, and generally demolish the chamber . . . the knights were reminded of the ferocity of the barbaric period they were supposed to inhabit; and this time, on Lear's overturning of the table, the stage exploded and sent shrapnel flying in a dozen different directions. Tankards whizzed through the air, hitting actors and ricocheting . . . set pieces were smashed, up-ended, bits of furniture and a chandelier above the rehearsal stage was splintered in a thousand pieces that came raining down on the company.

This kind of violence seemed gratuitous to many critics, as extreme as, in the other direction, a handful of quiet gentlemen meekly accepting expulsion. Lear's defense of their sense of propriety later, reasonable as it

---

*In Brook's film, this showed in closeups of a ripped wall hanging, a stained carpet, a wall marred with handprints, a broken vase.

is, must make him seem at best a poor witness, at worst already mad, if it follows a riot of uncontrolled violence. The political reality suggests visual imagery providing less a release through boisterousness than a building of tension. The fact of Shakespeare's design is that Lear will lose his knights, all but one of them; this—or the next—is the last scene in which they will accompany him. Among the possibilities beyond those suggested by the performances above: one by one they drift out, as the agon goes on, let go of the great wheel gone down hill, leaving Lear to face Goneril alone; or they are waved out, as by Gielgud's Granville-Barker *Lear* so Lear can face Goneril and Albany alone; or cowed by her, they desert en masse; or they resist, as loyal followers of the king, and are forced to withdraw. Lear's later speech, *Go, go my people*, will suggest that they—some?—have waited his orders, if not fought for him. If there is any sense of resistance, the visual imagery of division is served by the presence of Goneril's own armed men—men who will appear later in her army opposing Cordelia's—who have perhaps already quietly removed the knights' weapons, if not some of the knights themselves. All these visual possibilities are comments on character. A Lear who bows to power is different from one who withdraws before remonstrance. Without some show of force, Goneril's disciplining of her father-king must be seen as an achievement of her personality, and as a comment on Lear.

The design of Lear's character—and of the play's visual imagery—enforces his flight. As in I, i, his response to a frustrating antagonist is—passionately—either to order him from his sight, or flee. Lear's refuge now is inevitably the infantile threat to withdraw—I won't play, you'll be sorry; and he threatens it three times before he actually does run away—and thus repeats the flight-pursuit motif that repeatedly sends the defenseless in retreat from confrontation.

Lear threatens with words as well as withdrawal. His immediate expletive—*Darkness and devils!* (260)—begins with the word that will haunt him until, in his madness, he will discover his imagined source of it. Now he does not make the connection; but *darkness* attaches to an idea that haunts him, and accompanies his infantile retreat:

Degenerate bastard (262)

he calls his daughter. The echoes of this nightmare of illegitimacy, going back to *We have no such daughter* (I, i, 262–263), we have observed; they will sound again, and always in the context is an image of sexuality. Goneril is not only a bastard, but a degenerate bastard; and the image in his mind of her body, her tumescence, will break out more openly in a moment.

The symptoms of Lear's confusion, of thought interrupted by memory and passion, dominate the rest of the scene. Goneril's further explanation, as if she needs to justify herself, *You strike my people* ... (264) does not engage Lear's attention. The long questioning is ended; all now is declarative, exclamatory. He is on the gad: moving, leaving—

> Woe, that too late repents... (266).

To himself? To Goneril? To Albany, coming in? He is speaking now to everybody: to himself, to them, to his knights, to the listening world, with his complaints on ingratitude. *More hideous . . . Than the sea-monster* (268–269) looses a flood of animal images, this one sprung from the depths.

Albany is astonished. Lear's knights had noticed a great abatement of kindness in the Duke also. In IV, vi, Lear will fantasy killing his sons-in-law. Albany, so far an ambiguous man, still gives few clues to what he will become. He seems bewildered at Lear's anger, as if the situation is entirely new to him—a sign in his design of blindness? unwillingness to see? hypocrisy? He is distinguished by his inability to deal with the situation, and by his submission to Goneril. But subtextually this moment is the start of his illumination; in this first of his few meaningful scenes, the seeds of his growing awareness and responsibility must visually be planted, if at all. He must now be noticeably not only the "milky" man Goneril described, but also the Hamlet-like doubter whose change to decisiveness will so surprise Oswald and Edmund.

Albany's entrance crystallizes one climax of Shakespeare's superbly architected scene, one of the most powerful for sheer drama in his canon. But the fierce intensity of the remaining moments must be delicately articulated: they cannot be all bold brass and tympani, or the sustained note will dull the senses; modulations of character and expression are designed to counterpoint the short, sharp rhythms of action.

Three peaks make up this ascent: Lear's three threats to leave. Conventionally, the second, and then the third, should mount higher than the rest. Such is the power of the second, the famous *Hear, Nature* (284) "curse," that it has seemed to tower over the rest. Macready, experimenting with the revived Shakespeare text, reversed the two final speeches; Henry Irving, and more recently Donald Wolfit, have done the same. M. R. Ridley agreed, Wolfit wrote, that the "curse" is "far more impressive and dramatically correct if it follows rather than precedes." Again, this depends on the vocal and visual instruments used in the design. Sco-field, to match the uproar of his knights, intensified his *Hear, Nature* speech to a pitch higher than, afterwards, he felt was right, in terms of the whole design. Gielgud, on Granville-Barker's advice, deliberately quieted the middle speech and by this contrast achieved accumulation of power. Bassermann varied the emotional tone: the middle speech was "a father's pain," the final one all rage.

The physical imagery of the character design is crucial here. Lear threatens to leave at *Degenerate bastard*, but stays for the curse. Giel-gud's Lear, leaving, was held, and provoked to attack, by a burst of con-temptuous laughter from Goneril. Are there inner directed motivations for not going at once? Because this is an infantile threat that he hopes not to carry out? Because, as with some of the old-man Lears, he must summon strength to the action? Albany's entrance may serve, as it did for Macready: Lear leaned on the son-in-law for a moment, then gath-ered strength for the curse. Booth's* Albany tried to support him; Booth tore himself away. Both acts made visual expressions of Albany's char-acter. So did another by Scofield's Albany—no sympathy here—who busied himself righting the overturned table. Goneril's response to Al-bany's action, as well as to Lear's, will similarly contribute to the tension of character.

But the scene's development bears mainly on the Lear design; and as in all the play's crises, many oppositions cluster in the mosaic of that de-sign. The oversimplified Lear is easy to visualize here, as sentimental critics and actors—and Tate—visualized him: an old man, stung by the ingratitude of a loved daughter. Garrick was artist enough to realize be-yond Tate's cartoon some of Lear's further dimension: "violent, old & weakly fond of his Daughters," and also—Garrick disagreeing with a critic—a bit of an *Old Fool*. There is much more: love, hate, authority, submission, anger, grief, patience, rashness, reason, confusion, pride, shame, maturity, infantilism, violence, wisdom, folly, self-pity, weari-ness, energy, age, virility, approach, withdrawal.

One mark of Lear's sanity, his rationality, is his carefully argued de-fense of his knights. Albany has prayed Lear to be patient; and Lear cools for a moment. *Detested kite* (271) he calls Goneril; not as vicious as his first assault, but noisome in implication: the kite preys on small things, weak things, things made weak from sickness. Lear's *seeing* sys-tem is changing: he is beginning to penetrate outwardness, to see ugli-ness where he saw beauty. The rashness powered by his growing aware-ness of his error with Cordelia is on short fuse; but he manages the

*"Booth" is Edwin (as Kean is Edmund) unless otherwise noted.

patience Albany urges—he will himself pray for it later—to describe the worth of his men. His lines, with their succession of monosyllables, or words that insist on breaking down into separate syllables—particulars, exact, regard, support, worships—form the speech of a man reasoning, offering item by item, the k, t, and p enforcing a careful articulation:

> My train are men of choice and rarest parts,
> That all particulars of duty know,
> And in the most exact regard support
> The worships of their name (272–275).

And then patience gives way to remorse. Lear's underground, the sub-terranean current of self-attack that has only troubled his surface, now breaks out. He talks to himself now, of how Cordelia's small fault *wrench'd* his *frame of nature / From the fix'd place* (277–278). The frequent verbal imagery of the body under tension that Spurgeon observed is here matched by the physical assault that will be visited on the flesh:

> O Lear, Lear, Lear!
> Beat at this gate, that let thy folly in,
> And thy dear judgment out! (279–286.)

And he hammers at his head. At his mind, already like a vex'd sea. A Norwegian Lear held his head in his hands as if to keep the tempest from breaking out of his skull; he would repeat the gesture later, as the fiercer waves of madness washed against his brain.

Now he says *Go, go, my people* (281). Because they would resist? Because he would curse his daughter in private?—though this did not restrain him in I.1. The moment of the knights' going, covered by Albany's disclaimer of responsibility, gives Lear time to take breath for the curse. Scofield's face offered further motivation for it; at Albany's

> ...I am guiltless, as I am ignorant
> Of what hath moved you (282–283).

the fierce kingly stare turned sharply, knowingly, revengefully on Goneril.

The curse is evil. This appeal to "nature" reflects a deep ugliness—a human ugliness now still clothed in righteousness—that will expose itself finally only in madness. How critics can contrive to see Lear's concept of nature as somehow admirable—"the recognition of an order in Nature, Nature as a regulative principle . . . a principle of justice . . . the right order of things . . . takes for granted that parents are to be honored and human decencies observed"—how this can be believed after a fair reading seems almost incomprehensible.

Lear asks that his daughter be made sterile. By any concept of "human decency," this is a vicious, "antinatural" desire—that is still, in the dialectic of the play, and of life, part of nature. That it represents something even deeper in the Lear design will emerge in the storm, when the character will beg that all humanity become sterile in a cataclysmic orgasm: all germens spill at once. Behind this a deeper dialectic still: in madness, Lear will cry, *Let copulation thrive* (IV, vi, 117)—he will want soldiers born to kill live men. But this early response of Lear's to rebuff is, by attacking others, to cut *himself* off: not only from the next generation, but from the third. He has already denied one daughter, now a second—and would deny her his grandchildren. In his golden abdication, he gave lavishly to Goneril, Albany, and specifically, their issue. Now he as much as orders nature to interdict that issue—it *is* an order: he calls to nature, "Now hear this" and, in the imperative mood, commands

> Suspend thy purpose, if thou didst intend
> To make this creature fruitful! (285–286.)

Asking nature to suspend natural process is part of the incessant dialectic. If nature refuses this command, then accept this one: that a child of my child be "a thwart disnatured torment": that is, unnatural—for once more Lear bids nature against nature. The infantilism is unmistakable: you'll be sorry, you'll suffer as I am suffering. Danby's two-valued hypothesis, requiring that Lear's nature "take for granted that parents are to be honored and human decencies observed," in the face of Lear's indecent wish that his grandchild be a monster to his mother, demonstrates again how dangerous it is to try to make Shakespeare's work fit any neat, simplistic idea pattern.

What reason does Lear give for his topsy-turvy, fool's command that nature act unnaturally? That Goneril is thankless. Clearly she has threatened to reduce his entourage, thus reneging on his unilaterally ordered commitment (although a nod of agreement from Albany and Cornwall at his proposal in I, i would strengthen his design here) and she has denied his authority. But not reason motivates him; rather subtextual emotional outrage, compounded of the complex, clashing feelings of this tempestuous king, former king, father, fool, beggar, lover, child, man alone. The moment reflects Shakespeare's special mastery of multiple stimuli to sense, feeling, and thought. The fierce spectacle of father and child in confrontation stirs mindless ripples; the passions of the characters rouse echoing passions; the text compels engagement at some level of the brain with filial values. But there is no easy channeling of these responses: Lear's curse is pervaded by histrionic pity for his self, but he is also a truly pitiable object; he has a residue of love for Goneril, and, as John McCullough's (1832–1885) Lear suggested, loathes himself for loving. So Mantell's anger in the first part of the curse was undertoned with anguish; he seemed to be recalling all the tenderness of a happy past. After he rose to his height of fury at *If she must teem*, the counter emotions returned; he ended in tearful agony.

Goneril does not exist only as a foil to Lear here; she has an identity of her own, and is herself a design of opposites. This will also be true of Albany and Fool. The text scrupulously avoids dictating a fixed "idea" of their roles in the scene, so that extreme demands are made on the audience's response repertory.

Unfortunately, both theatre and criticism have sometimes preferred to narrow the confrontation to its sentimental (or, in the Brook case, to its antisentimental) elements. Given such a limited focus, Lear can be—and was often—made to seem here wholly pitiable, entirely wronged, Goneril a witch. Garrick, as Tate's Lear, could only suggest depth with his touch of Old Fool; and thenceforth through much of the nineteenth century, audiences nervous of ambiguity generally applauded Lear's pathetic image, even in the semi-restored Shakespearean text.

Garrick's strategy—there is a parallel strategy in criticism (e.g., that of Robert Heilman)—was to surround the curse with an aura of holy prayer. His Lear, poor old man, as he faced Goneril, leaned on a crutch; was this not sad enough? He stood rigid and silent for a moment, as if paralyzed at Goneril's affront; then he flung the crutch aside, and—in the words of an eyewitness:

> You fall precipitately upon your knees, extend your arms—clench your hands—set your teeth—and with a savage distraction in your look—trembling in all your limbs—and your eyes pointed to heaven . . . begin . . . with a broken, inward utterance; from thence rising every line in loudness and rapidity of voice, and at last bursting into tears.

The effect was tremendous: audiences "seemed to shrink . . . as from a blast of lightning." Samuel Foote, Garrick's faithful critic, found fault. He felt the tears were gratuitous—Tate's monarch was not a weeper. Reminded that Shakespeare meant Lear to cry, Foote retorted, Yes, but later. Foote also disliked the rising note; he advised a falling off of rage at the close, a melting into the pathetic. This was the same kind of impulse that Goethe saw in Schroeder's butchery of the play: to sentimentalize. Foote also saw indignity in Garrick's collapse at the end: said it was only half a collapse, because the actor was supported off, awkwardly.

Garrick cast a long shadow. The business of praying would be often repeated; in the twentieth century, Laughton, who presented a semi-priestly image anyway, prayed here as if he held a great invisible orb in his arms. Garrick's visual imagery, and the dialectic he effected between "those strugglings of parental affection, and powerful conflicting passions" (Thomas Davies), also became pattern. Edmund Kean threw himself on his knees, his silvery hair streaming,

> with his lank, bare arms extended, like withered stumps, threw his head quite back with the effort of a man nearly exhausted and breathless; the words spelled out syllable by syllable ... it seemed to be screwed out of the bodily frame as if by some mechanical power, set in motion by means independent of the will ... at the end the over-excited, exhausted form, sinking beneath supernatural exertion, seemed to crack and give way altogether.

But there seemed not enough dialectic in this terrible energy: it was all on two notes, William Hazlitt complained, highest and lowest, a speech of hate, rant, without relentings of tenderness, of the fond recollections that partly motivated it.

The obvious speech form was the elder Booth's—from a barely whispered start building to a crescendo of rage. Other actors were more subtle. Charles Kean, in the Garrick tradition, demonstrated the theatrical effectiveness of his initial Lear image of a kind, jovial, joke-loving old man, now moved to curse his daughter. This almost comic ancient seemed, with the instinctive return to the kingliness of his nature, the more terrible, the more pathetic. His dialectic, between love and hate, expressed itself in wrenching efforts to repress the passion driving his words out. He too kneeled, after throwing away the spear he leaned on. He began solemnly, prayerfully, in a fervid whisper, that rose to an outcry as, gasping, choking, he tried to suppress his passion. Down wanton, down. But it would not down. Kean ended in a "curdled whisper."

Somewhat similarly Devrient, having earlier emphasized the gentleness and tenderness of Lear, rather than the grand or the rash, seemed the more shocking now. Even so, his softness was dominant, and undermined him. He started off strongly, but while the curse became fiercer, his voice diminished in strength, as if, listening, he was gripped by the impact of his own words, and overcome by pain that a father should so have to speak to a child. The curse faded out, and he rushed off, not in rage, but in horror.

Macready moved between anger and agony. Old as his Lear was, he wanted his tears, when he wept, to be those not of a woman, not a driveller. Macready wanted the kind of tears that stained a man's cheeks. He, too, sank on his knees, and thrust his arms up toward heaven, strained upward with an intensity that suggested a curiously apt visual imagery: "like the talons of some strange animal trying to clutch a prey that is out of its reach." His voice mingled indignation, anguish and a sense of physical infirmity held up by a strong will; it faltered, then resumed, finally mounting to a high, startling screech, as if he were afraid his strength would leave him before he could say one curse more.

Their "oldness" shaped much of the pattern for these Lears. The mixture of an old man's love and hate, the struggle with age, brought them to a turning point. Having to find strength for this ordeal, they would have to find more and more for the savagery ahead. Booth, who until now seemed to have hardly enough energy to cow and strike Oswald, began the speech more in sadness than anger; it uncovered reserves in him as he went on, it welled in volume and intensity. His eloquent gestures served him: "the trembling hand that launched the curse seemed to fling the spirit of the words off the tips of its extended fingers." Bassermann, though awakened from his lethargy by Goneril's challenge, still was not fully vital; again and again his own words made him seem to doubt, the passion would fade, and the words would die on his lips. Klöpfer did not summon even passion: he spoke without tears, without shattering emotion, without flashes of majesty. Only his collapse immediately after exposed the intensity of the subtextual emotion he was squandering.

Some of the old Lears were clearly beginning to find their reserves of strength here. Irving, the most romantic, let the shadow of madness he felt in Lear energize the speech, emphasize the growing violence in the "violent weakness" he saw in the design. The curse was "a struggle of a worn and fretted mind, only lately re-aroused to great effort . . . the impersonation of will contending with weakness, of suffering striving to avenge, of a teeming mind racking a wrecked body, of agony wearily prolific in lofty but powerless excursion." Kneeling, his hands upthrust imploring heaven, he dropped them across his chest "as if conscious that he could not express his sense of wrong." The delivery owed something to the past: the speech was "not raved, it was gasped, or hissed word by word, syllable by syllable, as if torn from a breast panting with a last effort of rage and will." The words were deliberate, measured, weighted like a pious prayer until the voice choked with almost inarticulate rage; the physical imagery was frenetic: his whole frame quivered with excitement; the long tossing locks and straggling white beard waved round the old man's head like some whirling snowblast. "The keen eyes were lit with the fire of madness, those miserable and mistaking eyes were not miserable now, but glared . . . while the thin eloquent hands, with every sinew stretched like a cord, trembled in response to the agony."

Mikhoels, modern, less romantic, as he began to find his strength now used franker, more robust imagery. He felt that Lear was like Ezekiel, the most fleshly of prophets, who thought in earthy terms, wore rags, ate excrement. Thus, when he spoke of Goneril's womb, he slapped himself on the belly, loudly, so the house resounded with those slaps as he pronounced the curse. One motif in the running visual imagery he used was emphasized here; and one initiated. The first was his accustomed gesture of feeling for his crown. Time and again he raised his hand to his bare forehead, in despair and bewilderment, reaching for this old symbol of his identity. And now, for the first time, he wept—perhaps the first time in Lear's life, Mikhoels thought. Afterwards, he would begin to look for tears in other men's eyes—in the Fool's, in Kent's, in Gloster's. And in his own—this was a gesture he would repeat often, even when he was not speaking: he would check up—"You see, I am not weeping."

For the powerful Lears, the scene was a turning toward the disintegrative effect of acknowledged weakness. The more histrionic were pyrotechnic in their display. Thus, Forrest, after *Beat at this gate*:

> Striking his forehead, Forrest stood for a moment, a picture of uncertainty, regret, self-deprecation, and woe. Then a sense of the insulting disrespect and ingratitude of Goneril seemed to break in on him afresh, and let loose the whole volcanic flood of injured selfhood. Anguish, wrath, and helplessness drove him mad. He threw away his hat and staff, fell upon his knees. The blood made path from his heart to his brow, and hung there, a red cloud, His eyes flashed and faded and reflashed. He beat his breast as if not knowing what he did. His hands clutched wildly at the air as if struggling with something invisible. Then, with upturned look and hands straight outstretched toward his unnatural daughter, he poured out, in frenzied tones of mingled shriek and sob, his withering curse, half adjuration, half malediction. At first there seemed to be some method to his speech, as if his brain was striving to invent thoughts to express his anger, but his thoughts flowed faster until his mind became an uncontrollable temper of words. At the end, he was absolutely exhausted, and fell into the arms of Kent and the physician. By a perfect gradation his protruded and bloodshot eyeballs, his crimsoned and swollen features, and his trembling frame subsided from their convulsive effort.

This kind of violence was a tradition, even, as we have seen, among feebler Lears. It cut across national boundaries: thus Schroeder, the first

great German Lear—"his eyes were like lightning, his every muscle fe-
verishly trembling, his lips spasmodically twitching, his hands stretched
out as if he wished to tear down from heaven the fulfillment of his
curse." Spectacularly theatrical, these tirades awed and frightened audiences. But inevitably other, less showy means would be tried.

Salvini was the first of the titan Lears to intensify the power of the
curse with quietness. His Lear was an image of tremendous strength
cracking by repeated blows; he stood up to this one with formidable
gravity. He seemed to lose nothing—until the end. He uncovered his
grey head, and standing straight before Goneril, but without looking at
her, his arms uplifted, his face transfigured, in the midst of a great calm—
those about him shrinking in silence and dread—he seemed to commune
with the gods. Henry James thought there was a "touch of the sublime
in the wild mixture of familiarity and solemnity in his address to his 'dear
goddess.' The deep bass notes invested the curse with an awful solemnity." At the beginning every accent was a blow, like a sledge-hammer;
and yet Salvini would yield to passion, and pity, and at the end, at the
thought of ingratitude, his voice faltered. Finally, still without confronting Goneril, he wrapped his face in his mantle and strode out.

Granville-Barker rediscovered the power of "deadlier quiet," and under his guidance Gielgud exercised it. Gielgud's Lear, stopped in his intended exit by Goneril's contemptuous laugh, turned with terrible slow-
ness, raised his arms in invocation, and cursed Goneril with a quiet,
gentle, horrifying malignity, merciless in its restraint, modulating only
slightly to a crescendo. There would be a contrast between this arrogant
prayer, spoken rigidly upright, the palms up, as if calling down evil, and
the later, humble, beneficent prayer of the bowed head and body in the
storm. Gielgud's notes here: "Let go. The curse sudden, surprise the
audience. Speak nicely to Albany, going, then down to her. Strange,
not loud. Deadly. Ride it. Climax. Move backwards from her. Will not
go back on it. Slow exit." The muted effect was of something uncanny,
supernatural.

An earlier Gielgud had been fierce here. The German Krauss similarly moved from an explosive curse in his early performances to a "horribly low" voice later, only the twitching of his eyes suggesting the inward pressure toward madness. Carnovsky's fury, too, was repressed,
strenuously: he moved toward Goneril purposefully, the phrases
cracked out at her like gun shots. Scofield's Lear, holding his feelings of
love and remorse so far under they could only be sensed, advanced on
Goneril like a man who could attack. Some Lears have barely refrained
from striking Goneril; West clawed at her, as if to carve out, with his

fingernails, *wrinkles in her brow of youth*. These were not kindly old fathers, momentarily angered by vicious ingratitude: they were Lears as strong as their daughters, answering provocation with hatred that had as much ugliness as hurt in it.

Significant is Goneril's immediate response to Lear's "prayer." Albany's *Gods that we adore, whereof comes this?* (299) may partly be a wonder at the effect on Goneril. Her father has said almost the worst thing a father could, threatening, with almost supernatural power, her fertility, her womanness. Granville-Barker thought she was beyond being moved; if so, she might only respond with the "stolid contempt" of Booth's Goneril. But others have visualized her differently, often so in the theatre. (If she is pregnant, as has been suggested, the force of the curse might be intensified.) Forrest's Goneril, spectacularly responding through his spectacular curse, was "very much agitated . . . and at the end shrieks and rushes to Lear imploringly, who throws her off—She falls into Albany's arms and faints—Ladies and pages cluster around her." Irving's Goneril shrank from "the old man kneeling in the center of the throng, and after a harrowing shriek" hid her face in Albany's shoulder. More modern Lears have had more restrained effects: Laughton's quiet, almost conversational curse showed most of all in the effect it had on his Goneril: she was obviously shaken, it turned her stomach. Carnovsky's Goneril sagged, clutching at herself as if to ward off the blow; Irene Worth wept—this came over partly as genuine compassion for Scofield's Lear, and for the dissension between them; but even more as her own anguish that, at her age, she was childless, and wished she were not, and was hurt by his reminder as much as by his threat.

There is no overt evidence of strong feeling in Goneril's response later to Albany's troubled wonder at the situation; if feeling there is, it belongs to her visual imagery. On the other hand, she does not respond to Lear when he returns, except by silence, or gesture, either of which may express feeling, or feeling repressed. Her response partly determines Lear's character. If she is wholly unmoved, amused, scornful, Lear's curse is an exercise in futility, a comment on his helplessness. If she is revolted by what he says, or is frightened, or compassionate, it says something else.

The ugliness of the speech lies not only in its antinatural, destructive—and self-destructive—appeal for sterility, but in the images in the Lear design here. "The horror of sex first appears when he is mad," Empson suggests; but the note sounds now, when madness seems still marginal.

> Into her womb convey sterility!
> Dry up in her the organs of increase ... (287–288).

The first image is of the sexual act perverted—intercourse that destroys
life. The second extends, indulges the first. He goes on: *her derogate
body . . . If she must teem . . .* (289–290). A deep hatred of woman, an
impulse to anatomize—cut, dissect, plunge into—now hinted, will reveal
itself in his madness, as his regression to the ultimate darkness proceeds.
The tonic strain associated with Lear gives itself over to latent dissonances that echo into Goneril's fierce dominants.

Actors, we have seen, have hissed or gasped the speech—understandably, for it is charged with sibilants, line upon line, ending with the
spit of

> How sharper than a serpent's tooth it is
> To have a thankless child! (297–298.)

Lear's characteristic action is again flight. Whether helped out, as the
weary old Lears were, or proudly independent, his last words verbalize
apartness. His *Away, away!* (298) may refer to Albany, who is sometimes visualized as approaching, or even to Goneril; but his intention is
clearly flight.

Albany's bewilderment is another obscure step in his metamorphosis,
as must be his unspoken response to Goneril's curious—contemptuous?—
Never afflict yourself to know more of it (300), and her reference to
Lear's dotage.

Gielgud wondered how, when Lear was offstage, he would have
learned that fifty knights were to be *disquantitied*; Granville-Barker
said this was unimportant. But Lear does learn this: in the theatre, even
as he is moving off, he can be met, as he was in the Goldsby production,
with a knight bearing the news, or he may return with a scroll contain-
ing the order. This would suggest again the atmosphere of control Goneril could have set up visually from the very beginning, with her men
overbearing Lear's knights. Albany's present helplessness before this
manipulation would again be a comment on the character design.

Lear returns in tears. They may have begun to fall before his last exit;
they are now in force. Tears go with the sibilants continued from the
last speech into this one, intensified by the many f's, and interrupted by
the hard p's, b's, t's, and especially the k's. To the shame of being humiliated like a child is added the shame of weeping like a child—in utter
helplessness. That she has such power to move him; that he cannot manage the love and hate warring in him; that what seems to him kingly and
manly in him is being washed away in humiliation, so he seems to be
parting forever from his old image of himself—these accelerate his frus-

tration into apprehensions, yet unspoken, of madness. Now there is no pretence of prayer any more: this is frankly a *father's curse*. The powers of nature—blasts and fogs—are again called down against his issue; again Lear uses the penetration image:

> Th' untented woundings of a father's curse
> Pierce every sense about thee! (309-310.)

Pierce also that *most precious square of sense?* (I, i, 74.) The womb again? Only a woman bears an untented—unbandaged—wound. Now, instead of *out of my sight!* Lear threatens, in the words of Matthew, to pluck out his eyes if they offend him by weeping again—another of his childish threats that he will never carry out. His blindness is another kind; Gloster it is whose eyes will be plucked out—realizing the castration image, man's untented wounding.

Lear is of course wrong to imagine that Regan is *kind and comfortable* (315). Now again the man-animal images interfuse—kind Regan will, with her nails, flay Goneril's wolvish visage. The last line is the child's threat that he will so often repeat—you wait and see! you'll be sorry. But it has added meaning now, because of the Fool's comparison to Lear's formless figure of an O—nothing:

> Thou shalt find
> That I'll resume the shape which thou dost think
> I have cast off for ever (317-319).

It is a threat: Barnay, as he staggered out, shook his fist warningly at Goneril. Lear has been called a "passive" protagonist; in fact, he is intensely active, *choosing* options that enforce the play's movement. He initiates every agon, spews challenges, threats, curses, takes actions that compel him—and others—to further actions. Goneril will recognize his threat—possibly disturbed, possibly coolly composing her letter to Regan.

Again, Fool stays behind. Goneril orders him out—may chase him—providing Fool with a motif for later theme-and-variation:

> . . . more knave than fool, after your master (324).

Fool may have wanted to follow Lear, but be afraid—as in the Brook film—of getting past Goneril now that he is at her mercy. He may be trying to snatch a bit of food—thus underlining the privation he and Lear will suffer. Here, visually, Fool acts out his see-saw between practicality and loyalty. He follows Lear—and perhaps follows him perforce.

Goneril says to Albany, *Do you mark that?* (320) in response to

Lear's threat. If she does fear Lear's intention to resume the kingship—and before long, in Gloster's castle, she will learn of an actual plot to restore Lear to the throne, a plot perhaps related to letters Lear will send Gloster by Kent—the visual presence of her own armed guards, their suppression of Lear's men, would support this characterization. This would also fit into the design the fact of the absence of Lear's followers in what succeeds. Certainly Goneril proceeds as if her fears are real: she talks about what is politic and safe, she thinks senile Lear—again she uses *dotage*—and his hundred could *hold our lives in mercy* (337). Albany accepts that she fears, is afraid she may fear too far; she denies it: *I know his heart* (340). Then follows a curious threat aimed at Regan—and a clear indication that the two are not necessarily of one mind:

> What he hath utter'd I have writ my sister;
> If she sustain him and his hundred knights,
> When I have show'd th' unfitness ... (341–343).

The *if* hangs there as Oswald enters. But the tone implies "she'll be sorry." It is another note in the development of their rivalry—of the division between "the dukes."

Again Goneril speaks of fear, and scolds Albany for his *milky gentleness*. He is now seen for the last time until the great change in him three acts later. It is a glimpse of a man doubtful, aware of wrong done, hesitant to counter his dominating wife. He takes refuge in a pious couplet—not a typical scene-end rhyme, but a defensive, proverbial cliché. She starts to challenge him—*Nay, then*—and he backs up: Well, we'll see. In Carnovsky's *Lear*, the challenge was sexual: she went up to Albany, her arm around his neck, her hand moving on his chest, seductively. The great love he bore her was made visual, and it persuaded him. But in the Dunn *Lear* she shook off his loving advance, and he had to wait, humiliated and jealous, as she communed with Oswald. Significantly, when she sends her message to Regan, she orders Oswald to *Take you some company*—a man might not easily ride alone in this country in the night.

Shakespeare has taken great care in this scene to establish for Goneril an identity not subordinated to the Lear role. Her own drives begin to assert autonomy. The design includes her assumption of the power of the eldest, her overt rivalry with Regan, and her unspoken revenge on Lear for his indulgence to Cordelia: may her anger at Fool be partly spurred by Fool's resemblance—at least in relationship—to the exiled favorite? Her passions have some of the flavor of her father's, a power great enough to destroy her. The strong qualities in this female design emerge; and with them the first revelations of her contempt for her husband. He is not the man for her; and though she may now use him, exploit sexually his love for her, she scorns him, her fancy will build beyond him, may already, subtextually, be imaging someone in his place. In the pause after Lear leaves, Shakespeare—while providing a breathing space for Lear, before I, v, and for a tapering off of climax—gives Goneril time at center stage to assert, in her control of Albany and Oswald, and in what she envisions beyond, an independent dramatic destiny. She will not stop here, at the break with her father; he will become incidental to her; she is launched on a course that aims higher, highest.

To intensify the sense of the hero's isolation—a powerful motif in all Shakespearean tragedy—a compelling scenic image has been used to bridge this scene to the next, particularly in the European theatre: that of the castle doors closing on Lear—and Fool. Mikhoel's designer felt the sense of walling Lear out was at the center of the play, and his production design was keyed to the shutting of great doors. In the face of the blood-red castle Kozintsev designed for Goneril, doors three times a man's height closed on Lear. The king locked out of his palace, become beggar, his identity changed with his situation, has understandably been a folk-tale motif; here mythic impulse is made visual. From now on, Lear will be in flight, in night and storm, other walls will close against him, there will be no *place*, no territory on which to rest even for a moment, until he is led to the beggar's hovel.

Act I, Scene v

The design of Lear's lonely confrontation with himself, barely begun, emerges sharply in I, v. First his men may bustle in the background, and Kent's sturdy presence will provide company, but this quickly passes, and Lear is alone, shut out, outside, unattended, the tempest rising in his mind. Fool is there; but cold, miserable Fool now only half tries to outjest Lear's misery; half lances into it, and salts the wounds.

Lear needs no reminding of his folly. He responds now as much to the past as the present; the disjointed interjections of remorse and passion piece together, Jorgensen observes, into a kind of dispersed soliloquy. Intensifying inward forces distort his communication, until the accumulated pressure terrifies him—and Fool. Lear's multi-leveled responses, Fool's care to distract Lear, mixed with Fool's compulsion to instruct through hurt, and the wryness of the folk humor, make this an intensely threatening scene.

Its force is largely inward, as Gielgud found in working with Granville-Barker. In his earlier performance, the emphasis had been on the inwardness, and—somewhat sentimentally—on the compassion underlying the duet between Lear and Fool. Lear tried to concentrate on Fool's kindly-meant jokes, but was drawn back into himself. In the later performance the producer wanted a sense of Lear on the gad, impelled to flee from Goneril to Regan, driven by a mixture of physical and mental weariness, despair, and apprehension. Gielgud's note: "quick, not thinking of what he says. Walks continually to and fro. Stops suddenly . . . walk . . . stop again . . ." Where before he had been the fixed star, circled by the solicitous Fool, now he paced restlessly, Fool the pivot. Gielgud himself preferred the earlier pattern, the inwardness. So did Badel, Gielgud's Fool.

The design of the scene depends on the quality of Lear's mounting preoccupation. Fool's plot to distract him, the joke about a man's brains in his heels, has fairly been taken by acrobatic players as a cue for headstands and somersaults. An old Fool might try gymnastics and fail. Lear, scarred by his confrontation with Goneril, and feeling over his wounds, barely acknowledges Fool. An already slightly mad Lear, Booth, was lost in thought, moving subtextually beyond his momentary clear glimpse of his folly toward the more furious madness. The scene is a step toward unbalance in saner Lears. The storm within is such that Fool, sensing it, is often tentative, frightened by Lear's passion and distraction. The opening movement is generally very low-pitched, carrying over, in terse, earthy prose, reverberations of Lear's stormy departure from Goneril. Lear's visual imagery is most important here: all the passions of the curse are still alive in him, further charged with his growing apprehension of his sanity. Carnovsky showed this with nervous movements; Rudolph Schildkraut (1862–1930), by a mechanical way of answering, with the fixed stare of one looking inward. Wolfit's emerging fury showed in his handling of the whip, building to a fierce use of it. Mikhoels again evoked Cordelia's haunting presence with his aural gesture from I, i—the chuckle with which he searched for her. These chuckles were not for the Fool. Any temptation to simple sentimentality in the scene's humor is effectively interdicted by Shakespeare with Fool's bitter jests. He is moving down the animal scale in his jibes at Lear's daughters—and at Lear: crab,* oyster, snail. Fool's divided form never shows more than in these attacks: compulsively he is cutting himself off from the shelter that he will sorely need—that he already needs, in the visual imagery of some stage fools, huddling in the wind against shut doors. For now the sense of outside weather—of bitter cold and harsh wind—must be omnipresent. The wear and tear begins to show. Fool's through-line of action takes him to what may be his dying moment in III, vi—when he goes to bed at noon; and if I, iv had shown him already wasting, this following scene, sharpening his fears for Lear as well as for himself—the more for himself because of Lear's movement toward destruction—begins his physical decay.

In I, iv Fool's problem—and contribution to the rising tension—was to escape the mounting wrath he increasingly provoked; now he must work steadily harder to catch Lear's straying attention, evident in the monosyllabic, tangential responses. Carnovsky's promptbook note for Lear's mad, almost hysterical laugh at the first joke is "color of shame... brooding bitterness." The quality of Lear's *Ha, ha, ha!* ranges in possibility from an eager attempt to cast off despair with manufactured laughter to an angry or cynical retort to Fool's lame joke—and this, in turn, may provoke the new bitterness of Fool's taunts about the daughters. The taunts glance off: the insulting riddle about why a man's nose is centered in his face—with its recurrent image of smelling—misses Lear,

*The primary gloss is crabapple; but the animal implication persists.

lost in the silent inward trial where he stands self-accused and suddenly
pleads guilty aloud:

> I did her wrong (24).

He may mean Goneril, D.G. James suggests; but this seems unlikely.
Almost certainly he means Cordelia; still, there is an edge of ambiguity,
the undefined, the clouded center. Fool tries more sharply—lovingly?
bitterly? revengefully? all?—to provoke Lear to consciousness with
images of the shelter they are not to have—of the oyster and his shell, the
snail and his house. The word snail's *horns* sounds the sexual note that
will become compulsive with Fool; it revives Lear's anguish. Lear cannot play straight man, the inner trial proceeds, he is driven to articulate
a passionate defense:

> I will forget my nature. So kind a father! (32.)

So kind a father. He has cut himself off from one daughter with a terrible oath; he has banished another—wrongly, as he has only now admitted. His *nature* has been "unnatural"; and he must shield himself from
truth with this self-image. He knows he is slipping here, Carnovsky's
notes observe; he jerks himself out of his fantasy, forces himself to
practical matters, calls for horses. Fool makes a joke, asks an old riddle, and this time Lear anticipates the answer—the seven stars are seven
because they are not eight. Gielgud's note: "Angry. Heard it before."
Carnovsky's hand clutched his head—he was holding on. Scofield was
like a rock. There is bite in Fool's answer: *thou wouldst make a good
Fool* (39). Fool's jokes are not working, line by line Lear slips farther
away from communication, the center is not holding; failing, Fool is
more frightened. Alec Guiness, in his clown's white face, showed a
dejection at the misfired star joke that was both put on and real. And
yet, as Fool incites Lear to sanity, he baits him, too, and the pitch rises.
The scene builds: Lear's next speech to his inward fantasy is all exclamatory, and it suggests that Goneril may well be worried about his
intentions:

> To take 't again perforce! Monster Ingratitude! (40.)

Fool's lancing attempt to draw him out: . . . *I'd have thee beaten for being old before thy time* (41–42)—echoing the image of Lear caned by
his daughters—moves Lear still one pitch higher. Carnovsky at *How's
that?* (144) seized Fool, part angry, mainly clutching at a reality. "Sudden," Gielgud's note reads. One tension more, Fool's reminder to Lear
of his folly, and the scene comes to climax:

O! let me not be mad, not mad, sweet heaven (47).

Every line of the scene has led—mounted—to this terrible flash, that casts light backward as well as forward. Only now the unspoken fear is out. There was a special irony in the already-mad Lears glimpsing, lucidly, for a moment, the horror of the madness to come; for those Lears still clinging to sanity, the vision was one that had meaning for Everyman. The brain only bears what is bearable; more, and man enters—rules—a wholly different kingdom, chaos, certain uncertainty, the waiting darkness. Only Salvini, of the great stage Lears, refused to admit an approaching engulfment: his appeal to the gods for sanity was in effect a stern refusal of madness. Others felt the premonitory touch of the shadow, in voice and gesture. Carnovsky listened to the words as they came out, warning him that he would not have strength to endure his heartbreak. Gielgud's note: "Now afraid inside. Simple." The words came out in broken phrases. Olivier seemed to confront a prevision: his hand suddenly pressed his forehead, he whispered the speech. Scofield articulated the words singly, flatly, chillingly, as if he had little hope. Wolfit's Lear, provoked beyond bearing, letting his fury out at Fool's last gibe, struck angrily with his whip, lashed Fool with it—and the act itself helped wrench from him the plea that was now intensely a prayer: *O, let me not be mad.*

This is Lear's first appeal to *heaven* (now still *sweet* to him) in which the note of humility enters; like all the other appeals—prayers, orders, demands—it will be denied.

Lear's cry poises the scene at climax; in the dead pause following, the Gentleman enters. It is significant that only one Gentleman is left, the old bustle of attendants is stilled, even this one will disappear from Lear's immediate train.

The man's entrance is a present reality that can still return Lear to present consciousness; Lear looks, perhaps, to see if there are no other attendants, and then asks about the horses—impatient, angry, weary, abstracted, resigned, uncertain, depending on the design of the characterization. *Come boy*, he says to Fool; his tenderness for Fool seems to grow as his anger concentrates on his daughters, and his remorse on himself; he will not again, as he has so often, verbally threaten the whip. Lear calls, but in the theatre it is sometimes Fool who leads the way, ahead of the old man: Gielgud's Fool, still bent on distracting Lear, taking his cue from Lear's request, now made the chucking sound hostlers use to gentle horses, and drew the old man off. Carnovsky went out

still clinging to Fool as an anchor. Wolfit's Fool, cowering where he had
been lashed, ran to the whip, picked it up, and—as a dog would after being punished—put the whip back in Lear's hand. Lear put his arm around
him, and they went out together.

Sometimes cut, but contributory to Fool's dialectic, is his scene-end
rhyme, with its multiple erotic implications, perhaps accompanied by
visual gesture. Out of a context of madness he contrives a jest; the playwright uses it as a moment of alienation, a momentary interdiction of
intense emotional response, a relief through laughter, and a wry implication about the length of his own artwork. Fool talks to the audience:

> She that's a maid now, and laughs at my departure,
> Shall not be a maid long, unless things be cut shorter (52–53).

Act II, Scene i

The rivalry between Goneril and Regan, hinted at in the first scene, and again in I, iii, and I, iv, is stipulated now in the opening dialogue at Gloster's castle. Rumors spread of war between the dukedoms. This division will not be verbalized when the sisters meet; *the face of it is cover'd,* Kent will say (III, i, 20); but their physical imagery will declare it.

Night, rumor, quick movement—all's meet to the Bastard that he can fashion fit. Alone, his sentences come short, sharp, no complete thought ever more than a line long, the ideas jumping with exclamations, starting with the pervasive comparatives: *Better! Best!* This will be his momentary style: *Briefness and fortune, work!* (19.) He cries to Edgar, *descend!* and Edgar comes—comes down, on the way to the very bottom —not necessarily like a dog at call, as Granville-Barker says; but certainly an apprehensive man under guard, suspected by his father, going armed at his brother's advice. The bright, threatening dominant tonality associated with Edmund's rise colors the moment.

Edgar is hustled by Edmund's pace. Exclamations, questions, the racing tempo involving new dangers Edgar has never thought of: Cornwall comes hither now, *i' th' night, i' th' haste . . .* (25). Have you not spoken against him? . . . and when Edgar shakes his head, the Bastard—insisting on the division—tries the reverse: have you not spoken for him against Albany? Edgar says no in seven words, all he is given time for before he is rushed off.

Swift movement intensifies the tempo: Edmund must draw his sword on Edgar, he bids Edgar draw—often, in the theatre, draws for him. How far would the Bastard go to destroy the legitimate? He has said he has *one thing, of a queasy question* (18), that he must act. Is he designed to contemplate a quick killing, taking Edgar off guard, then to plead self defense? This clash must be seen in relation to V, iii. Edgar will turn out the better warrior then; will he now, in this brief rehearsal? will the Bastard's thrust be ambiguous, possibly a deliberate threat to Edgar's life, that Edgar must parry? Perhaps by knocking Edmund's sword from his hand? *Quit you well* (31), Edmund says—giving an extra meaning

to the verb? Edgar, turning aside Edmund's thrust, may acquit himself
better than he realizes. Edmund would be much safer with Edgar dead,
unable to exonerate himself. The Bastard will show no compunction
about putting his father's life in murderous hands, may intend this one
thrust a killing one. Or the latent conscience in him may check him at
the last moment. In any case, whether he contemplates murder now
or not, Edgar is for the moment unharmed, and Edmund hurries him
away, with more dizzying, staccato cries—in Kozintsev's film, Edmund
kissed his fleeing brother goodbye. Once more a character is caught up
in the tragedy's pervasive flight imagery. *Fly! . . . Fly!* Edmund urges;
Edgar is *fled . . . is fled*, he will not *'scape.*

Edgar's second brief appearance still reveals little, in the verbal part,
of his design, except that he is dazed by the suddenness of danger, the
confusion in the dark night, the curious play-acting of his brother. The
Russian Blok suggested that the milieu must suggest a dangerous world
where threatened sons must flee, as in *Macbeth*. Even if so, this brief
pivot of Edgar's action must reveal, as before, his characterization. His
coming change to a "sullen" Bedlam, and then to authoritative man,
will be meaningful largely in his distance from the young dupe's qualities he shows here: naivete? role playing? bookishness? drunkenness?
dissipation? uncertainty? weakness? The still incipient design must declare itself in a few flashing moments; partly the very speed of the scene
sustains disbelief's suspension: the audience, as hurried as Edgar, is swept
along in the haste, in the night.

The Bastard, alone, wryly cuts himself—the act, the words, the style,
his agility, his bravura collapse are usually darkly comic in the theatre.
He may go on pretending a mimic battle until someone comes. *No help?*
he cries, with just the right touch of piteousness—and Gloster enters, the
servants with their torches emphasizing the hazards of night.

Edmund seems to work a delaying action, to allow Edgar to get far
away; and so the tempo slows, as Edmund sketches a detailed picture:

> Here stood he in the dark, his sharp sword out,
> Mumbling of wicked charms . . . (38–39).

Chameleonlike, Edmund now is taking on the coloration of Gloster:
the mumbo-jumbo, the longer speech rhythms. Gloster is in a hurry;
Edmund tries to slow him with the show of his wound—Laughton's
Edmund fainted here—but finally must indicate which way Edgar fled—
pointing the wrong way usually, but not always. Gloster dispatches the
servants, and again Edmund returns to the portentous, sententious style
of his father. The lines are loaded with irony of both sound and idea:

> But that I told him, the revenging Gods
> 'Gainst parricides did all the thunder bend;
> Spoke with how manifold and strong a bond
> The child was bound to th' father ... (45–48).

The father-child climate is pervasive here. A dozen times in this short scene the word *father* sounds, mostly from the Bastard calling for help or mouthing propriety. The dialogue between the Bastard and Gloster sounds on the surface like true son and father. Edmund enjoys the irony of his "honesty" so much that he is tempted, in the theatre, to make it obviously comic; but its point is its earnest seriousness:

> When I dissuaded him from his intent,
> And found him pight to do it, with curst speech
> I threaten'd to discover him: he replied,
> "Thou unpossessing bastard! dost thou think,
> If I would stand against thee, would the reposal
> Of any trust, virtue, or worth in thee
> Make thy words faith'd? (64–69.)
>   ... I'd turn it all
> To thy suggestion, plot, and damned practice..." (71–72).

Gloster's immediate response mirrors Lear's: *no child of mine: I never got him* (78). The words—punctuated by the call of Cornwall's trumpets to set them apart—carry the overlying irony that Gloster talks lovingly now to the true Bastard—a "bastard" by behavior as well as birth—and calls him *Loyal and natural boy* (84)—merging the implications of illegitimacy, of naturalness, and the idea of natural goodness reflected in filial affection. Gloster is, as usual, on the gad; yet there may be a moment here when, before his commitment, the old man pauses, and seems to try to penetrate Edmund's disguise. But caution gives way to affection; Gloster's sincere gratitude to Edmund, his outpouring of love, can be so touching in the theatre as to focus sentiment on him at the expense of concern for Lear, as in the Porter production. To sustain the total equation, Gloster's shadow side must not be scanted. Still, Gloster's promises to make the Bastard his heir is genuinely a moving moment— partly because so tinged with irony—Edmund has topped the legitimate. "Now art thou my lieutenant." The beat holds for a moment on Edmund's triumph.

The flashing entrance of Cornwall and Regan renews the tension, and brings the two plot lines together. The *fiery duke* is borne in on his indignation; Regan is dressed surely to rival anything regal Goneril can put on. They have, the Folio says, attendants, probably armed men, for war is in the air.

Regan moves sweetly to Gloster, comforting him. Regan's manner is obliquely an attack on her father whom she implicates twice: was not Edgard his godson? Was not Edgar a companion with her father's riotous knights? Edmund, in a single modest sentence, says yes.

The Bastard's shift in tone belongs to the marvelous suppleness of his design. He will be what each character wants him to be. To Cornwall, he does not presume on his promised inheritance: he speaks with due humility, a deserving young man, as Cornwall decides—the lines almost overburdened now with ironic echoes of natural and filial relationship: *you have shown your father / A child-like office* ... (105–106); *Natures of such deep trust we shall much need* ... (115). Edmund offers absolute loyalty.

Even as he does so, visual imagery may be undercutting his promise. After Gloster points out Edmund's wound, the talkative Regan is conspicuously silent for many lines. What is she doing? Somewhere her sexual relationship with Edmund must have its seed, and where more natural (in a multiple sense) than here, where, womanly, she may cry out at the blood, may leave her older husband's side to bandage the young hero's arm. Edmund says he has seen young men cut themselves for sport—gallants in Shakespeare's time might do so to drink to their mistresses in blood and wine. So Edmund's cut may be winning him Regan. If they will not yet exchange oeillades, she may touch him, wrap his wound tenderly, with even a glimpse of the sensuality that will later envelop her. The Bastard is an artist at accepting a woman's attentions.

But Regan cannot remain long mute. When Cornwall begins to tell why they came, Regan interrupts, overrides, with her haunting, curiously domestic image of the blind, shadowed ambience of their world:

Thus out of season, threading dark-eyed night... (119).

Her speech to Gloster is kindly, queenly, wears the royal plural: *Our good old friend / Lay comforts to your bosom, and bestow / Your needful counsel* ... (125–127). Regan now, like Goneril, begins to assert a separate identity, suggested in her confident relations with these men. But little has been revealed of her shadow side; a naive spectator does not expect her to reject her father.

Act II, Scene ii

The night, the haste, the sense of the dark and the bitter cold, energize the opening. Oswald will speak politely of *dawning*; but the word may be conventional, or anticipatory, for Kent soon mentions the night, the moon shining. Kent has spent a long pursuit, he will tell Lear, dashing to Regan's castle, where his welcome was poisoned by the delivery of Goneril's letter. Now, before Gloster's castle, Kent races in ahead of Oswald, to punish him.

The craftsmanship is offhand: Shakespeare saves the details for later, where a pause will be useful, and now concentrates on stimulating action. The fierce, the angry, the ungovernable in Kent's design, evident in his confrontations with Lear, dominates the characterization: he asks for a fight, he bullies Oswald, who is less than brave. If Oswald is seen as a foolish Osric here, and Kent only the good, loyal servant, the easy comedy of the scene can cover the sting of Kent's savagery—Kent intends to kill a man. Excusing himself to Lear, later, Kent will apologize only for drawing sword because he had *more man than wit* (II, iv, 42) about him, will omit the bullying. But it is there, as is Oswald's unwillingness now to fight: Shakespeare was moulding both loyal servants in the round, balancing their qualities; when the critics or the stage distort them, when Kent is seen as a genial, teasing jokester, without purpose; or when Oswald is seen as a dapper nonentity; when Booth cuts the opening lines down to Oswald's entrance on *help . . . help*, to eliminate Kent's belligerence; or when Brook makes Kent seem entirely a bully; Shakespeare's intent is being edited. Kent is linked to the tonic modality, but in his design countering dissonances undercut the movement back to rest.

The elements are mixed through the scene. The danger to Oswald of Kent's rising anger is balanced by the comic verbal pyrotechnics of Kent's catalogue of denigrations, and his relish of them, and by the visual humor of Oswald's attempts to evade attack: in the theatre, Kent must draw Oswald's sword and force it in his hand (a gesture that may echo Edmund's with Edgar), and still he is unable to bring Oswald to manly battle. Kent, complaining that Oswald tries to seem more than

146

he is, that he disguises himself in false elegance (Kent himself a disguised *eiron*), sketches a distorted mirror image of the kind of sinful serving man that Poor Tom will describe. Kent attacks Oswald because he is a good servant—*super-serviceable*—implying that one can serve well too well, be *a bawd in way of good service* (II, ii, 18–19). Kent himself is now being super-serviceable—a bully in the way of good service.*

The scene builds to the kind of good, fighting climax Shakespeare enjoyed, with Edmund coming on, rapier drawn, to intervene. Kent by now has managed to involve Oswald in some kind of confrontation, for Edmund commands them to part, and Kent takes him on instead, Edmund's extreme youth emphasized by contrast with Kent's gray. Now the danger of the swordplay becomes quite real: these men are serious fighters, and Kent's *I'll flesh ye* (46), glossed to mean he will "initiate" the *goodman boy*, also has the unmistakable connotation of blade in flesh. When these two, who face each other across swords, last met, Kent promised to know the Bastard better—perhaps snubbing him; the Bastard promised to study deserving—perhaps promising himself revenge. The Bastard, for an instant, staring at Kent, may almost pierce the disguise, the earlier scene may momentarily be revisited. Then the duel. It may, for a second time, reveal something of Edmund's young fighting style; until the noise of the clash brings out the castle.

In the atmosphere of possible civil war, in this place where fugitives are hunted to death, the danger is considerable, and "servants," certainly armed, are directed to dash out with Regan, Cornwall and Gloster. *Weapons? Arms?* (47.) Gloster will cry—he who will soon welcome news of armed invaders in England to support Lear—as if a battle, rather than a duel, might be afoot.

The servants make sure it is no more than the duel, which Cornwall firmly stops. Between him and Kent now develops the mounting stichomythia that has characterized Kent's confrontations so far—he is possessed by quarrelsomeness. But special tension nerves this meeting: Kent's life is forfeit if he is recognized, and these people knew him well. If Kent drops his disguise—and one power of disguise in the theatre is the danger of its slipping—Regan and Cornwall will be his death. Goneril's behavior to Lear in I, iv had not provoked Kent to speech— the design may imply restraint with women, or deference before Lear, certainly his fear of recognition—but now he is man to man, and having more man than he can control, he breaks out.

There is humor in the outburst, in the new catalogue of imprecations,

*The implications of *service* in *Lear* are usefully examined by Barish and Waingrow.

and in the *agon* with the Duke. But basic motifs persist: underlying
Kent's diatribe on Oswald's conception—a tailor must have made him,
a stonecutter or painter could not have done so badly—is the running
question, What makes a man? Then, inevitably, the dialectic—the animal
images emerge: *beastly, rats, dogs, goose, wagtail. Wagtail* has typical
multiple implications: the foolish bird, the servile spaniel, the garbage
beast haunting the outflows of drains, the whore who sells her pliant
middle.

Kent's defense of passion is also multi-valenced. Shakespeare generally seemed to prefer feeling to repression, as did many of his contemporaries; and here Kent is clearly the favored character; but Kent is
made, still, to overstate: damning those who sycophantically "smooth
every passion," he not only cannot flatter, he cannot contain himself,
seems compelled to arouse trouble for his master. There can be too much
of speaking even what we feel.

The scene runs long to make its point. Tension is partly sustained
when servants must hold Kent off from Oswald, Edmund, and even
Cornwall. The crux of danger comes tardily, after the laugh when Kent,
who professes to be angered by Oswald's countenance, observes that
he has seen better faces than any now about him. Cornwall, with much
accuracy, describes Kent's ostentatious, truculent plainness, that he says
masks dishonesty in service. Among the variants of dishonesty abroad
in this milieu, Kent's is certainly one, as is his special kind of disserving
service to Lear. But the design enforces Kent to rouse at Cornwall's
focus on his roughness; and he endangers himself with the sudden high-
flown parody of rhetoric. Cornwall is understandably suspicious of the
elegant speech from this rough man, and Kent's disguise is now most
threatened.

The Duke, after examining him carefully, will have no more of him,
turns instead to Oswald, believes Oswald, will not listen to Kent, orders
the stocks. Cornwall's last phrase is archetypal, reflecting a motif that
lies deep in the psychic pattern of the play:

> We'll teach you (127).

The words are timeless. If they have an irony here, as spoken by a
younger man to an older, they more importantly reflect, though in-
conspicuously, the whole world of power enforcing submission, of the
impulse to punishment, to bequeath guilt and shame, that colors the
Lear fantasy.

I am too old to learn (128), Kent says; and he is: he will never learn,
for instance, the way to help Lear. Oswald's description of Kent's be-

havior in Goneril's palace, *put upon him such a deal of man* (121), reflects the excess which now involves him, and will be reprised when Kent confesses to Lear. A man can manifest too much of "man." How hard Kent fights the stocks now will be some visual measure of the "man" in him. *Man* here reciprocates with *knave*, so readily applied to both Kent and Oswald; and the animal inheritance is again touched on: Kent would not treat Lear's dog as he is treated; Regan will treat Kent, Lear's knave, so. Regan has waited until after Cornwall's decision to speak her contempt; she may also kick or strike Kent, as in the Carnovsky *Lear*. The intensity, the excitement of her words suggests the perverse energy that will fire her at Gloster.

Oswald has sometimes been seen taking visual revenge on the stocked Kent; perhaps the extreme use of Oswald for comic purposes was in the Phelps' production, where Oswald jeered at Kent, Kent threw his cap at him, and the frightened fop ran off crying "Murder, murder." Goneril's "gentleman," as Regan calls him, deserves better, if for nothing else than to support Goneril's stature. In the Scofield film, a more real Oswald pulled the stocked Kent's shoes off, emphasizing the ambient oppression of the cold that bit at the naked feet.

An important stroke in the Gloster design is now brushed in. Gloster seeks—humbly—to restrain the Duke his patron from stocking Kent. He "beseeches" Cornwall, reminding him of how the King will be insulted; the speech sounds his first notes about the poor, the kind of wretch punished for *pilf'rings and most common trespasses* (144), of whom Fool has sung, and with whom Lear and Gloster himself will soon have intimate acquaintance. Cornwall and Regan rebuff him; and Cornwall commands him to follow them out. Gloster will be seen here, and in II, iv, as humble to the point of servility before Cornwall; in the subsequent scene he will obey orders; here he pauses for a moment—the while looking anxiously over his shoulder?—to try to console Kent (is there any suspense of possible recognition between two old friends?) before hurrying off after his master, who *Will not be rubb'd nor stopp'd* (154). The man and master thread will have a recurring loop soon, when Gloster himself is pinioned in a chair by Cornwall.

This moment may involve connective tissue in *Lear's* action: Kent may slip to Gloster one or more of the letters he carries from Lear, and one of these may be the message, betrayed by Edmund, that will cost Gloster his eyes. Kent still has another letter from Cordelia (Shakespeare liked to use this kind of well-made play tool to tie together bits of plot).

Any "man" Kent has let off in harrying Oswald, fighting Edmund, debating with Cornwall, and then resisting the stocking—and perhaps the stocks themselves—has exhausted his old frame. His—rare—contemplative speech curiously inverts the dark-light dialectic: Lear escapes heaven's blessing to burn in the bright sun; less light were better. Yet he needs light to read by, for he must struggle in the dimness through the letter from Cordelia, already planning to come to her father's rescue. The speech is difficult; Granville-Barker didn't see how an actor could make sense out of the "obscure . . . corrupt" middle lines, and decreed a cut that would unfortunately excise the eloquent, motif-strong *Nothing almost sees miracles, / But misery* (155–156), and the plot-significant reference to Cordelia. Kent is himself so sleepy, so worn with cold, and so shamed in his prison, that his speech comes wearily: a last reference to night, fortune, and the great wheel, and he sleeps.

Act II, Scene iii

No scene break was indicated in Shakespeare's text for Edgar's sudden appearance; he could be "in another part of the castle grounds." His speech, however, suggests longer flight: he has learned that no port, no place, is safe for him. "Double" time is at work, suggesting an extended purgatory of experience paralleling a narrow actual chronology. Editors since the eighteenth century have generally separated the scene, so Edgar may be seen as "far off" or "in a Wood" or "another part of England." Whether near the castle or far, he has no relation to the sleeping Kent—except in the motif of flight imagery, here edged with irony, for Edgar reenacts Kent's run from a proclaimed death, while Kent himself lies imprisoned. The visual imagery, as before—and later—may well include the movement, in the background, of the shadowy armed men searching for Edgar to kill him. Men must run from killers in this world.

Edgar almost certainly repeats, also, Kent's onstage change into final disguise, or his new identity, too, may bewilder audiences. He needs to be recognized at first, because only once, in his last few words, does he proclaim himself Edgar, and by then he may be unrecognizable. The process of stripping before the audience is central, will anticipate Lear's action; particularly so if Edgar too must throw off conspicuously rich clothes to become nothing. On this pivot, Edgar's inward journey turns: he gives up, not only clothes and person, but also a way of life, from best to worst, and the peripety is evidently steep.

The mood is urgent: he has momentarily *Escap'd the hunt* (3), but, fearful of discovery, he tears at his clothes, the while building a picture of his new identity—or non-identity—to assure himself that his disguise will work. The picture extends the vision of poverty near the animal level, on the margin of crime, initiated by Fool and extended by Gloster. The theatre use of background images of the dispossessed, as by Kozintsev, can make this poverty visual: Edgar may take his place among other wandering outcasts, may emphasize his depersonalization by stealing a scarecrow's castoffs. He now couples his own incarnation of homelessness with the powerful verbal atmosphere of helplessness:

151

> ... with presented nakedness outface
> The winds and persecutions of the sky (11–12).

Edgar invites the hostility of the weather, of the biting cold that must be sensed through this and the next act. He almost delights in his shivering. More than disguise operates: Edgar now, like Lear who will *abjure all roofs*, is going all the way to alienation, not content—as he will be later —with a peasant's identity, but only with

> ... the basest and most poorest shape
> That ever penury, in contempt of man,
> Brought near to beast ... (1–9).

Man and beast are coupled again, and the issue is made flesh as Edgar grimes his face and strips down to a rag across his loins, disarranges his hair, and begins to stab his mortified bare arms to make them bleed— reinforcing the verbal and visual imagery of piercing, wounding, pluck- ing, cutting, pricking, which runs from the mockery of Edmund's self- hurt, through Lear's self-destructive impulses and Gloster's suffering, to the final punishing struggle between the brothers. The eagerness for suffering, for hurt, for degradation, to be not merely poor, but superla- tively so, is determined, almost demonaic: a feeling carried in the r's, b's, t's, and hard k sounds.

The ragged Bedlam beggar that Edgar changes into in this brief soliloquy was a non-person familiar to Shakespeare's London, vagrant from the St. Mary's of Bethlehem hospital, an intimate reminder of the poverty Shakespeare is beginning to set against the opulence of Lear's regal environment. Beyond this was the irony that, in life, these beggars would sometimes pretend lunacy as Edgar does, to get their living: the ambiguities of sanity, insanity, and pretence were a present reality to Shakespeare's audience. The shock value of Edgar's descent from nobility to nothing, from life's top to a bottom recognizable in the streets around the Globe, partly explains why the 1608 Quarto gave him second billing on the title page:

> *With the unfortunate life* of Edgar, *son* and heir to the Earl of Gloster, and his sullen and assumed humor of Tom of Bedlam.

Edgar's madness is not only pretence to foreshadow the reality in Lear; it has its touches of brilliant lunacy, madness in reason, as Lear's will have its reason in madness. Edgar is like Hamlet in that his ecstasy will sometimes carry him momentarily beyond pretence into the reality of the unreality he pretends. But he is not all Hamlet; Brian Murray, who played the role brilliantly with Scofield, found in it many more differences than likenesses. Where Hamlet vacillated, Edgar was active, non-reflective, met crises with decisions. "With Hamlet you say 'Wait, wait, don't act on impulse.' But with Edgar, it's all impulse; he acts on the moment." This was the knuckle of the through-line this Edgar would follow: a weakling in the first act, who read a book as he entered, becoming the man of action—and iron—who would end by killing his brother.

There is, in the design of Edgar's restless action, which grows frenetic in Act III, a movement between decisiveness and the irrational. His acts will often be convulsive, while his imagery will be in the direction of repression, punishment, pain, for himself and others. Even his greatest kindliness will be edged with a curious opposite, that, as he will say near the end, he recognizes as a fault. So the design requires him to act under compulsions that he does not understand; and their force may be made visual, in this self-mutilation here, with a brutal physicality that in the theatre sometimes has been manifested with a painful, masochistic attack on his vanishing self. His *assumed humor*, described in the Quarto as "sullen," meant, about 1600, "gloomy, moody, solemn," but also "sulky, obstinate, refractory." By Dryden's time certainly, and probably earlier, "sullen" also connoted "baleful, malignant." These qualities are certainly latent in Edgar's behavior. As Poor Tom, he will be bitter company both for himself and the sad father he professes to love.

Verbally, visually, Edgar in this scene embodies the *Lear* dialectic between reciprocating aspects of value, of economic, social and personal relationship, of human identity, of reality and appearance, summed in his words as he vanishes into further flight.

Poor Turlygod! poor Tom! (20.)

He tries out his new identity—perhaps on one of the pursuing men who may surprise him, seize him, scrutinize him, finally pass on. For now, he is safe. Madness in poverty not only enforces, it confers, anonymity; it is the perfect disguise, for it makes a non-person:

Edgar I nothing am (21).

Ultimately, any hope of a return to the tonic key will rest with Edgar. In the very circumstance of his plunging to the *basest*—a base lower even than Edmund's—he takes over from his brother the mantle of outcast hero. But now any hint of such a return is submerged in the dissonances of his condition. He is being born again, naked, into a harsh world, where he learns anew strange wawls and cries. He has a long way to go.

Act II, Scene iv

The Lear who enters here has ridden through the night—Shakespeare takes care to confirm the continuity—first on a fruitless errand to his daughter, now here: again, in the cold, suffering the persecution of the sky, outside the doors of a castle. (Fool may emphasize the early hour by waking Kent with a cockcrow.) Lear may—as in Gielgud, Kozintsev—have left Goneril's castle conspicuously dinnerless. He is dusty, cold, worn, far from the same man who roared into the warmth of Goneril's palace with such appetite from the hunt. He could then at least make a show of forgetting Cordelia; now his new wounds are too fresh. So even the most powerful of stage Lears begin to weary here; the old ones are holding themselves together by nerve, or are pathetically weak; the mad ones prepare to build to *fortissimo*.

Besides the Fool, only one Gentleman follows Lear now; and soon this one will be lost. The stripping is visually under way. Lear wonders why Cornwall and Regan have suddenly moved from their castle; Gentleman assures him that the night before they had no such intention. Lear must digest this strangeness; things do not go any more as he had ordered them.

The stocks where Lear sees Kent further disturb him. If Kent has been drinking, if he raises a flagon to his noble master, as sometimes on the stage, the disturbance is the greater. In their confrontation, Granville-Barker saw in Lear here "All the old dignity . . . the brusque, familiar give-and-take which true authority never fears to practice with its dependents." More likely not. This dialogue is designed to build in the troubled Lear a tension so fierce that at the climax it will almost suffocate him. His feelings are 'on the gad,' and Kent, with the provocation that discolors his loyalty, drives Lear on to the crisis.

Fool's mockery of Kent, with its images of beast and man in bondage, associated by sexual implications, does nothing to relieve Lear's outrage. Rather, it sets a tone for a stichomythia that almost inevitably hones a curious cutting edge on Lear's anger. Gielgud resented it at first, then experimented with it, nourishing the comic tone with lines fed at a

154

quick, rallying pace. Later in the run, playing the scene with deeper sincerity, I gave the replies slowly, as if unaware of their comic effect. To my surprise, the audience laughed more easily still. The comedy effect was obtained naturally, without stage trick, and the development of rage and indignation progressed more freely. A technical point arose, however. It was impossible to prevent a laugh on "Yes, they have." Up to this speech the dialogue could hold without interruption. Both Lewis Casson [Kent] and I used every known device to postpone the laugh until the next two lines were spoken: "By Jupiter I swear no," "By Juno, I swear aye" when the sequence was completed, but without avail.

The tragic laughter that comes from this scene depends considerably on Kent's role: he is not merely Lear's straightman, he is himself provoked, provoking, perhaps quite angry, more intent on the contest than on pleasing Lear. Lear's refusal to believe:

> They durst not do't ... (22).

voices a passionate hubris: *'tis worse than murther* (23) not to pay me proper respect. He thinks only of himself, has no sympathy to spare for Kent. The syntax embodies his losing attempt at self-control: after the swinging, fierce rhythm of the first three lines, he decelerates to the slower, lumbering final phrases. Kent picks up the earlier tone, extends the hissing sibilants, angrily covering his apology with reports of his hasty pilgrimage, capping it with thematic allusions that evoke Lear's errors and humiliations:

> Your son and daughter found this trespass worth
> The shame which here it suffers (44-45).

The persistent, threatening *shame* plunders Lear now; the agony of his speechlessness, partly a physical agony, is counterpointed by Fool's harrowing, motif-laden song, touched off by the image of deserting birds in winter (Fool ever fears and shivers in the pervasive cold), of the lack of clothes and shelter the poor must suffer. Fool harps on money and practicality: shrewdness buys filial love (though not his); poverty buys neglect; children turn blind, unseeing. The poor stay poor: the world becomes suddenly a sordid sexual metaphor, in the image of a brothel, with Fortune its whore, who opens her legs only to purchase.

Lear is one agony closer to death now, this time so oppressed that he can hardly breathe. The sheer physical strain is unmistakable; a "fit of the mother" has seized him, shakes him. He will die asking that the tight garment at his throat be unbuttoned (unless he refers to Cordelia), and here is planted the first visual image of that ultimate suffocation: *Oh!*

how this mother (this smother) *swells up toward my heart* (56). This is part of the design of age and the assault of weather and weakness that will beat at Lear until he can swallow life no more. The assurances of the tonic key in his opening Act I, i speeches are now almost obliterated in the gathering dissonances.

Even the fierce and mighty Lears must yield slightly here, though with an anger at yielding. Gielgud swayed, grasped at his breast, his voice strangled. Carnovsky had to suppress tears again, his marginal note was: "The *hysterica passio!*—goddamn it! An intense effort of control."

Lear will go in to his daughter, but alone; he turns back abruptly any who would follow—Porter's loyal Fool, always at Lear's shoulder, was hurt by the terseness of the command. But Lear wants no repetition of his public humiliation before Goneril.

For the last time, he enters the doors of a palace that houses a daughter. Other doors have been seen to shut against him; and these may be. He may have to beat against them—as he will threaten to beat at Regan's chamber door. (Gielgud, walking heavily on his stick, knocked the doors open with a furious blow and stamped inside.) He may have to brush past guards alert to the rumors of war, perhaps more alert because of the recent alarm in the courtyard. And note that Lear will not be allowed to stay long: a moment later he will be ushered out—unwillingly—by Gloster.

The pause after Lear's troubled exit is filled by the Gentleman, asking if Kent has done no more than he reported. Kent's offence is not honesty here. His denial—*None*—sets off again the pattern of figures so often linked to Lear's value system:

> How chance the King comes with so small a number? (63.)

The verbalization insists on what the eye has seen: Lear is deserted, the birds have flown to a warmer South. Practical Fool, with his simple, proverbial speech, from hurt feelings preaches a lesson he himself will not learn: the shrewd and provident who protect themselves from winter (the cold, again) have better noses than to follow him that's stinking. The word has been amended, intelligently, as *sinking*; but this misses the extrapolation of the nose and smell imagery elsewhere so specifically associated with defeat and corruption (smell his way to Dover, smell of mortality, the stink of Lady the Brach, stench, etc.). Fool celebrates his own ambiguity: to let go of the great wheel going down hill is shrewd advice, but let knaves follow it; he will not; he is a Fool.

Scholars have disagreed as to the altruism of Fool's motives here, and perhaps nothing is a better testimony to the purposeful ambiguity of the design. Knave-fool have been paired and opposed from I, iv; to Lear, Fool has been—tenderly, angrily—both; Goneril gave the words differently weighted, comparative meanings: *more knave than fool* (I, iv, 324). Most critics stress Fool's loyalty; Danby feels Fool "really does believe that to follow Lear to disaster is foolishness. Absolute loyalty is irrational . . . Folly is an alternative to knavery, but that does not make it a virtue." This may well be part of what Fool believes; but he acts his belief of the opposite, too. His is the most persistent dialectic of all. The only foolish thing about Fool is his loyalty to Lear. If on the one hand morality seems folly to him, he simultaneously embodies the saw that "the wisdom of this world is the foolishness of God." He is prophetic. Others

> Will pack when it begins to rain,
> And leave thee in the storm.
> But I will tarry; the Fool will stay (80–82).

Lear is now hurried out of the palace by Gloster, perhaps again in the presence, if not with the collaboration, of the armed guards. This is essential to the indignity of Lear's position: not only will his children not see him, the king is herded outside their *chamber-door* and will not again be let in. Father has become child. Lear may try to insist on the ritual of majesty—insist that Gloster and the others kneel to him; but the ritual is hollow now. Gloster, his fealty ambivalent, afraid of the fiery Duke, cannot get Lear out fast enough; Lear cannot bear the exclusion. He has heard a like excuse offered before:

> Deny to speak with me! They are sick! They are weary!
> They have travell'd all the night! (88–89.)

Perhaps even, sardonically, "*They* are sick! *They* are weary! *They* have travell'd!" for Lear himself travelled twice as far, wearily, unfed, sickening in mind and body. Exclamatory as Lear is here, his spleen cannot all be let out—the design is a mounting one. Gloster's shushing appeasements intensify Lear's anger, in a series of sharper waves.

The anger is evident enough, but because this is Lear, it is not pure. Mixed in it is still the anxiety, the hope for love, the pride, the new fear of the body, the old fear of the mind that brings him here. After the short, sharp thunders, one word at a time, as if he could not summon breath or thought for more—he will speak like this in his utmost madness—

> Vengeance! plague! death! confusion!
> Fiery! (95–96.)

there is always a receding, to a quieter tone:

> Why, Gloster, Gloster,
> I'd speak with the Duke of Cornwall and his wife (96–97).

These breaking waves have been imagined by scholars—and spoken on the stage—in moods from withering sarcasm to broken appeal. Actors have generally tried to move in a range of expressiveness here, not always correctly, according to an eighteenth century critic:

> When we see such starts of impetuosity, hushed unfeelingly over, without fire, without energy, with a look of affliction, rather than astonishment, and a voice of patient restraint, instead of overwhelming indignation, we may know, by the calmness we feel in our blood, that the actor is not enough agitated ... [When the occasion required] the sharp, the elevated, the stretched note, the exclamatory, the king mistook, like a dog in a dream, that does but sigh, when he thinks he is barking. [The actor] neither ... stiffened the sinews—nor summoned up the blood —nor lent a terrible look to the eye—nor set the teeth—nor stretched the nostrils wide—nor held the breath hard—by which last, Shakespeare had in his mind's view a certain out-of-breath struggle ... when angry, which is not only natural, but disorders, and stimulates the body, with the most alarming resemblance of reality.

Gielgud's note:

> The producer demanded four contrasting emotions in this scene: 1. The actual progression of events which must be experienced by the actor— the deep moral indignation. 2. The "rash mood"—outbursts of uncontrollable fury, checked continually by reason and attempts at patience. 3. The physical strain on the body—expressed particularly at two points: "Hysterica passio" and "Oh me, my heart, my rising heart!" and gradually leading to the climax when Lear, beaten, sinks exhausted into the seat. 4. The knowledge of the toppling reason; the fear of going mad. To these must be added the task of miming of old age in movement, pose, and gesture.

Lear's age, and the strength allowed to it, are severely tested here. The good old fathers—Charles Kean, for example—might feel Lear's full quantum of rage, and yet necessarily be limited in their violence. Klöpfer began to show effects of pain and rage on years: he began to stammer, to open and close his mouth as a prelude to speech he could hardly utter, his words would fail him, until his physical impasse began to find relief in tears of helplessness. To his credit, he developed these actions as symptoms of age rather than to evoke pathos, tried to avoid sentimentality.

The intensity of feeling that comes on Lear as a seizure gave the more powerful Lears more to struggle with, more range in the dialectic between age and strength. Olivier, who reverberated thunder in his sudden flashes of anger, moved subtly toward his madness by forcing down his recurrent *hysterica passio* with a sense of intolerable physical strain. Carnovsky, in his cataclysmic inner debates, began to let the merest touch of senility creep in to his voice (his note: "to be used sparingly").

The wave rises again when Gloster, caught between a bear and a raging sea, tries to placate his past master:

Well, my good Lord, I have inform'd them so (98).

Inevitably Lear mounts to a new breaking point, a new exclamation:

Inform'd them! (99.)

Olivier was thunderous, Forrest satirical, Carnovsky bitterly ironical, Edmund Kean feeble and indecisive. The zigzag of feeling goes on: thus Forrest was moved suddenly to tenderness at *The King would speak with Cornwall; the dear father / Would with his daughter speak* (101–102); the line carried deep feeling, an appeal for love. Here Lear clearly states what he regards as his two roles (Jorgensen speaks of his twin identities) and it is his awareness of his failure in both that vitalizes his anger, in another brief, mounting wave. Gielgud was steadily more intense in this scene, up to *My breath and blood!* (103.) His note here: "Recover, then hysteria again." Lear's whipsaw must be one modulation in the larger design leading to madness; this is perhaps most felt in Lear's persistent effort to beat down his rebelling mind and body. He is recalled to their infirmity at the peak of this wave:

Tell the hot Duke that—(104).

Perhaps the specific cue now is the felt suffocation at his heart, that he will be able to speak of in a moment, when alone. Junius Brutus Booth (1821–1883) particularly emphasized the connection between Lear's real illness and the Duke's pretense. Charles Kean's Lear desperately wanted to believe Cornwall's excuse; Gielgud seemed to be making excuses for Cornwall. The mind of Mantell's Lear showed its first crack here. He cocked his head, and seemed to argue with himself for a moment. His voice in the next line had a slight sing-song quality.

Lear is obviously speaking of himself, conscious of his frailty, as he reverses direction:

No, but not yet; may be he is not well . . .
. . . we are not ourselves

> When Nature, being oppress'd, commands the mind
> To suffer with the body (105-109).

The *we* is no longer primarily the royal one, but that meaning is echoed in Lear's self-involvement, his search for identity. If we are not ourselves, then who? The receding wave is longer now, because Lear is so deep in his own needs, so desperate to believe the lies that have been told him.

But the next wave is gathering itself. Lear notices Kent—in the theatre, Kent moves, or rattles his chain, and Lear's attention is drawn—and this sub-scene ascends to its climax. *Death on my state* (112) escalates, as with Olivier, to thunder. The phrase is indignant, but also prophetic, and—as so much in Lear—aimed against himself, self-punitive. Even the feeblest Lears exploit the new peripety. The speech hisses with sibilants and fricatives. *Give me my servant forth* (115) is fired at the closed doors of the castle. The mood is clearly exclamatory, Lear is evidently so furious, so regal and terrible in his anger, that Gloster, who would do anything to avoid the confrontation, goes in. Lear may have physically threatened the castle doors as he did before, as he promises to do at Cornwall's chamber door:

> I'll beat the drum
> Till it cry sleep to death (188-119).

The drum he beats may be his chest, over the heart that seems to be swelling to cut off his breath. "Physical," Carnovsky notes here. "Entirely new voice. Quick. Then stand still. Pay no attention to Fool. Closed eyes, hand to head." Mikhoels could only whisper the words

> Oh me! my heart, my rising heart! (121.)

This is a main station on the through line of Lear's bodily anguish.

Fool's jingle is curious, has been seen by William Empson as even malicious, partly satirizing Lear's habit of giving orders. It is the place where his portion of madness, provoked by his self-concern, and concern for Lear, is most grotesquely expressed. Edgar will pretend madness so well he almost enters it, Lear will lurch into it, but Fool owns inspired lunacy as a rightful aspect of identity. His advice to beat down Lear's anxious, rising heart

> Cry to it, Nuncle, as the cockney did to the eels when she put 'em i' th'
> paste alive; she knapp'd 'em o' th' coxcombs with a stick, and cried
> "Down, wantons, down!" (122-125),

is a metaphor of his design, and of the larger design of which he is a part: the whipping down of the life o' th' phallic coxcomb—eels with coxcombs!—the suppression of feeling, of procreation, of passion.

Fool labors to outjest Lear's agony; but this and his joke about the horse fed buttered hay fail him. The moment is a focus of many of the clashing emotions central to the play. Fool says one of his funniest lines that almost invariably outjests an audience's concern, and makes it laugh, but cannot down the wanton furies erupting in Lear, who is experiencing almost absolute anguish. The verbal joke masks a deep current of felt sadness; and fear, too: Fool, circling Lear, trying for the smile, failing, begins to sense something unreachable, that Lear's mind is slipping beyond him. The impudent Fool who dared Goneril's wrath is silenced; only in gestural imagery will he be of any use to Lear, will he let the audience know his grief, his fear, his sympathy, his anger, throughout this scene. No more words.

The painful pause that punctuated this clash of the comic and tragic is broken when Gloster returns with Cornwall, Regan, and servants—again, the Duke will be strongly supported. Duke and Duchess may be in nightdress, but in any case may wear warm outer robes that contrast with Lear's thinner protection against the insistent cold. Lear turns to face them.

The complex design of his response is evident in the variety of subtextual expressions in stage characterizations. The old Lears, the Lears touched already with madness, were most vehement, as if gathering their powers for their ordeal. Edmund Kean cried out when they entered, a kind of "terrible and indistinct 'Ha!';" and, where he had been feeble before, he built strongly to a spectacular ending of the scene. Devrient, who had awaited Goneril with the hopeful tenderness of a loving, bemused father, unwilling to be suspicious, now anticipated rejection from Regan, burst out almost at once in rage, fortissimo, and held to the high note—though not quite to the end. Gielgud, the titan, was unyielding. His note for his salutation, "No greeting. Cold." For Regan's

I am glad to see your Highness (129),

"Don't notice this." But his response, *Regan, I think you are* (130), "Tender, just (in his heart he knows)." Scofield brought to Regan, except for his added weariness, and the growing burden of knowing he had wronged Cordelia, the same toughness he showed Goneril. Most Lears, however, even the Olympian ones, felt more need for love than anger, out of their anxiety tried desperately to hope for—and yield to—

kindness. They moved between approach and withdrawal, in an accelerating alternation that foreshadowed madness. Thus Charles Kean, seeking consolation, caught between rage and tears; even Edmund Kean, fierce as he was, inevitably mixing tenderness with his suspicion. Edwin Booth was touching in his eager welcome of his daughter, and, consistent with his pathetic characterization, was as much disappointed as angry at her response. Irving, in the same tradition, yielded longer to softness:

> He is vanquished beforehand, and he knows it. With what sweetness, what patience, what heartrending desire to be calm! He tries to deceive himself, as he sobs on Regan's shoulder. He "gave the impression of helplessness, the most infirm and miserable of human weaknesses."

Even some of the most powerful Lears forced down their fury here to seek sympathy. Carnovsky advanced to hug and kiss Regan—recalling his lover's embrace of her in I, i, and so trying to recall, as he would in words, not only her obligations, but her love. Forrest clung to his Regan, obstinately tried to deny the rejection which she, in the nineteenth century tradition, cruelly and unmistakably offered him.

She is of course crucial to the equation. Cornwall and Regan have come out reluctantly, perhaps, as noted, as if from bed. The suggestion of nightclothes intensifies the subtextual father-daughter relationship, evokes implicitly some of the unspoken sexual motifs elsewhere touched on. Or daughter and son-in-law are fully dressed, giving the lie to their social excuse. Whatever Regan wears is "gorgeous," and she will perhaps display, in visual rivalry with Goneril, some evidence of her semiroyalty, even though muffled in the robe that keeps her from the cold. Cornwall barely speaks; if he is fiery, the fire is suppressed in sullenness. His one overt confrontation with Lear will be an angry one. Except for this, and the physical imagery by which Lear reveals his feelings for Cornwall, Lear concentrates on Regan.

Her evil is not obvious. Suspense is still part of the design: a naive spectator is not sure of what is to happen, can hope for help from Regan. Her obvious difference from Goneril, her particular style of dress, her more feminine mode of offering tenderness to Lear, her kind manner toward Gloster, and, probably, Edmund, have so far in the text masked her capacity for hurt and hate. Again and again she will *pray* her father to change, even *entreat* him. If at once monstrous, as in Tate and the nineteenth century, she makes an unnecessarily silly dupe even out of the most foolish-old-Lear image. In the theatre she has been most effective—

partly because it contrasts her with Goneril—when she has seemed sweet; in fact bittersweet, emasculating Lear with an insistent, tender concern. So Porter's Regan met him with laughing, maternal greeting. So Scofield's Regan showed genuine concern for him, as his Goneril had, was more embarrassed for her old father's *unsightly tricks* than angered by him. So Regan's design permits her also to be an entity, and not merely an accessory to her father in his tragedy.

Lear's words make him no easy father to love. He breaks out with his instant egocentric measure for all things: if you are not glad to see me, if you do not love me, you must be a bastard, your mother a whore. Wolfit particularly conveyed the obsessiveness of Lear's concern with legitimacy. The speech can be said without anger, with anguish—Olivier spoke with gentleness at first, partly the gentleness of misgiving, as if he feared another blow. Lear himself seems brought up by what he says; his self-pity overwhelms him, he asks frankly for sympathy, seeming to think of himself as a wronged Prometheus—the vulture Goneril, bird of prey, feeds on him, the thought almost suffocates him again:

> I can scarce speak to thee; thou'lt not believe
> With how deprav'd a quality—O Regan! (137–138.)

Beloved Regan . . . O Regan! Whatever the balance in Lear between majesty and humanity, between the father and child, the man and the animal, the sage and the fool, the fierce and the pitiable, however much the words are vehicles for his anger at Goneril, they are also an appeal for love, an admission of need, not only spiritual, but also physical. Beyond need, there is a felt fear; Forrest, playing the mighty, pathetic Lear, embraced Regan and would have fallen into her arms; he "leaned on her bosom." The old, the feeble, especially the weeping Lears were more frankly the helpless child and seemed the more to need comfort. Here Mikhoels' recurrent visual imagery—the gesture of reaching out to see if tears wet another's face—could powerfully point back not only to his own first weeping, but forward, to a different confrontation with both daughters in this scene, and farther, to the moment when he would find tears on Cordelia's cheek.

The more dependent Lear allows himself to be, the greater peripety in the design when Regan finally rebuffs him. Her first words are a defense of Goneril. Regan in the theatre has sometimes—as with Gielgud—been cold here; but her manner still seems so honeyed and solicitous as to sugar her intent, for Lear is as much puzzled as incredulous at:

> Say? how is that? (144.)

Regan's repeated apology for Goneril, her suggestion even that the riot-ous knights need restraining, provoke Lear not against her, but her sis-ter—and again the design is of a father cutting himself off from his gen-eration, revivifying the passion that has damned a daughter to sterility, or her unborn to disnature:

> My curses on her! (147.)

Lear's retort seems instant, and so Gielgud played it, with a deter-mined return to control, though he paced restlessly under the pressure of his feelings. The less secure Lears, still struggling beyond the need for love, moved more slowly: so Irving was half-impressed by Regan's defense of her sister, for a moment doubted the justice of his case; the outburst was, as often with the weak Lears, more touched with misery than fury.

One caution that continues to blunt Lear's perception of Regan's pur-pose is the need, made increasingly evident as the scene mounts, to keep her love. Her design reciprocates: her cloying, patronizing *O, Sir*, the repeated, *I pray you*, the sweet rhythms in which she reminds him that he is decaying, that nature—a sublime irony—is almost ready to give up on him. Hence, when he strikes back, he still aims at Goneril through her.

His gesture is magnificent: he kneels.* This echo of his posture for the curse in I, iv is a reverse of the visual imagery in I, i, when his daugh-ters may have, as usually in the theatre, knelt—Mikhoels made this a crude parody of their earlier bows and curtseys. It is also a forshadow-ing of another curse to come, and a reverse of his kneeling seriously to pray in III, iv, to beg forgiveness from Cordelia in IV, vii, to kneel by her corpse at the end. It is a focus of many thematic energies: the mighty king on his knees, the father become a child to the child, the old sub-missive to the young, the rich and powerful engulfed by the darkening shadow of poverty, becoming poor, without shelter and substance:

> Dear daughter, I confess that I am old;
> Age is unnecessary: on my knees I beg
> That you'll vouchsafe me raiment, bed, and food (155–157).

Lear speaks as if for a king and father to beg so would be unspeakable, impossible; and yet he begs now. He pretends to be begging Goneril; in fact he is begging Regan. He implies that Lear could not possibly want

---

*This is not Shakespeare's stage direction, except as implied in the text, and an actor might, as George Vandenhoff (1790–1861) did, stand straight. But this seems to miss important gestures.

for the bare necessities; but a prophetic apprehension undermines his pretense. The mockery is partly self-mockery.

Actors have been tempted to narrowed implications. For a great, powerful king to kneel to his daughter, with an undertone of earnestness to his begging, provides a special shock, as in Salvini's case. For a weak, warm old man to supplicate in sad earnest as Schildkraut did evokes pity—"only pity," a critic said. Anger belongs: Forrest "stood an instant in blank amazement, as if not trusting his ears; a tremor of agony and rage shot through him, fixed itself in a scornful smile," and, kneeling, he prayed savagely. With the common ironic tone went gestures of irony, first the kneeling, then, as with Gielgud, *Mark how this becomes the house* (154), with a stressed pride in the word *house*, he swept off his hat to bow before Regan. Kean, on one knee, gestured with his voice, suggesting depths of feebleness, despondency, mendicancy. Laughton, on both knees, raised both palms together in a supplication so intense it shocked Regan—who in this production was the hardest heart of all.

Regan's role in the equation is partly what Lear projects on it: the farther he lets his anger touch her directly, the more in danger he is of losing this last chance for love. Carnovsky tested her to the utmost: half sarcastically, half seriously, he went down on his knees, then on his scrabbling hands and knees—the doglike child-animal image for a moment incarnate in the old man—and his pretense carried him along into such passion and scorn that his kneeling became a regal, vicious insult to the speechless people about him.

The context is significant. Lear is sometimes imagined—or directed—to be alone with Regan, since theirs is a dialogue; but in fact Lear's passion and ultimate rejection are witnessed, are public, and so seem much more humiliating. Lear, to escape exposure, may try to lead Regan down and away from the rest. Regan may resist. Her reply is sharper, in blunter rhythms; but if she speaks of unsightly tricks, as Goneril did of pranks, if she speaks as to a child, the mood is still solicitous: *Good sir . . . Return you to my sister* (158–159). Laughton's Regan helped Lear to stand—physical imagery to go with the maternal tone. In other visualizations, Fool or Kent are there, or—weakly—Lear works himself back to his feet, rejecting assistance.

As he rises—if he does—he rises to another curse. Again the sibilants, the hard consonants, again the invocation of destruction for his issue. Again the curious concentration on Goneril's body, her youthful beauty. He calls on the cruelty of heaven—a heaven of stored vengeances—and on nature—a nature of painful punishments: lame my daughter, blind her, corrupt her beauty—to the end that, as in the I, iv curse, her young body will suffer as his old one does. The lines may be, ritually, in the form of a prayer, but are as vicious as in his earlier attack; and there is an added irony in their coming so soon after Lear's kneeling mockery of a prayer for substance. If he has continued to kneel, or if, in his passion, he slips back to his knee, the ambiguity sharpens. He will learn to pray better.

Lear has again invoked hostile weather against his kind: the taking airs, the nimble lightnings, the fen-sucked fogs. The weather will soon—may even start now to—come down on him, while his chosen target for its cruelty, his daughter, will be snug inside. Lear's tempest is linked to nature's, some critics believe; but nature waited through his first great storm in I, iv without, textually, giving any reciprocating sign although then, too, he invoked blasts and fogs. Shakespeare's text offers no such simple correlation between the passions of man and universe, will deny it as often as not. Indeed, the nature Lear prays to will treat him—and only him and his friends—with cruelty, will attack only when it has him within reach, never while he is sheltered. To this point in II, iv, any overt function of nature must be staged—or imagined—subtextually. Scenes so far have been set indoors, or out in the night; only nature's cold and darkness has been explicit.

As noted, the theatre has sometimes set the first scene outside, commonly in a Stonehenge-type milieu, and under a bright sun, as if to contrast the quality of Lear's pre-abdication life with what is to come—though warnings in shadow and sound of the outer storm may be sensed this early, too, and even in Lear's confrontation with Goneril. However, not until the dialogue with Regan does Shakespeare say that the storm begins to rumble faintly down; and the implication (unstressed) is not only that storms may accompany man's misery, but may also be part of an ironic world that is on watch to defeat an exceptional man's expectations. For, again, the storm will threaten only Lear himself, and those who love him.

Regan's response to the curse is a shocked, pious call upon kinder deities:

> O the blest Gods! so will you wish on me,
> When the rash mood is on (170–171).

To the honey of her filial manner, the holy is now added. Lear cannot even confront her, as he could Goneril; her intent is sheathed in softness. He must, he will see only the outside, her appearance of tender-hefted nature, and he clings to that. She shall never have his curse, he says—another promise not to be kept; he will see love in her eyes. Her manner is still sweet enough to give Lear hope. But it is his last hope; the rhythm of his curses on Goneril, Regan's mounting resistances, his responses, accelerate to a threatened break with the one love he has left. His lightning anger is momentarily masked, to break out in a moment; meanwhile multiple impulses cross in him. J. B. Booth's Lear "sounded the various stops of grief, of parental love, of irony, of indignation, of baffled but clinging hope." Olivier's Lear made a real effort to subdue his rash impatience, to make concessions, to try to understand; the undertone was of loneliness longing for affection.

Lear, in his anxiety, begins to bargain now; even the wheedling note comes in, as in his reminders to Regan of what she owed him. His plea is at one extreme Vandenhoff's grovelling sycophancy, at the other the tough, unyielding Scofield, or the emotion-grudging Porter. The dialectic within Lear was expressed in visual imagery by Mikhoels when, assuring Regan she should never have his curse, she knows what she owes him, his Lear reached out to caress her cheek, and then, as he went on insisting on her obligations, in a kind of frenzy, his hand kept pace, ambiguously, it was hard to tell if he was stroking or striking. Lear has sought Regan's eyes, which, unlike Goneril's fierce ones, he says, comfort, not burn—but as he looks into them, enforcing a verbal-visual motif, he begins to see into her, and in retreat he tries to justify affection not for its own sake, but for formal and material reasons.

Lear's speech breaks down into a series of thought-out, half-line phrases, a catalogue of his hurts and her reasons for loving him. Little ironies play through the verse: it *is* in her to do him all these hurts he says she won't do, she *will* oppose the bolt against his coming in. He reminds her of the bond of childhood, which he had found insufficient in Cordelia; the bargain he says she must remember she has forgotten. He begins to see in her face the reality of her rejection of him; and her response,

> Good sir, to th' purpose (183)

is a complete irrelevancy—Porter's Regan simply laughed it—that provokes, lets loose his deep anger, though still not aimed directly at her, but displaced:

> Who put my man i' th' stocks? (184.)

This comes out as a sudden break from his reasonableness, as unsequential as Regan's refusal to understand him. The cue may be a movement of Kent's—though a stiff Kent has often been carried off, for if he re-

mains he could not easily abide Lear's humiliation or be separated from
his master in Lear's exit into the storm. But the impulse may as readily
come from Lear's deep frustration. This is one of the frequent peripeties
from quiet to thunder that Shakespeare designs, and in the theatre it can
be a spectacular moment for unleashing Lear's chained violence, even to
a foreshadowing of incoherence to come. Edmund Kean made it a cry
of agony, the recollection of Kent's treatment fusing with his awareness
of Regan's rejection. Olivier, a master of peripety, jerked from the almost colloquial gentleness of his previous speech to fierce outbreak.

Thus the subscene comes to its climax—on a held note: Lear's furious
question is simply ignored. Nobody answers; he will have to ask thrice,
as he has of Cordelia and at Goneril's palace—threes are one of the play's
patterns—before getting a response. The peak moment is accented aurally with the sound of Goneril's trumpet.

The clamorous horn, Oswald's appearance, Lear's angry reaction, the
second ignoring of his fierce question about the stocking, herald Goneril's entrance. At once the weights in the equation shift. The precarious
balance in Lear between anger and fear, the need to love and the need to
strike out, the remembrance of power and the anticipation of poverty,
is finally upset, and despite his intermittent efforts to stabilize it, with
pleas, rage, humility, imprecation, even compromise, the disequilibrium
intensifies toward chaos. The dominant begins to overwhelm the tonic.
Of this moment, Lamb asked:

> What have looks or tones to do with the sublime identification of his
> age with that of the *heavens themselves*, when, in his reproaches to them
> for conniving at the injustice of his children, he reminds them that
> 'they themselves are old.' What gesture shall we appropriate to this?
> What has the voice or eye to do with such things?

Everything, we might answer. It is the visual image of a mortal man who
would be a peer to gods beginning to question their role, and his own,
for the first time, that nerves the irony of this moment. It is his visual
repetition of earlier, cruel or mocking prayers, usually kneeling—Lamb
never takes fair account of the central function of the tormented body
in Lear's agony—that links this crisis with Lear's past, and his petitions
in the future, when he will pray, probably on his knees again, in charity,
madness, love, or in a final defiance of the gods.

Lear is the center of many tensions now. Hostility is directed not only
at him, but through him toward other targets. Goneril's entrance brings
together the two sisters whose old rivalry has continued into a division

between their husbands' dukedoms. Their rivalling dress is symbolic of their pretensions, even if the face of the division between them is still covered. Both may wear crowns, as they confront each other. Kent will say in the next scene how they put on a show of harmony against their father; but the contention between them reflected in the love-auction of the first scene, and in their brief encounter at its end, emerges now in a curious way. Before, each sought to express most love for their father; now each will try to outdo the other in denying him. He is the same man, but not now a king; he stares, says the same kinds of terrible threatening things, but now he is empty of power, and to his daughters, involved in their own concerns, he is a nuisance.

Regan made sure, at the end of I, i, that Lear would stay first with Goneril; now each tries to push him off on the other. Their professed bosoms they now withdraw; they refuse him nourishment. Lear, trying to come between them—as Booth did physically—is doubly battered. He is both their victim and their tennis ball.

Some sense of his dilemma informs Lear's latest prayer to the heavens. Gielgud's note: "Noble, becoming helpless;" he staggered back, arms outflung, then covered his eyes raising his hands high in prayer. Lear no longer commands; a doubt creeps in. The ancient now pleads to gods he hopes exist and are decent. The fearful *if*:

> If you do love old men, if your sweet sway
> Allow obedience, if you yourselves are old,
> Make it your cause; send down and take my part! (192–194.)

He waits. Nothing. The heavens are silent, as they have been. No seconds. No sweetness. He must face the daughters alone, as man and father; his achieved and assumed powers have all slipped from him. His impulses to attack strive with his needs for comfort and love. He tries to shame Goneril—the weapon of giving shame, of guilt, of "you'll be sorry" seems still to him, coupled with the obligation to love, to have great power, because it wounds him keenly; when he sees that it blunts on Goneril, he tries it on Regan (Gielgud's note: "Desperate. Slow!"): *will you take her by the hand?* (196.) Regan will; the meeting between the two sisters, their pretense of affection, the formal pecks on the cheek, signify momentary truce only so they can oppose Lear with a common front. The moment is a doubtful one for Goneril: remember that at the end of Act I she was not certain Regan would support her against Lear.

Her growing sense of her own power, and the opportunity to make Lear finally sorry for loving a sibling better, move her to breed occasion: she is blunt, unyielding, she throws *dotage* at him. The word is spoken; age is unnecessary. This is his most absolute blow so far, it shakes him physically. He wonders that he can survive it:

> O sides! you are too tough;
> Will you yet hold? (199–200.)

The wrenching of the body, the shuddering of the flesh from the symbolic blow is visual, one more strain that will lead to disintegration. As elsewhere, Lear's harassed mind, fearful of intolerable inputs, turns to a safer outlet for rage: for the third time he asks who stocked Kent, and can snarl at Cornwall for doing it.

> You! did you? (202.)

To the Jacobeans, this confrontation would involve a train of expectation, as it would to a naive spectator. Might Cornwall be the next king? How does he stand up to Lear? He has been fiery with subordinates; how with the old ruler? Lear's speech—or his own character—silences Cornwall until the scene end. Gielgud's note: "Utter contempt." Gielgud, hands clenched behind his back, strode up to face Cornwall, spat *You!* passed, rounded on him contemptuously to finish the line. Lear may even initiate an attacking movement, evoking Regan's intercession, which again masks with sweet concern her resolute purpose. If she does not feed Lear the bitter medicine of *dotage*, she offers a sugar-coating no more to his taste, especially when her use of *father* betrays a scolding, maternal emphasis:

> I pray you, father, being weak, seem so (203).

She couples this insult with her repeated insistence that he go stay with Goneril.

Return to her? (209.) Now Lear is prophetic, he makes an oral vow that, ironically, will become more than true: rather he will declare his kinship with the animal, abjure all roofs, be a comrade with the wolf and owl. In fact, he will suffer the storm's fierceness while the lion and the wolf hide to keep their fur dry. Only fools and madmen will enjoy comradeship in it. Now the thought of animals, the unsheltered world, enforce him to think again of the spectre of poverty, of unsatisfied need, *Necessity's sharp pinch* (213). But to return to her!

Shakespeare twice repeats the phrase, giving the speech the development of an aria. Mikhoels reprised the phrase twice more, spiralling it up to a whipping outcry to emphasize his sense of this crucial choice confronting Lear; to go back to Goneril would be also to go back to the old order of things; to live with Goneril was worse than poverty, even

than humiliation at France's court. And yet there is still windy rhetoric
in his self-pity, in his threat to make them sorry with his suffering; his
balloon rather to be squire and sumpter to the detested Oswald is pricked
savagely by Goneril:

> At your choice, Sir (219).

His shame is not so much in the fact of this merciless rebuff as the mocking demonstration of the meaninglessness of his threat to suffer. Shakespeare is making retreat from Lear's position as impossible as possible, so
that the attempted retreat when it comes will plunge him into the profoundest humiliation.

He tries to put it off. His first response to Goneril's brutal jest is a
mastery of passion, urged by that other fear that has been haunting him:
madness. Again he tries withdrawal: I'll not see you any more. But where
before he has banished, now he will be the banished; being weak, seem
so, Regan said, and he does, now; for the first time he meets affront without verbal fury.

> I prithee, daughter, do not make me mad:
> I will not trouble thee, my child; farewell.
> We'll no more meet, no more see one another (220–222).

Lear might express this at the sentimental extreme, as by McCullough, as the abject, forsaken, utterly desolate old monarch; or at
the other, as Porter's tired, grim, hard-shelled old man. But the mixture of feeling that even Garrick, as Tate's Lear, conveyed—"rage and
tenderness, suppressed fury and affectionate condescension"—will not
let him hold any single emotional tone. So Booth's old Lear tried to speak
gently, but his intense resentment burst through the forgiveness, and
turned his pity to curses. Mikhoels, standing very close to Goneril,
stared at her as he acknowledged her his daughter, then, as if mistrusting
his eyes, reached out in his recurrent gesture to touch her face. The gesture suddenly brought him to awareness of himself, not as a figurative
being, a king, but as a material, physical thing; a puzzled gesture with
the palm followed, and then both hands came back to brush away the
cobwebs that had obscured his vision. For Mikhoels, this was a moment
both of insight and the beginning of irrationality, as if the last remnants
of reason were leaking through his fingers. Horrible thoughts were
crowding in upon him, and his gesture passed from trying to brush the
cobwebs away to a waving of the hand at Goneril, as if trying to brush
her away with all the images she had caused.

The bodily awareness Mikhoels emphasized is written into the Lear design: he must see Goneril now, and the passion that rises against her, and against himself, works out in imagery of the flesh: she is his tissue, his blood, or a disease in him, a plague sore, a carbuncle—*Kill thy physician*, Kent had said, *and thy fee bestow / Upon the foul disease* (I, i, 163). He cannot disclaim *Propinquity and property of blood* (I, i, 114), as he thought he could with Cordelia; he bears responsibility. The sense of corruption in his own blood, the perception that in him is the source of his daughter's behavior, revolts him, an anticipation of the disgust that will sicken him in Act IV, vi. Gielgud's note: "Rash mood. Then suffer in the head."

Against revulsion comes the countering impulse for survival, and Lear resorts again to psychic attack, the weapon of guilt:

> Let shame come when it will, I do not call it (228).

And then: *I do not bid the thunder-bearer shoot* (229). In the Carnovsky *Lear*, the first light rolls of thunder had just sounded, and Lear was disclaiming responsibility. Lear has still to learn that the thunder, which will not abate at his bidding, will on the contrary let loose when he does not bid it, and seemingly at him—almost as if the heavens insist on crossing him. Now he still speaks as if from power, but there remains the infantile impulse of the king-child: he will not tell tales of her—to Jove.

I can be patient (232), he says—again he is wrong: and he offers to take his hundred knights to Regan. Now begins the reverse auction.

Regan doesn't want him, and gives her social excuses—she is not prepared for his *fit welcome*. Listen to Goneril, she says, and her studied sweetness almost is broken—

> . . . those that mingle reason with your passion
> Must be content to think you old, and so—(236–237).

She checks, passes him to Goneril again:

> But she knows what she does (238).

What Lear will hear again is the word, not the feeling, and he attacks the word.

> Is this well spoken? (238.)

He is in retreat, and they hunt him down. Regan attacks with her barrage of sweet reasonable questions. They evoke an image that pervades the action of the whole play at the political and familial levels.

> How, in one house,
> Should many people, under two commands,
> Hold amity? (242–244).

The question casts an ironic light backwards to the very beginning, touches the nerve-center of the divisions that energize the Lear-Gloster actions, and will be echoed at the very end. Yet Regan still does not absolutely reject Lear: *Tis hard*, she says, *almost impossible* (244).

Goneril leaps in, to underbid Regan; Regan stipulates her reduction, with a grudging *if: If you will come to me* (248): twenty-five knights, no more.

Comparatives and quantifiers wrench the dialogue, *many, more, great, number, a hundred, fifty, twenty-five*—eating at the security Lear plays for.

> I gave you all—(252).

All or nothing, the stakes are becoming, as Regan pitilessly reminds him: *in good time you gave it* (252). This seems to be his base, his bottom; he has no leverage now, his price is as fallen as Cordelia's was. He had meant to set his rest—gamble his all—on her kind nursery; instead he bet on Goneril and Regan, and has lost. The temptation for the actor of the put-upon father victimized by ingratitude is absolute misery, gently reproachful pathos; so Edmund Kean projected "pure, touching simplicity, melting tenderness." At the other extreme is the stern obstinacy of Scofield's Lear, so insistent on his past gifts, so demanding of powers no longer his that some sympathy still is possible for the daughters. Lears more often stumble between these poles, moving, as Anschütz did, between love and hate, doubt and the need to believe, or as Booth did, among "tenderness, rage, astonishment, and distraction." Booth's old man was at a turning point here; the sense of kingship that he had joined to his pathetic age and troubled mind was beginning to desert him. He would appeal to Goneril humbly for a chance to go with her, for a sign of love. His attempts at a placid demeanor made all the more moving his erupting inward anguish. Carnovsky, less sentimental, projecting the bruised animal in Lear, reeled between daughters like a dazed fighter on the ropes trying to clear his head. Gielgud, swaying toward first one, then the other, as they batted him back and forth, finally lost control for a moment, cried out in abandonment. Mikhoels, concerned for the recurrence of physical imagery, made the scene a visual echo of the love-auction: he masked the depth of his wound with irony, half-bowed to Regan as she "entreated" him to bring but twenty-five, turned to Goneril, and then back to Regan as they bid down, with a mockingly curious expression and a shadow of his bows in I, i.

This pose covered the tragic agony at his stripping that other Lears in the theatre more openly poured out. As the comparatives intensify—

more, worst, double, twice; and the numbers that mean to Lear the garments of his status shrink to nothing—*five-and-twenty, ten, five, one,
nothing*—he begins to know the nakedness of that poverty to which the
great downhill wheel is dragging him. He fights for survival, physical
and psychical, plumbs a further bottom as, in his most degrading bargain, accepting a wickedness that is not worst—the speech is tense with
comparatives—he offers himself to Goneril:

> Those wicked creatures yet do look well-favour'd
> When others are more wicked; not being the worst
> Stands in some rank of praise (258–260).

Carnovsky, letting the image of the animal show again, now the animal
at bay, after *not being the worst* (259) spat toward Regan, voiced a savage, brute growl, and with a gesture of utter rejection turned with desperate expectation to Goneril. But—return to her! He forced a humorous
tone, but managed only a ghastly smile at *thou art twice her love* (262).
Laughton halted in a charged pause before he could get out the last
word. Gielgud emphasized the barely endurable shame of Lear's descent
to peddling himself; he turned his back on Regan, confronted Goneril,
but could not look at her. He covered his face with his cloak to shield
him from the humiliation and from the certainty of rebuff. Macready
hid his face in Goneril's arm. Scofield tried to make the offer a concession, as if from strength; for Porter it was a bitter negotiation. Olivier
could not stand still; he moved compulsively about his daughters. Mantell's daughters moved to confuse him further by crossing behind him
as he spoke.

To deny his oath, agree to go back with Goneril—to Regan's marked
satisfaction—would seem humiliation enough for a man once a king; a
naive spectator does not anticipate her further rejection, feels its sharp
edge, and that of each further step down which Lear is beaten, as his
knights are whittled away. Shock, shock, shock, coming quickly—the
reducing of Lear to nothing. Here is the cruelest overt attack in the play,
suddenly leaving Lear a thing helpless, unattended:

> What need one? (265.)

The daughters' staccato rallying builds to a charged pause that punc-
tuates this end of the beat: Lear needs time to absorb the blow. Its impact is visual: theatre Lears have suggested a concentration of feeling so
intense that the wound up body, denied physical reprisal on the daughters, anticipates another *hysterica passio*. With Forrest, the very intensity of his passion here, as he struggled to repress his rising anger, ren-

dered his Lear impotent. Gielgud reared back, to fall on a bench; Carnovsky recoiled, his eyes loathing Regan, and he made a cross-like gesture, a sound of disgust and horror. Macready threw his hat on the ground. Olivier was jerked again into motion; he could not stand still. Porter stood blank for a moment; and then, for the first time, this sternly anti-sentimental Lear, so used to demanding, turned to imploring.

The rushing dialogue, then the shocked pause, poises Lear at his great, climactic speech. The lines, modulated by so many contradictory needs and passions, are beautifully designed to allow him to recover momentarily from the humiliation of his rebuffs, and even more, from his shameful readiness to submit to Goneril. The tirade begins, unlike the earlier curses, on a note of pleading, of reason, before it leaps to imprecation.

> O! reason not the need (266).

The first lines have sibilants and explosives, but generally softened by the vowels and other consonants: *reason, poorest, superfluous*. There are many n's. Gielgud's gesture visually as well as verbally was defensive, hands fluttering, protective, a defeated tone coming into the voice. As Lear speaks directly to Regan, the vowels and consonants slow and soften further:

> If only to go warm were gorgeous (270).

Then, as his patience goes, the hard sibilants, the f's, the grinding g's and the hard k's work up the storm to be echoed by the elements.

The major challenge to the actor—or the imagination—is fitting the pitch of the lines into the play's form. The subscene, beginning with Goneril's entrance, has mounted swiftly in both action and motif to this culminating fusion of the two. The speech as it rises to its climax asks to be lifted, aurally and visually, above not only the foothills preceding it in this act, but also above the peak of the I, iv curses. The design is intensified by the countermovement of Lear's suggested weakness: his own sense of infirmity, his growing apprehension of poverty, his incipient madness, all now focussed on the certainty of his homelessness, his nothingness, his enforced kinship with the naked animal kingdom.

The speech is the second major pivot on Lear's journey toward madness, and how it is voiced largely determines the further design of character and action. One aspect of the father-daughter equation is generally articulated now: whether Lear is visualized as vigorous, weak, old, unbalanced, majestic, pathetic, his Regan and especially his Goneril are usually seen as having revealed their lack of love for him—though not yet their deeper evil. But even this is not invariable: in Scofield's *Lear*, the daughters offer the patience Lear does not have, and their speeches, ending *What need one?* are weary protestations to a very cranky guest whose churlish manners and those of his multitude of attendants have made him nearly intolerable. Appropriately, Scofield's Lear was still acerb, demanding, his concluding threats were uttered as if he had the power to execute them—when he knew he had not; he strode off at the end unyielding.

There is no need to see, in Lear's rejection, a representation of a break-down in Renaissance hospitality; the story of elder daughters turning on their once powerful father is timeless. In Shakespeare's design, Lear's character, not the inhospitality of the daughters, stimulates in him the cancerous insecurities that shake, and then unbalance, his body and mind.

Salvini's mighty Lear, who resisted through Act II the disintegrative forces let loose in Goneril's palace, begins now to break. Before this, angry—if lofty—passions dominated his responses, now grief and pathos do; even his great physical strength starts to decay. Gielgud's majestic Lear cracks, cannot maintain his dignity before his daughters, will rise in this speech from a whisper to almost a scream—and then he will flee. Carnovsky will demean himself to a grief-stricken, helpless supplication; frustrated, he will grovel and threaten like a bear. Olivier, driven manic by the rallying of his daughters, will move in frenzy toward his breaking point. Macready will follow this same escalating pattern, toward a screaming vehemence followed by a staggering helplessness. Forrest will try strenuously to check the curses rising to his mouth—then they will break out in a fierce storm. The weaker old Lears meet the challenge of topping I, iv more by intensity and contrast than by decibels. Charles Kean's very failing to match his earlier rage, in spite of utter irrational abandonment, suggested an ultimate exhaustion that intensified the de-sign. Laughton's curses carried an edge of power because of the intense quiet of his speech, a sign of tremendous effort at control. Redgrave's old, old man deliberately damped the speech, gave a sense that his Lear was being almost repetitive, tragic because so old and ineffectual. The onset of madness, implicit in the more resilient Lears, more frankly emerged now in these already touched by it, or by senility. Petulance now offset dignity in Booth's Lear; Irving, playing the feeble, foolish, despised old man, taunted by his daughters, let some of Lear's childish-ness show. In Garrick, as grief diluted and then displaced his rage, his face began intermittently to go blank with mindlessness.

That Lear still at first thinks he can reach his daughters on their level—the level of civilized people living gorgeously—sounds in his words of comparative value: *basest, poorest, cheap*. They mean more because we have just encountered Edgar's transformation into one of those basest beggars he mentions—Poor Tom.

Man's price is higher than beast's because of accoutrements, super-fluity, Lear can still say—as if to be a beast is the worst. He will learn, with Edgar, that there is worse. Now, on the meaning of *need*, his mind begins to shift. *If only to go warm were gorgeous* (270)—and the *if* is answered by the sight of a daughter's gorgeous dress, which owes the sheep wool, the worm silk, the cat perfume, and scarcely keeps her warm.* His mind shifts again, impelled by a vision: of love? of necessity's sharp pinch? of sadness?

> But, for true need—(272).

The shifting of the mind frightens him. The sentence is left gaping, open-ended, the vision clouded by the passion and the fear of passion that shakes him:

> You Heavens, give me that patience, patience I need! (273.)

Once more, he waits, and there is no answer; he will beg impatiently again before he learns that much more than patience is needed, and that the gods do not give.

He shifts to self-pity, a mood designed into the character when frustrated. Tears begin to come. Helpless, no seconds, he tries to reach his daughters obliquely, through an appeal to the heavens, where he also seeks sympathy. He hopes still that the gods may love old men—though they have given no sign of it.

> You see me here, you Gods, a poor old man,
> As full of grief as age ... (274–275).

For the first time he suspects these Gods may be *against* him, and he himself bids lower—asks only the power to resist his own weakness. Granville-Barker suggests that he abandons the struggle; but not yet. The *if* again—

> If it be you that stirs these daughters' hearts
> Against their father, fool me not so much
> To bear it tamely; touch me with noble anger,
> And let not women's weapons, water-drops,
> Stain my man's cheeks! (276–280.)

---

*Critics disagree on the implications here. Danby believes Lear contemns his daughter for being gorgeous; Heilman finds Lear believing that "gratuity in excess of need, of dignity, of honor ... distinguishes man from animal." Lear certainly does seem to believe the latter here.

Almost certainly the Gods fail him again; the subtext is of a man who
has wept before when humiliated by a daughter, weeping now again
perforce—customarily to the accompaniment of the first sounds of the
storm's rain. Lear's new tears lead actors to the speech's climax. Here
Mikhoels, who had touched his face—and others—to know if tears came,
now knew. Tears belong because Lear's mood is regressive; his beautiful
daughters he now addresses as women, women who might be ugly, old—
as old as mothers:

> No, you unnatural hags,
> I will have such revenges on you both
> That all the world shall—I will do such things,
> What they are, yet I know not, but they shall be
> The terrors of the earth (280–284).

The king-child is returning to the megalomania of youth, when they
told him he was everything; the speech is the anguished threat of a child
with no power, flinging magic words in an attempt to frighten his elders
—Porter pushed at Regan, too, in a futile gesture. (When Lear is seen as
smaller than the daughters, the poignancy of his regressed state is painfully felt; when taller, another kind of helplessness tortures his image.)
Like the child, Lear will never have any revenges, he will not—except,
ironically, in fantasy—do such things. Nameless horrors that crowd out
of the subconscious, unimaginable, uncanny, unspeakably destructive—
impossible—things. His speech by now has turned into hard monosyllables, or words that break down into monosyllables. The words may
come out, as with Olivier, in thunder, a torrential sound that splits the
world asunder, that "swept across the senses like Niagara . . . but in all
this raving music, one could still hear the tortured cry of a drowning
man"; still, they are words a child might use, as well as a man. Wawling
and crying at last like a helpless child—whether with great open sobs as
with Charles Kean, or the almost too-repressed signals of weeping, as
with Scofield—crying for his helplessness, insisting that he will not cry,
Lear is still not a child in that he has a man's perspective on the futility
of his boasts.

Once more he voices an unnatural curse, and accuses his kind of being
unnatural. His hand goes again to *this heart* that *Shall break into a hundred thousand flaws / Or ere I'll weep* (286–288)—and yet he weeps, and
the heart leaps under his touch, his mind cannot bear the massive assault
on his senses:

> O Fool! I shall go mad (288).

This is a rare prophecy of his—it comes true.

Lear is moved, as always when he cannot control a situation, to blast it from his sight, to withdraw, to fly, this time into the storm that has already begun to rumble and hiss. Salvini's was the classical theatrical imagery:

"You think I'll weep," he says, and a sudden fear seizes him, for the tears that have begun to choke his voice. He wrestles with himself; struggles with his grief; looks round in triumph. "No, I'll not weep," but he is still uncertain of the victory; the sobs, suppressed, are shaking his frame. "I have full cause to weep," he cries apologetically, as though foreseeing the end. And then, as if he had an enemy by the throat and were shaking him to death, he slowly gasps: "This heart shall break into a hundred thousand flaws or ere I'll weep!" Whereat the cataract of tears break from his eyes. He covered his face with his mantle, shuddered with horror at the sight he was trying to shut out, then falling on Fool's shoulder—a first slight sign in this giant of physical weakness—he cried in terror

O Fool, I shall go mad

and struggled out into the storm.

Gielgud also suggested the physical ravages setting in. He began the speech sitting, crumpled; then he rose, with clenched fists high above his head, to threaten the daughters. The effect used him up; he seemed broken, helpless, pitiful. His notes suggest a subtext of self-devouring rages and physical symptoms ignored. On the surface: "Collapse. Human, broken old man, futile. Suddenly looks at them. Wipes eyes." He backed away from his daughters (in an earlier production, he too veiled his face), moved into the exit arch, called Fool to him, held him close. The vision of madness seemed to paralyze him for a moment; *I shall go mad* came out flat, toneless, a chilling recognition of a fact; then he retreated through the archway.

Scofield made the final line so intense, so determined, that *I shall go mad* seemed less a pathetic prediction than a threat, as if he would lose his wits to punish his daughters. Scofield said No: "It was a dread, not a threat . . . unless perhaps as a threat to myself. It is a prophetic piece of self-knowledge." Yet it is also the last, the only way left to the child-king to try to "show them," to move these mother-daughters. They told him he was everything. If they care at all, they must respond to this emotional blackmail. But they do not care, even if he becomes comrade to the animals, or a squire to Oswald. He is nothing.

Mantell, at the height of his helpless anger and frustration, threw to the ground the walking stick he had stumped about with fiercely, and then the incipient madness flashed out again: at *O Fool . . .* he almost sang the word *Fool*, holding the sound; and he ended the line in a hoarse whisper, broken by throaty, exultant, demoniacal laughter. He kept repeating *mad* as he rushed off with Fool.

Mikhoels felt intensified the realization that all his old images of experience were shattered. "What was the sense of life?" Afflicted by doubts, he felt only confusion under his skull; he struck his fingers against his head, like arrows; he felt a pain in his head, and instead of beating it, holding it, or comforting it, he drew a cross over it, as if he would cut it into pieces—anatomize it. He knows now that he is going mad.

This moment is a downward pivot for the big Lears; they have at last confronted the vision of a counterforce, inward as well as outward, that size, authority, imprecation cannot touch. They leave now with minds and bodies wound-up toward a breaking point that will be visual one short scene later. Sometimes that point was reached here: Edmund Kean uttered a horrid, mad cry, and ran out as if his brain were on fire.

Kean had no Fool; Macready, restoring Fool to the acted text, gave the strong Lears a visual image central to the play: Lear fleeing with Fool, the most and the least thrown together; power dependent on weakness; foolish crumbling sanity sheltering with wise, bitter, tender folly. So Olivier suddenly dropped his voice, clutched at Fool for support, and they ran out in a wild, broken flight. Carnovsky's Fool put his hand in his weeping master's, and almost led him off, the two stumbling out with their arms about each other.

The weaker Lears had a different pivot here; this was their lowest moment, a nadir from which they would move toward a mad strength, and Fool became their only stay against collapse. Booth, suddenly quiet before his final cry, dropped his weary head on Fool's shoulder, and staggered off. Irving's last line was a wild wail, a surrender in the struggle not to weep, and he, too, was supported by his Fool, as he sobbed out his exit.

Fool's whole contribution to this scene, from Regan's entrance, has been subtextual. His fear of the daughters, and their power to expel him to the elements, to the cold that always threatens him, is poised against his concern for Lear. Knave and fool contend in him. He may shadow Lear with animal-like devotion, as Porter's Fool did, and withdraw into a pining reverie; he may mime his mockery of the powers that crush Lear; but he is afraid now, too.

How does the audience respond to Lear, as he passes into the storm? Critics suggest a wide range of possibilities. Josephine Bennett: "It is only a hard heart that could shatter into a hundred thousand flaws," so Lear's own unyielding pride and hard heartedness give meaning to his later wish to dissect Regan's heart. Irving Ribner suggests that Lear could expect sympathy for nothing he has done, but only for the viciousness toward him of Goneril and Regan, the pathos of his remorse for Cordelia, and the loyalty of Kent. Granville-Barker sees him otherwise: "all his errors . . . have partaken of nobility; he has scorned policy." Actors have been equally diverse, from Scofield's adamantine old man, most like the first conception noted above, to Salvini's noble one, most like the last. The design of Shakespeare's Lear is, we have seen, a mixture of these Lears, proud and simple, brave and fearful, hard and soft, noble and mean, loving and hating—a multiplicity of conflicting impulses. The final speech is a synthesis of these impulses. In the polyphony, flashes of the tonic still emerge to resist its own subversive tones as well as the bright dominants of the daughters.

Often, in the nineteenth century theatre, the scene—indeed the first act—ended here, to give Lear the grand curtain. But the remainder is indispensable, leading to a visual image that will define Lear's new condition. The daughters' separate, differing identities must continue to develop and move them, subtly, toward collision. Now they fence, agreeing, disagreeing. After the tremendous peak of the subscene climax, and the pause for absorbing it, Cornwall, ever practical, urges withdrawal before the storm. Regan still plays the hostess: there is not room for *the old man* her father and his entourage. Goneril, as usual speaking more directly, and more cruelly, plays the mother with the rod: it is his own fault, he *must needs taste his folly* (291). The final word, with its complicating cluster of meanings, is intensified by the verb: Lear must experience sensually, bodily, the consequences of his courage-passion-reason-foolishness-loyalty-love-hate. Regan cuts across Goneril with mannered sweetness: she will gladly receive her father, but no follower. Goneril, frankly, will not have him, and when Gloster returns says so: entreat him by no means to stay. Gloster's plea—the night, the storm—finds Regan topping Goneril now, though again in the guise of decorum, with a pious, personal appeal, beginning *O! Sir*—the salutation she had used to her father:

> O! Sir, to wilful men,
> The injuries that they themselves procure
> Must be their schoolmasters. Shut up your doors . . . (304–306).

Her platitude is, will be, true; but the operative words, proposed ostensibly in alarm lest the unaccompanied Lear bring his "desperate train" against them, are *Shut up your doors*. The warm world of interiors, of gorgeous shelter, is being closed to Lear. Subtextually, Gloster objects; he moves to bring Lear back, and in. Gloster's lord, Cornwall, the fiery Duke, will not let him. Cornwall's men, perhaps visually, interfere at the Duke's gesture, with Gloster's attempt to go out; and, as in the Carnovsky *Lear*, Cornwall's repetition of Regan's command may be angry, peremptory, final, allowing no disobedience:

> Shut up your doors, my Lord (310).

Gloster, caught between submission and loyalty—knavery and folly—submits. The doors close.

This whole scene has taken place outside Gloster's castle; Lear has only once, momentarily, penetrated inside; now in the wild night Cornwall describes, the favored ones withdraw from the storm, and the doors close. In the Globe, perhaps an inner below was thus sealed off, leaving the sound of storm to whip over the bare forestage that would be the cruel, natural world Lear had chosen to inhabit. As I noted at the end of I, iv, later theatres, and especially continental ones—as with the Mikhoels' *Lear*—made great closed doors a central visual image of Lear's alienation, his isolation from the society that he once commanded. Lear has sometimes been seen huddling in the outer shadowy edges of the stage, or even returning to the doors, playing out still his ambivalence between his needs to love and to hate. The German Ernst Possart, at the castle entrance, was stayed, and startled, by the loud click of the bolt as the doors locked against him; and only then he fled with Fool into the storm. Krauss, as the castle closed on him, acknowledged his humiliation in physical imagery: slowly, in a shambling step, majesty mocking at itself, a general who staggers away like a soldier after a lost battle, he retreated from the shut doors.

Act III, Scene i

Storm still, the Folio directs, as Kent staggers on to the stage. That Kent, stout and brave as he is, barely endures, is a significant measure of the storm's fierceness. The storm will push Kent, too, on a downward path; he will be near death as Lear dies. The weather is foul, so foul that the Gentleman, the beggar-king's last attendant, has been separated from him. Shakespeare's theatre could provide fine sounds of thunder and rain, and glimpses of artificial lightning, and the persistence of *Storm still* indicates that he used them lavishly.

A poor thing, a theatre storm, Bradley and other armchair critics have argued. Only if poorly done. Artistically designed, heard and seen thunder and lightning can instantly evoke urgent pity and terror, and carry a heavy freight of uncanny, symbolic stimuli, that evoke deep, even archetypal responses. Too much noise, or obvious pyrotechnics that call attention to their means, will undermine Shakespeare's dramatic verse; but so will poor speech. The playwright obviously counted on non-verbal—visual and aural—imagery to be articulated into the play as exquisitely as the trippingly spoken language.

The theatre has worked hard to serve him. Stage art can project a fierce lightning and thunderclap that awesomely evokes Lear's experiences of a natural world helpless before seeming supernatural power. Charles Kean achieved such effects more than a century ago.

> Black masses of hanging clouds drift across the sky, scudding before the gusty storm, disclosing glimpses of moonlight; the wind howls in an unearthly tone, something between a scream and a deep moan, vivid flashes of lightning, forked and sheet, now breaking in the distance, now gleaming in the very eyes of the actors, irradiate the darkness; the rain patters, the thunderclaps crash, appallingly.*

*"Charles Lamb held that the Lear of Shakespeare was beyond being acted, but this opinion—a poor compliment to Shakespeare, who wrote it for the stage—ought to be read in connection with the corrupt versions of the tragedy then supposed to be indispensable, and likewise, of course, the imperfect scenic appliance of 'Elia's' day. That the machinery with which they attempted to mimic the storm in the Kemble and Edmund Kean period was 'contemptible,' as Lamb declared, is likely enough. He would be a bold man, however, who would say as much of the storm

Critics, generally skeptical of stage storms, admired this one: for increasing "our reverence for Lear exposed 'to the pelting of the pitiless storm' all the more because the storm is so real, because the gloom is so complete, and because the venerable figure of the King is only shown to us by fitful gleams (in) . . . the flashes of lightning."

The modern theatre, sometimes distrusting realism, has explored symbolic or suggestive storm effects. Absolute silence, a kind of anti-storm, has been projected, as in the Laughton and Redgrave productions. With Laughton there was some speculation that his limited voice dictated the silence; he said no, in a storm you stop noticing noise, the storm was inside Lear. Sheeting rain and swirling cloud were only suggested by lighting; the actors moved in a controlled light, clear, solid, subdued, that emphasized the immensity of the surrounding darkness. Redgrave's silenced storm was a chiaroscuro world, a projection of intersecting lines, a stylized whirlwind, given body by the sounds and mimed resistance of the actors to the verbally imaged hurlyburly of the elements.

The unheard storm has not satisfied audiences; and a lack has been felt, too, in thundery scenes that had none of the movement of weather against men, as in the Gielgud production; or that missed the sense of the tormented air about Lear, as in Olivier's storm. Shakespeare wrote a scene to stir the senses, and, whether by realistic or stylistic means, eye and ear need rousing to experience the attack of the elements. Brook, for the Scofield *Lear*, brought the storm to his bare, impersonal void by lowering from the flies three copper thundersheets, rusted metal banners that rumbled and quivered with the thunder. The physical force of the storm was suggested by the miming of the crouching, huddling actors. In the film, Brook intended a contrast between the storm within and without:

> The storm grows more and more savage. Gradually, it will be impossible to tell how much it is the real world undergoing this epic convulsion, how much the landscape is the inside of Lear's mind. For the images become less and less narrative, more and more strange, surrealist

---

which rages at [Irving's] Lyceum. This is a storm indeed. The scene is a desolate heath, swept, as we feel, by furious blasts and beating rain, and illumined by coruscating lightning as dazzling in its brilliancy as the rolling thunder that accompanies it is terrifying. With this loud weather, the passion of Lear, like a sea 'swelling, chafing, raging without bound, without hope, without beacon or anchor,' has a strange affinity. He is something more than the old man that Lamb saw turned out of doors by his daughters on a rainy night, and tottering about the stage with a walking-stick. His sorrows and wrongs, so strange, bewildering, and overwhelming, assume a grandeur that seems to lift the whole conception above the plane of the purely theatrical" (*Times*, November 11, 1892).

though never apparently fantastic. The ground cracks open, roots painfully are wrenched to the surface, roofs are carried away, walls burst
outwards, great doors fly open, shutters snap their catches and bang
apart, flames mount among branches, wells overflow their pitchblack
content, but out of the gashes and scars in the earth come scorpions,
ants, spiders, snakes...two views intermingle, the ferocious images
that Lear sees, the equally frightening but more prosaic viewpoint of
the Fool, for whom the storm is nothing but wind and water and cold.
[Near the hovel] the images are hallucinatory. What [Lear] sees lit in
flashes of lightning could well be a rock, a stone, a stump, a bush—but
could equally well be some agonizing human shape, a limb, a face, a
burnt child, a screaming mother, and the alternately black and fiery
horizon could be that of a scene of war.

The heath, in a modern Antwerp *Lear* (1969), was a kind of moon-
landscape; the characters like travellers driven off their course, adrift in
space. In Sweden (1921), stone blocks in the mist gave the impression of
a cemetery. Lear made his great storm speech beside an illuminated
rock that might have been a gravestone. In Bucharest (1970), a corps of
actors represented, in a ballet, the unchained forces of nature. For the
Goldsby *Lear*, Toshiro Ogawa designed images, in greens and blacks, of
tormented nature, and spun a projection of them around the walls of the
auditorium, so that the audience was itself, like Lear, in the eye of the
storm. Electronic sounds and streaks of light poured through rents in
the cyclorama in Herbert Blau's Actor's Workshop production (San
Francisco).

The test of realism—and of anti-realism—is whether what is visualized
in the theatre or the mind supports the dramatic experience without
calling distracting attention to itself. In place of storm effects, some recent productions have used music, usually modern, composed for the
occasion. The 1971 Norwegian *Lear* began with the light tinkling of
bells, and built to the whistling and crash of a full orchestra; while the
doomsday motif of the chorus, that was chanted in earlier climaxes,
sounded through. Music alone has not seemed to convey the feel of live
thunder and lightning that Shakespeare stipulated. The required realism
seems to be a spectacular sight and sound, molded to the action, that
strikes terror without compelling disbelief. To these effects, audiences
yield readily.

To make the weather tangible is a risky thing. Lear and his companions are designed to feel wet, wet through to the skin; will the sound
of rain bedraggle them enough? Fog—that Lear twice calls down—may
be introduced to the scene, as, effectively, by Henry Irving; actors may

come on somewhat drenched; how much more rain may be represented
or visualized depends on the art of the whole. A sense of the force and
effects of wind, unless excessive, is readily fitted into the experience of
cataclysmic terror. Actors will mime—readers imagine—the bitter cold
Fool laments.

If there must not be too much realism, there must, also, not be too
much anti-realism. Integral to the storm scenes are the details of the tangible body suffering from weather: men shiver as they strip, wear rags,
go naked. The great lyric and declamatory arias are interspersed with
homely, mainly monosyllabic, exchanges.

> Come on, my boy, How dost, my boy? Art cold?
> I am cold myself. Where is this straw, my fellow? (III, ii, 68–69.)

The play's dialectic form enforces this see-saw between loftiness and
simplicity, the heights and the depths. The storm which frames this dynamic is both apocalyptic and immediate, hinting at Olympian assault
but stipulating tangible, bodily misery in the *little world* of unaccommodated man, drenched, ragged, stumbling, cold. Lear described an opulent kingdom in I, i; dialectic is made visual in this stormy bare heath,
with scarce a bush.

The division in nature is echoed in the division within Lear, and
among the people of his kingdom. Division is visual in Kent's cautious
fumbling in the storm toward the dimly perceived other figure: Kent
both searches and is in flight; he moves forward tentatively. *Who's
there?* Lear? Friend? Enemy?

This question, to be often echoed, holds Kent still and wondering, as
it does the audience, until the other stormbound figure is discerned. In
the Gielgud production, the two cloaked men seemed to be anxious to
hide their identities from each other. Kent, even in this crucial moment,
with so much important information for Cordelia, and though he finally
recognizes the Gentleman, will not—dare not?—disclose himself.

The dialogue, mime, and spectacle, by making the storm so terrible,
makes even more frightening the image of the tempest within Lear. He
contends with the elements, Gentleman says; Lear does see himself in
battle, and will personalize the enemy later as this *contentious* storm. He
is furious, as the elements are: the blasts, with *eyeless rage*—echoing the
motif of unseeing, often under the stress of passion—tear at him, he tries
to *out-storm* them. He has offered to be a comrade to the animals, but
now all we may hear of them are their voices, mixed with the storm; the
wolf knows, as do the bear and lion, to come in out of the rain, as Lear
does not; the old man *runs*—as he will later—*unbonneted,*

And bids what will take all (15).

Again, the motif of infantilism: all right for them, let it go all; wager it all—set his rest—on this throw. All or nothing.

Kent specifies the split in the nation, confirming Curan:

> There is division,
> Although as yet the face of it is cover'd
> With mutual cunning, 'twixt Albany and Cornwall (19-21).

The masking motif, that runs through the verbal imagery, suggests also the kind of visual image that has governed—and will govern—the appearance of amity between the sisters. The speech builds on motifs of disguise and sight: of spies—what great ones have them not?; of cunning; of covered face; of what may be seen in the differences between the Dukes; of their hard treatment of Lear—and again the enigma of appearances, the hint of the unknown, of

> ... something deeper
> Whereof perchance these are but furnishings—(28-29).

Kent speaks of France's party, and then, for the first time, the focal site for so much of the forthcoming action: the ultimate aim of the old men, their hopes for security or heartsease, the battleground for all the dialectical forces in the play: *Dover.*

Then, once more the storm and the return to the search: peering, seeking, for Cordelia, for Lear, for illumination:

> ... he that first lights on him
> Holla the other (54-55).

Act III, Scene ii

Lear contends against the storm, with many subtle weapons. His habit is command—and at first he would command weather; but command rebounds, and dissolves into self-pity, anger, scorn. Theatrically, as Carnovsky has observed, and many actors have conveyed, the contention may be a dialogue between Lear and the storm: the response of the angry elements may range from anthropomorphic ejaculations to the fiercely impersonal snarls, growls, and retorts of unhuman nature. The storm's language is most archetypal when most pre-verbal, when its casual terror stirs old fears of unspeakable threats and dangers. Lear can speak to the storm, but he cannot outshout it; when he tries in the theatre, he fails, must fail, because the little world of man, of king, is nothing to weather. The dialogue between man and Nature is visual, too: man moves, as in the play, from darkness into light, the blaze of lightning or the colder white of the moon, and then, as the storm shifts, into darkness again.

Most importantly, Lear himself, with his Fool, contends visually with that Nature on which he has called twice so peremptorily, and then tentatively, and now in near hysteria. Image echoes word: the massive old man tows along his slighter Fool—usually small, child-like, yet shrewder, knowing enough to come in out of the rain, so that the roles intermix, old man plays child and fool, Fool plays wise. Nature savages old manchild, and child-old man, shut out from the house. All the elements—earth, air, fire, water—contend with them physically, the nimble lightning darts at their eyes; they are stricken, beaten to the mire; the rain comes to wet them once, and again, and again. All the first tones are dominant, shifting into pure atonality; no hope for rest seems possible.

The quality of Lear's resistance in this unfair contention—unfair because he mistakes his antagonist and wastes his force on the assault of the elements while suffering ambush from within—is determined by his design in the total action. The Lear who is weak, very cold, already partly unbalanced must begin to find unexpected strengths in his ordeal; the power and violence he discovers in his combat with Nature and reason dignify him. The titanic Lears begin to deteriorate under the erosion

188

within and without; their way is down, toward the feeble bliss of the reunion with Cordelia. Here may be seen the pitfalls of extremes in the early visualization of the character: a Lear too old and weak cannot plausibly ride the storm, a Lear too stalwart cannot be subdued to the image—even self-image—of a poor, infirm, weak old man, unless a massive factor of self-pity is thrown into the equation.

Then this scene must be articulated into the design of the larger action. Lear has climbed three high moments: his three curses and disavowals of his daughters. In decibels, in intensity, and in emotional temperature the scenes have had some cumulative relationship, as do the calculated outbursts of drums in a symphony. Lear's next two scenes seem almost all timpani, deep horns, and high strings fortissimo; and yet they must be modulated so that the volume and force, the pitch and tempo of the storm will not only develop to sub-climax, but also lead forward to the intense dissonances of Lear's madness in IV, vi which must in turn yield to the allegro of IV, vii.

In the dynamic of the theatre, for which Shakespeare designed the equation, Lear's apparent strength must determine the extent of and quality of the opposition. Salvini's Lear was to be of such inner power that his sufferings could never quite drive him beyond sanity to madness; they would begin to corrode his immense physical powers so pitilessly that at the end his dying would seem the inevitable result of insupportable physical weakness. Most of the hardy Lears—Scofield's oaken figure—would stay sinewed enough that their killing of the slave that hanged Cordelia need not seem—as with weaker ones—only the last flare of a dying candle, but a capable act; the fall of this Lear's mind, from the very vitality of its passions, makes a resounding crack. The foolish Lears —Laughton, Mikhoels—began to move upward, find a wisdom, and it seemed to give their old bodies strength. In the old, old Lears, the very weak, and those touched already with madness or senility—Redgrave, Irving, Rossi, Booth—the fire of madness would inflame them to a lambent strength, and its ashes leave them exhausted. In the nineteenth century, the "mad scenes" might be cut and telescoped—Booth deleted Lear's determination to be patient—to intensify the crisis of madness, the idyllic sequel.

Lear's confrontation of the storm that has so buffeted Kent and Gentleman, and now Fool, acts out the dialectic between the apocalyptic and immediate. Little as his little world of man is, this man is a giant in it; against the greater world of the elemental universe he may be nothing, but his assertion of somethingness guarantees his heroic dignity.

Where Lear is, is stage center. Whether he strides in, as Salvini did, or is found in a kind of tableau with Fool crouching near him, as with Wolfit, he is the foreground, the figure behind which the encompassing world must only serve as ground. Wolfit preferred his grouping, set among gigantic masses of rock, so Lear could "tower as he should." But Gielgud, using this design, seemed too far back at first, and this, as well as the stillness of his position next Fool, took some size from his hubris. Then, as he moved, he seemed the center of the storm—or the storm seemed centered in him.

How far have the physical accoutrements of his status been stripped from Lear? If the storm has torn away, or defaced, some vestiges of royalty, he has still many sufferings to go before he will strip to the unaccommodated skin. Some raggedness there will be now: Mikhoels' gown hung from one shoulder, a rag, and his doublet was open at the breast. Carnovsky's broad-shouldered coat of animal fur was slashed and bedraggled—any covering this Lear owed the animals made him seem more animal than ever, even when the flesh showed through. Body flesh, as Porter observed, had to be made up as the face and head would be, if the skin were to show four score and upward; Porter's own Lear was already physically humbled by the storm, his dress shamed by a universe apparently determined to make a grotesque of him. A Japanese Lear, his white tunic blown about him in the wind, seemed wraith-like, hardly of this world.

The conventional, romantic Lear inherited from the nineteenth century faced the storm mainly in the guise of an anguished hero suffering undeserved ill-treatment. Forrest suggested the grand image:

> His eyes aflame, his breast distended, his arms flying, his white hair all astream in the wind, his voice rolling and crashing like another thunder below, he seemed some wild spirit.

Olivier, a restless Lear—he did run unbonneted—moved like a tall ship driven before the storm, wandering the whole storm-swept heath of the stage, and as the sound dropped, the light found him out, his voice, intense but never lost in a shout, challenged the storm. Irving railed fiercely, as fitful gleams of light crossed him. Scofield's assault on the storm—made visible by mens' resistance to it—was as much in his voice as his body:

> Blow winds ... (1)

was a mighty, sustained cry, the first vowel extended, an aria of anger. Under the harsh lights of Brook's bare stage, he—and the echoing thundersheets—roared the sound of fury. Scofield felt Lear took the storm on as a king, in the last burst of his hard-driving manhood, the last shriek of his self-hood in sanity.

Gielgud, following Granville-Barker's suggestion, sustained the image of the storm mainly with his voice; though, great singing instrument that it was, it seemed not enough to incarnate the turbulence Shakespeare designed. So, too, with Laughton and his silent storm; there was sense enough, in his feverish voice, of the storm within, but he did not—as did others, Ayrton for instance, flinging himself here and there across the blasted heath—assimilate that inner tempest with the outward torment. In the silence, his monologues were sometimes so philosphic as to seem almost conversational.

While no Lear could outshout the natural violence, a fearful intensity had to speak back to it; Devlin's voice rose "as if he were the spokesman for mankind against malignant nature." Even the senile Rossi was fierce here. Yet volume was not all; Kean, one of the most declamatory of actors, lowered his voice to make nature listen to his first cry, and Charles Kemble (1775–1854) spoke with "a gloomy carelessness."

The speech itself is all dissonance: at once tantrum, challenge, command. Lear personalizes the forces loose in the storm, now as destroyers, later as the instruments of gods, as summoners, as persecutors. Partly he is daring the storm, "let it go all, destroy everything, blast my poor old head, go on, see if I care"—literally: after me the deluge. But more, the destructive, self-destructive impulses that drove Lear to curse his daughter, to interdict his own issue, consume him again. He who fears madness now almost asks for it: burn my head—my brain. He who asked nature to pervert the natural in his daughters, now urges nature to suicide: *Crack Nature's moulds, all germens spill at once* (8). The mood is outraged revulsion with a world that has dared to treat him badly. The hissing that marked the curses of his daughters continues, braced by the sharp w's and the hard, crackling assault with k's, b's and t's:

> Blow winds, and crack your cheeks! rage! blow!
> You cataracts and hurricanoes, spout
> Till you have drench'd our steeples, drown'd the cocks!
> You sulphurous and thought-executing fires,
> Vaunt couriers of oak-cleaving thunderbolts,
> Singe my white head! And thou, all-shaking thunder,
> Strike flat the thick rotundity o' the world!
> Crack Nature's moulds, all germens spill at once
> That makes ingrateful man! (1–9.)

The sexual undercurrent rumbles through the speech: drench'd steeples, drown'd cocks, the thick rotundity of the world struck flat—Nikolaus

Delius sensed the implication of the rotundness of gestation, and indeed the cosmic womb seems stipulated: nature's mould, that must be cracked in one mighty thrust so all the semen of posterity may be spilled out. Nature's orgasm is sulphurous—has a stench. Lear touches here an image that the subconscious in the character design has been tracking since his first rages and will follow further—a compelled hunt, in terror and fury, for the source of life. The sexual loading of the image is evident when compared with Macbeth's similar figure where aggression dominates:

> ... though the treasure
> Of nature's germens tumble all together,
> Even till destruction sickens (IV, i, 58).

The pause while Lear looks to the heavens and waits for his world to end at his command is filled, reasonably, by the voice of unreason. All sounds, verbal and sub-verbal, are dissonant now; Fool, always an atonal element, jars rhythm and harmony. Fool wants no share in Lear's quarrel with the universe. Fool is cold, wet, shivering; he who is the sworn enemy of hypocrisy prefers it—*court holy water*—to the rain. In and ask thy daughters' blessing, he begs: and exposes the naked paradox of his plea:

> ... here's a night pities neither wise men nor Fools (12–13).

Which is the wise man, which Fool? Whichever, their dilemma is pitiless: the fool who would not be a knave, the wise man who would not be a fool, cannot tolerate the court; yet the storm would drive them to it. That they might possibly return—that perhaps they have a choice still—helps nerve this scene. But Lear shakes bodily misery off, now; he will say his inner storm is so violent he cannot feel the other. Fool's suffering is physical, intolerable, he will die soon, beaten, it seems, by the exposure that is now, visually, beginning to debilitate him. Often, as with Gielgud and Wolfit, Fool crouches at Lear's feet through this early storm; or follows Lear, though not always as closely as Porter's Fool, who continued to shadow his master like a monkey. Olivier hugged his Fool to comfort and shelter him. Scofield's Fool sat hunched, staring beyond the audience, beyond time, unwinking, a spectator at the world's disaster, and his own, that no words could halt.

Lear ignores Fool; Lear has asked for annihilation, and is rebuffed—as all his commands, pleas, adjurations to greater powers are rebuffed by the *thought-executing*—mind destroying—fires he has called down. In every speech, now, the storm within Lear will disorganize him, give hints, in the erratic sequence of his thoughts, of the chaos to come. If at first he anthropomorphized the adversary, now he brutalizes him, *rumble thy bellyful, spit . . . spout.* The speech whipsaws, one idea doubling back on another, to effect self-pity: "you hostile elements are not my children; I don't blame you for unkindness, I never gave you anything, you owe me nothing; go on then, hurt me all you want to"—especially in the context of spilled germens, there is a sexual undertone in this last, of nature's orgasm:

> . . . then let fall
> Your horrible pleasure (18–19).

But the dalliance of the powers of nature savages Lear:

> . . . here I stand, your slave,
> A poor, infirm, weak, and despis'd old man (19–20).

There is indeed some self-recognition in this; the king begins to see himself a subject, a simple man; but what most colors the speech is his sense of wrong done him, of the conspiracy to persecute him. Again the doubling dialectic—not he the slave, but they:

> But yet I call you servile ministers,
> That will with two pernicious daughters join
> Your high-engender'd battles 'gainst a head
> So old and white as this. O, ho! 'tis foul (21–24).

Subtle echoes from Lear's experience mark this further zigzag toward unbalance. Cordelia, he had said, had better not have been born than not have pleased him better. Now he is the rejected one, some formidable cosmic pleasure showers discomfiture on him. Unbonneted, he invites the elements to make him suffer: "Go on, hurt me," he says; and then, "how foul of you to do it." He does not entirely beg for pity; but he says, "see what a pitiable object I am."

Here lies danger for the Lear visualized as unwaveringly kinglike and stalwart in the storm. Salvini, upright against the hurricane, vigorous in his defiance, seemed powerful enough still to organize a war against his tormentors; for such a Lear, the inapplicable cry of *poor, infirm, weak* is self-pity *in extremis*. Lear here must both recognize a truth of his frailty, and overstate it.

For a Lear conceived as not yet mad, the notes of self-pity merge with the tones of the irrational, hints of reason slipping, though still in control. So Carnovsky, wrenched by compassion for his injuries, enduring new assault from the storm, muttered on as he shielded himself and Fool

"foul . . . foul . . . foul." Mikhoels, lifting a forefinger to search out the
unseen—one of his echoing gestures that could recall his teasing with
Cordelia and his search for tears—related the past to his next indictment
of the enemies of the gods, and carried subverbally his movement toward the outbreak of revelatory madness. Gielgud emphasized the sharp
see-saw from elation to self-conscious misery. The gentler, "feeling"
Lears, like the Bulgarian Georgi Stamatov (1893–1965), focussed
throughout on Lear's sensitive suffering.

Fool must give up pleading sense, must play fool again, labor once
more to outjest the storm in his master. He makes a plaintive allusion to
shelter; is led to sing a sex-joke as most calculated to distract Lear. As
cruel as his jokes usually are, this one reminds Lear of his poverty, and
the source of it in generation:

> The cod-piece that will house
> Before the head has any,
> The head and he shall louse;
> So beggars marry many (27–28).

The phallus that spawns and makes no provision for itself will be attacked by blood-sucking insects. Multiple images converge; king become homeless beggar; man, linked again to the least of animals, is harassed and leeched in his fatherhood, his sexuality. Lear's sweet prayer
to poor, houseless wretches will stir an echo of this foolishly housed-
houseless codpiece. The concentration on the genitals, that will recur to
Lear in his last madness, leads now to the dialectic between lust and
love—illumined by what Fool's gestures?

> The man that makes his toe
> What he his heart should make,
> Shall of a corn cry woe,
> And turn his sleep to wake (31–34).

If there is much antisexual in this, as Danby observes, there is still one
part in Fool's mind that will sing yet for love. *What he his heart should
make* . . . Lust may end by making the phallus sore; but love is possible,
its consummation much to be desired. This is as close as Fool will come
verbally to letting the mask of cynicism drop, the tenderness show. He
saves tenderness for his gestures.

Fool's coda is alive with echoes that sustain the dialectic:

> For there was never yet fair woman but she made
> mouths in a glass (35–36).

The vanity of Regan and Goneril proclaims itself—the motif was made visual in that performance where Regan, making up her face to be beautiful for a younger Edmund, tried mouths in a glass. But the glass will be held too, to the fair Cordelia's face, and the lips will be silent, no mouths made.

Lear ignores Fool. Self-involved, speaking only to himself, for himself, he persists in trying to make the universe sorry it has mistreated him, as he is sorry. *'Tis foul*, he cries, and waits for surcease; but no pity, only storm still. There is a hubris that is at once kingly and infantile in his pronounced resolve—note that he seems to answer an unspoken provocation, as well as a wanton inward impulse that he is trying to down:

> No, I will be the pattern of all patience (37).

This is Lear, in his immense, storm-defying ego: not merely patient, but, superlatively, the archetype of patience. How brilliant the stroke now, as king-child echoes the stance of petulant king's child in the first scene:

> I will say nothing (38).

The descent from declamation is touching; Olivier, with a change of voice, brought a rift of humor to this peripety. Fool, Lear's audience, registers the irony in what was said.

In a pause of silence that Lear flings at the parental powers, he waits for them to treat him better for saying nothing than he treated Cordelia. Storm still. Kent's figure suddenly appears, again in the dual poise of flight and search. He would find the king, he would avoid arrest and death again. A cautious: *Who's there?* Fool gives a fool's answer:

> ... here's grace and a cod-piece; that's a wise
> man and a Fool (40–41).

This is the dialectic of man, stretched to its limits: man is love and lust, wisdom and folly. Fool may be describing Lear alone, after his fashion of mocking his master—now personified as codpiece. Fool may be describing himself, too; or, of course, opposing pairs, among Kent, Lear, himself. Then the ambiguity spirals: which is lust, which love, which wisdom, which folly?

Kent describes the storm again, stipulating the assaulting dissonance of fire, air, water, and the claps of thunder; *man's nature cannot carry / The affliction nor the fear* (48–49). Kent's demonstrated bravery authenticates the terror of the scene; and emphasizes Lear's ignoring of it. Lear's "nature" is now "unnatural"; he will bear the unbearable. His has been a solitary struggle to keep the patience he promised; he cannot do it, as he cannot keep quiet—as he cannot do anything he commits himself to. He must impatiently say something. Men are on trial, they are in danger of the kind of punishment he has handed down, now he is on trial, he must defend himself, but first he is prosecutor: to palliate his own case he furiously indicts all the others, all those who have the guilts he denies in himself. *Let the great Gods* (49)—he does not address them directly now—punish, punish, punish *them*—the hidden liars, the hypocritical incestuous, the "others" who are secretly vile, who have hidden guilts—they'll be sorry—but not me: I plead extenuation:

> I am a man
> More sinn'd against than sinning (58–59).

Kozintsev's Lear accused Fool, and then Kent, of the crimes he enumerated. Carnovsky, breaking from his two followers, who were trying to quiet him, made the speech a fierce accusation against the gods for harassing the wrong man. Gielgud cried it as his strength ebbed, with the resignation of a man feeling deeply wronged, appealing for a kindly judgement.

Lear has been likened to Prometheus; he is different, more complex. No god, he has brought darkness, not light; he has nailed himself to his rock. The design is less Prometheus than a failed Zeus: he would take vengeance on all who oppose him, particularly the young. He will not recognize in himself the secret faults for which the "others" must be made to pay. His obsession with trial and punishment is now, through III, vi, nearly absolute—counterpoint to the design of madness in IV, vi, when he will at last drop his insistence on trial and sentence, and exonerate all.

Through the shell of Lear's self-involvement Kent at last penetrates. By insistence, by urgent voice, by touch—Gielgud's Kent forced his cloak on Lear's shoulders (a gesture that goes back to Macready), Forrest's Kent held Lear's hat on the white head—Lear is made to perceive the storm, the reality of being shut out from that *hard house*. Again, Lear descends from the apocalyptic to the monosyllabic simple: he comes to himself—

> My wits begin to turn (67).

For the Lear who has feared but resisted madness to now, the taste of it is suddenly in his mouth. For a tough Lear like Scofield, it is a moment of terrible recognition; for a more pliant one, like Gielgud, of piteous bewilderment. And yet there is perhaps an expectation of freedom to come in madness, a fool's hope—as in Lear's exposing himself to the storm—that here may be the escape from the tempest in his mind that makes him run.

He holds on to sanity by concentrating on the present. Now comes his concern for Fool:

> Come on, my boy. How dost, my boy? Art cold?
> I am cold myself (68–69).

Lear's earlier kindness to Fool has been, except briefly in I, v, coated in jest, and spiked with anger; now he is only tender, thinks first, for once, of someone else. Startling, the peripety from fury to love; and inevitably touching, even with the hardbitten Scofield. Macready's girl Fool, Miss Horton, responded by wrapping her coat around Lear.* Salvini emphasized the reverse business, often copied, of taking off his mantle and throwing it over the shivering Fool, and folding Fool in a large, paternal embrace. Fool may be near collapse, now; Lear (or Kent) may have to carry him—as Lear will carry Cordelia. Then Lear himself feels the bitter cold—Edmund Kean, shocked, shivered as from a fever, he was not ague-proof.

> Where is this straw, my fellow?
> The art of our necessities is strange,
> And can make vile things precious. Come, your hovel.
> Poor Fool and knave, I have one part in my heart
> That's sorry yet for thee (69–73).

But for true need . . . Lear is learning poverty—in one part of his divided heart. Enforcing sanity on himself, against the clamor of those other parts, he communicates now with a unique clarity and directness. Briefly a return to the tonic seems possible, harmony seems promised; Lear speaks out of love, and Fool answers with rare acceptance, versing to the "Hey ho" song of *Twelfth Night* a stanza on patience in adversity for all who have—and who here has not?—*a little tiny wit*:

> Must make content with his fortunes fit
> Though the rain it raineth every day (76–77).

True, boy, Lear says, acknowledging his own tiny wit? His acquiescence to resignation? Yet the old fury is latent; when Lear tells Kent to lead them to the hovel, often, as with Gielgud, it is with the suggestion that he is concerned—as in the next scene—only with shelter for Fool: who, in some visualizations, as in Charles Kean's, is already far gone in illness by now, staggering off in Lear's arms.

*In the long blank, with Tate, of Fool's banishment from the stage, Lear had to lavish fondness on Kent. Bastard language went with bastard action: thus Forrest— "Dead as I am at heart, I've one place there/That's sorry yet for thee."

Fool's tailpiece rhyme has often been cut, in the theatre as in the
Quarto, as much for its indecency as, presumably, for interrupting action. Bradley would have liked to think it spurious. But it fits with the
dialectic form, the incessant posing of opposites, and Fool may sing it to
amuse Lear as they find their way out. If momentarily before Fool spoke
for the heart, he is returned now, on this night to cool a hot whore, to
his overt cynicism: whether things are as they are,

> When priests are more in word than matter (81)

or reversed,

> When nobles are their tailors' tutors (83)

or idealized,

> When slanders do not live in tongues (87),

Albion will come to great confusion. Fool describes both the Lear
world, and the world it became, that of Lear's audience; and he gives a
final dissonant fillip to the anachronism by promising that Merlin will,
later on, make the same prophecy.*

*Busby finds earlier examples of this form of fool's prophecy in Frog in *The
Faire Maid of Bristowe* (1605) and Haphazard in *Appius and Virginia* (1575).

Act III, Scene iii

The glimpse of Gloster and the Bastard hurrying on, in whispered consultation, insists on the night—they bear candles; on the danger implied in their huddled exchange; and on the upward movement of Edmund—the poor outcast bastard now wears richer garments, perhaps even something recognizably Edgar's. He has begun to top the legitimate. He is his father's pride, his confidant, caressed, the object of his concentrated affection.

Gloster is, as before, caught between pity and policy, between loyalty of the heart and head. He would have all well, but for his compassion for Lear, his house has been confiscated, he has been threatened with *perpetual displeasure*. (The background presence of Cornwall's men may make this visual.) This echo of the grim "pleasures" of power articulates not only Gloster's danger, but also Lear's, now clearly outcast, a poor homeless wretch. He is out in the bitter cold; the rising, ornamented Edmund is in from it. Gloster's deep, almost desperate fondness for this only son left to him emphasizes Edmund's ascendance.

The Bastard responds, always, as his father would wish. *Unnatural dealing* (1), Gloster said; *Most savage and unnatural!* (7) says Edmund. How savage and unnatural is this loyal and natural boy will appear in a moment, when he serves them whom he now calls savage and unnatural. There he will betray "nature" in the interest of "loyalty"—and an Earldom. Yet he must seem earnest now; may even seem truculently, fearfully earnest, so that a naive spectator, not having sounded the depths of his villainy, still has a chance to be surprised at it. Leering villainy here would deny suspense, as well as Edmund's real depth; though his profession of loyalty may, by its very energy, hint at the masked division between this son and his father. Edmund is partly his history; his revealed capacity for concealment is a mine under Gloster: it shadows Gloster's revelation about the division between the dukes, the subversive news of the power *footed*—on the move—to rescue Lear, and Gloster's trust that his son will share in baffling Cornwall.

Gloster has made his decision, will help the king. Partly because the old politician knows of the invasion to help Lear; but the essential loyalty works, too: he will die for it, if necessary. Now he is on his way, will be dressed—as Gielgud's was—to go into the storm, and has only confided hastily to Edmund in passing. He asks Edmund to convey to Cornwall and Regan the now-familiar excuse of the people of this world who would avoid the unpleasant—*I am ill and gone to bed* (18). A quick survey of the sullen storm within his house, an ear tuned to the storm without—and possibly, borne by the wind, a faint strain of Fool's lament on the eternal rain; and then his last line, echoing his sense of the uneasy, haunting ambience, and his tender care for his son:

> There is strange things toward, Edmund; pray
> you, be careful (20-22).

With a touch, an embrace, he goes to face the lightning. The Bastard, watching him leave, is still an unresolved character: in the pause, still poised in the posture of embrace, he seems to have a choice of paths: loyalty or treachery. He chooses, and the choice—betrayal—seems at once inevitable; it

> must draw me
> That which my father loses; no less than all:
> The younger rises when the old doth fall (25-27).

This is so true it is touched with the dark comic: the tone of humor colors his villainy still. Edmund will hasten the natural overturning process; he is playing for all, as Lear is; and the means to back his wager is beginning to fall into his hands. Fortune's wheel is on the upswing for him. His strong dominant note rises triumphantly.

Act III, Scene iv: Part One

The scene cuts abruptly, with the speed of film, to the outer storm that Gloster will enter, where Kent, Fool, and Lear now struggle toward the hovel. They are in flight; their lives are in danger; the ambient shadows may be alive with the daughters' men, who seek Lear's death, with Gloster's men, seeking Edgar. But Lear's flight is mainly from inwardness: where before he ran, now he is slower moving, absorbed, heedless of the danger, the storm. He is a stage nearer disbalance.

Brave Kent once more declares the terror—and ambiguity—of the unnaturalness of nature:

> The tyranny of the open night's too rough
> For nature to endure (2–3).

Lear will endure it. He will not be shepherded—Gielgud's Kent, leading him, turned to find Lear standing, rapt, unmoving. But inwardly Lear cannot rest, and the restlessness shows: his next short, monosyllabic cries are as much to Nature and to himself as to the entreating, tender Kent—with whom, as so often, he is at odds:

> Let me alone (3).
> . . . . .
> Wilt break my heart? (4)

He is in tears, moved by his own suffering, but sensitive to Kent and Fool: Trevor Nunn's design for this scene was to have Porter, as Lear, gaunt and haggard, yet carry Fool on in his arms—an omen of the end, when he would carry in Cordelia: *And my poor fool is hang'd* (V, iii, 305).

Lear cannot be still: he images himself between a bear and the roaring sea. Carnovsky saw the word "shun" as the key to this dialectic: a beast on one side, angry nature on the other. His hand went to his forehead, and, unable to quiet the storm within, the fingers traced circles in the air to reflect the whirling of the mind—a gesture related to Mikhoels' recurrent imagery of trying to find, with his forefinger, the mystery that eluded him. Lear defines obsession:

> This tempest in my mind
> Doth from my senses take all feeling else
> Save what beats there (12–14).

The reality of the body is crucial to the image of Lear now. His whirl-ing mind refuses the messages from the body; he does not even know he is cold. The overloaded feverish mind ravages the flesh; as the reason slips, is checked less surely, slips again, the overextended body begins to decline, toward the utter exhaustion of III, vi. Thus Gielgud's emotional crisis showed the marks of his weeping, of his physical and mental ex-haustion: the storm has shamed his elegance; his hair, wild and deranged, suggested the pathos of once kingly presence. He moved into a meta-physical world: "His whole bearing is gentler, suggesting no longer the outward grandeur of defiance, but the finer struggle of the soul . . . there is a strange, detached tone in his voice." Gielgud's note: "Move away from them all. Words tumbling out."

What beats in his brain, he says, is *Filial ingratitude*—and the thought, unleashed, hurls him violently into a see-saw from one thought to its counter.

> Is it not as this mouth should tear this hand
> For lifting food to't? (15–16.)

The recurrent language of bodily assault, in this case the cannibal imag-ery, is linked with the visual: Carnovsky, with a horrible laugh, brought his fingers to his mouth to bite them. Then the speech breaks up into shards of cross-purpose:

> But I will punish home:
> No, I will weep no more. In such a night
> To shut me out? Pour on; I will endure.
> In such a night as this? O Regan, Goneril!
> Your old kind father, whose frank heart gave all (16–20).

The tumbling words move him from the passion to call to trial, and to punish, to the equal passion to suffer, to make the world sorry for his state. In self-pity, he fantasies himself as innocent as a child:

> old, kind . . . whose frank heart gave all . . .

He stops—he cannot bear the implications of what he has said. Not only filial ingratitude but also inward anxieties torment him. To have given all without return is intolerable to him: the problem of giving or not giving is a central motif in Lear's design. The self-doubt in the design that will plague him may emerge now, in the unspoken thought that his

self-image is a lie, that he is not kind, that his heart is not frank. This may
help remind him of how precarious his sanity is:

> O! that way madness lies; let me shun that;
> No more of that (21–22).

The tension throughout is sustained by the familiar comparatives of
quantity and substance: *nothing* and *all* sound often, supported by
much, many, more, poor, little, small, better, greater, dearer; and by
more numbers: *one, first, three, thrice, six, seven, nine*. Questions again
pervade the dialogue: questions mainly of searching, of quest for identity, for a base.

The design of the scene requires that Lear's attraction to madness, and
his fear of it, now be climactic, his last strenuous resistance to unreason
before he breaks. Thus, to Gielgud, it was a vision of absolute horror,
prophetic of the reality to come. Irving's Lear, already shadowed by
insanity, made visual his perception of how he must escape his thoughts:
he literally shunned them, with a sudden, wayward rush forward, as of
a man in dream-horror fleeing from an image that almost stops his breath.

Only by a tremendous wrench is Lear able to return himself to present reality. This is his last peripety before madness—although an audience is not yet to know this, and welcomes his concern for Kent and
Fool, his insistence that they take shelter first, as a sign of the mind stabi-
lizing. A titan Lear still acts the king: Gielgud bade Kent take shelter
with a regal courtesy, and stopped kindly to touch Fool. Other Lears
descended further toward humanity: Carnovsky at first forced the facade of regality as he knelt—with a half-laugh—to pray; but his gentler
impulses overpowered him, he turned away, hid his face for a moment,
broke into tears again, then suddenly embraced Fool, tightly, with a
deep feeling of pity and tenderness, in an unmistakable softening of
character. The good old Lears were all sentiment here, particularly in
their care for Fool.

Similarly, in the prayer itself, Gielgud knelt majestically in what was
unmistakably mire. Granville-Barker wanted him to cross himself, but
after a few performances he reluctantly dropped the business, deferring
to critics troubled by the inconsistency of a Christian symbol in a pagan
play. But Gielgud felt that the gesture, like the beating of his breast
(which he retained) genuinely belonged to the solitary prayer on the
windswept heath.

The prayer, so far in spirit from his earlier adjurations, moves Lear
into a different dimension. As with Macready, a new world seems to
have broken in on his mind. He is alone with his best thoughts: Laugh-

ton, though he spoke facing the audience, seemed to withdraw into a
privacy illuminated by the simplicity and belief of a child. Scofield
seemed to be praying hard for insight. But the insight does not necessarily confer balm: so the Russian A. F. Kistov (1903–1960) seemed,
with revelation, forever banished from the paradise of ignorance.

Deep compassion, but not a note of self-pity. Poverty and need have
been apprehensions up to now, but largely theoretical: Lear could reason not the need. Now he knows better; his prayer will echo his growing apprehensions and the persistent, practical preaching of Fool (*the
codpiece that will house before the head has any . . . how shall your
houseless heads . . . ?*). Now he has learned the art of necessity, that
makes vile things precious; need has compelled his attention—and he has
responded, breaking at last out of the cage of his ego. His very kneeling,
the visual gesture always before so fierce or mocking, now so generous,
sets the moment apart. And his tone: he will no longer make demands of
the gods, or even plead with them; this—a last prayer—is addressed to
men, urging pity for the defenseless, a plea to the prosperous to share
their excess. Lear no longer asks the gods to make men more just; now
he asks that men do as much for the gods. The final anal image (*take
physic . . . shake the superflux*) is curiously collusive with Lear's own
spiritual purgation.

The storm beating down on him, unsheltered, enforces on his body a
sense of the misery of poverty (his experience is made visual in the Kozintsev film by the wretches he glimpses in the shadows); still he does
not include himself among the poor: he prays for others, finds only fault
for himself:

> Poor naked wretches, whereso'er you are,
> That bide the pelting of this pitiless storm,
> How shall your houseless heads and unfed sides,
> Your loop'd and window'd raggedness, defend you
> From seasons such as these? O! I have ta'en
> Too little care of this. Take physic, Pomp;
> Expose thyself to feel what wretches feel,
> That thou mayst shake the superflux to them,
> And show the Heavens more just (28–36).

The archetypal action of the powerful humbled to insight seems to be
realized; and a naive audience can, at this redemptive vision, anticipate
serenity. The true tonic note sounds clearly for a moment.

But Lear must journey beyond easy tragic redemption, on and on. In
none other of the major tragedies is hope so often evoked, and then an-

nihilated. In the prayer, Scofield said, Lear has been asking how: you houseless poverty, how can you—unsheltered, unfed, unclothed—be helped to defend yourself from storm? Show me how; and the only answer, Scofield said, was to go mad.

Show the Heavens more just, Lear ends, and with the shaken confidence of his experience, he looks into the void and waits for the answer. The fearful double retort is made suddenly, shockingly visual and aural by Mad Tom: in Lear's world, there is no defense, there is no justice. The moment is like a blow. Tom's sailor cry heralds it, with its reminder of the flood, of rainstorm, and even deeper, the mythic implication of depths from which water-creatures emerge:

Fathom and half, fathom and half!* (37.)

Sight and sound harrow the sense of Lear—and of Fool, Kent, the audience. Almost always here Lear is visualized slipping—or breaking—into madness, and the reason is not only that Poor Tom appears, but how. His uncanny cry, knifing out of the hovel, drives Fool screaming from the shadows. Fool has loyalty enough to warn Lear away; but his flight—to Kent's arms, as the lines suggest? to Lear's? to safety far across the stage? to a stumble and Tom leans over him?—is for life:

Help me! help me! (40.)

Kent and Lear start; Lear's balance is tested. A brief stare of vacancy may reflect, even this early, as with Edmund Kean, the physical shock. More often, what has shown is crisis: the suddenly renewed pressure on the mind. The cracking may even begin here. Gielgud pressed agonized fingers to his forehead, trying to quiet the rising inward storm; he screamed and looked toward the hovel through spread fingers, as through the bars of a cage.

Kent offers Fool a supportive hand, dares question the unknown; Fool utters one of his rare unadorned reports:

A spirit, a spirit: he says his name's poor Tom (42).

Edgar still would, unseen, frighten them away with cry and groan. Kent's *What art thou that dost grumble . . . ?* (43) (a reprise of the play-long search for identity) insists on appearance. The three wait fearfully for what will emerge.

The apparition that erupts on them—something like a man, but mud-

---

*Gielgud's *Stage Directions* prints an interesting variation (he says accidental) that has curious implications:

Father and a half! Father and a half!

daubed, nearly naked, pierced in flesh and mind, shrieking, fleeing an invisible Fury—frightens, shocks, scatters Fool and Kent, drives Lear back dismayed. The threat was more than symbolic, imaginary: as Shakespeare's audience knew, so dangerous were some of these wandering madmen that the law formally dealt with injuries they inflicted when used as entertainers. Edgar plays possessed as monstrously as he can—in the Cobb *Lear*, he beat himself with a weed whip—needing, under cover of the shock he causes, to calculate his chances of being recognized, his chances of escape. His own reason may not be safe.

Lear's mind, assaulted by a sense of rejection and mistreatment; wracked by the rain, lightning, and thunder so fierce Kent calls it unnatural, unbearable; suffering an accelerating accumulation of feelings of self-doubt, shame, error, and an upthrust of impulses he has always repressed; now, suddenly, harrowed by a vision of the shrieking madness that has been terrifying him with foreboding—Lear's mind yields.

Madness

Lear's madness governs not only his—and Edgar's—characterization; it organizes the drama. When Lear is ejected from the womb of kingship, he must confront and test reality; when reality becomes unbearable his mind evades, doubles back, encounters his self, flees. How the inner and outer forces that madden him converge on him, stagger him, overwhelm him, then recede, return, will determine the shape of the play's long center, and abrupt end.

In the simplest pattern, Lear's madness is seen as brought to him by external cruelties: mainly his daughters' ingratitude, with the savagery of nature striking final blows. This is a simplified character design, of innocence corrupted: a sentimental vision, almost all Tate left of Lear, that infected much of eighteenth and nineteenth century stage and critical interpretation (and survives beyond—Wolfit, most lately, championed it). Actors of genius, like Garrick and Kean, would inevitably find their way deeper, in Pyrrhic triumphs over Tate, but the essential action remained corrupted: a good old man, maddened by cruel daughters, was returned to life and sanity by his true child.

Once Macready "restored" the text, actors had to project verbally some of the rooted inward impulses to Lear's mental dissolution. The sentimental image did still sometimes persist, in other kinds of innocents: childlike, or a touch unbalanced from the first; or sometimes—because very, very old—foolish, weak, hardly responsible. Thus Devrient acted out Schlegel's vision of Lear's childish madness in I, i; so Booth; so Irving. Given this start, dramatic logic would force, when madness broke out, an upward movement toward intensity, strength, a vision of wisdom. Foolish old Mikhoels, fussy old Laughton, take on dignity, stature; old, old Bassermann, Redgrave, are nerved to tower fiercely once more in their madness. The Lears who begin pitiful with touches of unreason now declare madness magnificently: so Devrient's uncertain old man becomes a commanding king for the first time. The contrast with their beginnings intensifies the effect of their outbreaks, as when Charles Kean's mild senex, so foolish and fond, turns archetypally fierce.

This interpretation made good one popular critical view of Lear as growing, learning from his madness. Much road to grow there was; the steps proceeded through the shocks of banishing Cordelia and Kent, of feeling banished by Goneril and Regan, up to the prayer for the poor; then, in these Lears, the mind was fired by the lightnings of madness, more than darkened by its passions. Intensity held and mounted to IV, vi, an inspired, hectic apex.

For the more majestic, powerful Lears, madness intensified the action but usually the character movement was perforce downward. The awful apprehension, in absolute lucidity, that insanity threatened, foreshadowed a mental and physical destruction to come. Where the weaker Lear would rise to a violence of madness on sheer nerve, this tougher man had grudgingly to give way, and it was his blanks of uncontrollable weakness, the shattering aberrations forced on him, that were most moving.

It is doubtful that Shakespeare meant Lear's madness to carry a positive value, to be instructive, regenerative, as is sometimes argued. Levin Schücking, opposing, went too far in insisting Lear is no better after madness; for the design will show Lear able to love Cordelia, to recover briefly that giving impulse of kneeling and praying in the storm. But the madness is a painful interruption; his mind's furious hyperactivity will leave Lear drained, as it would in life; he will have regressed to the helpless innocence of the dependent child when, with Cordelia, in IV, vi and the beginning of V, iii, he briefly resumes the learning begun in III, iv.

Nor did Shakespeare use the madness for a moral lesson; nor—as Orwell would have it—as a mask to express safely dangerous "socialist" opinions about society. Gloster does not have to learn through madness; and Gloster is quite sane when he prays for a better distribution of wealth—as indeed Lear is, too, in III, iv. Lear's reasoned-mad damnations of hypocrisy, false justice, and court dissipation needed not insanity to be voiced—or staged—in malcontent drama. Shakespeare created this madness—it was in none of his sources—to fit the multiple dialectic that is *Lear*.

The movement in some stage Lears from weak to strong, in others from strong to weak, is a response to the dynamic of the characterization. The Lear design lives on contrast; monotones—as in the Phelp's Lear, where there was insufficient difference between the sane monarch and the weak, infirm, despised man; or in Spranger Barry's, where the transitions were without force—negated the dynamic.

The visual expression of this dynamic has ranged, as has the madness itself, from simple outward manifestations to deep inward expressions.

On the surface level, realistic actors by mimicking the gestural manner-
isms of lunatics, have sometimes portrayed not Lear but any asylum
inmate—and occasionally, indeed, madhouses have been studied for
Lear models. The result, as in Rossi's case, could be so flat-toned a drivel-
ing, drooling, slack-mouthed idiot that to English audiences he must
seem intolerable.

Distinguished Lears conveyed the inward experiences, and the motives, for madness. So Gielgud, who first tried to lose himself in dodder-
ings and twitchings, turned to a more studied restraint: "the prevailing
note must be kingly dignity." If these actors were influenced by models
—as Paul Scofield was from an experience of madness in his environment,
Garrick by the madman down the street who had let his baby slip and
fall to death—what they conveyed was not so much the manner as the
method of unbalance: the apprehension of unreason, then the uncertain,
wavering hold on reality, then the insistent guilts, resentments, fears, re-
gressions. Often actors, from Garrick to the present, have suggested the
changing states by intermittently dropping into vacancy—in abstraction, isolation, alienation. Occasionally, as with Charles Kean, momentary hints of this abstraction interrupted Lear's tirades even before III,
iv. The vacancy could be seen to reflect a somber inwardness: as
with Edmund Kean in his dreamy state, his mind making weak efforts to regain reason, but shadowed by the sense of the compulsive
agony ready to break out; or, as with McCullough, the felt awareness of
the mind slipping, the reason not working, the brain going over and over
a hurt, obsessively; often followed, as with Macready, by the pathetic
effort to force sanity back. In the full dialectic, returning lucidity would
energize the face, reason and unreason would struggle, alternating rage,
cupidity, craftiness, with sudden, open-hearted tenderness—the voice of
love, never entirely stilled, sometimes heard crying under the howls
of hate.

There are recurrent gleams of the old authority—Lear trying to resume his dragon shape; and descents into childishness. Old associations
and delusions may paralyze him; then paroxysmal hallucinations. Thus
Prucha's Lear: his eyes and his mouth, now harsh and wild, again tamed
and shy; now proud and again on the brim of tears; gestures changing
from sovereignty to vagueness; his hands pointing somewhere in command, and then suddenly losing direction. Shakespeare drew even comedy into the design, grotesquerie edged with irony and sarcasm. In madness, Lear moves toward being Fool, riddling, jesting, posturing, even
clowning, sometimes playing—and being—fantastic; and some actors—
Olivier, Charles Kean, Carnovsky—deliberately evoked the laughter,

with its shadow of pain. But Lear's linked manic moments may become suddenly demonic, terrible: fierce, even dangerous irritation over trifles, the strength of will retained, as with Booth, when the strength of mind failed. The sequence of moods is often subterranean, subconscious; efforts to connect them by obvious, logical association in criticism, or the theatre—again as with Booth—may diminish their reverberations. Better the implication of an irrational, emotional symbiosis among the erratic manifestations of the released inhibitions.

Only Salvini, among the distinguished Lears, denied the fact of madness in Lear. At most, Salvini felt, Lear was temporarily unhinged by outside forces: by ingratitude, the elements, the sense of man's degradation. Certainly he was not mad at first; there would have been no great crime, Salvini wrote, in treating an insane man as Lear was treated; and Lear's quick cure in IV, vii indicated that he could not have been wholly mad even at his worst; so Salvini let the action move on an axis of physical deterioration: the mind only wavered, but the mighty frame began slowly, visibly to decay.

Overt, stark physical manifestations accompanying Lear's madness are stipulated in Shakespeare's design: the erratic physical movement, the hallucinatory gestures, the restlessness. While excessive realism, or physical rant, are corruptive of the design, the eloquent language of head, torso, and limbs is as essential as the verbal gestures. Often not easily accessible to the reader's imagination, this language in the theatre stirs multiple responses. Thus, the old white head: unbonneted, the seat of madness, where the brains feel cut; the hands often go to it—the self-beating at the end of Act I echoed by fingers fumbling at the forehead, as by Carnovsky; hands throwing the long white hair off the temples, as by Forrest and Edmund Kean; hands stroking the bald dome, as by Porter; or reaching for the lost crown, as by Mikhoels. Garrick's head spoke silently more than Tate's miserable words gave him to say: he moved it very deliberately; his eyes were fixed, or if he turned them on anyone, he made a pause, and looked fixedly at the new object, in his strange, mad world.

Perhaps hardest of all for the imagination to visualize are Shakespeare's intentions for—and the actors' use of—Lear's eyes, those organs so central to the play's theme, so significant in Lear's blind staring search for inward sight. Often the actors' eyes, like Garrick's, looked at objects and did not see them; or saw through them, as if trying to peer beyond the limits of the world; or perceived—and made the audience perceive—hallucinations as fearful presences; or closed on horrors too terrible even to be hallucinated.

The mark of a king, Lear would say, was his stare; his angry eyes flash up to the fierce heavens, seek to wither his imagined daughters; then range in bewilderment and sometimes glee over the terrifying society of outcasts and phantasms that surround him. Carnovsky's most telling recurrent bodily imagery was his persistent piercing, squinting examination of his mysterious world. Kean's mad gaze was terrifying because his eyes smiled with half-gladness as he spoke the most horrible things; Devrient was said to convey the whole course of his madness almost entirely with his eyes.

And with his hands—Lear's hands, that Shakespeare directs to such activity—to tear off his clothes, cling to Edgar, shoot imaginary weapons, point to phantoms, mime violences, make strange, incantatory gestures. They are extensions of Lear's inner turmoil, speak their own language of madness: in their revealing signs of the king-beggar gone irrational, impotent; in their heightened or lessened energy, their occasional uncontrollability, in their wavering and uncertainty that convey, as the eyes do, the agonized, erratic thought—so Edmund Kean's hands had their own wandering, searching motion, as if looking for something lost; so Mikhoels repeatedly reached for the discarded symbol of power.

Punctuating the visual imagery of madness are its sounds, Edgar's as well as Lear's: the nonverbal signals actors have used of incoherence, excitement, despair, raging delirium: monotonal utterance, mutterings, moanings, piteous cries, growls, croonings, shrieks, commands, weeping, idiotic laughs, pleading. The speaking voice itself signals the difference between normality and madness, as when Devrient said some of the most painful words not with pain but as if with a curious joy.

Lear's agony when he is irrational contradicts the occasional conception of his madness as an escape, a freedom. It is an escape into nightmare; unable to *meet the bear i' th' mouth* (III, iv, 11), Lear sinks in a roaring sea, the sea of the subconscious, where monstrous impulses tumble and abrade him. Obsessively he seems almost, as with Carnovsky, to coddle them, to be their nurse as well as their prisoner. Lear knows, though, how unfree this freedom is when, momentarily, lucidity awakens him: he is cut to the brains. The effort both to sustain his delusional system, and to end it, exhausts him: what is almost most heroic in Lear is his struggle against the refuge of unreason. He never stops being Lear, must not, in the theatre, even when mad. Scofield felt Lear's sense of the accumulating burden of his error maddened him—and yet Lear would struggle back to assume it again.

Gloster, in his anguish, could wish for madness to escape lucidity; but the design of his mind, for all its suffering, is far short of Lear's million nerve ends that sustain a universe of malign perceptions. Early on, Gloster would unstate himself if he could resolve his doubts about Edgar; later, to end suffering, he would settle for suicide. The design of Lear's tremendous *elan* never allows him to surrender to madness, even in the depth of madness itself; and he will yield willingly to death only when, in IV, vii, he offers to drink retributive poison at the hand of Cordelia. In the depths of his unreason, Lear might seem to smile at his lunatic wisdom, as Charles Kean would, but as the edges of delusion dissolve, the pain of awareness always returns.

The uniqueness of Lear's madness emerges in contrast with Edgar's manufactured insanity, apparently a copy of the familiar, contemporary Bedlamite beggar's madness—or of the pretense of it. Edgar mimes the masochism of possession—conventional sexual and social guilts and devils ride him—although, as noted, as the counterfeit sometimes merges with a reality of unbalance, his excitation soars, he seems touched with true irrationality. Lear's madness issues from the very sources of his character: if it has moments of the wise, sweet and pathetic, it is mainly aggressively erotic and hostile, sadistic: he would punish, knife into flesh, kill, kill, kill. The naive spectator anticipates—dreads—some act of violence; this is not a harmless madness.

As Lear is hurtled down from king to man toward brute animality, startling insights emerge—but not because Lear's madness is necessarily wisdom: his perceptions of mankind at its worst are felt so sharply because discolored by his feverish perspective. There is no stopping point, no base; the cutting edge of truth changes as Lear changes. In IV, vi he proposes to embrace a world without values as a way of getting revenge on the world that rejected his values; but his most brilliant, most cynical vision of human depravity is contraverted by the near-idyll of his reunion with Cordelia—as this vision, in its turn, will be contraverted.

What Mikhoels called "polyphony"—simultaneous contrasting or opposed notes in the Lear chord—he sensed in the multiple impulses that held Lear wavering between a madman's fantasies and the revelations of reality. Lear's mind is in mutiny: old ideas are collapsing, new ideas struggling to be born. Thoughts are not connected by ordinary logic: they evolve in abrupt impulses, the very gaps between linked by a "musical tinge of absence." Mikhoels voiced Lear's lines now in a decisive affirmative, now as a protesting, shattering interrogation, now in low and solemn tones—fit for awakening, imprisonment, or death. The subrational continuity led to the central philosophical meaning Mikhoels saw as the new thought forced on Lear—that man is a "forked animal."

Madmen, in fact, do sometimes have lightning insights. Partly because, as Walter Freeman, a psychological physiologist, observes, the mind becomes fragmented, the usual interconnections do not enforce normal perception, hence what is familiar is perceived as strange, and characterized afresh. So psychotics may have startling artistic visions. In Freudian terms, with the lifting of psychic censorship the mind can indulge in what it has hitherto suppressed—for that which we most desire we may, as "civilized" beings, profess to loathe and deny. In Shakespeare's design, Lear gives voice to repressions hinted in his early speech; he can revel now in what before he could not endure.

In his delusions and hallucinations he sometimes turns philosophical, but never does he call on the gods. An extra undertone of irony, then, infuses the hallucinations and adds ambiguity to the madness design: when he talks so confidently to what he cannot see, is he any more mad than when he spoke to the invisible gods—who also do not reply?

As rationality and repression are stripped from Lear along with his other social garments, he moves toward a psychic and physical nakedness that stirs repressed archaic responses. When he confronts in himself a poor, bare forked creature akin to animals; when he speaks with the impunity of an irresponsible, greedy, megalomaniac, self-pitying child, he incarnates two archetypal images of the madman—animal and primordial infant. The naked lunatics of the "wild man" legends are of this company.

The lunatic's likeness to beast and child was formally stated, Bernard Diamond and Anthony Platt have observed, by Henry de Bracton, Chief Justiciary of England's highest court, in the thirteenth century. A madman was held inculpable because he was like a young child, and not distant from a brute (brute meaning not wild or carnal, but of a lower order than man): a beast that wants discourse of reason. This is not the madman image Shakespeare dreamed elsewhere, gently, as akin to lover and poet; in *Lear*, the harsh, obsessive, savagely irrational dominates the design. The difference here between man and beast, as the *Ayenbite of Inwit* would say, is that the former has understanding—a point that would be extended in *The Anatomy of Melancholy*: "beasts cannot reflect on themselves." In Lear, the division is dramatized in those excruciating lucidities when he looks out for a searing instant from his dark abyss, reflects on himself, knows what is happening in his mind, and flees back into the roaring gulf of his terrible madness.

Another irony: the irresponsible—the animal, madman, infant—is a nonperson. No one can tell him who he is. Hence the motif of the archetypal, megalomaniac king-infant, declared in the absolutism of I, i and

continuing residually into Lear's crafty impunity in IV, vi: *They cannot touch me* (IV, vi, 83). Only his conferred role gives him identity
as king.

The exact point at which Lear breaks into madness has been vigorously debated. Schlegel's contention that Lear was mad from the first
found, as we saw, some theatre followers. Mantell's first crack came after he recoiled from confronting the *fiery duke* in II, iv. Empson sees the
onset of insanity (and so Edmund Kean played it) at the end of this
scene, with the self-pity of *I gave you all* (II, iv, 252). But most critics
and actors choose that fearful moment in III, iv when Poor Tom suddenly appears. Even here, the crossover is not necessarily violent; unless
the earlier hints and fears of madness (Kent's *when Lear is mad* (I, i,
146), Lear's *his notion weakens* (I, iv, 236), *beat at this gate* (I, iv, 280),
let me not be mad (I, v, 47), *O Fool, I shall go mad* (II, iv, 288), *my wits
begin to turn* (II, ii, 67), and the incoherence, the momentary abstrac-
tions) are designed to lead to so great a smash. Some actors, like the
German Schroeder, carefully articulated a step-by-step transition toward madness; some, like his countryman Ferdinand Fleck (1757-1801),
made it seem to come suddenly, unexpectedly. Scofield tried acting the
moment when unreason had ripened for emergence.

For those stage Lears carefully rational up to Poor Tom's outbreak, a
terrible irony attaches to this turning point, as the precise moment when
Lear is least distorted by self-interest, when he is most sane, has purest
insight—in his prayer for the poor, naked wretches. In the unbalanced
Lears, the prospect at last of lucidity beckons here. But once more, the
answer to prayer is *No*; the powers that made Lear again deny him,
make him mad at the moment they might finally love him. To a naive
spectator, this prayer, coming so sweetly after the vicious prayer curses,
has seemed to promise serenity at last, surcease. Then at once chaos is
come again, and the endless peripety goes on. The momentary promise
of the tonic is drowned in the dissonances inherent in the tonic itself.

That Lear is not really started on madness until III, vi has been suggested by Coleridge and Norman Maclean; Sholom Kahn pushes the
ultimate moment to IV, vi when the Quarto stipulates *Enter Lear Mad*.
(Kahn qualifies by acknowledging an "encroaching madness" in III, iv,
"reason in madness" at III, vi, and "furthest madness" in IV, vi.) Much
depends on the design of irrationality in Lear's actions. Is his sudden undressing in III, iv violent insanity, or only a response of humane insight?
Is his anger at Poor Tom's daughters ironic? satiric? in deadly earnest?
madness? Is his philosophizing with Tom a first insane sign, as Joseph

Warton thought? Is Lear's prose a clue to the madness design, as Milton Crane's sensitive study speculates? Many of the irrational speeches are in prose; but Crane wisely observes that this is not invariable; and it may again imply the wavering of the mind. In many cases, notably in IV, vi, speeches printed in prose in both Quarto and Folio could as easily be versed. As important as the rhythm is the lexicon; from now on Lear will mainly forego the great ringing declamations, in which he spoke to deities, using words for their magic power, for the simpler speech, often monosyllabic, of a man talking to a man.

Actors who begin Lear as sane—including all the modern ones who discussed it with me—invariably began to shatter at Tom's entrance. This is a cataclysmic moment: the unaided imagination cannot easily encompass the sudden, intolerable pressures of sight, sound, and feeling that converge on Lear. In the theatre, particularly to naive spectators, the scene becomes genuinely terrifying.

Whether the madness comes abruptly, or in delayed shock, the stripping of Lear's reason is unmistakable now; but as in so many places, the line between insight and unreason remains ambiguous. This is important to the design of the larger action. Granville-Barker argued that character could not be developed in terms of lunacy, that Lear was no longer a motive force and that the III, vi trial scene was probably cut in the Quarto because it did not work theatrically. But it does work in the theatre; and it contributes to developing Lear's character in terms of lunacy—mainly as measured by his war against it.

A naive spectator is caught up in this war: he does not know if Lear will ever win it, will ever be sane again, and must be involved in each new battle. There is no single climactic scene, as Bernard Beckerman observes, but a series of intense moments. These are carefully modulated. In the first, III, iv, Lear still carries over the compassion of his prayer; in the second, III, vi, he is obsessed with punishment of his daughters—the other side of a desperate defense of his own guilt that echoes his plea of innocence in the storm; in the third, IV, vi, he has progressed to revulsion for all society—and, ironically, to acceptance of it. There is a physical movement, too: the hyperenergy of the first scene is diminished at the end of III, vi; IV, vi is a resurgent, manic gavotte, before collapse and the near-allegro of IV, vii. Peripety persists; between the last two mad scenes a witness in IV, iii raises hopes: Lear is *in his better tune* (40). The snatches at reason are as essential to the action as to the characterization: the naive spectator is led to hope: Now! Now! he may regain sanity, serenity.

Countering this motif is always the threat of events. The external dangers that helped impel Lear over the edge accelerate. He flees into the storm, where madness comes, then he becomes a hunted fugitive, caught in the same flight and pursuit imagery as Kent, and Edgar, and later Gloster. The danger hounds him from refuge to refuge, until, when at last he can sleep, and a rest might save his crumbling sanity, he is forced from his rude shelter into the maddening night. In IV, vi, his own sense of his danger is another reverberation of his latent lucidity: he knows he is pursued, believes he is in danger; he runs.

To give Lear's madness a scientific classification is meaningless. It has been called mania, obsession, senile dementia, melancholy dotage, runaway narcissism, schizophrenia, paranoia. Symptoms have been cited: the quick wrath, hallucinations, delusions, incoherence, fantasies, the undressing, the feverish sexuality of the language, the repressed incestuous impulses. These are reflections of life experience that contribute to the verisimilitude of the unique design of Lear's madness: the confrontation and testing of fearful, unaccustomed reality, the flight to illusion and hallucination resisted sternly and at last climactically in a battle where the outcome is never sure. Again, by comparison Edgar's imitation of familiar Bedlamite madness, unresisted, helps define the characteristic Lear struggle. Edgar pretends to be possesed by a demon. Lear, at contact with Edgar, briefly submits to possession—by a demonic, punishing self. And then wrestles with his demon to the death.

The developing intensity of the encounter defines the madness and extends it. The ominous power in Lear, as he commits the terrible act of banishing Cordelia—an appointment with madness as Albert Camus observes; his capacity to apprehend and struggle against insanity's onslaught; the encroaching selfness that seems to doom his resistance to it; then the mingling of reason and unreason, so ambiguously that sometimes they can hardly be distinguished—reason in madness, madness in reason; the very real danger that Lear may break out into insane, brutal violence; the pauses in the conflict, when the lucid mind shudders at what it perceives: through such wrenching, pitiful, frightening peripeties the sanity of the universe, as well as of Lear, is cast in doubt.

Act III, Scene iv: Part Two

Poor Tom's apparition maddens Lear partly because Tom incarnates Lear's most dreaded imaginings: to be a houseless, naked companion to the wolf and owl, to liberate the beast residing in man—in Lear himself. The *thing itself* is not merely man—it is *id*, man naked, irrational, careless of social accommodations. Mad.

Edgar, for safety's sake, and for deeper motivations built into the design, plays the part of madness intensely before the king he knows—and has perhaps served. The more intensely because his suffering is real, as well as calculated. He does hunger, the winds that blow through the hawthorn do freeze his bare limbs. He really does dream of a warm bed. He must be visualized as outfacing a truly bitter sky in near naked-ness, as Shakespeare stipulates: Edgars, well-covered, even in rags, have not served the play well in the theatre, have not cut Lear to the brains with the living image of his fears. The visible, anguished, animal body enduring physical pain is again central to the ritual design, though its caperings and language may be grotesquely comic: "a desperately hu-morous and purposefully exorbitant creature," said Alexis Minotis, who played the role in Greece.

Lear's first—of many—questions extends his obsession with *all* and with *daughters* over the line into paranoia:

> Didst thou give all to thy daughters?*
> And art thou come to this? (48-49.)

The question is sometimes asked in the theatre with some wryness; more often Lear, sliding through shock to his new perspective, looks at—and often clings to—Edgar with an almost childish sympathy, a deep com-passion, a fellow-feeling, a delighted fondness, even admiration, and asks his questions earnestly, intently, as if—with Laughton—the whole secret of life lay in the answers. To Macready, Tom seemed a focus for remembering all the history of his own wrongs; though Forrest seemed to forget his own misery in his compassion for the Bedlamite: he spoke affectionately but with the dignity still of a king surrounded by his

*Granville-Barker wanted Gielgud to hold a dead silence before the first speech, and then say, in a voice not used before, *Didst thou give all....*?

court. Olivier sheltered Tom's shivering nakedness with a fatherly care, as he had sheltered Fool. Gielgud's note: "Face each other. Still."

A sense of kinship between the two developed, as with Irving, who followed Tom closely, studied him with a hungry curiosity. The kinship deepens: as the Dionysiac rises to the surface in Lear, a subconscious—often subverbal—communion binds him to Tom, even as to a son, a child. This becomes visual, pathetically, in the loosening of his bond with Fool, whose vitality now steadily diminishes. Tom becomes—plays—fool. Fool's jealousy may begin to show at once; though one sweet theatre Fool tried gently to rub Edgar's grimed face clean.

Edgar has shocked the trio no more than he is shocked by them. Suddenly he confronts his king—was he of Lear's own retinue?—bedraggled, almost unattended, evidently mad. The shock is psychic, though physical danger lessens: at least this strange little company does not threaten pursuit. Edgar must recognize the irrationality and perhaps even the pathos of Lear's question; but in his complex response, he offers nothing now, and very little later, of compassion or support. He will later express sympathy in asides; he will claim that he became *pregnant to good pity*—but he is not delivered of it with Lear as generally he is not with his father. If he had been characterized by drunkenness, a trace of it may remain. *Sullen*—the Quarto description—aptly characterizes him now. He hardly at all—and never in this scene—offers a comforting or assuring word to Lear. Does he want to infect Lear with fiends? He certainly forces on Lear's troubled mind a fearful image of suffering madness, suggesting—via the metaphor of possession—Tom-Edgar's inclinations to suicide even in church: *knives under his pillow . . . ratsbane in his porridge . . . dragged through fire, flame, ford and whirlpool, bog and quagmire.* (His dallying with self-destruction will be echoed in his father's suicidal moments, and his own thought of it in V, iii.)

Edgar's pretended agony is not all pretense, all counterfeiting. His design suggests the undertaking—or enduring—of a process that he will see as a purification, but that must appear as ambiguous to an audience as Gloster's, or Lear's. Edgar is involved in a transitional phase that will end—he will say in the play's last statement—in compassion and a determination to speak what he feels, not what he ought to say. Now, probably, he speaks both: for he is truly vexed by that foul fiend that has been plunging him toward nothing. He may flee frantically back and across the stage, as a Norwegian Edgar did, to escape a fearful hurt. The fiend's seat may be in Tom's head—as Lear's is in his head—(though Minotis slid his hand down his half-naked backside to keep his devil from entering there). When Tom snatches at the fiend,

> There could I have him now, and there . . . (61–62)

does he—as Lear does—beat at his brain, where demons lodge? Or at the persecuting air? Or at the pricks, real and imaginary, that the fiend plagues him with? Or may Tom, practising imaginary swordstrokes on his "fiend," echo his brief passage at arms with Edmund, and prepare tactics for the final encounter with the Bastard? Symbolically, Tom may be closing in, too, on that fiend of his shadow side that is symbolized by his masochistic possession: he may be coursing—cursing?—*his own shadow for a traitor* (57). His inner division parallels the Lear-Gloster agonies, but is unlike in being almost wholly inward. The transition from what he was to what he will be is more subterranean, revealed in perceptions (no worst, there is none); but still masked in motivation— why torture Lear and Gloster so much?

The extra dimension of Edgar's pretence of madness imposes an insistent purposefulness on the design. His irrationality is mainly deliberate, his ravings contrived. While he may sometime, like Hamlet, shelter so enthusiastically in pretence as to be engulfed by it, while his crowings of cold and hunger are evidently genuine, the design requires that his madness be familiar enough,* and artificial enough—the street Bedlams he imitated were known to use various frauds to get more leverage for their begging—to set off Lear's true disbalance and Fool's professional kind. The borrowing from Harsnett suggests Shakespeare's intention that the fraudulent in mad Tom be apparent. An Edgar in the theatre who does not provide this dimension, who does not occasionally —visually—withdraw from the Bedlam role to observe its effect on Lear and Gloster—as indeed Shakespeare made him do verbally in asides (with whatever ambiguity of dismay or satisfaction)—risks blurring the design. The worst theatre Edgars have been those so determinedly mad that their lunacy seemed as genuine as Lear's.

Lear still harps on *daughters* and on *all*, in language moving steadily toward prose as Crane observes; the prose of madness?

> What! has his daughters brought him to this pass?
> Couldst thou save nothing? Woulds't thou give
> 'em all? (63–64.)

"With sad dignity," Gielgud notes. "Pity now new."

---

*So familiar, the words were set to music by Orlando Gibbon (1583–1625) in a "London Cry": "Poor, naked Bedlam, Tom's a-cold, a small piece cut of thy bacon or a piece of thy sow's side, good Bess, God almighty, bless thy wits" (see Sternfeld).

Fool's line, one of his few remaining, that would take the sting from shame by mocking it, cannot outjest Lear's madness, which swerves past, to curse Edgar's imaginary daughters with the old energy. Kent's insistence on reality is so severely rebuked that he will remain silent until Gloster appears:

> Death, traitor! nothing could have subdu'd nature
> To such a lowness but his unkind daughters.
> Is it the fashion that discarded fathers
> Should have thus little mercy on their flesh?
> Judicious punishment! 'twas this flesh begot
> Those pelican daughters (70–75).

Matter and impertinency mix. Beyond the obsession about wicked daughters is the undertone of guilt. Lear talks justice, but he thinks in his old pattern of punishment—here self-punishment. (Carnovsky's note: "serves him right."). Lear's cue is the thorns piercing Edgar's flesh—Booth plucked one out, and moved to tear his own flesh with it. Word and action echo the motifs of children as diseases of the body, of cannibalism, of the beastly beasts—louse, vulture, young pelicans—that feed on flesh and blood, of the ugliness of sex, begetting. Empson will see something sordid in an old man beginning to find sexuality so exciting; but this has from the beginning been a subtextual impulse in Lear's shadow side, latent in his confrontations with his daughters, but always offset by countering dialectical elements.

Pelican, pillicock: the begotten suggests the only begetter, the phallus, to Poor Tom; his cry may be a Bedlam noise, or a song refrain, or an animal call; but it may also be the sounds accompanying the sexual act, as Pillicock mounts Pillicock hill.

Does Fool sense the direction of Lear's wandering? In this next to last of his few lines in the long scene, he is again more sensible than Fool:

> This cold night will turn us all to fools and madmen (79).

Edgar still does nothing to lighten the cold night's burdens. Madman preaches morality, perhaps in the posture of priest—was this a mark of the Bedlamite, who must have heard (and pretended) morality enough —echoing the pontifical manner of Fool's teaching in I, iv, and Lear's preaching in IV, vi? The words are pious, commandments mixed with adjurations; they carry an inherent irony, aimed at his father—honor your parents, but fie on adultery—as well as an overt irony. As if to insist on the absurdity of the beggar preaching—and the absurdity of this night—Edgar suddenly lapses into his beggar's whine: *Tom's a-cold* (83).

The playlong pursuit of identity is focussed in Lear's characteristic question when he meets a stranger:

What hast thou been? (84.)

Tom's confessional is layered in ambiguity. Edgar as Tom is a fraud; Tom is playing a Bedlamite fraud; Edgar-Tom is describing a man he never was: the kind of professionally sinful man whose public, auto-biographic soul-searching, then as now, could capture the attention and compassion of a street-corner audience. Tom's righteous tone, his ministerial, sing-song rhythm presumably would encourage charity from sympathetic listeners (Edgar may have his beggar's hand out now, and be collecting). But there remains the undertone of reality, of the true voice of Edgar, shaping what he says, meaning it. The dapper, lecherous "serving man" he describes might be Oswald, might be Edmund; but the word *service* extends in *Lear* from role to human function: all men serve: as servants, sexually, socially, politically. Lear serves, Gloster serves, Edgar himself serves. How much of Tom's confession of failed serving is Edgar's own? How much the outburst of repressed fantasy? How much revenge, how much self punishment? How much addressed to Lear, how much to himself? If his early character was visualized as dissolute, given to drink, careless, Tom's Puritanism, however, calculated, can now function as a transition toward the stern, austere man Edgar finally becomes. An early Edgar naive and bookish begins now to assert a fierce Mosaic identity: his "thou shalt nots" belong to his character as does the harsh disciplining of Gloster. He does not forgive his father for his goatish disposition, for serving the lust of his mistress' heart, for doing what Tom now calls *the act of darkness with her* (87–88); Edgar will remind his dying brother that Gloster—then dead—lost his eyes for begetting Edmund in a *dark and vicious place* (V, iii, 172).

The undertone of Edgar's true involvement in his masquerade sounds also in his insistent condemnation of fine clothes, *proud array*. He has stripped himself of raiment to bring himself to nothing; the whole burden of his sermon now is ascetic self-denial. He extends verbally and visually the poverty imagery Lear and Fool have been building; symbolizes the divesting motif that will strip home, rank, and rank's panoply from Kent, all that plus eyes from Gloster, and everything from Lear, leaving him near naked, in mind and body, before the end.

Tom's madness of manner through the sermonizing may be visualized as ranging from an austere ministerial parody to the frantic flight from

possession that becomes panic at the end, with the break into inco-
herency. Redgrave's Edgar flickered bat-like at him from the shadows.
Mikhoels' Edgar, edging toward the margin where man and animal meet,
became the sinful beasts, and voiced their noises: *hog in sloth, fox in
stealth* (94). At his miming of *dog in madness* (95) Mikhoels picked
up the barking, and imitated it, louder and louder as Edgar finished, Fool
joining in. Lear continued his barks through the great following speech,
making visual and aural his great hurt: bark! bark!—man is a beast, we
are all fakes, we poor two-legged animals pretending to be human. The
barking, Mikhoels felt, was a concrete expression of the subtextual
emotional imagery.

Lear's great response to Edgar's nakedness Ribner has called "the lowest point in [Lear's] delusion" and J.S.H. Bransom "the highest reach
... of his intellect. ..." In fact, it is a series of gestures, the last cancelling
the first, that mark dialectic phases in Lear's battle against madness. Lear
begins seeming to win, and ends in retreat. In the first gesture, he looks
beyond the transient vision of his recent unanswered prayer. The
heavens will not be just; better be dead than live as Tom does, houseless, in looped and windowed raggedness.

Then, in the second movement, a new vision emerges. As he saw
partial truths in that illusory world where gods seemed to reign, he now
enunciates a different partial truth for a world that seems without justice, heavenly or otherwise: civilization is corruption:

> Is man no more than this? ... Thou ow'st the worm no silk, the beast
> no hide, the sheep no wool, the cat no perfume. Ha! here's three on's
> are sophisticated; thou art the thing itself; unaccommodated man is no
> more but such a poor, bare, forked animal as thou art (105–111).

As I am, Lear would say. To Scofield, this came with soft, musing despair; to Carnovsky, it was a tragic insight; to Gielgud, a philosophic
vision; to Irving, a fascinating discovery.

Then comes the third movement, that visually as well as verbally
stipulates Lear's divestment of the garments of culture and of consciousness. He would go naked into the world of the subconscious, of the underground ungoverned impulse; the anarchic. Only in irrationality can
Lear accept absolutely his animal identity: so his resistance to madness
must again dissolve. Though in his rational mind he knew he were better dead than like Tom, he has swung about in these few lines to embrace and share Tom's unadulterated animality, his nakedness—his
vulnerability.

This evokes Lear's second major disrobing, repeating—ritually?—his

I, i abdication when he shed other borrowed garments: *Here I divest myself*:

> Off, off, you lendings! Come; unbutton here (111-112).

Lear will again, at the end, request help unbuttoning (then possibly for Cordelia); now it is an order: to his little entourage? or to Edgar? or to the stubborn garment he would strip off?—or even to himself? (Kozintsev's Lear pointed to his head—*unbutton here.*) He is in a kind of tantrum. Knowing how terrible it is to be naked in the storm, he *will* now be naked, no more furred gowns, he will show them, he will be brother—not merely companion—to wolf and owl. The unnaturalness of nature has led Lear to a changed conception of the nature of man, of nature itself. Superfluity that may be good to satisfy need is now bad, because it sophisticates. Lear moves, again, between *all* and *nothing*. Since there was adulteration in his former world, then all must be adulteration in it. So he chooses a world of nothing. The language itself is reductive, negative: the prose is wonderfully stark, simple; and in the few lines there are six *no*'s, two of them stipulating that man is *no more* than the least, the worst.*

The irony of illusion is insistent: Lear is moved to accept the animality of man not by the true thing itself, but by a fraud: a pretender to madness. Lear thinks he can now accept himself as simple man; but the design insists that he go on feeling his kingship. Lear's insight is thus not only partial, a limited perspective, but also based on an illusion. But it makes easier his madness, his flight to the terrible freedom of nakedness.

Kent and Fool rush to stop Lear's disrobing—sometimes grappling with him, swaying in a mass, as with Gielgud, sometimes scattered in pursuit across the stage, as with Porter. Usually a kind of primitivist dignity surrounds Lear's tearing at his garments; but Porter's was deliberately grotesque, unheroic; he dropped his trousers partway to reveal long white old legs; hobbled, by the trousers caught at his knees, he stumbled about trying to strip until Kent and Fool overpowered him. The wrestling with Lear's impulse—especially if played as the impulse of a madman—builds to a strenuous subscene climax.

Fool's urgent warning of Gloster's advent freezes the action. The rain

---

*A sentimentalized Lear tears off his garments to give them to Tom. This would extend the impulse of the prayer, but it softens Lear's descent toward the animality he will embrace in IV, vi. Here he wants only to shed—not share—all lendings, all superflux. Shakespeare dramatizes what Claude Levi-Strauss calls the archetypal dialectic of myths: between nature and culture, between man's urge to transcendence and the animal inheritance that will not let go. The terms of the dialectic oppose and fuse in the art of this moment.

and the cold have set Fool to riddling again—prophetically: in this night
wet enough to swim in, the spark of an old lecher's heart were not
enough for warmth. It is a capsule of Gloster's life. Then the alert:

> Look! here comes a walking fire (116–117).

The four fugitives hush—or are hushed. Light in the darkness may be
dangerous. Any intruder from the sophisticated world can mean death.
To the naive spectator, this is a frightening moment. Only when the
light slowly comes on, carried by Gloster, is there some relief—and
then still not for Edgar, Gloster's prey.

Edgar attacks. This first harassment of the father who has pursued him
exploits Gloster's susceptibility to superstition. He is a devil, Tom says;
his evil involves clouding the sight, making the eye *squinny*—the motif,
here used symbolically, is prophetic as well as descriptive. Lear will say
to Gloster in IV, vi:

> Dost thou squinny at me?
> No, do thy worst, blind Cupid . . . (IV, vi, 138–139).

The word includes the whispering *w* sound that weaves through the
speech, drawing out the expletives, and preparing for Tom's slow,
plaintive, self-pitying:

> . . . and hurts the poor creature of earth (122).

To expel this hurt, Tom chants a saint's charm, ending with a fierce
exorcism by word, and perhaps flashing voice and body, that must
frighten Gloster, always easily set on the gad, now highly agitated—his
wits *craz'd* (174), as Shakespeare will stipulate. He is as startled as were
Fool, Kent and Lear at Tom's first appearance: the more so because
Edgar makes a direct attack on him, and because, in the shadowed,
stormy night, his half-stripped king is being quieted by such strange attendants. Gloster, in his agitation, may well back away.

Lear's characteristic inquiry into identity now has a mad note—that
may sound through shock, bewilderment, amusement, anger. Gielgud,
from the shifting mass of three bodies, shot out an arm to point wildly
at the intruder: *What's he?* (129.)

Kent is ready for defense. The on-guard questions pile up. *Who's
there? What is't you seek?* (130.) Gloster: *What are you there? Your
names?* (131.)

Staggered by Edgar's assault, Gloster's interest—he has not yet recognized Lear—centers on the mad beggar. He will later say his son Edgar
comes into his mind, perhaps because he hears the echo of a trick of Ed-

gar's voice—that Tom may betray, and then cover. Tom insists on his
mad identity, in a rhythm of phrases echoing his masochistic resolution
to be nothing, worst. He eats and drinks what is revolting, suffers pain
and punishment. The dominant consonants—s, t, v, f,—are soft, and let
him dwell on his self-pity. But he cannot let Gloster get too close:

> Beware my follower. Peace, Smulkin! peace, thou fiend! (145.)

Troubled Gloster—puzzled still to be reminded of his lost son—asks
Lear, ironically:

> What, hath your Grace no better company? (146.)

No better company than Gloster's own son? Tom's retort curiously
mixes the devil's role with Lear's own recurrent motif of the dark:

> The Prince of Darkness is a gentleman (147).

The irony of this in the *Lear* context—of the Prince of Evil, but also the
gentleman seducer, he who dallies in the dark and vicious place—evokes
from Gloster a nonrational, associational response rather than a logical
one, as if, again, some unrecognized note in Tom's voice and meaning
commands the old man to muse, oracularly:

> Our flesh and blood, my lord, is grown so vile,
> That it doth hate what gets it (149–150).

Edgar responds on the same subterranean level, repeating his initial experience of rejection:

> Poor Tom's a-cold (151).

Gloster wrenches himself to the business at hand—providing Lear
food and shelter in despite of Goneril and Regan—but by now Lear is
hypnotized by Tom. In the theatre, Lear gazes at his *philosopher* fascinated; or imitates him; or walks apart with him; or forces him to con-
verse. For sympathy, because of his ragged garments? Because Tom ex-
presses feeling so readily, suggesting to the envious Lear a Montaignian
rejection of Senecan stoicism? From the Horatian epistle (II, i) about
the poet able to move his auditor through a wide range of feeling and
imaginings, "who makes me at Thebes one minute and the next at
Athens"? None of this is needed to explain the poetic—and theatrical—
effect of the king who never before listened to anyone, now appealing
for oracular knowledge from a mad beggar in rags:

> First let me talk with this philosopher.
> What is the cause of thunder? (158–159.)

This was a common philosophical speculation: edged with meaning here from Lear's old feeling that he could command thunder; from the conspiracy of thunder to join in high-engendered battle against him; from—perhaps even at this moment—a new assault of thunder that has held the quartet momentarily silent; and not least because there has been thunder in Lear's own head—the tempest that will not give him leave to ponder on things that would hurt him more. So Carnovsky, at the question, beat with his fingers on his forehead.

But more often the irony is compounded by the earnestness of Lear's search for wisdom from another. So Gielgud kept step with Edgar as they walked up and down, treated him with noble reverence, bowing and gesticulating with an air of majesty and profound understanding. Scofield asked with the utmost intensity, as if to know this were to know everything.

Thus the titan, preserving regal dignity. Another visual pattern—Garrick's business—was to play with Edgar in the hovel straw, as the Keans and many subsequent actors did, with an imbecile dullishness, the question seeming more foolish than pregnant.

In either case, old fools are babes again. The younger rise as the old fall. The unnatural is natural. Edgar becomes tutor to two of the oldest and most powerful men in the kingdom. And his tutelage will be severe, and painful—no kind nursery.

The scene is difficult, complex; so many elements must converge. The physical imagery, sometimes in mime, often frantic; the aural design—storm, mad cries, the "who's there?" calls, Lear's new tones; the action, nerved by Gloster's urgency to lead the three from dangerous discomfort to a comfort perhaps more dangerous, because forbidden—all these threats must be articulated toward the climax. Figure and ground must shift quickly, as Shakespeare's focus shifts; the kaleidoscopic images must not blur.

Gloster's urgency and agitation do not become apparent verbally until *His daughters seek his death* (167); but this is the subtextual impulse that drives the scene on, the more energetically as it is baffled by Lear's dalliance with Edgar. Usually the two are at first forestage, for the full value of their mystery.

What is your study? (162).*

*Jorgensen suggests the stress on *your*: Lear, whose own study is unkind daughters, asks a fellow scholar about *his* specialty.

How to prevent the fiend, and to kill vermin. To avoid physical and spiritual distress; but the words still aim at Gloster, too.

Lear is both concerned with stilling the fiend in his own head and wanting to kill certain vermin; *kill, kill,* he will later cry. He draws Edgar apart to learn more. (The movement may echo earlier movements when he tried to deal privately with his daughters.) Macready whispered:

> Let me ask you one word in private (164).

Edgar nodded smilingly, and they murmured together.

This now clears the forestage for Kent and Gloster. Kent adds to the urgency of flight the element of Lear's condition in a loyal euphemism:

> His wits begin t' unsettle (166).

The strain on Gloster, that must have been expressed visually throughout the scene, now breaks out in his language. After expressing his concern for the banished Kent—may Gloster, too, make us wonder for a moment if he has guessed Kent's true identity?—he reveals his own disturbed state, reverberant of the parent-child alienation motif so pervasive now:

> Thou say'st the king grows mad; I tell thee, friend,
> I am almost mad myself. I had a son,
> Now outlaw'd from my blood; he sought my life,
> But lately, very late; I lov'd him, friend,
> No father his son dearer; true to tell thee,
> The grief hath craz'd my wits (169–174).

Gloster's agitation is such that he must pour out his anguish even to this rough fellow, whom he calls friend. His softer remorse, said here in simple, touching language, and implying evident visual anxiety, can again, if overplayed for the tempting tears, threaten to overbalance an unsentimental Lear characterization. Gloster's abruptness in his changes of verbal direction are useful both as characterization and to provide cover for Edgar's separated philosophical dialogue with Lear. Edgar may hear as far as

> ...now outlaw'd from my blood (171),

and move abruptly away. If he hears more of what had driven Gloster mad, the ambiguity of his behavior, disturbing later, emerges now.

Gloster wrenches himself again to the main business: rescuing Lear.

He would send Edgar back to the hovel, as unfit company—again, rejecting his own son; but whatever peremptory tones Gloster may use,
whatever rough gestures—even to pushing away his beggar-son?—

> In, fellow, there, into th' hovel (178),

Lear clings:

> With him;
> I will keep still with my philosopher (179–180).

Gloster finally yields—Tom may go along—but, frightened of pursuit,
pleads for silence. *No words, no words: hush* (185). Lear acquiesces: so
Gielgud, still showing his magnificent courtesy to Edgar, offered him
his arm, yet, like a child, put a finger to his lips, made a hushing sound.

But not Edgar. In spite of danger, or as if he would call danger down
on them, he sings his mad jingle. Whether Childe Rowland comes to the
dark tower (Folio) or the dark town (Quarto), the one a more male
image, the other female, darkness, again linked to uncanny secret places,
remains his destination. Does Tom look at Gloster as he smells an Englishman's blood? At Gloster, who soon will be bleeding at the eyes? Does
Gloster, as he tries hushing Tom, have any presentiment? Any further
reminder of his son?

Tom has the last word. Silent Fool is usually seen separated inexorably
from his master, following forlornly behind.

Act III, Scene v

Resistances are closely packed into this short scene's language and action.

Cornwall, who may have been roused by Edmund from sleep, begins by stipulating his planned violation of hospitality:

> I will have my revenge ere I depart his house (1).

The Bastard, showing the pious face Cornwall wants to see, empties two key words of their meaning: he fears censure because *nature* gives way to *loyalty*. Nature here seems not the goddess Edmund prays to privately, but that gentler divinity that blesses familial bonds. In fact, however, the Bastard is following his pragmatic deity; he gives way not to loyalty, but disloyalty.

Shakespeare's poor grammar obscures Cornwall's response, which seems meant to say that Gloster's *badness*, and not only Edgar's evil, provoked Edgar's attempt to kill his father. Edmund's piety pours out in further paradox characteristic of the play: *How malicious is my fortune, that I must repent to be just!* (9–10.)

The Bastard forces the damning letter on Cornwall's attention—reprising the tactic he had first used to fool Gloster—while piously bemoaning his need to do so; but a moment later, he is reminding Cornwall of how significant the letter is: *If the matter of this paper be certain, you have mighty business in hand* (15–16).

Cornwall responds with the appropriate reward: the Bastard is Earl of Gloster. Ritual enforces density: Edmund may kneel to the Duke, who, with a sword to the shoulder, confers the title. The kneeling sardonically echoes a recurrent posture in the *Lear* tapestry.

Again, this warm interior may be pierced by a faint whisper of Fool's song to the wind and rain. Told to seek Gloster, the Bastard indulges in an aside so extravagantly villainous it is absurd—absurd enough that Shakespeare carried it no further: *If I find him comforting the King, it will stuff his suspicion more fully* (19–20). Overtly, the Bastard's piety candies out again in a restatement of the nature-loyalty proposition:

229

> I will persever in
> my course of loyalty, though the conflict be
> sore between that and my blood (21–23).

The delighted Cornwall familiarly *thees* and *thous* the Bastard, offers himself paternally as a *dearer father*. Edmund keeps a straight face. To achieve another paternity may indeed be part of his design; as may be the impulse to make love to the wife of this new father; and to conspire in killing the older husband of the other sister he might wed. The Bastard's indirect destruction of his own father is not all that links him to the Oedipus story.

Act III, Scene vi

Kent says to Gloster

> The Gods reward your kindness (5).

Gloster has provided a roughly furnished place; but it is a shelter, with cushions and stools, much better than the hovel. Once more the gods will deny, or cross, a direct appeal: Gloster goes off in the darkness to blinding.

He may brush past Edgar, whose speech now reverberates motifs: *Frateretto calls me* (6), he says; and Frateretto is taken to be one of Tom's fiends, because he is in Harsnett, Shakespeare's anticlerical source, but the word echoes *brother*, too, *little brother*: who tells Tom Nero was *an angler in the Lake of Darkness* (7). Again, the dark, the illicit, with a connotation of the sexual abyss where evil is got—Nero angled in a dark and vicious place. Gloster, a prince of darkness, leaves; but Tom and Lear remain in the obscure, subterranean world from whence hidden impulses threaten chaos.

Edgar does little to relieve the agony; but his

> Pray, innocent, and beware the foul fiend (7–8)

while it may be addressed to all, or to Fool, may be as well meant for one of his rare supports to Lear, plunged in the terrible innocence of madness. Lear is a stage further into darkness: where before he misinterpreted reality, now he is visualizing unreality; hallucinating. He does not respond to cues; he pays no attention to Fool, who, now close to disappearance, if not death, tries desperately with his riddle—is a madman a yeoman or gentleman?—to recapture Lear's attention from Edgar. Lear's answer

> A King, a King! (11),

though it has mad logic—this king may be more mad than any man of lower rank—is more significantly a response to some challenge heard only in Lear's brain. The king who cannot be recognized because naked must try to declare his identity. Gielgud asserted it indignantly; the Nor-

wegian Lear straightened and flung up his hands, in a suggestion of his
Act I gestures, that would bridge this outburst to the mad assertion of
royalty in IV, vi. Here Lear may seize Fool's bauble for a sceptre, and
stare with all the remnants of his majesty. That he is a king Lear will
often, in his madness, remind the world; the very madness of his kingship will be a comment on the pretensions of royalty—no wonder *Lear*
was not staged in England when George III seemed insane. The madman
is your true king—he knows he is everything. Yet Lear does not entirely
give way, as Edgar does in pretending the conventional madman. Lear
struggles backward toward sanity, and has glimmers of it even in his
hallucinations. Then

> To have a thousand with red burning spits
> Come hizzing in upon 'em (15–16),

seems to plunge him into Tom's imagined hell. The thousand, equipped
satanically, are fellows of Tom's fiends. But that they may also be Lear's
soldiers—he will be after recruits in IV, vi, and will mime war—suggests
that men may be devils too, and *kill, kill, kill*. Lear would punish home.

The fiend pursues Edgar. We are reminded, in the Quarto, of the actuality of his hunger: to the devil in his belly, crying for food, he
must say:

> Croak not, black angel; I have no food for thee (33–34).

All four must feel starved by now and their hunger may be accentuated
by their falling on what scraps Gloster has given Kent to parcel out.
Lear would make sure that Tom gets a share.

Fool, even more jealous of his supplanter, masks his hurt in self-
hurting epigram that reflects on his own folly as well as Lear's:

> He's mad that trusts in the tameness of a wolf, a
> horse's health, a boy's love, or a whore's oath (18–19).

The man-animal imagery, linked to madness, will pervade the scene.
Brook's film externalized what the three "see": Lear sees his wicked
daughters, on trial, dissolving into the dogs; Edgar sees "his own obscure
erratic imagery, while the Fool sees nothing but the literal facts—a shed,
a cat, and a three-legged stool."

Lear assumes the topmost human role: he is the king, empowered to
judge. Mad king, mad judge. To Gielgud, the thought came suddenly,
at random, as he was swinging a stool in his hand. Cobb seemed to begin
by clowning, as if on one level of his mind he was putting on a show.
Klöpfer pensively took the stand of a copper kettle from the hearth, and

slowly balanced it on his head: the circle with its three iron legs had the mock appearance of a crown. The linkage of this hallucinating Lear with his earlier self was established by Mikhoels with other recurrent imagery: he repeated gestures of I, i, by counting imaginary courtiers with his fingers; by directing Fool to his old place; by hallucinating—with the same show of laughter and great joy—his discovery of a hiding Cordelia; by imaging his stool a throne, and climbing up on it with remembered ceremony. The irony is the greater because this king, once so gorgeously dressed, is now so storm bedraggled: thus Mikhoels' gown was gone, his doublet tangled, hardly covering his frail body; one arm was naked.

Lear's mind, following the erratic track of his internal dialogue, suddenly commands action: he will try his animal daughters, *she-foxes*. He graciously names as judges madman and fool—*learned justicer*, and *sapient sir* (though Fool may be unwilling, as with Gielgud, to share a seat with Edgar).

Whom does Edgar see standing, glaring? Lear, hallucinating the image of the beautiful Goneril he both loved and hated? Tom's fiend? Edgar connives at Lear's hallucination:

> Want'st thou eyes at trial, madam? (24–25).

Asking does she dare to be seen? Can she outstare the fiend—or Lear? Does vanity drive her to be admired even there? Or—a twist to the sight-insight motif—is she, blind, finally ready to see?

Edgar's starting snatch of song is commandeered by Fool, jealous; and Edgar retorts, in sibling rivalry: *The foul* (fool?) fiend haunts him with a nightingale's voice. Edgar is a visual image of the accumulated poverty-madness motif as he speaks comfortingly to—and often pats—the ravenous black angel in his stomach. His madness remains purposefully erratic, theatrically rich in the dark comic.

Kent cannot stay Lear's confusion, though throughout he tries valiantly, tenderly. Untrue to his promise, he is least unmannerly when Lear is mad. From speechlessness, Lear turns to command. He prepares the trial with great dignity, urging Fool, Kent, and near-naked Tom, *Thou robed man of justice* (37)—the clothes motif inverted—to their places. Gielgud solemnly set their stools, and bowed grandly. Now these four, playing their troubled roles—king become mad beggar, Edgar become pretended mad beggar, Kent become rough Caius (though his diction now seems more Kent again), Fool become a dying victim of his folly of loyalty—try the daughters.

Lear's hallucinations have a terrible reality in the theatre. As

Granville-Barker suggested, equal value must be given to the real and imagined characters. An actor like Scofield does in fact see what is not there so intensely that he makes an audience see it. His three companions almost see it; their jests are partly defenses. An uncanny air touches all their acts and sounds: thus Edgar's simple song about the shepherd carries implicit warning: an alarm must be sounded, if lambs are to be saved. His

> Purr, the cat is grey (46)

sustains mystery: he does not say *purr*, but purrs, evoking the image of a witch's familiar, the gray beast. It may indeed, as Kittredge suggests, evoke the old proverb—or its archetypal mood: When candles be out (at night) all cats are gray.

In this atmosphere at once uncanny and terribly real, Lear formally arraigns Goneril. He swears an oath—a false one—reprising his earlier oaths, back to I, i. His manner depends on the state of his battle with madness. A Russian actor, Serge Zakariadze (1909–1971), made the daughters dolls: he picked them out of the air, as if dangling puppets, and presented them to the judges. When Minotis played Lear, he, Fool and Edgar moved about the imaginary daughters in a kind of ritualistic rhythm, and the lights spun with them: "a flame enveloping the hurricane whirl of the three madmen," Minotis said. Mikhoels echoed his I, iv gesture of trying to see Goneril plain; his hand swept across his eyes, as brushing a film away. Carnovsky, in and out of hallucination, began with some assurance, his hand raised to swear truth:

> I here take my oath ... she ... (47–48),

then became bewildered, his mind sought for the next words through a long pause, as he finished haltingly

> kick'd the poor King her father (49)

and sat sadly down. When Fool beckoned the stool to approach, Carnovsky's affirmation was still self-pitying; Gielgud—he turned topsy-turvy his earlier fear of her with command: *Is your name Goneril?* (50) —deep in hallucination, was judicially reasonable:

> She cannot deny it (51).

Central to the design is Lear's compulsion to self-attack; he will "see" the painful images his own mind creates and compels him to see.

Fool's attempt to jest Lear back to sanity,

> Cry you mercy, I took you for a joint-stool (52)

again fails. Lear is intent on accusing Regan: *here's another*. But a stool moves, is moved; or the drama in Lear's mind itself evokes a new punishing pattern: his daughter grieves him by escaping his punishing of her. His impulse is to war, killing; he scents corruption—all omens of his descent to IV, vi. Any possibility that Lear might be playing a game in this trial scene seems destroyed by his violent anxiety now:

> Stop her there!
> Arms, arms, sword, fire! Corruption in the place!
> False justicer, why hast thou let her 'scape? (54–56).

Gielgud, a moment before a commanding chief magistrate, watched his prey slip through his fingers, and was suddenly shrunken, trembling, a childlike old man. He cried out wildly. Carnovsky's transition—and Zakariadze's—was of a man seeing something disappear before his eyes; he saw Regan, and suddenly he was looking into emptiness—the actor's art made both unrealities tangible. Carnovsky wrung his hands with anxiety at what his mind projected. Salvini, the more active Lear, rushed down toward the footlights, clutching emptily at nothing, trying himself to arrest the fugitive; he blamed Fool—as false justicer—for the flight. This was a minor peak in Salvini's characterization of waning strength: his energy would rise again, but the bursts were on a descending scale. Whatever early comfort this punitive fantasy gave his Lear would not come again.

The extent of Lear's anxiety is perhaps reflected less in Kent's *O pity!* (58), and his urging of Lear—by now with unintentional irony—to resume his boasted patience, than in Poor Tom's stereotype cry,

> Bless thy five wits! (57)

because here said, perhaps for the first time, sincerely. At last Edgar will give Lear some sympathy and support. His tears mar his counterfeiting. For the first time, he is moved by someone else's plight. He says what he feels: *Edgar he something is*. This is a major pivot in his characterization: he will not be wholly merciful yet, he will be cruel even when he is kind—but he has begun to have compassion.

Lear needs it. He is deep in hallucinatory self-pity. The new scene may seem to change before his staring eyes, or his eyes shift to phantasmagoria; the design requires that the image his mind commands him to experience is still persecution, despair. He now affects the archetypal figure of the exiled beggar-king forgotten by his palace hounds: *See*, he says, *they bark at me: Tray, Blanch, and*—building to the third, the meaningful one of the triad, with the loved name—even *Sweetheart*

(63). Gielgud broke down, wept hysterically, in Kent's arms, in utter misery.

The association returned Mikhoels to awareness of his own animal nature, and he was barking again, Tom joining in.

Again, if the sound of pursuing hounds is sensed as accompanying the persistent flight imagery, this recurrence has multiple reverberations . . . *all are fled* (73). If Tom is still conspiring with Lear's madness, he is now also developing a supportive mood—he makes to *throw his head* at Lear's imagined persecutors (Booth's Edgar threw his straw hat). His charm against them is a dwindling catalogue of animals, and reflects a desperation: his pretense as Tom is running down, his horn is going dry. That also he may literally have no more liquor to drink, that he is being forced to confront sober reality, may be significant for a characterization moving from early dissipation toward ambiguous compassion.

Lear's struggle against madness nerves his next speech:

> Then let them anatomize Regan, see what breeds
> about her heart (77–78).

This is mad, but metaphor, too. Lear, now wrenched free momentarily from hallucination, could here be poet as well as lunatic, or some of both. The repressed urge to invade the female body he has intimated when evidently rational; again the irony is that he is only mad in context—as visual imagery normally makes clear. Mikhoels was reminded of his clash with Regan—his hand suddenly lashed out at Fool, striking-stroking him in the same way. Most theatre Lears act out dissection: plunging the hand in the imaginary body, holding up the heart, striking it with the imagined knife (Mikhoels' Edgar held his hand from stabbing), finding hardness (Gielgud's hand felt the unyielding surface of the stool he held), finding it perhaps too hard for a knife to enter. All these gestures of dissection and penetration have multiple implications: the grotesque is set off against the eminently reasonable.

> Is there any cause in nature that make these hard
> hearts? (78–79.)

This is a flare of energy, as well as insight; a flare ominous of the collapse to come—Carnovsky whimpered the line. Newly engulfing irrationality unsteadies Lear. To Edgar:

> You, sir, I entertain for one of my hundred; only I do not like the fashion
> of your garments: you will say they are Persian; but let them be chang'd
> (80–83).

If Edgar had indeed been one of his knights, the moment has an extra poignancy; Lear now knights Edgar a second time, in a regal gesture made absurd only by the context; Lear's newfound compassion for the poor may invest it. In the previous scene Cornwall named Edmund an earl in an echo of this visual ceremony; the irony intensifies because there the costuming signaled splendor, here a king of rags knights a mad beggar, and quibbles inversely over his "Persian" elegance. Is war meant to be in Lear's mind here, as it was in Cornwall's? *Kill, kill, kill?*

Carnovsky started to rip off Tom's poor garment—he felt the line could explode as a cry of sudden rage, far out of proportion—but was too tired to finish. Similarly, Cobb reached out to touch his new knight, but missed him; Edgar had to catch the limp arm in his hand. Gielgud gestured with exhausted courtesy, a king nerving himself to complete a royal task. Now all reserve dissipates; Lear merely submits when Kent leads him gently to the cushions. He lies down as if on a canopied bed, and king becomes almost child again, playing a child's game:

> Make no noise, make no noise; draw the curtains (85–86).

Gielgud feebly closed imaginary drapes—Edgar and Fool have also mimed doing it for Lear—and then peered through them for his *so, so.* Carnovsky, cautious, acquiescent, very tired, collapsed to rest. Cobb rested his head on Fool's lap, looked vaguely at the figures surrounding him before closing his eyes to sleep. Dunn's Lear clapped hands to ears, as if all sound were terribly painful, and screamed the words. Macready let the speech run off into babble; but the last line, that Carnovsky spoke in a long, tired sigh,

> We'll go to supper i' th' morning (86–87),

has some of Fool's mad grace; like the rest of this scene's ending, it prepares for Lear's next fey appearance, when he will himself assume the riddling, paradoxical style of the vanished Fool. It is itself a kind of fool's farewell to Fool, and Lear may hold him, say it directly to him.

Fool signals his disappearance in this late center of the play with his own riddle:

> And I'll go to bed at noon (88).

There is no rest for the weary. Pursuit threatens, in Gloster's hurried entrance from the storm, but even more in the *high noises* Edgar will mark: perhaps only the symbolic discords of the great, but also the noises of hounds on the scent? of armed men again hunting fugitives? Gloster is as usual on the gad: Lear's murder is plotted, even a half-hour's delay means his death, the death of all his followers, hurry, hurry to Dover. This urgency presses against another almost as great: Lear's wits are gone, Kent says, sleep and rest are his chance for healing, otherwise—? The conflicting urgencies create tension that must sustain the image of Lear's precarious safety and sanity through his long absence to IV, vi.

Gloster overrides Kent: Lear must be troubled, if he is to live. The drop of a convenient forestage curtain, as with Gielgud, conveniently avoids transferring Lear to a litter, and carrying him off; but this diminishes the aura of danger in the flight motif. For practicality, the cushions Lear sleeps on may cover, be part of the litter used to transport him; the carrying off keeps the touching image of the utterly exhausted old man sleeping through the bustle of escape: so, as he was borne off, Macready's fingers were seen to relax, and straw fall from them; so Forrest could be heard *snoring*—so impressively no laughs came.

Saved, too, is the image of the bedraggled Fool, almost too weary to rise, following after at Kent's command, lending a useless, dying hand to the portage, or, unable, carried out or left behind. Badel's final imagery here—he remembered Gielgud suggesting it—was suddenly to find himself alone on the stage, the others all gone; and like a lost, frightened dog to look about for the scent, and cry "Nuncle Lear, Nuncle Lear" to the emptiness.

Like Lear, Fool has been worn by the exile, and the storm; unless his disappearance now portends mystery, the noontime bed will certainly be a grave; he has been declining to it through the cold he hates so much, the savaging storm, the fear of pursuit, the flight, the estrangement from Lear. In the theatre, young Fools are likely to be dying of strain and exposure, older Fools of weary age, both of too much mortality.

Edgar, left alone, contemplates his earned insight; but still a modified insight. He has less compassion for Lear than gratitude: seeing another's misery has lessened his own.

> But then the mind much sufferance doth o'erskip,
> When grief hath mates, and bearing fellowship.
> How light and portable my pain seems now,
> When that which makes me bend makes the king bow;
> He childed as I father'd! (109–113.)

The last equates Lear's evil children with Edgar's cruel father; but it bears the prophetic implication, too, that Lear regresses to childhood as Edgar moves toward maturity, toward fathering his own father. Edgar is still mainly concerned with his own fate, his return to his rightful place; and, as pursuit nears, he goes stealthily back into the dark:

Lurk, lurk (118).

Most modern productions break the play in half after the next scene; some place the intermission here, as in Jan Bull's Norwegian Lear, where the iron curtain that lifted to open the play came down even more smudged and rotted, spotted with yellowing implications of insanity and disease. The storm sounds and music that opened Bull's next act would be pervaded again by gossiping whispers of the chorus.

Act III, Scene vii

Immediate preparations for war charge the opening of this scene, and the next act. Noises are high. Cornwall is on the gad: Albany must be warned urgently to arm, festinately. Communication between allies must be swift. The traitor Gloster must be caught, at once. Regan would hang Gloster, Goneril blind him: Cornwall reserves to himself the decision—though he will, in fact, do what his strong-minded sister-in-law says. There is an air of triumph, command; the mood of the dominants, emerging here, threatens to obliterate the tonic.

New magnificence ornaments the scene. Edmund is dressed grandly as the Earl of Gloster he intended to be; he will aim higher, to the crown itself. His would-be consorts, Regan and Goneril, now frankly assume the trappings of majesty: with the planned death of Lear, nothing now but their own dying can keep them from playing—and now dressing—competing queens. This rivalry is one intensification of the division between them; another now emerges: Goneril is to go off alone with the splendid new earl, and Regan cares enough to notice and recall later how they are eyeing each other. They were so absorbed, in the Cobb *Lear*, that an angry Cornwall had to shout, meaningfully, *Farewell* to get Edmund's attention, and to urge him to hurry: *Farewell, my lord of Gloster!* (13.)

Regan does not speak words, listens in pregnant silence to Goneril's triumphant *Farewell, sweet Lord, and sister* (21) as she makes off with Edmund. This rising dissonance between the sisters will importantly sustain the tension of the next two acts.

The mood of haste, intensified by Cornwall's prodding of Edmund, is further nerved by more flight and pursuit imagery: the hasty entrance of Oswald, the news of thirty-odd knights, *hot questrists* racing toward Dover to join other well-armed friends in support of Lear; the urgent, repeated order—the "fiery" Cornwall often repeats commands—to recapture Gloster; the pressed search for the old earl. The questrist knights do not materialize—except as they may appear in the war supporting Lear—but they serve here to sharpen the sense of imminent conflict, and to exacerbate Cornwall as he faces Gloster.

Now a new—without the *form of justice*—trial: a reverse mirroring of III, vi, for here the young woman, Regan, indicts the old man. At last Shakespeare allows a full revelation of the evil in Regan's design: she who spoke so tenderly to Gloster about the "treachery" of a son, will now with warp'd looks revile him, pluck his beard, in some theatre versions offer other indignities—throw his torn hair back in his eyes, spit at him, strike him across the face. The shock is the greater when Regan is— or is seen as—an outwardly beautiful woman whose visual facade, too, suddenly cracks, as her cruel sensuality develops. In Regan's design is new motivation for cruelty: her growing antagonism toward Goneril, her irritation at Goneril's grand exit with Edmund. She is provoked to her worst.

The seizing and blinding of Gloster is savage. A Japanese Cornwall began by brutally knocking him to the ground. *Bind fast his corky arms* (29), Cornwall says, and at the merest delay characteristically repeats: *Bind him, I say* (32). Regan, intense: *Hard, hard* (32). Gloster's subservient social mask: *Good my friends . . . guests . . . friends* (30–31) finally drops; he retorts. The clash builds, in language of war, to staccato stichomythia. Syntax subordinates to passion: Cornwall and Regan hurl questions, *thou* him insultingly, the language tightens to single words, phrases. The question, *To whose hands have you sent the lunatic king?*, offends Gloster, he shuts his lips against their *Speak*. They force an answer.

> Cunning.
> And false.
> Where hast thou sent the King?
> To Dover.
> Wherefore to Dover? Wast thou not charg'd at peril—
> Wherefore to Dover? Let him answer that.
> I am tied to th' stake, and I must stand the course.
> Wherefore to Dover? (49–54.)

The verbal assaults accompany visual imagery. Cornwall threatens Gloster physically, as with a knife at his throat; Regan slaps him, pulls his head back by the hair. Gloster's major answer merges the fury of unleashed resentment with his customary compassion; the hard k's and explosive b's are softened by the h's:

> Yet, poor old heart, he holp the heavens to rain (61).

The sight motif, so foreboding here, echoes in word and sound: *see thy cruel nails* (55) . . . *his poor old eyes* (56) . . . *the sea* (58) . . . *I shall see / The winged vengeance* (64–65). *See* Gloster shall never, as Cornwall

says—certainly never divine revenge. Gloster is as wrong about his gods
as Lear. His gods intervene as little. His cry, as an eye is gouged out,

> Give me some help! O cruel! O you gods! (69)

is finally, if ambiguously, a cry of the forsaken: Why hast thou . . . ?
Gloster's physical anguish—the arched body, the cry from the vitals, the
despair—must be terrible, only less terrible will be the second eye's loss.

Cornwall's sadism, he had said in reverberant imagery, was not fit for
Edmund's beholding. Not for any beholding, many critics and producers of the play have thought. Too cruel to see—although seeing is the
very point of it. Samuel Johnson grieved for Shakespeare's excess, could
not "apologize" for the "extrusion"; the nineteenth century theatre preferred to delete it. That Gloster should be blinded is well enough accepted, often on the moral notion that, in Heilman's words, "perhaps the
final guarantee of his insight is his loss of outward sight." But this very
much oversimplifies the character's design. Gloster's blinding urges him
at first only to suicide, and such insight as he will attain is precarious and
intermittent. He stumbles when he is blind, too. There was visual irony
in the Norwegian scene when sudden flashes of blinding light accompanied the plucking out of each eye. In this play, sight and insight are as
ambiguous as all other aspects of life: nothing is guaranteed, nothing but
pain and death.

Cornwall's animal savagery, besides sustaining the pervasive ambiguity of the sight motif, serves a significant dramatic function. A naive
spectator at *Lear* confronts unexpectedly, and with brutal shock, an
uncompromising violence. Until now, the working out of the archetypal myth might still have been hoped for: the good child might still
rescue the troubled old father before real harm might come. In *Lear*,
the only actual violence has been verbal, emotional, or theatrical—as in
the pursuit of fugitives, or in Lear's madness; or, as in the Kent-Oswald
duel, semi-comic, abortive. Now there can be no easy, bloodless solution
any more—as there could not be, for instance, after Polonius' death, or
Duncan's, or Roderigo's. Lear is in mortal danger; the arbitrement is like
to be very bloody.*

So the cruelty—Gloster uses the root word three times—is inexorable.
An almost intolerable visual blow is intended. From bleeding sockets the
eyes are torn out—Antoine used blobs of *vile jelly* indeed to suggest the
crushed organs that Cornwall stamped upon. At Colorado, Cornwall
gave the plucked eye to Regan, and she smashed it in her clapped hands.

---

*One naive spectator's comment was, I think, worthy of the play's dialectic:
"Gloster's blinding was an eye opener."

At the Porter *Lear* at Stratford, I saw a large, muscular man faint at this scene, and have to be carried out. There is no return now.

In the theatre, Gloster is often strapped to his chair for the first gouging with his back to the audience, the angry faces of Cornwall and Regan showing, but it has also been done face forward, front and center. Usually a thumb gouges out the eye—Orson Welles closed up for this on television, made it grand-guignol. Rumelin saw a chair leg used for the blinding. Directors have sometimes taken their cue from Cornwall's

> Upon these eyes of thine I'll set my foot (67)

and staged the assault on a Gloster recumbent—Brook gave Cornwall golden spurs, and one roweled out the eye.

Regan urges full blinding, Cornwall—the repeater—savaging on:

> If you see vengeance ... (71).

The good servant intervenes. Cornwall calls him what he called—will call—Gloster: *villain*. A subtle linking of clash of class with character, extended when the servant becomes *slave*. The motif is stipulated at Regan's *A peasant stand up thus!* (79.) The action is as swift as the lines: Servant mortally wounds Cornwall, Regan kills servant, "slave"—(from behind, the Quarto specifies). She may take a dagger or sword from someone; Kozintsev thought she kept one in her dress. The servant, dying, to Gloster, in sight imagery:

> My Lord, you have one eye left
> To see some mischief on him (80–81)

Cornwall, also dying, reprises his *see shalt thou never* theme, and gouges out the other poor eye. Wounded as he is, this is a last effort: he must stagger back to do the thing—Gielgud's Cornwall crawled. A Polish Regan gave Cornwall a hairpin to strike with. Both symbolically and physically this completion of the blinding intensifies Gloster's anguish, lifts the scene pitch higher.

The great rush of action pauses for a moment, but its power persists. Bleeding Gloster calls on Edmund, learns from Regan—sometimes screaming, or whispering—of his villainy, cries pathetically of the wrong to Edgar (though Gloster does not—ever—curse the bastard as he cursed the legitimate).

> Kind Gods, forgive me that, and prosper him! (91.)

There is no forgiveness. Regan, ordering him cast out, perhaps stripping him of his earl's robes, evokes the stench image:

> ... let him smell
> His way to Dover 92–93).

Still, in the subsiding action, the power persists. The measured unbind-ing of Gloster; his painful rising to his feet; the full sight of his bloodied eyes; his unseeing stumbling, even crawling; all this, often acted in dead silence, provides one of the fiercest moments of the play.

Neither Folio nor Quarto instructs Regan to help Cornwall out, as he bleeds apace: her design justifies the chilling response seen in the Laugh-ton *Lear*: the terror and pain in Cornwall's *Give me your arm* (97) told how mortal his wound was; but, her mind on Edmund, she ignored him, swept boldly past and out without so much as a glance. He staggered back, groping for support; no one moved to help.

Much is made by redemptionists of the brief interlude of kindness among the servants, as they plan an unction for Gloster's bleeding eyes, and to get Poor Tom to lead him: "common humanity in its bravery and charity with its simple, stumbling talk." But these servants are of the same mixed cloth as the rest: only one intervened for Gloster, and he died for his decency; now the others help when it is safe to do so. Their language is as conditional as their acts, pivoting on *ifs*: *if this man come to good* (99) . . . *if she live long* (99). Yet they do help; and there was calculation in Brook's version which, like the Quarto, cut the kindly talk. The scene—as it often is—was set to precede the intermission. Glos-ter, trying to feel his way, a ragged cloth thrown over his head, stumbled into callous servants who buffeted and jostled him. With houselights al-ready up, the audience, forced to participate in wasteland, sat in the full glare as Gloster, trailing bandages, wandered upstage and out, a broken figure in a cruel, heedless world. Very powerful, but as one-sided as sentimentalism. In the center of the dominant mood, the playwright planted countering notes that promise, if not a return to the tonic, a hint that the tonic may exist. Only a hint, as Gloster is thrust out of doors, to join the homeless, the unsheltered.

Act IV, Scene i

Edgar is in flight again—still. Armed manhunters perhaps filter through the shadows, searching for the fugitive prizes. Any sound threatens, any movement sends Edgar scurrying for concealment. It is against this apprehension that he cries *yet*:

> Yet better thus, and known to be contemn'd,
> Than, still contemn'd and flatter'd to be worst (1-2).

Folio puts a comma before *to be worst*: better consciously despised and be worst than fooled by flattery, to be ignorant of being worst. Pope's period after *flattered* clarifies—but perhaps loses meaningful ambiguity, as in Quarto's subtler punctuation, above: worst is to feel flattered at being worst. Edgar has preened himself on degradation as Edmund has on topping; is this a further glimmer, building on Edgar's vision at the end of III, vi, of re-ascension? To be nothing—the lowest—is no longer base, but rather *a* base—a bottom from which to rise. Now emerges, in this humorless soliloquizer, almost a touch of exultant humor, hope:

> The worst returns to laughter (6).

Dashed, as always, by the next movement: an awful sight approaches. Again, Shakespeare's simple use of entrance for suspense. Edgar, frightened by the sound of men, starts to fly, looks off:

> But who comes here? (9.)

And well before the appearance, the terror of it writes on Edgar's face. Peripety:

> World, world, O world!
> But that thy strange mutations make us hate thee,
> Life would not yield to age (10-12).

Meaning: "Except for painful circumstances, we would be always young, never wish to die"? Or: "We are reconciled to age so as to die sooner"? But perhaps most likely, in Edgar's angry mood, "Our very hate of the fickle world is what keeps us alive." Edgar hates well.

What appears terrifies: not only Gloster's patched, bloody eyes, but his inner torment, externalized as he tries to wrench free from his patient, peasant guide—another good servant—whose first line protests Gloster's pulling away:

> O my good Lord! (12.)

Gloster's goodness glimmers through his torturing pain and misery: beyond his suicidal impulse, his need to be alone and grieve, he wants no harm for the old guide. His tones see-saw from frustrated anger, *Away, get thee away* (15), to the kinder, *good friend, be gone* (15). The hard *g* of *get* softens in the *good*; the opposites merge in *Thy comforts can do me no good at all* (16).

Once more Gloster must not be made to appear too kind and sympathetic in his suffering, lest he unbalance the equation with a more sinewy Lear; his compassion is always tinged with self-pity, shadowed by his suicidal despair.

His complexity is crucial now because it must reciprocate with Edgar's ambiguous impulses. Those who see Edgar simply a noble and good son may miss the evident cruelty of his behavior. His resistance to insight is emphasized by the imagery, as well as the naked appeal, of Gloster's response to Old Man's solicitous hanging on:

> Old Man: You cannot see your way.
> Gloster: I have no way, and therefore want no eyes;
>   I stumbled when I saw (17–19).

This has meaning, not only for himself but also for Edgar. So also:

> Our means secure us, and our mere defects
> Prove our commodities (20–21).

The "see better" imagery, linked to an echo of the cannibal, seems aimed directly at Edgar:

> Oh! dear son Edgar,
> The food of thy abused father's wrath;
> Might I but live to see thee in my touch,
> I'd say I had eyes again (21–24).

Does Edgar hear? And therefore see? A concern for emphasizing Edgar's "goodness" may move a producer—or a visualizing critic—to protect Edgar from hearing and knowing his exoneration. But such knowing would not alter Edgar's behavior, as it will not on Dover cliff. The speech is crucial: because only here does Gloster make clear that he has been *abused* (literally; also "deceived"), so Edgar can perceive Edmund's villainy. Probably it is this perception that causes some shock to Edgar, some movement, or sound, provoking Old Man's fear, and perhaps his move toward flight, and the recurrent, anxious identity question,

> How now! Who's there? (24.)

But Edgar's response, aside, is still entirely ego-centered, self-pitying, unseeing:

> Edgar: I am worse than e'er I was.
> Old Man: 'Tis poor Mad Tom.
> Edgar: And worse I may be yet; the worst is not
>   So long as we can say "This is the worst (26–28).

Meaning not only: "as long as I can say it, things could be worse," but also, in this context, "things will be." He goes forward, hand outstretched—for alms, for compassion.

Language is dense and reverberative. Old Man, mirroring the Lear image, describes Edgar: *Madman and beggar too* (30). Gloster's reply

> He has some reason, else he could not beg (31)

suggests not only that a beggar must be minimally rational but also have some motive, some need. The concern for the poor and for social justice that Swinburne perceived in *Lear* informs Gloster's design here. It is linked with man's capacity to love, and also with his animality: Gloster recalls the last night's beggar, who made him think both of man his son, and man the worm—the very least animal.

His bitter

> As flies to wanton boys, are we to th' Gods;
> They kill us for their sport (36–37)

has sometimes been taken for the play's theme. No; it is part of the zigzag of Gloster's design: he is blaming the Gods now for all that man the worm does to his kind. This is not insight but inblindness; unseeing has not helped. About the gods it says: if they exist and have power, then indeed the man-worm's case is desperate.

But it needs no gods to explain casual cruelty: Gloster has himself been a "wanton boy"; Edmund, too; Edgar's design, that included exacerbating Lear's madness, now compels an option of kindness or hurt, and the choice is both—Edgar, too, will be sometime a wanton boy. There is a kind of compulsion in it:

> Bad is the trade that must play the fool to sorrow
> Ang'ring itself and others (38–39).

Bad indeed—in a multiple sense: unpleasant, difficult, but also cruel, teasing, deceiving, even evil—one allusion is certainly to the wanton gods, as well as to men. Why fool—play fool—not with wise foolery as Fool did, but with cruel deception? Why play wanton boy? The *Lear* equation is subtly, glancingly mirrored: where the bad children made a show of giving love, Fool made a show of withholding it, and so did Cordelia—except that on meeting her beaten father, she alone will offer love unstintingly. But not Edgar.

Why does Edgar withhold love, deny his identity, play fool, deprive Gloster of his dream of seeing Edgar in his touch? Blaming himself later —he is a steadfast blamer—Edgar will call it what it obviously is and much more: a fault. For what motive? Even if he has not heard Gloster's cry of love for him, Gloster's power to pursue is obviously gone, Edgar need fear him no more. Then why withhold? Revenge? Punishment? Sullenness? The man-worm's god-like cruelty? Edgar's "fooling" is masochistic as well as sadistic—*ang'ring itself and others*. Something of the design of Edgar's complex ambivalence, that will lead him while "nursing" his father to torture him—and himself—will show in his physical imagery, and especially now. Naive spectators were divided in their expectations: will he take his revenge on his father? Or will he offer comfort by revealing himself? He remains ambiguous, presents Mad Tom.

Tom acts mad, perhaps must be it a little. "I think we are really meant to doubt his sanity," Empson suggests. Probably we never believe him mad, as Lear is mad; but the shock is severe, and even more severe is the inner struggle. This now externalizes: in action that Gloster cannot see, Edgar has shown in the theatre the pain of his compassion. He may not at first be able to look in the bleeding sockets, may pass his fingers before them to make sure Gloster cannot see. From a feeling that is part revulsion, part recrimination, part aching sympathy he may extend a sheltering hand that does not touch. When he touches, it may be as in the Cobb *Lear*, as of a child coming suddenly up behind, a quick nudge, then away. *Alack, sir! he is mad* (45), Old Man must explain.

Old Man continues a foil for Gloster's anguished, erratic mood. *Get thee away* (41), Gloster has said again, then checked himself, asked for clothes to accommodate the *naked* Tom (the adjective, sounded three times, asserts poverty, man's condition, Edgar's state, the stripped son) who will lead him. He overrules Old Man's objections in echoing imagery:

> 'Tis the times' plague, when madmen lead the blind (46).

Then, the customary command:

> Do as I bid thee ... (47)

checked again, with the kinder

> ... or rather do thy pleasure (47).

Finally, firmly, a touch of the old arrogance again,

> Above the rest, be gone (48).

When Gloster and Edgar are alone, Edgar's antagonism-compassion builds to explosion. He cannot daub it further—disguise, plaster on a false coat, act—and yet (compulsively?) he *must*. But his old song is made to fit new reality:

> Bless thy sweet eyes, they bleed (53).

There is still external danger—Old Man has said bravely that he will bring clothes *Come on't what will* (50)—and Tom may already be trying to drag the blind, way-feeling Gloster out. The rising tension, inner and outer, mounts to a powerfully reverberative outbreak of Tom's madness. *Poor Tom hath been scar'd out of his good wits* (56) is true enough; and his benediction seems for himself: *bless thee, good man's son, from the foul fiend!* (57.) Harsnett's five devils that have inhabited Tom are harnessed to an old theme: thou-shalt-nots, against murder, stealing, and especially adultery. *Mopping and mowing* may well imply sexuality, *lust* certainly does, and the adultery motif swells to the possessing of chambermaids and waiting women. Shakespeare thus uses Harsnett to confirm Edgar's obsession with the sexual, and especially here, in the face of the primal adulterer, prince of the dark place: was it then a maid, or a waiting woman, with whom Gloster sported to make Edmund? Are we to sense that this is why Tom-Edgar fondles this sin?

It may touch Gloster now on a raw memory, force an anguish greater than his physical wounding, for Tom's dialectic swings quickly now from hurt to compassion:

> So, bless thee, master! (63.)

and he briefly gives up taunting for care.

Gloster rides his own see-saw, between self-pity and compassion. He forces money on Tom—again, ironically, being generous to a banished son—and so continues to strip himself: like Edgar, he will see himself the lowest, nothing, even lower than Tom.

> ... that I am wretched
> Makes thee the happier (65–66).

Then, with characteristic reversal, calling on the gods who sported with him, he reinvokes the social justice motif—the dream of bringing into balance the world's *more-less* dialectic—reprising the anal and perception imagery of Lear's prayer:

> Let the superfluous and lust-dieted man,
> That slaves your ordinance, that will not see
> Because he does not feel, feel your power quickly;
> So distribution should undo excess,
> And each man have enough (67–71).

Gloster, a lust-dieted man who did not see because he could not feel, prepares to purge himself. He reveals his purpose to Tom. Surely he wants leading to Dover to go to his king? No . . . where Lear would never yield, Gloster surrenders readily: led to his brink, he will embrace capitulation, death.

A naive spectator expects Edgar to respond to his father's suicidal wish with disclosure, assurance, love. With—in—a world of ambiguity and ambivalence, Edgar comes to his decision:

> Give me thy arm:
> Poor Tom shall lead thee (78–79).

He guides his stumbling father, sometimes gently, compassionately, sometimes hauling him along in flight, but always cautiously, for armed men still search this world for fugitives, and their shadows may even be seen. Gloster stumbles after—toward what goal, the naive spectator wonders. Toward Dover? Suicide?

Act IV, Scene ii

The residual sense of war and manhunt becomes visual in the splendid presence of Goneril and the Bastard. These two will now be the prime movers of the assault on Lear and the throne; they will sound the rising dominant tones that power the disequilibrium of the play until Lear's return.

Compelling in their themes is the sexual note, sometimes latent and tenuous, sometimes urgent, that flows toward Lear's mad IV, vi climax. This sexuality, in the persons of Edmund, Goneril, and Regan, has sometimes, by moralist critics, been equated with simple lust, as if these depraved creatures could only love obscenely. But this again oversimplifies Shakespeare's complex designs. He takes care to stipulate that these "villains" have grace and beauty; and he gives them worthy language. Goneril, embracing Edmund, as she welcomes him to her castle—perhaps so warmly partly because Albany has not come to meet her?—earns as much dignity for her passion as for her aggression. She is no Cordelia, to love tenderly; but she is designed to care for Edmund intensely. In her fashion, she gives him all—she will take seriously his bravura, *Yours in the ranks of death* (24), and march with him there. To see her as simply lascivious or serpentine is another way of reducing the whole *Lear* equation to a morality. Goneril's passion, like her ambition, is oversize, Lear-size; she would be a queen with a king of her choice. She has some of the stature of Lady Macbeth—whose love was not necessarily lust because she was an accomplice to murder. Goneril's emerging individuality, establishing a line of action not solely dependent on Lear's fate, is important in sustaining the anti-tonic notes of this fourth act. *Lear* is thought of as having plot and subplot; in fact another plot begins to develop here—the Goneril-Regan, Edmund-Albany complication—to intensify the dialectic of the action. These four drive hard toward their own tragic denouement, and none with more force than Goneril. Powerful and passionate, she yet has touches of grace and humor: a character designed to say, as she does, such lines as *Oh! the difference of man and man* (26) has a claim on the audience's humor and sympathy, as well as its fear.

251

The Bastard's motif carries its own polyphonic tensions. He has been interested—expedient?—enough to draw *oeillades* from Goneril in public; the Gloster sensuality may impel him as much as ambition to couple with Goneril, and both motives may show as the two embrace now, revealing a relationship that already has considerable history.

Edmund's contrast to Albany is stipulated visually, economically. Handsome Edmund's arms around Goneril are masculine, assured, where paler Albany has been civilized, intellectual, tentative. (In a 1970 Polish *Lear*, a passionate Edmund tore at her dress, uncovering her breast.) Another contrast, between the early Albany and the new one, is stipulated verbally, interpolating the long gap between I, iv and this scene: bewildered Oswald suggests the extremes of this man never *so chang'd*, in dialectical terms that reflect the play's polarities. Values are, in a clothes image, *wrong side out*: Albany can be calm at the invasion of a foreign army, unpleased to see Goneril—*the worse*; shocked at the *loyalty* of Edmund's betrayal of Gloster; offended by what he should like.

Goneril is reminded of Albany's indecision, his meekness, his femininity:

> I must change arms at home, and give the distaff
> Into my husband's hands (17–18).

No shallow, lascivious slut says the lines that incite the Bastard to vast ambition—and passion; sinister as their import is, they are worthy of Lady Macbeth:

> ere long you are like to hear,
> If you dare venture in your own behalf,
> A mistress's command. Wear this; spare speech ... (19–21).

She gives him a favor—Gielgud's Goneril a ring, but more often, and more effectively in the theatre, a scarf of some kind, that will function as a visual image later. Goneril reaches to embrace him. Cobb's Goneril linked Edmund to her in her extended necklace:

> Decline your head: this kiss, if it durst speak,
> Would stretch thy spirits up into the air.
> Conceive, and fare thee well (22–24).

There are sexual reverberations in *stretch thy spirits* and *conceive*; but it is a grand speech, and Edmund answers grandly, prophetically, the familiar sexual pun enriching the panache:

> Yours in the ranks of death (25).

"Falsely chivalrous," Granville-Barker says. But this assumes a Goneril so obtuse, or perhaps besotted by attentions from this handsome—younger?—man that she is blinded to obvious dissimulation. Part of the Bastard's design is the chameleon quality of seeming sincerely what people in power want him to be. He will wear Goneril's favor proudly. Shrewd Goneril believes in him:

> My most dear Gloster! (25.)

Again, her tribute, as he departs,

> Oh! the difference of man and man (26)

is heartfelt, and often evokes sympathetic audience laughter. The naive spectator does not yet know of, or even suspect, Edmund's attachment to Regan; Edmund does not yet know of it himself, unless a hint came when she bandaged his arm; he seems now, whatever else his capacity, a well-matched lover for Goneril. *Her* woman's services are due such a man.

Not so Albany. Against Goneril's fire and strength, he has seemed, indeed, a usurper of her bed, her body. If not the fool she calls him now (and twice more in the scene), yet he has been without force or even forthrightness: Lear's knight had felt (I, iv) the coolness in the Duke as well as Goneril. Lear acknowledged this, and the memory of it urges him, in IV, vi, to dream of stealing upon his sons-in-law to kill, kill, kill. Albany clearly does not satisfy Goneril maritally: now she can hardly bear his touch. Carnovsky in his notes wondered, "Albany cold to Goneril? Not sexually roused? Part Puritan? Is she too hot for him?" So far, only a misleading outline of Albany's milder side has appeared; now the dialectic of the design, the polyphony, the moulding and shading are foreshadowed.

Goneril tenses to meet him, may again pointedly exclude him as she confers with Oswald—whose shock at Albany's change has warned of conflict. The spectators' eyes swivel to Albany's entrance, the interpolation is complete, confrontation is ripe. Goneril's ironic

> I have been worth the whistle (29)

evokes an animal image, as it rebukes him for not meeting her—does she still hope for a passion from him? But Albany is indeed in a stern Puritan mood, his sermon is prophetic: disbranch unnaturally from the material sap and you wither, come to deadly use. No hint of love, but an ironic echo of what Gloster and Lear have done—disbranched children. Goneril finds the text foolish, but she can no longer overbear Albany. He preaches on the theme of the unnatural with some of the intensity, imagery and disgust of Lear himself:

> Filths savour but themselves . . .
> Tigers, not daughters . . .
> Most barbarous, most degenerate! (39–43.)

He calls, like Lear, on revenging gods, again evoking more wild animal imagery:

> If that the heavens do not their visible spirits
> Send quickly down to tame these vilde offences
> It will come,
> Humanity must perforce prey on itself,
> Like monsters of the deep (46–49).

Albany last, in I, iv, begged the *Gods that we adore* (299) to explain the Lear-Goneril conflict. Here his theology is prophetic of a godless world: if there are gods, and they do not intervene, man-monsters will try to destroy man—as indeed, in this play, man-monsters do, no gods intervening. Cambria (Albany's original) in the old *Leir*, might meaningfully say, "The heavens are just," for in his play, goodness triumphs; Albany's Gods seem to exist only to mock petitioners.

Albany's own position is, of course, ambiguous. Neutral to Lear or worse in I, iv, he allowed the *Good old man* to go angrily out into the night—the act for which he now flays Goneril. Albany believes Lear wronged—yet he will fight against him. So the design, as with the other characters, has its built-in restlessness, unresolved inner conflict. His very excoriation of Goneril may have in it a subtextual resistance, a yearning back toward the love he expressed in I, iv, that intensifies his fury.

Goneril opposes opprobrium with grandeur. "Beast . . . as she is," an alarmed critic writes, "she rises . . . to the level of an unclean and a criminal Joan of Arc." Her evil is matched by her passion. No Christian she, as she blames Albany for bearing "a cheek for blows"; but she speaks of honor like the great captains in *Henry IV* and *Macbeth*. She seems to call her husband *villain* here in the class sense Cornwall used, for his indecision, his failing of his role:

>   Where's thy drum;
> France spreads his banners in our noiseless land . . .
> Whil'st thou, a moral fool, sits still, and cries
> "Alack! why does he so?" (55–59.)

Implicit here is the ironic accusation that he will suffer cuckolding—and more—from Edmund. But the *moral fool*—a striking value inversion that awakens the whole folly-fool-knave complex—is what stings Albany: devil he calls her, more deformed than fiend. *Fool* again, she retorts, and provokes to the full the indulgence in invective which is the chief expression of passion in Albany. If he offers almost the first new tone that promises a return from the unsettling dominant strains back to the tonic, there is still no clear note, the undertones of sexual animality discolor the harmonic thrust. Albany calls Goneril *self-cover'd*: an image of disguise, the fiend masked by the woman's form—her *feature*: but implying also, in the Elizabethan *cover'd*, something monstrous, self-copulating, self-engendering. Albany maddens at the terrible impulses crowding him: his *blood* urges him savagely to

> ... dislocate and tear
> Thy flesh and bones (65–66).

Except for the cannibalisms, no fiercer animal image occurs in the play—though it recalls Gloster's vision of how Goneril will, in Lear's *annointed flesh stick boarish fangs* (III, vii, 57). *Be-monster not thy feature* (63), Albany has said; from his subconscious, his own monster threatens to overwhelm him.* Multiple implications of Albany's design inform the subtext: his *great love* for Goneril, his evident failure to satisfy her, his hesitant, perhaps Puritan quality, his repressed animality. His very manners change: he suddenly *thou's* her, in this context a degradation. Passion and repressed passion, struggling, may move him so far, as in the Phelps' *Lear*, as to take Goneril by the throat, threaten even more —sexually undertoned?—physical violence. But it will come to nothing. Goneril knows it, and there is provocation as well as scorn—and scornful laughter—in

> Marry, your manhood—mew! (68.)

This second short feline assault, the tigercat offering herself to his impotent assault, may indeed drive him to the verge of the animal outbreak he threatens. Shakespeare builds the scene to a crisis where Albany *must* attack her or break—except that the messenger, rushing in, restores his control over his divided humanity.

This and other non-Lear scenes in Act IV have been found, by some critics, dull. Not if the identities of the principals are clear, freely

*Note how Shakespeare turns to character use the *Leir* line: Perillus to Gonorill: *peace thou monster ... thou fiend in likeness of a human creature.*

emerge, freely act out their inner and outer impulses. They incarnate some of *Lear*'s core polarities.

Civilization lives in Albany's response to news of Gloster's torture. The monster submerges. The deceptive tonic note sounds: Cornwall's death means the gods above must after all be justicers. But the hope is as ironic as the echo of mock justice of III, vi—Gloster's other eye is gone, too. Brook's Albany, at the news, had to turn and vomit: civilized man, restraining his own impulse to tear flesh, revolts at another's actual deed.

The dreaming Goneril weighs the chances of her imperial vision: the *building in my fancy* (85) is of sharing a crown with Edmund. Now the dominant note of the sisters' intensifying rivalry sounds sharply—will Regan get Edmund first, destroy Goneril's fantasy?

Against this Albany represents a contrapuntal movement toward tonic: he will take revenge on Edmund for Gloster's blinding. Five times in the short passage *eye* and *eyes* sound, as if to reprise the insight motif: if so, what Albany perceives is that Edmund is to be punished, and that a man, not the Gods, must see to it.

Act IV, Scene iii

The movement toward the tonic now takes on a lyric tone, that will be identified with Cordelia. Here it is conveyed through the Gentleman; and the sweetness of his tone is so cloying that some critics have wished the scene banished, and some producers have banished it.

But consider the Gentleman's verse as characterization, especially in its contrast with Kent's crisper verse. Kent's direct question, establishing the absence of the King of France, looses from the Gentleman a flood of speech, ornamented with elegant redundancies: the trouble in France imported *so much fear and danger* (5) the king's return *was most requir'd and necessary* (6). The description of Cordelia has some of the courtly delicacy of that perfumed lord who so infuriated Hotspur. There is a touch of Osric in this Gentleman, a touch of the court poet with his artificial antinomies, that are pretty echoes of the deeper oppositions of the play:

> . . . she was a queen
> Over her passion; who, most rebel-like,
> Sought to be king o'er her (14–16).
> . . . patience and sorrow strove . . . (17).
> Sunshine and rain at once: her smiles and tears
> Were like . . . (19–20).
> As pearls from diamonds dropp'd. In brief—(23)

He is not, of course, brief:

> Sorrow would be a rarity most belov'd
> If all could so become it (24–25).

The Gentleman's characterization subtly projects the elegantly sincere: he is a vehicle for introducing a positive tonic-oriented image of Cordelia, to counterpoint the last impression of a stubborn daughter measuring out love untenderly. Yet there are undertones of Cordelia's hostility even in Gentleman's earnest, sentimental version of her tearful "parting" cries. (Cordelia herself never speaks in these fluttery rhythms; we assume a courtier's embroidery, but trust the substance which evokes a tearful ghost):

> Sisters! sisters! Shame of ladies! sisters!
> Kent! father! sisters! What? i' th' storm!
> i' th' night? (28–29.)

Shame. Lear called Cordelia a shame of nature, Cordelia would load shame on her sisters, now Lear beats himself with shame. Obsession with this demon of the Lear family haunts *the poor distressed* king who is now *i' th' town*—an echo of the Quarto's *dark town* to which Rowland came? For Lear it is dark: sadly, when he is sometime *in better tune*, when he briefly wins in his battle against madness, sanity only reminds him of his guilts which, most rebel-like, become king over him, push him about: a *sovereign*

> ... shame so elbows him: his own unkindness ... (43)
> ... these things sting
> His mind so venomously that burning shame
> Detains him from Cordelia (46–48).

Mingled threads of tonic and dominant end the scene. The armies of the sons-in-law are afoot; Kent has some secret mission to undertake, but Lear may be united to Cordelia.

Act IV, Scene iii

We have been prepared for Cordelia, but in what image? At the head of her armed soldiers, is she dressed for war? Her tenderness in the midst of steel is one of the bittersweet dialectics here: a lyric note shadowed by drums of war.

But expectation surrounding Lear's image is primary: we learn his *better tune* has yielded again to the dissonance of shame, he is *mad as the vex'd sea*. So we are being prepared for his IV, vi entry, wearing the crown Cordelia describes—another image of poverty mocking royalty, and inevitably, with its spiky nettles, an echo of the thorned crown: of the forsaken, of the pretender who is real, of the sufferer for all.

We would not need to recognize the weeds to sense their mockery: enough that they are twice so named, *furrow weeds, idle weeds*; they are *rank*, their hard k's and t's assault us. Edmund Blunden tells us more: "the *nettle* that throngs about graves, the *hemlock* with its fame for poison and narcotic, the sickly and usurping *darnel*."* One cuckoo flower, Kenneth Muir notes, is the Bedlam cowslip; another was used for convulsions, epilepsy and other diseases of the brain; the bitter *fumiter* was used in hypochondria.

Bring him to our eye (8), Cordelia orders. She will give all she owns—her *outward worth*—to help him. But *seeing*, again, is ambiguous. The doctor promises relief:

> Our foster-nurse of nature is repose (12)

(evoking the nursery image Lear initiated); he knows drugs that giving rest, *Will close the eye of anguish* (15). So seeing may equal pain, unseeing surcease.

When the messenger comes rushing in to warn of the British army's approach, Cordelia takes time to pray sweetly, probably kneeling—as a Japanese Cordelia did—to reprise visually this important ritual motif in

---

*Darnel, "eaten in hote bread, maketh the heade giddie." Thomas Cooper, *Thesaurus Linguae Romance & Britannical* (1565) cited by T. J. King, *Notes and Queries*, CCXIII, 141.

259

the play. She asks nature to nurse Lear, to save him from his *ungovern'd rage*.

Cordelia's need to excuse her invasion of England motivates her *Luke*-like

> O dear father!
> It is thy business that I go about (23–24).

Her *earthly* father, she stipulates lovingly:

> No blown ambition doth our arms incite,
> But love, dear love, and our ag'd father's right (27–28).

Then martially she leads her soldiers—Gielgud's Cordelia drew the messenger's sword—marches forward toward love, toward war. The threads are still mingled.

Act IV, Scene v

Not only Cordelia seeks Lear, the enemy does, too, and this scene may open on Regan in the field, her own armed men on the march, visual reminders of pursuit imagery, as well as of the atmosphere of war.

Usually, however, editors place (the Quarto and Folio do not) Regan and Oswald in a castle, perhaps still Gloster's. Regan presumably grieves for Cornwall, is in fact dreaming of Edmund: so Gielgud's Regan sat at a table, in deep mourning, but painting her lips and cheeks as she talked to Oswald, whom she had made to sit next her.

Sensual as Regan is, she is also shrewd. As she sets out to seduce Oswald to her party, her inquiries stipulating the atmosphere of war prepare slyly for her first key question:

> Lord Edmund spake not with your lord at home? (4.)

Edmund is all she thinks now. For his pursuit, to kill blind Gloster, she finds Regan-like extenuation: *In pity of his misery* (12). But also, practically, *to descry / The strength o' th' enemy* (13–14).

Oswald's attempt to get away—he has perhaps tried before, only to be held bodily—evokes so overt a gesture by Regan:

> I'll love thee much,
> Let me unseal the letter (21–22),

that often, in the theatre, it is accompanied by physical imagery: she comes close, may caress, even kiss him, as she reaches for the paper, perhaps searches him for it. The language about the love looks between Goneril and Edmund is intimate, and can be made more so by her manner, especially a meaningful

> I know you are of her bosom (26).

His abrupt *I, Madam!* (27) may be played as an easy joke for a frankly effeminate Oswald—to James Kirsch, it reflected Oswald's doubt of his own masculinity—but Oswald's loyalty to Goneril suffices for the design, and gives him more dignity. Regan now fills in a blank:

> Edmund and I have talk'd
> And more convenient is he for my hand
> Than for your Lady's (30–32).

If true, this provides them a history, too.

What Regan sends to Edmund by Oswald may be letter or some token of favor. Edgar will find no second letter, but he may find a scarf or "napkin" and, ironically, take it to wear when he duels with Edmund —to the latter's confusion.

The link to the next scene: Regan promises reward for Gloster's death, Oswald is at one with her here and goes off to seek, as well as carry.

Act IV, Scene vi

Oswald has gone one way to search for, and kill, Gloster; Edgar, stealthily, leads him out another. Other men are out seeking Gloster; before the scene ends, Oswald will find him, and claim his reward.

The imagery of pursuit colors Edgar's choice of paths. Gloster's coming "fall" has seemed to demand an open place to which Edgar must expose him with some apprehension; so Edgar may lead him in circles on the open stage, to demonstrate how safe it is; but among hiding places, even in trees, or among rocks, would do as well, and would emphasize the unreality of the cliffside Edgar imagines. Since the area is Dover, he may even be leading Gloster toward a sandy beach.

If Edgar gives comfort physically to Gloster, nothing in his language shows it. Gloster wants to reach the top of his hill—an ironic top; Edgar pulls him along—*look how we labour* (2). Edgar is fooling a blind old man, deceiving his senses: his cruelty is mysterious and provoking to a naive spectator. Why lie to the suffering father? Gloster thinks the ground even, thinks his guide is better spoken, cannot answer yes to the false questions that so haunted Keats:

> Hark! do you hear the sea? (4.)

Edgar then blames Gloster for not perceiving what is not there:

> Why, then your other senses grow imperfect
> By your eyes' anguish* (5-6).

Edgar's cruelty cuts deep. Gloster, clinging to any shred of certainty he can find, repeats his belief that Tom speaks better than he did—and in fact Tom very obviously does—but Edgar baldly, boldly denies it, making no effort to daub it further with words. He seems still in Tom's sullen mood.

> You're much deceiv'd: in nothing am I chang'd
> But in my garments (9-10).

You're much deceiv'd—this is the only true thing said; the rest is lies— and worse than lies: it unsettles Gloster's trust in his own perceptions.

---

*A close verbal echo of *close the eye of anguish* (IV, iv, 15).

The only base of the blind man's knowing, hence of his new identity, is cut from under him. He can only slowly puzzle in his darkness, try to understand how his senses can be so wrong.

If he reaches out, in visual imagery, to try to "see" Edgar by touching, the disguised son offers no comfort. Edgar hurries him along, speaking with a designed lucidity impossible to the Bedlam; especially the lyric story of the immense height, the fearful fall. What Edgar describes is a world grown small, diminishing; it may reflect the shrinking of the whole *Lear* world, but specifically, here, it is an imagined scene that only the sharp-eyed, sharp-minded could see. Gloster's frustrated, turning face must show his amazement at the growing keenness and eloquence of his companion: Tom-Edgar's speech is frankly now in literate verse, it murmurs with many m's and n's, the b's, s's, and sh's softened, the whole colored by a climate of seeming, of imagined seeing that is in fact *deficient*, fraudulent.

But Gloster must believe, must stand at his imaginary verge, must reward his beggar-son, must—characteristically—ask the *fairies* and *gods* to prosper him, must ask to be left alone—and again Edgar deceives, seeming to go far off, but staying to rationalize the torture: he *trifles* with his father's despair—to cure it, he says. But, as he exacerbated Lear's madness, he has—perhaps still touched by the shock of his pretend-madness?—intensified Gloster's despair.

How despairing Gloster is—evident more in visual than verbal imagery—emerges in his prayer. Kneeling, probably, to echo earlier gestures of appeal, he is still on the gad—he tells the gods he could hardly live without defying them—and then not long. He asks them to watch him die: one more petition denied.

He pauses to bless Edgar. Again, silent Edgar hears. A naive spectator, caught up in the mystery of Edgar's behavior, waits again for his response. Will he now reveal himself? Will he ever? We who know the play anticipate Edgar's eventual disclosure, though we may wonder why he does not immediately say who he is, as we know Cordelia will in a like situation. But suppose we did not know? What would we anticipate? A naive spectator begins here to feel, "If not now, probably never. Then what new deception will Edgar impose? Is Edgar getting revenge on his father? Does he want him dead?" The moment passes; Gloster, kneeling or rising to his full height, flings himself forward.

An actual fall from some height has been visualized; but almost certainly Shakespeare intended only the flat stage, to stress Gloster's illusion. Theatre Edgars have sometimes circled to catch Gloster as he falls, to make clear to audiences that the scenery described is wholly illusory.* But if Gloster's is an absurd world, his ruined suicide is not, as Kott would have it, an absurdity. This is a stage of fools, not of clowns. Gloster is not a clown. His design demands the choice of a death in fact; the design is countered by Edgar's intense, complex motivations, much too meaningful for absurdity.

At Gloster's collapse, Edgar's language is curiously detached: imagined dying, he says, may indeed kill one ready to die. Gloster is so quiet: *Alive or dead? . . . Thus might he pass indeed; Yet he revives* (45–47). Revives to what ambiguity of feeling in Edgar? Again, a naive spectator waits for signs of love at last. Edgar offers no comfort, no kindness, unless physically. In a new voice, to match his new masquerade, he asks the recurrent identity question, *What are you, sir?* (48.)

Gloster wants to die; Edgar bewilders him further with the seeming of the great *miracle*, the harmless fall, again undermining his father's trust in his own perceptions. *Do but look up* (59), he says, and this is taken to have symbolic meaning; but in fact it can only frustrate Gloster, who has no eyes, who can only stare helplessly, (angrily?), at his guide-tormenter who reminds him of his mutilation. In the zigzag of his feeling for the gods, Gloster now grieves that he cannot escape them in suicide:

> 'Twas yet some comfort,
> When misery could beguile the tyrant's rage,
> And frustrate his proud will (62–64).

"False miracles" were being exposed by such contemporaries as Harsnett and King James himself, Elton observes; if Edgar's falsehood here had the same connotation of fraud to Jacobeans as Poor Tom's madness, his unkindness to his father cuts more sharply, and emphasizes his curious deviousness: he is a deliberate deceiver; if his ends are better than Edmund's his means are, by design, as false.

Gloster at first rejects the miracles of Edgar's petty gods, who preen themselves on doing tricks men cannot. Edgar bears him down with the story of the monster-devil that led him to the suicide attempt. Edgar may symbolically be parting with a diabolical part of himself; if so, he retains part, for he plays on his father's superstition as casually as Edmund did; and Gloster, in bewildered fear, submits to Edgar's gullings:

---

*The Brook film uses only close shots of the scene to this point, so the naive viewer would have no way of knowing Edgar's plan until a long shot after Gloster's fall. Then Edgar carries an unconscious Gloster down to Dover beach.

> I do remember now . . .
>   That thing you speak of
> I took it for a man; often 'twould say
> "The Fiend, the Fiend": he led me to that place (75–79).

Gloster, reversing again, abdicates responsibility to the supernatural, promises reform:

> Henceforth I'll bear
> Affliction till it do cry out itself
> "Enough, enough," and die (75--77).

This essay in noble stoicism gives some assurance of a return to the tonic. Isolated, these lines suggest—have been so taken—as evidence of *Lear*'s moral lesson. But the play insists on being much more: inevitably character and action demand reversal—and so, in a few moments, Gloster will wish for the escape of madness.

The polyphony of the Gloster-Edgar design has deepened as the scene builds to climax. Gloster's conflicts are clearer: he would live, he would die; he would trust his perceptions, he would be fooled; he would believe in supernatural support, he would deny it, damn it. Coloring his polarities is the ambiguous climate of his relationship with "Tom": blind father led—nursed—by disguised son, staring at him with bloodied, unseeing eyes, sensing a communality, struggling to identify it, deceived, failing.

Darker ambiguity shadows Edgar's design: he asserts kindness, but acts cruelly; he promises a cure of despair, but withholds the obvious remedy—his acknowledged identity, and love; he reconciles his father to "reality" with persistent deception. He has metaphorically prepared his father to accept the image of a mighty fall from a lofty height to a base, a bottom, where at last Gloster can stand; but he urges the blind old man to look up without disclosing the one solid reality that might reconcile Gloster to never seeing. Mary Rosenberg suggests that perhaps Edgar would evidently wish to reveal himself at every chance, but emotion would be seen to overcome him—all he *can* do is *daub it further*. Certainly impulses to love and support move him; but they seem clouded by motives of revenge and punishment. Edgar has brought his father close to death, and soon will take him all the way. Edgar, the actor, indulges the bad trade of playing fool to sorrow.

The subscene, built to Gloster's transient rebirth, breaks at another of Edgar's startled looks offstage. Again, the threat of danger passes, the threat of the awful is on Edgar's face as he watches an extraordinary,

dismaying phenomenon approach. *Bear free and patient thoughts* (80)—
he has just said—and instantly such thoughts are impossible.

Lear's appearance justifies Edgar's dismay. Absent since III, vi, but
actively present through the reports of his shame, of his better tune, then
worse, of his crown of flowers, Lear's entrance is yet unprepared for.

Multiple images converge in his implosion: the king who was running
unbonneted, the mock king, the nature king of flowers and rags, the
bridegroom, the fugitive, the beggar, the fool, the child, the madman—
strenuously mad, mad as the vex'd sea.

Edgar, awakening an echo, sees him first as unaccommodated man; and
safer sense would indeed not accommodate him thus: in his crown of
flowers and weeds, dressed—or undressed—strangely: ragged, in remnants of his old regal garments, or even half-naked, as Mikhoels was, the
doublet now all gone; or in some picked-up nondescript garment, like
Laughton's white gown. The clothes deny the kingship that Lear needs
to assert—three times in this scene. Before Garrick, Lear often carried a
straw scepter, might wield as a sword a sapling, or a straw as Forrest did,
might lean on a tree branch as did Kistov and Gielgud—who also wore
round his neck a chain of flowers that recalled his royal chain of office
in the opening scene. Lear might brandish Fool's bauble as his badge of
royalty. His whole entrance parallels, almost parodies, his first appearance (Granville-Barker suggested "caricature" of I, i to Gielgud), reflects his will to resume the shape he has cast off. Yet he is trying to
escape punishment again, he is clearly a fugitive—Olivier came in running on bleeding feet—hence the protest, usually taken from Quarto:
No, they cannot touch me for coining; I am the king himself (84).

One changed word may make the appearance even more disturbing.
Folio says:

> They cannot touch me for crying;
> I am the king himself.

For *crying*. Lear, the king who has wept, who will soon weep again and
speak many times of men who cry—Lear who has been sometime so
shamed he must cry, and more ashamed for crying, Lear whose recent
offstage anguish has been dominated by shame, may now be struggling
against tears as he comes on. Strongly now the child in the king-child
will emerge: in the moments of regression, in the remembrances of the
birth cry, in the simple language that seems to speak almost directly from
the subconscious. Lear's weeping may be another sign of this. He has felt
keenly that his daughters—unnatural hags—have become his mothers.
That he should cite his royalty to escape punishment for his tears makes

his appearance the more poignant. *Why this would make a man a man of salt / To use his eyes for garden water-pots* (197–198). Edgar might well call it a *side-piercing sight!* (85).

If *crying*, then Lear's

Nature's above art in that respect (86)

follows "naturally," with multiple meaning: he is a king by divine right, he is a flower-crowned nature king, he must cry because art cannot suppress nature. Only then he turns to the soldiers he has impressed, to pay them.

Because he does this, editors almost universally adopt Quarto's *coining*. It carries meaningful implications of sexuality and counterfeit; but the smoothness of the sequence does not necessarily commend it: in mood and action as well as language, violent dialectic persists in IV, vi. Thus humor streaks the dark madness, sometimes has even been seen overlaying it: so Granville-Barker's note to Gielgud: "Happy king of nature. No trouble. Tremendously dignified." Anschütz chuckled his way in. But generally light only shafts darkness. Carnovsky's Lear made the underlying pain the deeper because of his sudden moments of seeming to enjoy madness: so he flung twigs to Edgar and Gloster for press money—as Macready, a century before, scattered flowers. The undertone of anxiety never disappears. Zakariadze murmured a tune that would haunt him through the scene: Tom's "Pillicock sat on Pillicock hill." Mikhoels reached for his absent crown, found only weeds. Scofield, in his ragged royalty, held to the stern image of the throned king he believed he was. Salvini came in distraught; making the transition he projected from king to father to man, he seemed to be asking "Who was he? how came he here?" Porter manifested overtly Lear's battle against insanity: he struggled toward what he did not understand.

The battle shapes this middle third of IV, vi. Impertinency seems to give way to matter; but the promise of a return to the tonic is undermined by latent dominant notes. Matter reflects a bitterness toward sexuality, toward all life, that will force an emotional confrontation with Gloster; beyond will lie a hopeful, if weary, vision of acceptance—until the tragedy's incessant dialectic interrupts. The climate is of a fluid, subrational world: so Gielgud's "expressions, as the fleeting smiles without apparent reason, show a mind unrestricted by consciousness. Throughout, there is an intuitive balance between nobility and childishness, mental chaos and spritual illumination."

The connections between Lear's thoughts are at first violently er-

ratic; as he fights back to sanity, sequence and syntax become temporarily normal. Prose mainly accompanies the early irrationality, as Crane
observes. Quarto proses almost all Lear's lines; but Folio verses many
later ones without difficulty, and could easily have done more. We do
not need Johnson to break down the long *every inch a king* (110) speech
to verse. The wavering of the language from verse to prose itself, as
Crane suggests, measures Lear's wavering; but so too in the verse itself:
the syncopation of the iambics, leading to the timpani of the spondees,
orchestrates Shakespeare's most powerful dramatic poetry.

Underlying Lear's impertinences is the fantasy of revenge through
war—an impulse that will soon fuse with volcanic images of lust. A sub-
logic weaves a skeleton of pertinency out of the shards of ideas and feelings; studious efforts to explicate all the tendons, either in criticism or
in the theatre (as by Booth, laboring associative detail) may diminish
the felt nonrational unity of the scene. As before, Lear makes connections in his mind as he sees relationships in things invisible and visible,
sees them all with the same actuality: so Carnovsky, always peering hard
at the mystery of reality, stared as intensely at what was not there.

Giving out his coinage—the coinage of his imagination, and counterfeit—to his soldiers (sometimes, in the theatre, one careful piece at a
time, more often lavishly) or to Gloster and Edgar, whom he may use
as his targets all through—leads him, arm outstretched, to observe the
failure of one impressed soldier-archer: Edgar with his staff? Gloster,
his hands helpless? Any poor houseless wretches, who may have gath-
ered, as in Kozintsev's film, to watch and share this new misery? Some
unseen presence, as Lear reviews his troops? In this formidable moment,
the king-captain is distracted by a tiny mouse, and the army waits—ironically at *Peace, peace!* (89)—while he offers the homonymous *piece* of
cheese. The resurgent child is active here, but the motive is complicated:
Gielgud gently fed the mouse, but Cobb slapped at it to kill it. Lear's
outflung hand—perhaps now at an imaginary glove fallen, or the imaginary glove slapped from the hand—suggests to Lear a thrown gauntlet;
the tiny mouse rears to the stature of another childish image—a giant.
Frightened by his own fantasy, he calls up his halberdsmen for support.
A vanishing thought returns, war and killing are in his mind again, he
aims his bow, he pursues with his eyes the flight of an arrow, whistles
it onward—*i' th' clout, i' th' clout* (92). Clout is often glossed "target" by the editors; but it may also mean a kind of loin cloth* cov-

---

New English Dictionary: 1551— ". . . they use to go naked, save a clout about
their middle." 1568— ". . . leaving them neither shirt nor clout."

ering the genitals, symbolizing a special, revengeful kind of mark for the arrow in Lear's mind. Lear follows the imaginary flight until his eyes bring him, suddenly, face to face with Edgar.

How *Give the word* (93) is given depends on the immediate Lear design. A show of surface humor enables a pleasant joke. Edgar responds, with more or less compassion, *Sweet marjoram* (94) (another source of brain medicine, Blunden reports) and Lear is satisfied: Carnovsky ordered *Pass* not because he got the word he wanted, but because he liked it; Gielgud applauded Edgar, smiling. But Lear may have more serious doubts of this stranger in his armed camp—this stranger who was recently (in III, vi) the poor Tom he studied and cared for. His philosopher. Scofield stared hard at his Edgar, who felt disguise almost pierced by the look. This is an important ambiguity: may Lear be seeing Mad Tom? The Edgar who was perhaps one of his knights? The possibility carries more energy when Lear looks—perhaps later, perhaps more sanely—from Edgar to Gloster. Is Edgar a threat? Dunn's Lear, warrior and Quixote first, seized Edgar's staff and tried to force him down, as he had Kent in the first scene.

Gloster's recognition of the voice draws Lear's attention. Lear may have looked at Gloster before: but it is the essence of his state that he perceives—or seems to perceive—the same thing differently from moment to moment. A sudden cry of mad recognition, *Goneril, with a white beard!* (97) can provoke an easy laugh; but the line may be a cry of fear, or a horrified exclamation, as with Gielgud, who rubbed his head in pain—the brain hurting. In Lear's last fantasy of Goneril, she kicked him, she is a source of danger; the image also suggests transexuality, the distaff side turned threatening man, white-bearded, a hag, old, wise, knowing more than he. The fantasy may be in Lear's own mind: Salvini did not look at Gloster, but saw his invisible daughter in the air. The image of the hag daughter as mother (and father?) moves Lear strangely toward reality, sanity. The child emerges strongly here; so Louis Calhern (1895–1956) tried deliberately to seem, sound boyish. Lear's speech is regressive, but it is coherent; the syntax straightens, the ideas develop, he has a flash of knowing himself less slenderly. Time for him has the fluidity of the subconscious: when he was a child, a beardless youth *they* —the daughters-mothers he did not yet have, his court, his world, even the Gloster he now speaks to—flattered him sycophantly. They fooled him. When the rain came to wet him *once**—as if the recent storm were distant in memory—when the thunder ignored his bidding (Booth made

*Ella Freeman Sharpe determines that this reflects a time when the baby Shakespeare wet and dirtied his little pants. A critical misdemeanor.

this third affront the climactic evidence of rejection), there he *smelt* 'em out (the word is a subterranean link to the next sexual-disgust speech). The lines are often prosed, as per both Quarto and Folio; but the rhythm is unmistakable, the syncopated iambic sounds through to the end:

They told me I was everything; 'tis a lie, I am not ague-proof (106–107).

The involuntary shiver that racks Lear, the unaccommodated man, is partly physical. Very much physical. The powerful Lears are on their way toward the decay that will end in death, the weaker, older ones more and more are nearly broken, and are forced to summon dwindling reserves. But the shiver, and the resistance to it, is psychic, too: not to be everything is to be nothing to a Lear who had believed he was everything.

This speech, microcosmically, parallels the scene's larger design: Lear seems, after an agony of letting go omnipotence, to approach rebirth as a man. When Gloster recognizes Lear's voice—*Is't not the King?* (109)— peripety allows the macrocosmic movement to develop:

Ay, every inch a king (110).

He resumes his former shape—or a mirage of it. Does he put irony in this? In his first lines of the scene, with all their erratic juxtapositions, a sense may be conveyed that on some level of his mind he enjoys the humor of his ludicrous antics; but he will soon be grimly, furiously serious.

Sometimes actors—Edmund Kean, for instance—have made *Ay, every inch* derisive, as if Lear knew he was powerless. At the other extreme, and more frequently, has been a resurgence of earnest dignity, as with Macready, a gesture asserting true royalty, insisting on the ritual kneeling; so Carnovsky repeated his imperial salute of I, i. Calhern, from his regressive, boyish mood, moved back to his aura of kingly maturity. Barton Booth "assumed the God, and grasped his sceptre of straw like a thunderbolt." Scofield persisted in his grim assumption that he was never anything else than king: the statement seemed fact; this was its madness.

A physical resumption usually accompanied the psychic: sometimes the weedy crown, awry or fallen off, was restored to the head, or Lear might try to fashion a new crown out of twigs and leaves. In the titans, the moment was almost the last great summoning of energy, a rising again, as by Forrest, to the full height and pride of I, i. Salvini stared for a moment as Gloster's meaning penetrated, then he straightened, a giant again, broke a great branch from a blasted tree, and waving it as a sceptre spoke the line fiercely—and yet a polyphony was heard, a touch of sarcasm, as if sanity knew better. In the more foolish Lears, who are now rising to their highest point of vision, a new dignity may clothe their resumed majesty. Laughton, slouching, his head sunken, soft and old, brought himself erect, spoke with a new certainty. Usually the line is a direct response to Gloster, but Gielgud said it quietly, as if to himself; and Irving, in another stage of his madness that persisted throughout, deliberately avoided a sense of returned youthful energy, spoke dreamily, as if for a moment an old memory had wakened his mind.

However spoken, the posture somehow echoes and mocks the many, ineffectual attempts to command submission by stern and angry eye. Yet this is the immediate touchstone of a king, the mad king says:

> When I do stare, see how the subject quakes (111).

Now mad king exercises kingly powers:

> I pardon that man's life. What was thy cause?
> Adultery?
> Thou shalt not die: die for adultery! No:
> The wren goes to't, and the small gilded fly
> Does lecher in my sight (112–116).
> Let copulation thrive; for Gloucester's bastard son
> Was kinder to his father than my daughters
> Got 'tween the lawful sheets (111–119).

Lear resumes here the shape of justicer—again the trial design, the climate of punishment or forgiveness. Gielgud mimed the court situation: he listened as an imaginary bailiff told the defendant's crime. This sinner may be one of Lear's hallucinations; it may be Edgar; but more likely it is another instance of Lear seing Gloster in a new shape that suits his whirling mind. Even if addressed to the empty air, the irony bites at Gloster; it draws most blood if Lear confronts him without knowing him. Or without seeming to know him: for the lurking image persists that this cruelty is not gratuitous, that in some level of his mind, perhaps very deep, Lear recognizes and is punishing his old courtier—perhaps for sycophancy as well as lechery. He could hardly hurt more. Gloster, perhaps on his knees in front of his king, may well quake after, if not before, Lear's attack.

Cruelty's motivation begins to emerge. Lear is driven: by suppressed impulses, fears, needs that have partly powered his rages toward his daughters. Subconscious commands swim up toward consciousness, as the images of adultery and his daughters intertwine. No daughters of his, he has called them all; Wolfit's key to Lear's passion, this obsession with the "lawfulness" of his progeny, surfaced here.

Now Lear would punish the bad ones, get soldiers to war against them. War and lust link. *To't, Luxury*—the word itself is an orgy. *Yond simp'ring dame . . . That minces virtue* (119–122) seems hallucinatory; but the matter is sane, if verging on hysteria, its pertinency hurts. Lear may again be looking at Gloster, the bloodied eyes and beard suggesting the uncanny sexual implications of

> Whose face between her forks presages snow (121).

Forks might suggest something other than legs, but, especially given the echo of *poor, bare, forked animal,* that meaning certainly dominates this "contaminated" metaphysical figure, fused from melted fragments of sensual images. How powerful and uncanny is suggested by the Victorian sensitivity to it: thus Furness curtly disposed of William Warburton's glossy gloss, "between spread fingers": "unwarranted, but I have no inclination to emphasize an unsavory question by discussing it."

Minces virtue carries the extra load that other reverberating words do now: the woman affects purity, but at the same time she mangles it. Out of the festering, secret place in Lear, long sealed off, feverish images, with multiple implications, emerge. Visions of animal lust transpose to humans copulating. *The wren goes to't . . . the small gilded fly . . . the fitchew . . . the soiled horse.* Wren, fly, fitchew become common symbols of promiscuity—fitchew an easy slang for whore, as in *Othello.* *Soiled* is usually glossed as lustful with spring feeding, but it carried also the sense of moral and sexual licentiousness.

Now the ultimate repressed, unholy thoughts break out. Woman becomes both more and less than animal; above the waist—in the head? the heart?—she is the Gods'; below, a Centaur, human-animal, sexual monster—the fiend's. As the sense of the *forefended place* (V, i, 11) ignites his imagination, Lear's disgust grows orgiastic:

> . . . there's hell, there's darkness (129).

The shadowy trail ends, a fusion of echoes of the dark, of stench. *There's* darkness. Loathing, revulsion, agony, crack Lear's syntax, overwhelm him with smell images that bring him to nausea.

> There is the sulphurous pit—burning, scalding,
> Stench, consumption;* fie, fie, fie! pah, pah! (130–131).

*I am strongly drawn to Quarto's *consummation.* The one word embraces so much of Lear's dialectic.

The monosyllables are, of course, not voiced as such: they are inarticulate sounds of physical disgust that may be accompanied by grimace,
spitting, vomiting.

Mack would deny the insistent physicality: building on Empson, he
argues that we must be appalled by an old man's ridiculous and sordid
obsession if this is acted "psychologically" on stage with appropriate
gesture and facial expression. "We lose altogether its emblematic and
morality-based dimension as a meditation, an oration in the tradition of
De Contemptu Mundi." Of course we lose this. The speech is nothing of
that kind; it is a unique manifestation of a particular dramatic character
in the stress of an artistic design intended to arouse audiences. Appalled
we are, and are intended to be: not by the sordidness but by the whole
terrible passion that has agonized this oversize representation of tangled
human needs and wants. Lear must spew out his disgust—not only at his
castrating daughters, but at all women, all who beget, all who consume
men with their sex—all who have attracted him. Lear will preach; but his
very preaching is discolored by the madness that frames it, by the dialectic that seems to repudiate it. Any spectator who prefers a "meditation or oration" here to being appalled will do better in a church.

Matter now gives way to a pertinency that seems impertinent. Up to
the crisis of this subscene, Lear has been coherent and sequential; as a
jeremiad, what he said has been sane. Now he shifts; but whether to a
deeper insanity, or a mockery of it, or both—or to simple imaginative
metaphor—remains ambiguous. Lear is beginning to take on the manner
and matter of the vanished Fool: he speaks reason in riddle and metaphor.

> Give me an ounce of civet, good apothecary,
> To sweeten my imagination.
> There's money for thee (132–134).

This has been said in the theatre with humor, with serious, gracious dignity, and with the same kind of desperation as went before.

Again the outstretched hand—that Gloster would kiss; and again the
ambiguity: madness, metaphor, or both?—

> Let me wipe it first; it smells of mortality (135).

A great, a dangerous line; spectators screwed up to an unrelenting tension may want to laugh at it, and will unless it is powerfully controlled.
It can be whispered; it can be said with a laugh, as by Cobb, his hand
wiped on the rags of his dirty robe; more often it comes out darkly, an
expression of the *stench-consumption* thought. The hand—Lear may

bring it to his nose, wonderingly, bitterly, with disgust—has, though it is every inch a king's, something of the smell that has just sickened him, perhaps the smell of vomit. What he wipes it on is equally mortal.

Gloster's return to dismay is a measure of Lear's apparent madness. Moments before, Gloster declared himself armed against affliction; now he is afflicted: *O ruin'd piece of Nature!* (136.) Lear becomes the microcosm of Gloster's prophetic vision—the great world will wear out so. Nature is helpless, no gods intervene.

Gloster asks the identity question,

> Dost thou know me? (137.)

Lear plays Fool to Gloster's sorrow. A bad trade. He picks unerringly at the most sensitive spot—he recognizes Gloster's eyes, they remind him of *blind Cupid*, a sign of indiscriminate love, and worse—brothel love. Adultery again. I'll not love, Lear promises.

The battering of Gloster continues: Lear holds up a challenge—imaginary or some fragment of leaf or paper—for him to *read*. He can no more read than look up. If the tragedy can be made to "say" anything about life, Edgar's pitying comment comes closest:

> ...it is,
> And my heart breaks at it (142–143).

To this, there is no countering, no dialectic. Everything positive in the *Lear* universe is transient, or shadowed: hope, love, bond, philosophy, the gods. The tragic universe *is*—and good hearts—as much as human hearts may be good—must break at it.

Lear punishes on. In Gloster centers an agony of failed sight, painfully sharpened feeling. Sense and sensitivity clash, resolve. Were all the letters suns (sons?), Gloster could not see; but Lear, staring into the sightless eyes, perhaps pushing a twig at them, commands again, *Read*—so violently, in Dunn's *Lear*, that Edgar moved between to protect his father. Gloster, his irony—and pain—grotesque:

> What! with the case of eyes?
> *Lear.* O, ho! are you there with me? (145–146).

The obvious gloss: do I understand you, you me? But the literal meaning persists: are we blind together? Minotis touched the blood and tears on Gloster's cheeks, then moved his stained fingers to his own eyes—in a gesture that some Lears would approach with the weeping Cordelia in the next scene.

Lear-Fool rides it out, in Fool rhythms, still relating money to insight:

No eyes in your head, nor no money in your purse? Your eyes are in a
heavy case, your purse in a light: yet you see how this world goes (146–
149).

Does Lear suggest that Gloster may see better? Gloster synthesizes
many motifs, physical and psychic, as he reaches out to touch and understand Lear:

I see it feelingly (150).

He not only sees physically and psychically with his feelings; in extended meaning (New English Dictionary) he also sees truly, under-
standingly.* This is madness, in the world Lear now inhabits: a world of
lust-dieted men, who do *not* see because they will not feel. Lear's vision
is moving toward the pragmatic cynicism of Edmund, in the paradoxing
idiom of Fool. A judge is interchangeable with a thief: *handy-dandy*,
which is which? *Handy-dandy*. The whole structure of order Lear believes in comes crashing. Rank, character, value amount to nothing more
than the chance of a child's game—which concealed hand? *Handy-
dandy*: king or beggar, bastard or legitimate, sane or fool—which is
which?

The old standards collapse—order, justice, chastity. A dog's obeyed
in office—Gielgud and Carnovsky barked— so much for *The great image
of Authority* (160). The beadle who whips a whore shares her lusts—
handy-dandy. The garments of rank, once so important, seem now only
disguises: furred robes, gold, armor the sins of the powerful,** while
the ragged are vulnerable to a straw—Forrest took one from his crown
to demonstrate—but *handy-dandy*, which is which?

Lear himself is focus for his diatribe: the great image itself, his robes
gone, a beggar, barked at by Tray, Blanch, and Sweetheart, burning
even now with repressed lust—he is anybody, nothing. He is the ultimate, unaccommodated man-animal, reminding us of Erasmus' saw: even
a king changes his disguise for the common act of begetting. To Enid
Welsford, this is a version of the culmination of the *sottie*, the feast of
fools, when the rulers of the world "are revealed in cap and bells." Lear
now sees human life as a vast *sottie*.

If all do sin, if one is like another, sinner and sinned against, *handy-*

---

*Marvin Spevack observes this. (*Explicator Cyclopedia*, 277–278.)
**Heilman makes a case for Folio's *Place sin with gold* rather than the customary
Plate—*place* here in the sense of putting a sinner into office where he is immune to
the scrutiny of justice. Heilman cites a similar use in *Timon*, IV, iii, 28ff. (*Explicator
Cyclopedia*, 278–279.)

dandy, then the old passion for punishment fades. Forget the gods and their criminal enemies; Lear takes it on himself to exonerate all:

None does offend, none, I say, none (170).

None . . . none . . . none! The rising, furious emphasis suggests that Lear needs to forgive so as to forgive himself, too; needs to obviate the compulsion to punish. Jan Bull's Lear, who wore a crown of thorns, rather than weeds, spoke this standing between Gloster and Edgar in a triad suggestive of Christ between the robbers. But this is no Christian forgiveness for all stone casters: *I'll able 'em* (170) Lear declares, meaning also that he empowers sinners to sin, he emancipates the *id*-world, let impulse, wickedness thrive! He begins by giving the adulterous Gloster an imaginary writ—*Take that of me* (171)—that will subvert justice, *seal th' accuser's lips* (172), exempt Gloster from punishment for begetting Edmund.

Again, Gloster's response is a measure of Lear's mounting tension. The blind one begins to weep; Lear's leftover feeling spills on him, brings a recurrence of anger at evil:

Get thee glass eyes;
And, like a scurvy politician, seem
To see the things thou dost not (172–174).

Whether this comes as a snarl, or in a light tone—Irving spoke with a kind of hollow mirth, Charles Kean with a comic sarcasm, an almost idiotic humor—it hurts deeply. Then, as Gloster breaks down under the shock and the cruelty, the subtextual tenderness emerges from Lear's anguish.

Only more touching than what happens next are the reunion with Cordelia, and the final deaths.

Now, now, now, now (174).

Lear gently comforts the weeping Gloster. He gives Gloster something to do—*Pull off my boots* (175) (sometimes an echo of his boots pulled off in the beginning of I, iv). Lear may in fact be barefoot, but needing to rid himself of the last of his formal garments, as Olivier was, or Gielgud, who suddenly felt the pain of the unreal boots, and called frenziedly for relief: with a sigh of *so* as Edgar came to his aid, as Edgar also did for Carnovsky. But the focus is Lear-Gloster, and the sorrow shared by the two old men. Cobb absently plucked at Gloster's white hair, fondling him. Olivier took Gloster in his arms. A Japanese Lear, so exhausted by his passion that he had fallen to the ground, looked up in a sudden, lucid recognition of Gloster; he crawled toward his old friend, and the two embraced. Scofield, a deep, sane sorrow written on his face, also embraced Gloster (who pulled at his boots), held the blind head in his arms; spoke patiently, as to a child; his lucid compassion motive enough for Edgar's

> O! matter and impertinency mix'd (176).

Touching as the moment was, Scofield felt it was a final purgatory needed to preface the brief serenity of IV, vii.

Scofield's offer of his eyes, for Gloster to weep with, was earnest, and yet rational. Lear shifts between the bitter fool and the sweet one. He does offer his eyes, but he seems also to be saying, riddlingly, Gloster would have to see misery as Lear had to know his suffering. Lear may himself be weeping again, as he offers to pluck out the eyes that once offended him for shedding tears (I, iv); he may be saying, "Here are eyes that know how to weep." A naive spectator fears for a moment that he may try to blind himself.

What comes next seems pure matter: the design revives the compassion of the III, iv prayer, but substitutes for its vision of hope—since lost in disillusion—a vision of acceptance, of the patience that has so long eluded Lear. For the moment, Lear may be patient: so Laughton, perching quietly in a farm cart, Olivier sitting swinging his legs, Scofield gently nursing Gloster's head. If Lear did recognize Gloster earlier but denied it—this ambiguity persists—he acknowledges him now:

> I know thee well enough; thy name is Gloster (179).

Here is another touchstone of Lear's madness. Does Lear suggest, as Cobb did, a kind of sly, crafty cleverness—as if he knew all the time? Or is this a sudden rift in his clouded mind, as with Scofield? The comfort he gives is rational, bittersweet: we were born to cry, to leave the warm womb for the cold, shelterless air:

> Thou must be patient; we came crying hither;
> Thou know'st the first time that we smell the air
> We wawl and cry (180–182).

Lear himself may be weeping now—they cannot touch him for crying; and Gloster weeps afresh, *Alack, alack* (183)—for the matter, and perhaps also what seems the impertinency of Lear's offer to preach, and for what must come after. Lear plays Fool—echoes Fool's stance of teaching in I, iv—and also the ministerial note in Mad Tom; but his repeated, fondled wisdom belongs to his special design, a wisdom of the king-

child, reaching back to the time when they told him he was everything
and yet he cried—the third time the word sounds, and the idea.

> When we are born, we cry that we are come
> To this great stage of fools (184–185).

Stage of clowns; stage of dupes; stage of foolish, flawed mortals; stage of
the foolishly idealistic, of sweet fools, of moral fools, of bitter fools, of
knaves. In a world of fools, all men pursue their kinds of folly. The very
lucidity of this painful insight is unbearable to Lear. His brains hurt
again, his own tears perhaps shame him, a mad hostility dominates again.

The usual gloss for his next mindwandering was taught Garrick by
The London Magazine:

> Lear . . . would not preach with his hat on, but bareheaded, as was the
> custom. He therefore takes off his hat and begins his preachment . . . but
> by the time he has got to this great stage of fools his thoughts are turned
> . . . he breaks out into "this a good block!" i.e., a good hat.

The hat may be an imaginary one—Dunn's Lear took off his weedy
crown and saw it as felt—or a real one. Macready had "borrowed" Gloster's hat—Cobb took Edgar's—and used that. *Block* has also been made a
preacher's stump: Brockmann climbed on it to preach, Schroeder tried
to, but was too weak. The "hat" gloss presumably leads to Lear's feeling
its soft material, and devising his delicate stratagem—Gielgud excitedly
whispered in Gloster's ear

>   to shoe
> A troop of horse with felt; I'll put't in proof,
> And when I have stol'n upon these son-in-laws,
> Then kill, kill, kill, kill, kill, kill! (186–189.)

Six *kills*. The cry of soldiers charging. Any sweetness gives way to savagery. King Lear leads his troops at both hallucinated sons-in-law. His
gestures range from the imperious signal of a general to the vicious attacks of a murderer, or the crafty ambush of a schemer: part madness,
part fantasy, part lucid intention. His voice may be a whisper, or a
scream. Booth punctuated each kill with the stab of a straw dagger; Scofield manipulated his boots as if felt-shod approaching the enemy; Gielgud struck out with his arms: "Build to revenge," his notes say. Dunn's
Lear, shocked at his words, covered his mouth with his hand. The see-
saw of the scene, carrying Lear's battle with madness to a peak of disgust, to another of disillusion, and another of compassionate acceptance,
accelerates now to the passion for hostility that suddenly brings Lear to

face indeed armed inrushing soldiers attracted by the vehemence of his cries. This troop is the imagined enemy as far as Lear knows—and as far as naive spectators know, at first, as they watch Lear surrounded. What is hallucination, what real?

Then the audience recognizes Gentleman, who says *Your most dear daughter* (191)—and Lear is fearful: of degradation by Goneril? of shame before Cordelia? The shock brings a bridge to reason. He feels trapped by those he would have ambushed—Carnovsky laid about him with a twig, Salvini was furious,

> No rescue? What! a prisoner? I am even
> The natural fool of Fortune (192–193).

Natural fool—born to be Fortune's fool, to be played with; also material for jest: the king a prisoner. Lear's tears are on the way; his rationality is painful.

> Use me well;
> You shall have ransom (193–194).

This much sanity is hardly bearable:

> Let me have surgeons;
> I am cut to th' brains (194–195).

Pared on both sides, and nothing left in the middle. He does not hear Gentleman's reassurance, he mistakes the attentions of the physician. The tempest in his mind does not give him leave to ponder reality. At the sense of aloneness, of helplessness, the tears come freely:

> No seconds? all myself?
> Why this would make a man a man of salt,
> To use his eyes for garden water-pots (196–198).

The courage, the humor returns. They cannot touch him. He weeps without shame, makes a sex pun on the death he prophesies:

> I will die bravely
> Like a smug bridegroom. What! I will be jovial (199–200).

He resumes his shape, perhaps fits his crazy crown—or pieces of it—again on his head:

> Come, come; I am a king, masters (201).

Their ritual, familiar kneeling to him may frighten him—or give him the opportunity of escape. *Then there's life in 't* (203)—they must catch him. He runs. Some theatre Lears have not: Booth allowed himself to be led, because running seemed to him undignified; Zakariadze, chanting "Pillicock," marched out somewhat as Phelps had done, making the soldiers his followers rather than pursuers. But this leaves no suspense: the return to the tonic must still be frustrated, a naive spectator still fears for Lear's safety if he escapes his helpers—so most Lears run away, unbonneted, still in flight, still pursued.

The manner of his evasion may, briefly, release the audience to wistful laughter. Gielgud ran as if playing a game: Olivier kept a touch of humor in his escape; even Salvini, his anger gone, skipped and ambled away, huddling his clothes about him. Irving's run was famous, one of the most touching expressions of his mad Lear: defiant and terrified, ungainly, without a shred of dignity, he scuttled out in a scared, eccentric, lunatic shamble.

The Gentleman, in his insistently courteous way, grieves for Lear, informs Edgar of the coming battle, leaves. Gloster, in another suicidal agony, begs the Gods to end his life before he himself tries to do it. Heaven is *gentle* now:

> You ever-gentle Gods, take my breath from me:
> Let not my worser spirit tempt me again
> To die before you please! (218–220.)

Edgar's curious *Well pray you, father* (220), especially the last formal word, moves Gloster once more to inquire into identity: *What are you?* (221.)

Will Edgar reveal himself? Again, no: he is a poor man, whom suffering has fertilized, made *pregnant to good pity*. Pregnant, but hardly delivered of it: he who never forgives his father's adultery now grudges him the comfort of knowing his guide is Edgar. Certainly Edgar's pretense that he is curing his father's despair no longer has currency. Flight must be resumed; Edgar leads his father on. Gloster ironically gives thanks to heaven for its benison—and, as usual, a moment later seems to be meant to suffer for his belief. Oswald appears, sword out, to claim the prize of Gloster's eyeless head.

Gloster gives up, at once, his resolve to live, seeks death—*Put strength enough to't* (232) he begs Oswald. Edgar, in the mask and dialect of a rustic, intervenes. Gloster does not speak during the fight—can only show, visually, his amazement at Edgar's new disguise—but he may well, as in the Nunn *Lear*, try to circumvent Edgar and force himself against Oswald's sword, in a grotesquely tragic effort to die. But Edgar, in this first evidence of his fighting skill—unless against Edmund—kills Oswald. Often, in the theatre, with a savage blow of his staff, or by taking Oswald's sword from him, as in the Cobb *Lear*, or forcing him down on his own sword, or dagger, as in Gielgud's. Folio and Quarto are no help: the lone direction is Quarto's "he dies."

Oswald's dignity survives. He has rested on rank, called Edgar *peasant*, *slave* and *villain*; but his last act, after asking to be buried, is loyalty to Goneril: deliver her letter. As he dies, the repetition in his last words is curiously touching, individualizing:

> O! untimely death.
>
> Death! (252–253.)

Edgar spares no kind word for Oswald's loyalty to *the vices of his mistress*, though he would rather not have been death's man. He speaks, in his philosophical style, of opening Oswald's letter:

> Leave, gentle wax . . .
> To know our enemies' minds, we rip their hearts;
> Their papers is more lawful (261–263).

Vicious the letter's message, but not its style. It asks Edmund to kill Albany—not out of absolute lust, but also because (and Goneril may have made this clear long before) she cannot bear Albany's lovemaking.

Shakespeare uses a letter again to wind the two plots together to their end. Edgar will do the winding: characteristically, he excoriates Goneril and Edmund not merely as murderers, but as *murderous lechers*.

Gloster, sad to be undelivered of life by Oswald—*What! is he dead?* (256) is a tragic cry—turns inward. He envies Lear's madness; his own *vile sense*—a sexual undertone?—is too *stiff*, makes him suffer. Where Lear resisted madness, Gloster would embrace it. His *ingenious* feeling of his huge sorrows is usually glossed "conscious," "acutely aware"; but the word already meant inventive, skillful, and suggests a clever destructive inner force contriving to remind Gloster of, and intensify, his misery.

The drums of war sound, Edgar must drag Oswald off—to rake him up in the Dover sands. Then flight again: Edgar leads the stumbling Gloster away—to a friend, he says, though the friend does not appear. Another pretense? Edgar's two actions have been combined in the theatre: thus, Brook's Edgar handed his staff and Oswald's sword to Gloster, who held tentatively the familiar things, now so strange and useless to him, while Edgar slung Oswald over his shoulder. So the procession went out, Gloster holding on to Edgar, his sword, and his stick.

Act IV, Scene vii

For the first time since I, i, the tonic sounds strongly, a promise of rest, a glimpse of certainty after so much disharmony. Literally as well as figuratively this music is heard: for the doctor has ordered a melody to quiet Lear's spirit. After the frenzy of madness, the barely heard music comes as a boon, slowing the tempo, enabling long, feelingful pauses, a pastoral. Appropriately, the sun shines—after all his troubled night, Lear will see fair daylight—though the scene is often played indoors, sometimes in a tent, to follow an old editorial insertion. Perhaps some hint of France, to make Lear wonder if he is there: Cordelia's attendants—or, as in Nunn's production, she herself—may wear martial costume, French blue; the war is afoot. Signs of war and poverty already oppress the scene in Kozintsev's film. Houseless wretches and armed men move uneasily in the open, bedraggled courtyard to which Lear has been carried.

Only anxiety for Lear seems to discolor the scene's first words. Cordelia thanks the Kent who supported her so sturdily in I, i, and Lear afterwards. But low key tension persists in the language of measure and comparison, and in Kent's concealed reason for continuing disguised. The scene develops strong emotional growth, and expectation, in both textual and subtextual drama. For all its quiet mood, it is not an idyll: it is, as are the other pre-catastrophe scenes with Cordelia, bittersweet. Gielgud and his cast were told to play for "reality, complexity, and suspense." His note: "There is serious danger, or was in my case, of the actors allowing the pathos of the scene to swamp them, so that they play it all in pathetic and noble voices, sentimentalizing the quality and strength of Shakespeare's conception."

Cordelia's prayer to the Gods, one that seems transiently to be answered, takes its energy from supporting and opposing the aural imagery of the music:

> Cure this great breach in his abused nature!
> Th' untuned and jarring senses, O! wind up
> Of this child-changed father (15–17).

Child-changed looks two ways: changed into child, as well as changed
by child. Lear's *nature*—his human condition, as well as his person—has
been breached in body as well as spirit.

Some productions show Lear on stage when the scene opens, but
Shakespeare designed him off for the suspense of his entrance. The doctor motions him to be carried on, with Cordelia's permission, and her
evocative question: *Is he array'd?* (20.)

Better than the doctor's answer is the vision of the gently borne sleeping old man. This action, its settling down, gives time for silent response
to the pastoral image. Often Lear is arrayed in a purity of white; but he
may also, as Prucha did, wear—and ironically not recognize—royal robes
like those of I, i, when he last sat on a throne-chair among subjects.
(Folio specifies a chair; if Lear is carried in, or simply appears, like Irving on a couch, the design itself is diminished, and some of the visual
value of his face is lost). Traditionally, Lear's white hair, now trimmed,
gently frames the ravaged face. He has been drugged, and he sleeps
deeply—the actor's projection of a profound slumber, as by Irving, has
been as important to the image as the apparent actuality of the
hallucinations.

Louder the music there! (25) the doctor orders. But not too loud—
Redgrave once complained that its volume forced him to raise his voice
too high. Only loud enough to sound under Cordelia's own low voice—
for she has her longest affection-filled speeches now. As Muir observes,
she is more warmly eloquent to Lear when he cannot hear her. *Dear
father* she calls him—and *father* twice more—and she medicines him tenderly with a kiss—not omitting meanwhile to scorn her two sisters.

She pauses—to see if and how he will awaken. Her indignation sharpens as she sees—and may, in the theatre, touch, or kiss—his *white flakes*,
his face, his *thin helm*. Was this a face, she asks, to oppose to the storm?
Of Lear's own part in this opposition she does not speak: her concern is
all for his mistreatment; he is her mistreated child—*poor perdu*. She
echoes Kent and Gloster: her enemy's dog, biting her, would fare better. Her emotional turbulence, the *quick cross lightning* of her words,
is reflected in the shifting of dominant alliterations: f's, d's, k's, p's, w's,
s's. Then:

He wakes; speak to him (42).

The urgent watch by Kent, Doctor and Cordelia intensifies the suspense
of Lear's slow return to consciousness. Rossi took a full minute—a long
time in the theatre—to open his eyes, and begin to focus them. No moment in the play concentrates more emotional energy in subtextual

arousal. Moved observers in many countries describe the power of the
acting: thus, of Schroeder:

> He lay there. Corpse-white, peaceful, eyes tight shut, breathing lightly
> through open mouth, hands drooping by his side: soon quicker breath-
> ing showed his approaching awakening. Feebly he raised his eyes and
> dimly looked around at those standing by. Cordelia speaks to him. His
> gaze, still mad, halts on her face. A faint memory of his outcast daughter
> flits through his mind, and under the delusion that he has been lifted
> from his grave she seems to him like a happy spirit. His eyes dwell longer
> on her sweet face, and there is more light in them, more life at the mem-
> ory. But his spirit is still chained, he thinks it is a delusion of madness.
> Doubtful, he shakes his head, and as he looks again around him and sees
> himself surrounded by strangers, he thinks himself the victim of trickery
> and deception: a stranger to himself, he doubts his own existence too.
> His searching glance, the moving grief that shows in his every expres-
> sion, the mournful tone of his voice, all this shows his state of mind. And
> as he begins to see Cordelia in more living, more convincing truth, he
> recognizes the old beloved ring of her voice as it begs and entreats him.

Cordelia speaks no longer as loving child, but in courtly submission:

> How does *my royal Lord*? (44.)

And as he very slowly focuses,

> How fares *your majesty*? (44.)

She has reason to be anxious about his health, but more. He last swore
never to see her again, he had no such daughter. So: will he be sane? And
if so, in what mood? Slowly, he speaks. Ambiguity still: is this madness?
Hallucination? Metaphor?

> You do me wrong to take me out o' th' grave;
> Thou art a soul in bliss; but I am bound
> Upon a wheel of fire, that mine own tears
> Do scald like molten lead (45-48).

Half-circle the wheel had come for the Lears who began titanic,
tough, autocratic, tyrannically angry. The descent from the arrogance
and harshness of I, i to this pale anxiety effects the ultimate power of
dramatic contrast. So Salvini, so mighty at first, now humbled himself
absolutely, self-reproachful, abandoned to his fate. He had gone the
whole way from king to man. Scofield seemed shrunken, older. If his
voice did not gentle, his manner, suffused with unpretentious humility,
did; the hard, unforgivingness transformed into an aching need to be

forgiven. Forrest's vast, arrogant early gesture gave way; all his auto-cratic force spent, his hands began to move in unpurposed benediction. Gielgud's contrast was on shorter rein: having so recently stressed the happy freedom of madness, his return to sanity—in the mode of "reality and simplicity"—was bewildered, troubled, he was fretful—even at first "a bit sulky," as per Granville-Barker's direction.

For the Lears who had seemed mad at first, this was at last a moment for "a vision of sanity." The *great rage* stilled, they could for a while see, feel, clearly. Much expectation accompanied their awakening: might they finally leave madness behind? Booth extended the suspense by awakening first to a vacant stare, and then burying his head in his hands before he looked up. Irving moaned and stammered out his first words. Rossi visually worked his way out of the mists of memory before he could speak. For Klöpfer, the words seemed to come unconsciously, without his will.

If the good old father Lears no more than returned to themselves, as Charles Kean did—to "the instinctive kindness of his nature"—the de-velopment of the inward character design, and its possibility for the fu-ture, was minimized. Though the tonic is felt in this scene, subtextual dissonances must persist: if nothing more the momentum of the dialectic ensures apprehension of peripety. Laughton's "father Lear" did look ahead in this scene: the new vision and dignity that first awakened in his prayer in the storm, and then informed his madness in IV, vi, seemed to carry over into his sanity: as he spoke his look straightened, his eyes steadied, he rose in stature.

You do me wrong (45).

Healing as the idyll is, there is yet a beautifully designed *agon* in it. Cruel father, now humiliated, is rescued by rejected—and prodigal—daughter. What might be a fairy tale ending is saved by the resistances and apprehensions subtly inlaid. *I did her wrong*, Lear had thought of Cordelia, and suffered burning shame. Now he opens his eyes to a vision of her, and: *You do me wrong*.

The words come hesitantly, and may, as from Carnovsky, pause here. Lear has wakened from a drugged sleep, after a nightmare reality. "Groping" most often has described the hesitant response to the star-tling change in his environment: the faltering mind, the slowly focussing eyes, the seeking hands, the halting voice, the tears falling. Lear begins, as was said of Irving, "slowly to piece out the puzzle of his personal identity"; and his first remarks have an old, faint touch of reproach and self-pity, as well as *burning shame*, especially

> I am bound
> Upon a wheel of fire (46–47).

Lear's wheel has been related to archetypal, mythical, and classical allusion; but these seem less sources than sharers with *Lear* of a common source. Many images may converge here. Kirsch considers the archetypal circle (Mandala) figure, visualized—as in Ezekiel and Indian *Tankas*—as relevant combinations of wheel and fire; and he translates the Epistle of James into the allusive "the tongue defileth the whole body, and setteth on fire the wheel of nature." Elton notes Renaissance figures of a wheeling, burning sun. These may be supplementary to what is central in the Lear image: the twisting, fiery wheel torturing. Literally, prisoners racked on an actual wheel would, if also subjected to fire, suffer a kind of ultimate torture. Metaphorically, they may turn in the tortures of hell; they may suffer on Fortune's wheel. In the context of the play, Lear, himself, Fool's great wheel running downhill, has reached bottom. The Ixion myth is relevant, but not for correspondence of incidents: Ixion was bound on his wheel for an overt act—boasting of adultery with Juno—quite unlike Lear's; nor is Lear understood to be wheel-racked because he begat daughters like the Centaurs Ixion fathered—by now Lear seems to have forgotten Regan and Goneril, and will brush away later references to them.* What is exciting about the Ixion metaphor is Ovid's description of him as both pursuing and flying from himself: a tremendous, fertile image implicit in Lear's—in human—action. But even this kind of allusion, if intended, could only support the immediate image of the helpless man bound upon the familiar, fearful throne-chair, weeping for his unspeakable pain. Such pain, his tears come so hot, so heavy, that they scald the fire.

To cut through the pain, Cordelia presents herself again—the identity question, in a new guise, asked again with a subject's deference, as if she still is apprehensive of her reception:

> Sir, do you know me? (48.)

Not metaphor, surely, but hallucination, Cordelia concludes from his answer.

> You are a spirit, I know; where did you die?
> *Cordelia.* Still, still, far wide (49–50).

Let him alone awhile (51), the doctor says; and they wait as he seeks to know in the simplest of poetic language if this is Lear. *Where have I been? Where am I?* (52.)

Then, the self-pity:

---

*Though they—all women—were to him, in IV, vi, centaurs below the waist.

> I am mightily abus'd (53).

Abus'd is generally glossed "deceived," "deluded;" but the implication
of torture persists. Lear would *die with pity / To see another thus*
(53–54).

He reprises the scene in I, iv, when, before another daughter, he
sought to reassure himself of his identity, to hold off fears of his weaken-
ing consciousness:

> This is not Lear! ...
> Does Lear walk thus? (I, iv, 234–235.)
> ... lethargied? ... waking? (I, iv, 237.)

And he might then pinch, or prick himself with a pin, to *see*. So now:

> I will not swear these are my hands: let's see;
> I feel this pin prick. Would I were assur'd
> Of my condition! (55–57.)

Cordelia, addressing him still by the formal *Sir*, kneels for his benediction. In the old *Leir*, a succession of ritual kneelings and blessings
sugared the reconciliation; Shakespeare compresses the moment, as he
does the scene, to save sentiment from sentimentality. Cordelia kneels
to ask benediction; Lear kneels to her: an echo of much earlier kneeling,
but mostly a touching ironic reprise and reversal of his gesture before
Regan. Cordelia may not allow him to kneel, as in the Phelps *Lear*, but
without the double reverence much is lost. The visual image concentrates intensely the motifs of dependence, of father-child relationship,
of the submission of the old to the young—the nurses, guardians. In the
theatre, the image of the once-absolute ruler kneeling to the loving
daughter who seeks his blessing wrenches at the feeling. In a Lear who
had been as unyielding as Scofield, the gentleness and humility were almost unbearable.

Only more pregnant the next moment: the simply spoken helplessness
of the old king-child; his slowly clearing perception; his hesitancy in
accepting himself and hence his shame before Cordelia. So McCullough:
dazed, forlorn, piteous:

> Pray, do not mock me (59).

(Edmund Kean: a pathetic expostulation bordering on despair.)

Lear is practiced in mockery, in kneeling to mock; he now has a
child's fear of mockery, of being laughed at, *shamed*. Only very circu-
itously, apologetically, will he come to what lies in his heart:

> I am a very foolish fond old man. (60).

Fond is usually glossed "in dotage, soft headed," but it carried also the familiar sense of soft-hearted, of caring: hence, the folly of loving. Now Lear can utter his old, haunting terror:

> I fear I am not in my perfect mind (63).

(Macready: with a world of misery and hopelessness.) Lear moves slowly, but with a felt purpose, toward the crucial fact of his identity. Other things are minor: not knowing Kent, lodgings, time, his garments —his *king's* garments? But one recognition he hardly dares acknowledge —this is his great fear—he might be jeered at, shamed again:

> Do not laugh at me;
> For, as I am a man ... (68–69).

He may pause at the last word, remembering that he speaks no longer as a king:

> I think this lady
> To be my child Cordelia.
> *Cordelia*: And so I am, I am (69–70).

Lear's speech mounts in bursts toward its climax. He fights his battle to hold sanity word by word—Bassermann seemed to pause at every one, testing the reality of each before stepping out to try the next, hesitating, despairing, recovering, going on. To know Cordelia is to know sanity— but also to know the fear of rejection, as he will next say. This hedges the sentiment. So Bassermann's bravura love sob at the last words seemed excessive. Salvini moved from despair to wonderment to intense relief. Booth, sick and weary, looked doubtingly, questioningly, from Kent to the physician, almost afraid of the ultimate daring to know his daughter. Kean, fond of violent reversal, after despairing uncertainty, shrieked out his recognition.

Visual imagery has been spectacular here. Devrient only clasped his hands, as if in prayer that he saw aright; and Gielgud, his voice full of love, flung out his hands to Cordelia, who knelt to him, seized the hands, and caressed them. Mantell reached out to stroke Cordelia's hair—but could not look her in the face. Classically this has been an opportunity for Lear to take Cordelia in his arms: so Salvini's fatherly embrace. Booth held her, and rocked her from side to side; Bassermann, too—re-calling I, i, when he held her on his lap on the throne. The embracer has been Cordelia, too: Edmund Kean staggered, sobbing with tenderness and joy, into her waiting arms, Irving laid his head on her bosom like a tired child, with a sigh of content—he was, at last, setting his rest on her kind nursery.

Verbally, Cordelia preserves her gentle formality throughout. Part of her dialectic is that, loving her father, she still cannot easily, in his presence, speak her love. Something inhibits her: something subtextual, partly a resistance to the subtextual demands he makes on her. The essential Lear character remains in her design: when Lear tries to apologize, she will not voice any words of endearment. One effective actress was described as "tongue-tied" here. The design enforces some distance in Cordelia, as it will in V, iii; countering this is her insistent sympathy, that visually breaks through: a true Lear again, she weeps. Does she do this partly because her design includes her felt disability that keeps her from offering the open love her father seeks?

> *Lear*: Be your tears wet? (71).

His gesture may echo his tenderness with Gloster in the previous scene. Garrick reached out to touch Cordelia's cheek, and many actors have followed suit. Irving tasted the tears on his finger.

Then absolute submission. For the only time, Lear accepts death. After her embrace, her tears, some self-pity colors his offer to drink her poison: *I know you do not love me . . . You have some cause* (73–75).

> No cause, no cause.
>
> Am I in France?
>
> In your own kingdom, Sir.
>
> Do not abuse me (75–77).

Again, the double meaning: do not dupe me, do not misuse me. Seeking to locate himself, reminded of his kingship, he flees into introspection—thought, mind-wandering, melancholia, self-pity, a new threat of madness—that isolates him. The battle for sanity is precarious: so Macready seemed to lose the power to retain the new image of Cordelia, reality seemed to fade away before his eyes.

Cordelia is so moved she cannot speak; the doctor comforts her. Faint signs of the *great rage* dormant in Lear are hinted in the design: the doctor cautions Cordelia against reviving the past. This until-now subtextual undercurrent of the danger of returning madness is one of the dominant notes that has tensed the idyllic scene. Cordelia sounds another when she gets his attention and, characteristically, addresses him formally:

> Will't please your Highness walk? (83.)

He rejects kingship, insists on his frail humanity. Formality he does not want. It is as if he senses her insistence on the form of the bond, some withholding in her over the old injury:

You must bear with me. Pray you now, forget and forgive: I am old
and foolish (83–84).

Gielgud spoke the words cheerfully. But other Lears were troubled;
Macready, struggling against overwracking imbecility; Rossi, grief-
stricken and desolated by his condition; Cobb, almost shaking Cordelia
as he demanded forgiveness; Scofield, only after a long pause, a look
meaning many unspoken, unspeakable things. He did not need help off,
nor did Gielgud, moving out with "soft dignity"; nor Laughton—Cordelia was a queen following a king, no mothering. But Redgrave's old
Lear went slowly across the wide stage weeping with Cordelia, and
Irving's Cordelia supported and guided his feeble, tottering steps, in
kind nursery.

The uncertainty that has shadowed the tonic tone of the scene now is
overt. As Scofield's ambiguous look denoted, their exit does not have
the feeling of an end: Lear's mind is still a battleground, and the concern
of Kent, the Doctor, and Cordelia as they shepherd Lear out intensifies
the underlying apprehension.

That another battleground awaits is immediately stipulated. *'Tis time
to look about* (92); Edmund, leading Cornwall's army, allied with Albany's power, comes on apace. Gentleman, again carrying a slight touch
of the comic, tells Kent that Kent is rumored to be elsewhere. Kent
ironically puts him off. All will hang on this battle, Kent muses; and,
as Gentleman has warned, *The arbitrement is like to be bloody* (94).

Act V, Scene i

Men armed for war, in all their sound and panoply, color the stage, confirming Gentleman's warning. This large pageantry will, as before, give way to intimate insets: which will be followed by spectacular confrontations involving the whole stage—modulated, again, by intense emotional cameos.

Edmund, magnificent, sets the initial tone as he leads his forces in, and looks for his ally. His characterization of Albany casts light backward: contemptuously, he wonders if Albany has been able to hold to his last decision:

> He's full of alteration
> And self-reproving* (3–4).

Isolated with Regan—usually alone on stage with her—Edmund graciously accepts her love. Clearly their relationship has developed: so much farther, in the Goldsby production, that the two had recently come from bed, Regan still half naked—making a kind of sense of *Now . . . You know the goodness I intend upon you* (6–7). Jealously, sensually, perhaps with gestures, she tests him: has he found the way, with Goneril, to the *forefended place*—that place of darkness? Another echo: Edmund:

> That thought abuses you (11).

Regan pursues her imagery: has he been *conjunct and bosom'd* with Goneril? No, he swears—by his honor. The Bastard's honor.

More sound and sight of war—Albany, Goneril, and their army enter. Private war, too—Goneril would rather lose battle than Edmund to Regan.

Albany's inner division, marked by Edmund, manifests itself. The situation has its own ambiguities: a French army, on English soil, fights for the right. Edmund leads troops—Cornwall's and more, his father's—that may resent his supplanting of Gloster. Albany is whipsawed by con-

---

*Quarto's variation, "He's full of *abdication*," deserves more consideration than Greg gives it. *Abdication* has more energy, and is curiously prophetic.

flicting values. His speech breaks into erratic phrases. He will fight, but reluctantly. He fights against the king, but for the kingdom. He could not be valiant unless honest—and his rationalizations demonstrate how very much he doubts the honesty of his present motives. He is full of *alteration and self-reproving.*

The Bastard's *Sir, you speak nobly* (28) might be satirical; but his chameleon-like adaptiveness suggests as easily a romantic response to seem to match Albany's in sincerity. Regan is unmistakable: "Why so much quibbling?" Goneril, too: "Let's fight the war, not each other" (a glance at her rivalry with Regan, too?).

Albany yields to their scornful practicality, and he and the Bastard agree to plan strategy; but the private wars continue. Perhaps because Albany is somewhat older than the others, and because they have a common front against his scruples, he is isolated—as Goneril and Oswald have previously isolated him. The tension is overt: Albany is angry and uneasy with Goneril; she is openly contemptuous of him, builds in her fancy on her secret, pledged bond with Edmund, grows murderously jealous of Regan.

The next cryptic lines make sense in the context of this jealousy:

> *Regan:* Sister, you'll go with us?
> *Goneril:* No (34-35).

Goneril may assume Regan speaks the royal plural; Goneril's intent is to stay behind with Edmund. But Regan's *us*, Regan may now reveal, includes Edmund; after Goneril says *No*, Regan can take his arm to leave with him, and taunt Goneril: *'Tis most convenient; pray go with us* (36). Goneril's

> O, ho! I know the riddle. I will go (37)

would be her surrender; but from her subtextual determination, we may assume also that this may be the moment in her design where she recognizes Regan's priority with the Bastard, and plans to kill her sister.

Sounds of war continue. The Lear army approaches. Edmund, Regan and Goneril sweep off to their public and private battles. Edgar, disguised, a new Edgar who has come a long way from the dupe of the first act, now strong, authoritative, intercepts Albany—who characteristically stops to talk with one so poor. Edgar's manner is compelling enough for Albany to accept Oswald's letter; then, the duel arranged, Edgar fades away before—perhaps because he sees—Edmund's coming. However, if Edmund is delayed—if Albany has time to read the letter— a new tension develops between him and Edmund, and helps motivate his terse reply when Edmund, the picture of Mars, thirsty for triumph, urges attack.

Alone, the Bastard savors his success in love and society. He is frankly playing now for the throne. The way to it requires marriage to Regan or Goneril, and one must die to make this possible. If Regan dies, then Albany must die, too—let Goneril manage this. In any case, Lear and Cordelia must die. There is still a touch of humor in this soliloquy, but the mood behind it is grimly real: the Bastard has come from base to within a hand's grasp of the very top, and there is no jest in his final couplet: he means nothing to stand in his way.

Act V, Scene ii

Folio's opening direction projects Lear into the ongoing war:

> Alarum within. Enter, with drum and colours,
> Lear, Cordelia, and Soldiers, over the Stage,
> and Exeunt.

This suggests that Lear himself may wear some kind of arms, be part of the battle by leading "loyal" British soldiers, as well as French ones. The image bridges the gap between the weak, confused old man of IV, vi and the imprisoned philosopher of the next scene. If he is more the former—feeble, vague—he is a helpless onlooker, who watches the war in bewilderment. If more the latter, with returning strength, he may wield his own sword powerfully enough to explain his killing of the slave that hanged Cordelia. His garments will be royal. He is once more the image of a king.

The Lear party may already be losing the battle in the Quarto stage direction:

> Alarum. Enter the powers of France, over the
> stage, Cordelia with her father in her hand.

This may more accurately describe the intended business: the old man only a bystander, led along by his daughter who is perforce with her troops, a defeated Joan of Arc.

The theatre usually cuts this mime, brings on, amid the sounds of battle, Edgar leading Gloster (mirroring, in juxtaposition, Cordelia's guiding of Lear).

Edgar has not found the promised friend for Gloster, now offers his father little comfort. *Pray that the right may thrive* (27)—which is right? To the audience this is ambiguous; to Gloster meaningless. Edgar's new promise—again to be broken—depends on another frightening *if—if* he returns, he will bring comfort. And *if not?* The contingency remains unspoken; Gloster can only guess at it, dismayed. *Grace go with you, sir!* (4.) Folio has Gloster respectfully wish his mysterious companion.

295

Where Edgar does go during the battle we never learn. Like Kent, he seems withdrawn from it, as if Shakespeare held off engaging these two "loyal" figures in a battle that reflects the play's dialectic: where "right" —the restoration of Lear—depends on "wrong"—a foreign invasion.

Gloster sits alone as the war rages. Producers have sometimes staged conventional battles here, sometimes unconventional ones. One "primitive" production used arrow and stone-throwing machines that fascinated spectators so much it took their thoughts off the action. More stylized and swift was Nunn's ballet-like dance of silvery lances moving to electronic music, in minuets of attack and defense behind Gloster— who sat forestage, head upthrust, listening to the war with a silent scream fixed on his face. The Bucharest actors who had mimed a balletic storm now similarly projected a battle scene. Kozintsev's battle was veiled, behind a transparent scrim; but Edmund came on in triumph, past realistic dead soldiers and the carrion of horses.

The text suggests no sight of battle, only sound: Alarum and retreat. This absorbs the war quickly into the flow of action, an admirable restraint. So Brook's Gloster, alone on the vast, empty stage, filled only with maddening sounds of war, sat in his rags, trying to sense the unseen world: twitching his face to test the blindness of his eyes, sniffing at the air, listening, a wasteland figure in a void.

Edgar returns, his promise of comfort broken, and the flight imagery is enforced again. *Away! ... away!* (5.) Twice he tries to seize Gloster's hand, to hurry him off; the old blind man stays. *A man may rot even here* (8).

Edgar preaches again, succinctly. *Ripeness is all* (11) suggests the acceptance of what life offers—a concept equally at home in Christianity and paganism, Elton observes. It is of course a universal metaphor, wherever growing things ripen. But the image contains the dialectic of the play. Behind the implication of acceptance—and the even more optimistic one of fullness—broods the darker meaning. Edgar, who at V, iii, 184 will grieve that he had not had the courage for suicide, now says:

> Men must endure
> Their going hence, even as their coming hither (9-10).

He is not, as Lear was in IV, vii, saying: endure your coming hither, we are born to cry, we must be patient. Edgar is preparing Gloster to die— to endure his *going hence*. Ripeness implies fullness, but also the moment when the growing thing is plucked—before the rot decays it. Making *ripeness* an unalloyed religious affirmation, connoting an "acceptance of order as the final reality" (Heilman), a learning "to accept with a deep inner joy" (James Jones), may miss the dialectic of the play, and the momentary image. What man must learn, in the *Lear* world, is to live with disorder; there is no help from heaven, joy is transient, patience is the best to hope for, and not likely. Gloster allows himself to be pulled off, saying Folio's

> And that's true too (11),

another of his see-saw yieldings to a delay in dying.

Act V, Scene iii

Hardly has the one old man been hurried off the stage than the other is driven on—before the victorious Bastard, and his troops: *in conquest,* Folio stipulates.

Yet Edmund's order to imprison Lear and Cordelia is not at once obeyed. Edmund's position is, as he will say, touchy, his rising political ambitions endangered: Lear's age and title have charms to *pluck the common bosom on his side* (50), and Gloster's troops may be seen as not happy to serve him. Hence Edmund's speech is a mask: he says he wants the two held for the *pleasure*—the horrible pleasure?—of the proper authorities; in fact he will order them killed. His face by now has become a mask of power, of terrible will. His long drive to the top may be focused in his handling of Lear's crown, which he may have taken from the old king. The crown will be a central visual image from here on: Edmund, trying it on, may seem to confirm the initial expectation of the naive spectator that the maltreated outcast youngest would indeed come to power.

Meanwhile, his pretence of consideration, Lear's visual rejection of any immediate hostile move—he may exercise his king's stare—and the growing friendliness of his British subjects toward their old king-prisoner, give Lear and Cordelia time to speak. Cordelia, still formal, still untender in face-to-face speech, addresses Lear as *King*. A man could as well have spoken her first conventionally rhymed Stoic lines, extending the adjectives of measure begun by Edmund: *some, good, greater, first, first, best, worst.* Her last line is characteristic Cordelia, to the inflections:

> Shall we not see these daughters and these sisters? (7.)

Lear now sounds one of the play's last tonic notes. How truly, depends on the character design. If Lear is seen as greatly enfeebled here (Bradley), weak, helpless, relapsed into childishness (Schücking)—he has been played this way, by actors as far apart as Macready and Wolfit —only faint echoes of the promise of rest may be heard. If Lear is clearly sane again (Jorgensen), even the proud old warrior-king restored

(R. W. Chambers), a strong hope for spiritual, if not material, serenity resonates. Some version of the latter mode fits best the persistent dialectic of the design.

On stage, the good old Lears—like Charles Kean—who recovered their geniality in IV, vi, intensified it here. The Lears touched from the first with madness had a further glimpse of sanity. Here was dramatic contrast; and even more contrast enlivened those Lears, titan, tough, human, who found or contrived a warm or exultant joy in supporting Cordelia, and envisioning a prison life with her. This radiated from Mikhoels, even though he was brought in—as was Cordelia—with hands tied. Lear had never been more free, Mikhoels felt: he had at last found a sense of beauty in man. Mikhoels'-Lear's compulsive gesture of reaching for his crown fell from him; he had outgrown it. His voice was jubilant as he described the life-to-be in prison. Gielgud, too, came in serene and joyful, with a light step. Granville-Barker wanted the speech "like a polka, sung in every possible range and variety of tone, but lightly, like a boy of nine telling a story to a child of six." Gielgud liked the movement that developed—a half-walk, half-dance down to the footlights, Lear swinging Cordelia's arms in his in a childlike minuet. As Mantell *laughed / At gilded butterflies*, his hands reached out like a child's for the winged things.

But the bright vision is shadowed, actors and critics have observed. There is sweetness in Lear's encouragement, but the context is bittersweet again. So Scofield's Lear was dignified, explanatory, an austere teacher to his weeping daughter. Calhern tried to project the duality of Lear's vision: a dream of a kind of timeless beauty, discolored because it was only an old man's dream, and wronged his daughter. Lear rejects reality: he will not see *these daughters and these sisters*. His four exclamatory *no*'s may contain elements of anger, fear, revulsion; certainly suggest, in context, the impulse to escape. Better—in a kind of joyful invitation:

> Come, let's away to prison (8).

He offers his young daughter, separated from her husband, a life with her old father in a cage: a fixed life, where they will sing like birds (a first gentle use of bird imagery; the last reference was to the wrens who *go to't*). Lear would repeat forever the tableau of IV, vi—and the child's barter for love he first proposed in I, i:

> When thou dost ask me blessing, I'll kneel down,
> And ask of thee forgiveness (10–11).

Perhaps they kneel to each other again, as in a Japanese *Lear*. *So we'll live* (11), he says: as if this is life, and they will have it forever: in an isolated world, where they can magically laugh at meaningless courtiers, and talk with them, too. In this idyll, they will go deep:

> And take upon's the mystery of things,
> As if we were God's spies (16–17).

No need to see anything blasphemous in this one possible reference to one God, or in this assumption of godlike insight: Lear's fantasy is full of magic, of wonder, as in its stipulation of power over time as well as space and mind:

>   ... we'll wear out,
> In a wall'd prison, packs and sects of great ones (17–18).

Lear may be painting so gentle a picture partly because Cordelia, for all her Stoicism, has been weeping: too much even—ever—to speak again. He himself voices the other, painful side of his prison image:

> Upon such sacrifices, my Cordelia,
> The gods themselves throw incense (20–21).

This is his last gesture for the benison of divinity; it will turn out hollow, and unless he is firmly self-deceived, a dominant undertone of his doubt may now sound. Cordelia's tears do not stop. *Wipe thine eyes* (23) may be accompanied by a gesture reminiscent of his comforting of her in IV, vii (and of comforting Gloster in IV, vi.).

Cordelia weeps partly because her design stipulates "loving wife." What Lear says may be a reminder of her love—half she has to give, at least—for her unmentioned husband. Her weeping at Lear's vision of a different kind of marriage, a life *a deux* in prison, with its undertones of an all-demanding relationship, kind nursery and more, that she resisted in I, i, opposes a note of painful reality to his fantasy. A Swedish Cordelia (1929) was praised for standing uncomfortably, awkwardly here, arms at her side, not returning her father's caresses, mute in feeling as well as words.

As in their opening encounter, Cordelia cannot speak; can only say nothing. Nor can she escape; hence Lear's triumphant

> Have I caught thee? (21).

Some felt resistance in her, perhaps some movement, from Edmund's guards, rouses the old dragon:

> He that parts us shall bring a brand from heaven,
> And fire us hence like foxes (22–23).

Ambiguity, again: only the heavens could part them—but heaven imagined as acting the role of hell.

Lear himself may be weeping now, echoing his tearful, ashamed refusal to weep in II, iv:

> The good years shall devour them, flesh and fell,
> Ere they shall make us weep: we'll see 'em starv'd first (24–25).

Spoken with his old virulence, with his old compulsion to punishment and revenge under the mask of justice, this one prophecy, ironically, comes oracularly true: Edmund, Goneril and Regan will die in success; and they will make Lear weep again.

Come, Lear says, as if the decision is his to make. On stage it has been, as he has calmly or fiercely denied shepherding; he may make a ritual of it, bowing to Cordelia, extending a hand for her to take, before they march off as in a royal progression; or Edmund has enforced their going, as he has their coming; or respectful or fearful guards have gently led them off. Neither Folio nor Quarto directs an exit; but the mood of the scene suggests that Lear leaves freely enough to initiate another peripety: all may yet be well, it seems to a naive spectator, as Lear leads Cordelia, as Gielgud did, apparently to a prison's safety.

The Bastard promptly blasts this easy hope, rearouses anxiety. The man-animal motif, revivified lightly in Lear's butterflies and birds, is brutally intensified in Edmund's unaccustomed terse, staccato, time-conscious prose phrases, reflecting the desperate intensity of his ambition now:

> Know thou this, that men
> Are as the time is; to be tender-minded
> Does not become a sword; thy great employment
> Will not bear question; either say thou'lt do't,
> Or thrive by other means (31–35).

Are men only as the time is? How do they differ from animal? The captain:

> I cannot draw a cart nor eat dried oats;
> If it be man's work I'll do't (39–40).

Edmund means to do king's work, and, as suggested, this can be made visual: he may have taken Lear's crown, may have, during the Lear-Cordelia dialogue, tried it on, or may do so now. He will like the fit.

The captain and Edmund may be surprised by the magnificent sweeping, sounding entrance of Albany, the sisters, and all the troops. The entourage, loyal British, will provide the ground on which the main figures play out their tragedy.

Edmund is ready to grasp the crown; Goneril and Regan, the crown and Edmund. Albany, the only tonic element, hides at first his anger and hurt over Goneril's letter. The four may pause for a formal, ritual acknowledgment of victory: here Goneril can (in the theatre sometimes does) provide drink, with a poisoned cup for Regan—who may otherwise be sickening as she enters, and need support or a resting place, as in Gielgud's *Lear*.

The deep dissonance that disturbs this meeting may at first be visual: Albany's spiritual isolation from the rest, his men perhaps now cutting out—if they have not before—and dismissing Edmund's troops, as Goneril's, in I, iv, may have dismissed Lear's. Albany begins with praise for Edmund's valor—significantly the credit goes not to the gods, but Edmund's god, Fortune; then peremptorily demands Lear and Cordelia. Edmund, unaware of the mine laid under him, assumes—speaks with—equality (and echoing imagery): their captives could *turn our impress'd lances in our eyes* (51). Lear's *age* as well as his title, has charms.

Always alert to the opportunities of time, the Bastard suggests delay, in dignified words:

> At this time
> We sweat and bleed; the friend hath lost his friend,
> And the best quarrels, in the heat, are curs'd
> By those that feel their sharpness (55-58).

It is a thoughtful speech, the speech of a would-be king, reflecting Edmund's sensitivity to the undercurrents swirling around him, his readiness to play role.

Albany is at last absolutely firm: he takes Edmund, not as the brother he would be, but a subject, Now the rivalry between Regan and Goneril, that began in I, i, culminates. Regan, using the royal *we*, claims Edmund's rights, as her surrogate, to brother Albany. Goneril shows her hand: Edmund exalts himself. When Regan insists that *she* gives Edmund the right to royalty, *he compeers the best* (70), Albany for the first time shows humor, with a sour joke on Edmund's ambition, the punch line of which only he knows.*

> That were the most, if he should husband you (71).

Regan's retort awakens many echoes from the earlier acts:

> Jesters do oft prove prophets (72).

*Quarto gives the line to Goneril, and so intensifies the sisters' rivalry.

So does Goneril's imagery:

> That eye that told you so look'd but a-squint (73).

Regan, deathly sick now, in worthy words, and with a gesture of love, formally makes Edmund her *Lord and master*. When Goneril objects, and Albany says it is not her business, Edmund can now boldly, arrogantly *thou* him. Albany reacts with insult: *Half-blooded fellow, yes.* He halts the ritual drum that would establish Regan's investiture of Edmund, with, curiously, *hear reason*. Not reason, but hurt and anger move him: he will half-confess that he is a cuckold. He arrests Edmund for treason, and links to it his own beautiful wife—*gilded serpent*. Again, the curious, bitter humor erupts in sarcasm to Regan:

> For your claim, fair sister,
> I bar it in the interest of my wife;
> 'Tis she is sub-contracted to this lord,
> And I, her husband, contradict your banes.
> If you will marry, make your loves to me,
> My lady is bespoke (85–90).

The mean joke goes on too long, impelled as much by rebuffed love as anger. He brushes aside Goneril's arrogant *An interlude!* (90.) Freely using *thou*'s, he challenges Edmund, is nobly answered.

The difference in design between the two sisters has intensified with their rivalry: Regan, always more feminine, ends by speaking lines worthy of a romantic heroine; Goneril, under the pressure of shameful exposure, becomes harsher, more masculine, more terrible. Regan may, at some point, recognize, with a look at Goneril, the source of her poisoning; may, being led out, make some last gesture of clawing at her sister; but the design is mainly characterized now by her softness, her femininity—being ill, she will not trade insults with Goneril—and her devotion to Edmund. Her sickening in Olivier's production was a shock, an omen of the death she struggled with, that momentarily stilled the stage. Brook saw her at the extreme of yielding, "creeping ignonimously off like a squashed spider." But she has committed herself to the Bastard; and her dying must draw some response from him that edges his relationship with the other sister. In a Japanese *Lear*, he rushed to kneel by her.

Goneril's arrogant jabs at Regan reflect not only her response to the triangular tension, but also a larger design: a mounting nervousness that will end in her passionate, self-destructive act. She stands apart, as in the Scofield *Lear* markedly alone, in a kind of trance, inward anxiety intensifying, watching doom come.

The ritual of the duel is spectacular, and suspenseful: trial by combat —succeeding a scene of trial with words. In Quarto, Edmund, not to be outshone, calls along with Albany—perhaps simultaneously—for the herald. The stern challenge to Edmund is read. The rousing trumpets sound twice, no champion appears, a naive spectator sees Albany prepare for the fight—then the third trumpet is answered, and a masked fighter appears: pat, like the catastrophe of the old comedy.

Normally the unknown is in bright, unidentifiable armor, helmeted, plumed (in Brook's film, he strips a dead knight), motivating Edmund's

> ... since thy outside looks so fair and warlike (142).

But Nunn's Edgar startled spectators with his peasant costume, his helmet of stark burlap sack, with deep eyeholes. Edmund's design has required that he conform with a show of panache to social norms, yet his new independence might have freed him from obligation to fight a peasant.* Nunn's Edmund carried it off by describing Edgar's "fair and warlike" outside ironically; but the line jarred, and this and Edgar's lack of armor made the moment uneasy.

Herald has asked the persistent identity questions of Edgar:

> What are you?
> Your name? your quality? and why you answer
> This present summons? (119–121).

My name is lost (121)—"I nothing am"—the unknown has replied; then with the most chivalric terms has challenged Edmund's eminence at the very top, in language that gives the Bastard full credit for his ascent, but reveals a dangerous knowledge of his means:

> Despite thy victor sword and fire-new fortune,
> Thy valour and thy heart, thou art a traitor,
> False to thy gods, thy brother, and thy father,
> Conspirant 'gainst this high illustrious prince ...
> A most toad-spotted traitor (132–138).

Edmund's answer in print seems easy and immediate; but in fact what he has heard must be unnerving and must show on his face, before his helmet is on. Who is this man who knows all his secrets? His answer, finally, as elegant as Edgar's, foregoes the identity question, *In wisdom I*

---

*Too, the stranger's identity in Nunn's production was now unmistakable. Almost certainly this would be Edgar, anyway; but for a naive spectator a doubt was possible—particularly since Kent, like Edgar, having been absent from the war, could also be a candidate. Edgar without armor seemed almost impossibly vulnerable.

should ask thy name (141), but indicates that his time-conscious mind has considered the practicality of procrastination—and dismissed it: this unknown master of his mysteries must be dispatched.

> What safe and nicely I might well delay
> By rule of knighthood, I disdain and spurn (144–145).

Folio simply says *Alarums. Fights*, Quarto nothing. Then Edmund is presumed dying. If the duel is accepted as having a foregone conclusion —the "bad guy" inevitably defeated by a "good guy," Edgar, who has shown little skill at arms before—the battling must be merely ornamental. Then a stylized confrontation, like a stylized battle, eliminates the strain of life-like swordfighting. But suspense need not be abjured. In the Brook *Lear* the two men were hard to tell apart: a battle of giants, Murray, the Edgar felt: both men grotesque and sinister, in nearly identical suits of heavy armor, with six-foot broadswords, almost too heavy to wield. They pressed against each other in one straining confrontation; then they sprang apart, Edgar made one mortal thrust, and Edmund fell. When the duel is realistic, the fencing must suggest actual danger—one of the most difficult techniques of visual theatre—or disbelief is evoked, and the scene is wasted. There must be a *fight*, not merely swordplay. Shock can come through suddenness: in the Cobb *Lear*, Edmund struck hard three times against Edgar's shield, breaking it, then Edgar stabbed him through. Traditionally, the duel has been longer, and more formal. Macready's soldiers, forming temporary lists, crossing spears in a semi-circle around the fighters, suggested the tournament quality conventionally projected. Such cliches as Edgar knocking Edmund's sword away and letting him retrieve it (Edmund doing the reverse) have lost fashion; recently the savagery of both fighters has been emphasized, they are in to kill—in the Dunn *Lear*, Edgar knifed the fallen Edmund repeatedly, and had to be dragged off. Edmund does not always fight villainously: when Jan Bull's Edgar fell and Edmund waited chivalrously for him to rise, Edgar rushed suddenly at him and stabbed him unprepared. At Colorado, Edmund finally pulled Edgar's sword on himself.

One possible clue to the fighting: Albany's *Save him! save him!* (151.) Save Edgar, momentarily in danger? disarmed? Johnson thought, "Save Edmund to get his confession," implying that the victorious Edgar must indeed be pulled off from killing.

Goneril might well own the words, cried out for her lover. There is no lust in her passion now, but a desperation, as Albany will say a hysteria, as it was with Gielgud's Goneril, that will drive her to suicide.

This is not sudden; it has been building, from the moment of the victory council. As she has shown more hardness, arrogance, even flippancy—*Holla, holla!* (72) ... *An interlude!* (90)—she has also been coming closer to breaking. In Edmund's death she glimpses the crashing of all she had built in her fantasy, and usually she falls with a cry on his dying body. She cares not for Albany; and when he tries to frighten her with her letter, she tries to tear it as much from frenzy as wishing to destroy it. Quarto is probably right in giving her, rather than Edmund, the heedless

> Ask me not what I know (160)

for immediately after her exit Albany sends someone to *govern* her desperation.

That he does so indicates—beyond its value for suspense—that Albany has much more dimension than "revengeful husband." He cares; behind all his fury at her lies a subtextual commitment that will move him even beyond her death—and that will do much to sustain the scene until Lear's return.

Edmund's dying becomes him; he speaks with grace, characteristically refers to *time*—what he has done, *the time will bring it out*—and finally broaches the identity question:

> But what art thou
> That hast this fortune on me? If thou'rt noble,
> I do forgive thee (164–166).

Edgar, as he takes off his helmet, at last speaks in his own person; but the message is still Tom's, intent on punishment for sin. *Let's exchange charity* (166), he says—and after reminding Edmund of wrongs done, utters lines that are among the least charitable, the most sullen, in this angry play:

> The gods are just, and of our pleasant vices
> Make instruments to plague us;
> The dark and vicious place where thee he got
> Cost him his eyes (170–173).

Edgar's impulse to charity has seemed to some critics his true motivation. "Yet Edgar is in reality both humble and gentle" (Kenneth Myrick); "[This gives] Edgar confidence in their [the gods'] moral nature" (Charlton); Edgar "eases his [brother's] last moments by offering ... comfort in the only terms Edmund is able to comprehend ... his own *lex talionis* formula" (Elton). But the shadow side of Edgar's fierce, troubled design still functions. The character has too much validity to be merely humble and gentle; Edgar's "confidence" in the trickster gods' moral nature for blinding a man for adultery—are all bastards to die, all adulterers to lose their eyes in his theology?—is a measure of his own bitter morality; he offers Edmund no ease, rather reminds him of wrongs done, even blames him for being a bastard. But this is secondary—mainly he uses the occasion to attack his father's sexuality again. Most significant is the characteristic, echoing imagery, recalling other *darknesses*. Not only adultery bothers Edgar, but its locus, which is not described easefully: the *dark and vicious place*. Tom-Edgar's puritanism, welling up from the same deep source as Lear's revulsion—*there's darkness ... stench ... confusion*—condemns Edmund for ever being, his father for the sin of his making, in that terrible *place*.

Edmund, once more taking on the coloration of his environment, once more intent on pleasing, agrees, his words an echo of Gloster's perfunctory acceptance (*And that's true, too*) of Edgar's last sermon about enduring death:

> Th' hast spoken right, 'tis true (173).

A teasing punishment by the gods was Edgar's cruel notion of their "justice" (with its family resemblance to Gloster's of divine, wanton boys, sporting with men's lives). Edmund responds at a tangent: his divinities are Nature and Fortune, and he has pursued and fled from himself on the latter's wheel from base back to base.

> The wheel is come full circle; I am here (182).

He lies dying while Edgar, embraced and questioned by Albany, tells his *brief tale*—a very long one. Edgar's mood has some of Gloster's zigzag—he is his father's son. Preacher against suicide, he yearns for death now:

> O! that my heart would burst! (182).

Why did he live after his flight?

> O! our lives' sweetness,
> That we the pain of death would hourly die
> Rather than die at once! (184–186).

Ripeness is not all. The swings in Edgar's dialectic intensify. Thus the opposition of "Life is sweet—how can we bear its pain" (which refracts his earlier "our hatred of life keeps us alive"). A moment before he has condemned his father's adultery; now he mourns for him. Edgar says he nursed his father—verbalizing the mirroring of Cordelia-Lear—but never tells the deceptions and tortures of that nursing; only that he

> became his guide,
> Led him, begg'd for him, sav'd him from despair (190–191).

But Gloster, in this nursing, went from one despair to another—and another; Edgar confronts at last—and at least—the strange omission that might have finally steadied his father:

> Never—O fault!—reveal'd myself unto him,
> Until some half hour past (192–193).

By then Gloster could not bear the news. His heart, Edgar reports—in the echoing dialectic of the play—

> 'Twixt two extremes of passion, joy and grief,
> Burst smilingly (198–199).

How are we to understand Gloster's *grief*? Because of the wrong he had done Edgar? Because Edgar had waited so long to tell him? Or, perhaps, because Gloster finally realized how much Edgar had, in fact, been fooling him? In effect, Edgar's way and time of telling killed his father. Edmund's false warning to Gloster was oracularly true.

Shakespeare's next twenty-odd lines do not much help the scene's momentum. Edmund's dignity since the duel partly prepares for his determination to do some good; but his request to hear more, presumably at some visual strains evident in Edgar, is awkward and labored:

> You look as you had something more to say (201).

So is Albany's cowish reply:

> If there be more, more woeful, hold it in;
> For I am almost ready to dissolve,
> Hearing of this (202–204).

Quarto wisely cuts Edgar's rejection of Albany's plea, and his attenuated description of Kent's agony. They diminish both the tension of the moment, and Edmund's plot against Lear and Cordelia—great thing of the audience by now almost forgot. The language, though tensed by many characteristic comparatives and superlatives from *top extremity* to *worst*, has no sustaining poetic energy. The reported Edgar-Kent meeting seems not only unncessary, but also to detract from Kent's touching appearance later. Important only is the clue to Kent's deterioration:

> ... the strings of life
> Began to crack (216–217).

But this, too, will be communicated better visually.

Tension resumes with Gentleman's inrush. His characteristic shouts, evoking overlapping cries from Albany and Edgar, lead to one of the most difficult lines in the play for modern audiences to take seriously, unless very carefully controlled, about the bloody knife:

> 'Tis hot, it smokes (223).

Gentleman's message is shaped for suspense, revives audience concern for Cordelia:

> It came even from the heart of—O, she's dead (224).

A naive spectator may wonder if *she* is Cordelia; but Albany is not thinking of her. His *Who dead? speak, man* (225) to the halting Gentleman elicits the answer he seems to expect, and perhaps fear. He is silent with pain as Gentleman goes on, and Edmund hurts him more with the brilliant pun on sex and death—Edmund will die bravely, like the smug bridegroom of Goneril as well as Regan:

> I was contracted to them both: all three
> Now marry in an instant (228–229).

When Albany recovers, it is to ask that the bodies be produced. Why? Later, lined up on the stage around Lear, they will repeat, in tragic parody, the initial court scene, and so round out a design; but a personal motive insists, too; Albany will see the dead woman for whom he had his *great love*.

This judgment of the heavens (231)—Albany speaks so when he approves of what happens—*Touches us not with pity* (232). Thus the text: but will his visual language not betray something else, when he looks at the dead face? His pauses and silences suggest as much .

His involvement with his own repressed feeling through the lines after Goneril has left may partly motivate his shock when Kent, entering, mentions Lear. Albany is forced to focus.

> Great thing of us forgot! (236).

But once the dead sisters are brought in, Albany immediately forgets again, at the sight of Goneril.

> Seest thou this object, Kent? (238).

His hurt is deep.

Edmund's next line is sometimes used, in the theatre, for his exit, it so condenses his drive for approval:

Yet Edmund was belov'd (239).

This is his measure—two killed themselves for him. He had come far, this boy who had been away nine years, and was to be sent off again.

His boast is brutal to Albany. *Even so*, Albany acknowledges. Reminded of his great love, great hurt, he takes one last look. Then, *Cover their faces* (242). In his distraction he has, for the third time, so forgotten Lear and Cordelia that he is only reminded when Edmund, more tender-minded after the evidence that he is lovable, invokes his temporal sense:

Nay, send in time (247).

Albany, unthinking, panicky, now urges haste: Edgar and Edmund must think for him, send Edmund's token. Albany utters another of the play's many prayers that are unanswered, if not rejected:

The gods defend her! (255).

The shock of rejection is immediate, designed: Cordelia's limp body is brought in by Lear. The gods provided no defense.

Edmund's body is carried out as Cordelia's is borne in. The youngest die here—the "bad" young son, the "good" young daughter. Lear passes Edmund: the old king, and the would-be young one, both at the bottom of the wheel.

Edmund may pause to watch Lear, thus preparing for the entrance—but Lear has no eyes for Edmund. His whole energy is concentrated on his mourning, as he carries Cordelia in his arms—the roles once more reversed, father nursing daughter.

For the old weak Lears, the burst of energy unleashed in killing the guard sometimes lasted into this entrance: so Booth, recovered to a sanity and power not approached before, strode froward in a fierce passion, weeping, moaning, howling. Macready, too, rushed in furiously, almost recklessly*—yet his strength ebbed, he had to yield Cordelia to the arms of two of his guards.

*Thus, Fanny Kemble, one of his Cordelias: "Macready certainly was aware of the feeling of his fellow actors about his violence, and want of personal self-control on the stage; for as he stood . . . ready to rush in with me, his Cordelia, dead in his arms, he made various prefatory and preparatory excuses to me, deprecating be-

More conventionally, Lear comes in solemnly, often with great effort, sometimes real, as well as apparent. When Edmund Kean, with a great deal of courage, decided to be first to restore the death scene to the Tate version he moved awkwardly, short as he was, carrying his Cordelia, and some among the audience were amused. Gielgud's portage was easier with a concealed sling which made it seem that he carried her on one arm. This was one of Granville-Barker's favorite inventions to give Lear the appearance of massive strength. Cordelia lay limp in Klöpfer's arms as if taken down from the cross of life. Scofield came on almost unconscious with rage, his Cordelia's neck clearly marked—as with a red necklace—by the hangman's signature. Scofield yielded a sense of the inward suffering that carried through from IV, vi; outwardly on his hard frame the blows that sagged him slightly seemed more psychic than physical, the bludgeoning of despair. He had the physical strength when needed, but he had used almost the last of it; like all Lears, he had only a little further to go. His *howl* was the more touching because it came from so granite a character design.

An old, old Lear, like Redgrave, nerved in midplay to the strenuous energy of madness, calmed to dependence in IV, vi, and to philosophy as V, iii begins, now can be so exhausted that he can barely stand, his last rages the guttering of a dying candle. By dramatic logic, the same deterioration may culminate the physical design of the titan Lears, affording a shocking contrast, where gentler Lears have shown less change. This was dramatically demonstrated when two of Bulgaria's foremost actors alternated as Lear. Stamatov was, in I, i, a "feeling" Lear, full of love, more surprised than angered by Cordelia's *nothing*. His madness was an agony of experiencing the cruelty of man and nature; awareness ended in a despair that crushed him. Vladimir Trandafilov (b. 1891) made the longer descent from egotistical, autocratic king to degraded beggar. Hot tempered, irritable, absolute in authority in I, i, he stormed fiercely against the storm, was furious against the unjust world, and ended exhausted by his struggle.

So, too, Forrest's magnificent strength finally failed him; he could hardly carry Cordelia in, he was slack with hopeless exhaustion. Salvini was even weaker, at the end of the long downhill slope he had designed:

---

forehand my annoyance at being dragged and pulled about—saying, that necessarily the scene was a disagreeable one for the 'poor corpse.' I had no very agreeable anticipation of it myself, and therefore could only answer, 'Some one must play it with you, Mr. Macready and I feel sure you will make it as little distressing to me as you can,' which I really believe he intended to do, and thought he did."

How is it credible that an old man, broken down by so many disasters, and on the point of rendering up his soul to God could possess such Herculean strength [as to carry Cordelia?] . . . Lear, not allowing anyone but himself to touch the beloved body, must drag it in with difficulty.

Drag it, Salvini did, with failing energy; Welles would do the same a half century later—though his vocal energy seemed to belie this sign of weakness.

The threefold howl itself makes demands on Lear's strength, from the first terrible cry, that may sound before Lear appears, and arrest all action—including Edmund's leaving. The howls intensify in pain, if not in pitch and volume, whether in a full-bodied voice, like Gielgud's, or a high, cracked one, like Laughton's. *Howl* is not articulated usually as a word; rather, as a voiced pain, often an animal ululation, man-beast merged in an aural-visual image of visceral suffering too fierce for verbalizing: an anguished cry (Karl Mantzius), a quiet sobbing, by a Japanese Lear, a deep baying (Redgrave), the wail of a wolf (Krauss), of a mourning dog (Cobb). The sound may echo the mad king's earlier barking.

When a Lear does cry the word "howl" he may mean, as Porter did, to keen an order to the dumb men about him: *Howl!* Mikhoels was long at this: he first carefully, silently, laid Cordelia down and knelt by her, looking for a sign of life. He turned to the circle of men—to whom could he show his grief? He approached Albany—gestured haltingly—passed beyond to the line of soldiers. *Howl*, he ordered, in a low wail, but the men, absorbed in their own suffering from the battle, had no sympathy to spare him. Then he turned toward the audience, raised his hand high over his head, palm down, hovering, as if to shield himself, his mouth opened for a terrible moan, but all that came out was a long drawn-out, high-pitched *ah-h-h*—the cry of a sickened child.

Usually, in the theatre, Lear comes directly forestage, where he lays Cordelia down—if no litter is hastily provided—on his own knee, as Edmund Kean first did, or on the ground, so he can kneel beside her. Kneels once more—not to ask her blessing, as in his vision, but to beg her to return. The severed noose sometimes still hangs around her neck, as with Irving and Booth; she lies limp in his arms—the head of Olivier's Cordelia swung like a puppet's as he held her. Lear may clasp her to him, nursing and rocking her, his little child. A throne on stage, in which Lear could lull Cordelia, as Bassermann did in I, i, can reinforce the note of reprise that echoes throughout the scene.

Some such inner struggle as that Mikhoels suggested must go on—Lear still battles to quiet the tempest in his mind, as Olivier emphasized.

In some Lears it would give him no leave to ponder on other things, in others it would edge him again into unbalance that seemed almost welcomed.

Rage, grief, desperate love, ego, pride, abstraction, stupefaction share in the dynamic that shunts Lear bewilderedly toward death. Now even the weakest Lears find energy for anger at the silent men around him.

> O! you are men of stones (257).

The fury of the first line in Olympian; and yet Lear's language, as always in this last of the play, is simple, hardly two words have more than one syllable. He will pray no more to gods—rather he wants such a vocal assault on them that *heaven's vault should crack* (259). And not only a vocal one: *Had I your tongues*, he says, *and eyes* (258). He still trusts the power of a fierce stare, as once more he confronts the sky.

Rage gives way, in the dialectic, to ultimate grief, in a world where gods give no hope beyond the grave. The speech could hardly be simpler:

> She's gone for ever.
> I know when one is dead and when one lives;
> She's dead as earth (259–261).

Then grief yields to sudden hope, Lear sounds the first of a series of false tonic notes: perhaps she is still alive. He asks for a *looking-glass*— a grim metaphor for the whole search for identity, echoing the image of women who make mouths in glasses (III, ii, III, v), the image of "Lear's shadow" (I, iv).

> If that her breath will mist or stain the stone,
> Why, then she lives (262–263).

A tremendous *if*. Not only Lear hopes, but the naive spectator does. Shakespeare's own first spectators must have: especially if they knew the old play that preserved Cordelia alive. A tremendous moment of suspense.

Hope is dashed against the dismay of Kent, Edgar, Albany. If they, too, have waited, with some hope, for signs of life, if they have given him the "stone" to reflect her breath, they first let the audience know despair.

> Is this the promis'd end?
> Or image of that horror?
> Fall and cease (263–264).

No mistaking this implication: her certain death, Lear's fool's hope, reflect the final dissolution of the world, chaos, the Last Judgment.

Lear's balance between sanity and madness is reflected in his visual imagery. A clearly mad Lear hallucinates the looking glass—to the horror of the mourning onlookers—and fantasies the feather he now holds to her lips—thus Calhern, picking nothing out of the air. (Granville-Barker suggested a feather floating in space—but a Lear reaching for this invisible mote would give the same impression of hallucination.) If the onlookers know from the first that Cordelia is dead, suspense fades, tension centers on character in these Lears. Saner Lears, clinging to reason, operate more realistically: Booth demanded a feather of Kent, Salvini plucked an actual plume from a soldier's helmet, Redgrave used a wisp of his hair, Forrest a strand of Cordelia's. An old Lear whose hand shook might indeed see a stirring as from breath.

Lear's imagining that Cordelia breathes, if he is not clearly mad, sounds another false tonic, can still raise hope in a naive spectator—hope strengthened if, as with Gielgud, a madly joyful prospect shows on Lear's face.

> This feather stirs; she lives! (265).

Then the *if* on which his world pivots:

> ... if it be so,
> It is a chance which does redeem all sorrows
> That ever I have felt (265–267).

No such chance. In the pause, hope slowly dies. Kent is moved: *O my good master!* (267). Lear rejects him, in the old pattern of banishment from sight: *Prithee, away* (268). "Strong," was Gielgud's note. Lear does not hear that this is Kent; he is intent on keeping Cordelia alive. Irving kissed her, worked with his lips to breathe life into hers; Forrest tried to fondle her alive, with paralyzed hands; Olivier pumped and pumped his hand against her heart, listening for breath.

As hope fades, rage resumes—so Mikhoels erupted in a kind of animal fury:

> A plague upon you, murderers, traitors all! (269).

The obvious first targets of his wrath are the bystanders; but he may be speaking to the gods too. Or only to the gods—they have failed him again, and finally. Then, unbearably, to himself: *I might have sav'd her* (270). Not only now, but long ago, long ago.

Now, in the sanest Lears, the repeated shocks disjoin the rational process. Mind moves erratically, swings dialectically. Desperate hope swallows rage again, her name, whispered? cried? called as if from far off? comes out in plaintive music, the syllables sharply defined:

> Cordelia, Cordelia! stay a little (271).

Again, a naive spectator rises to the possibility of the false tonic. Like Gloster, the audience is wracked between extremes of possible joy and grief. Lear hears something from Cordelia's lips (the actor makes the surd real):

> Ha!
> What is't thou say'st? (271–272).

This is one of the ironic reprises of I, i: King Lear, surrounded by his court and family, waits for a sign from his most loved daughter. He begs, listens for any word, as he did before, now excuses her for her silence.

> Her voice was ever soft,
> Gentle and low, an excellent thing in woman (272–273).

The mind swings: agonized memory, searching out self-justification, finding pride, escapes from the terrible fact before him.

> I kill'd the slave that was a-hanging thee.
> *Gentleman.* 'Tis true, my lords, he did (274–275).

The old dragon revives for a moment:

> Did I not, fellow?
> I have seen the day, with my good biting falchion
> I would have made them skip (275–277).

That he can summon reserves of physical strength, even now, is another dialectic in the design. The oldest Lear had to have energy enough for the killing; though he may now be able to do little more than muse at it. Irving's momentary show of violence was only a spasm; Booth, half-childishly showing the power of a sword thrust, overbalanced, almost fell; and the submission with which he received the help hurried to him told how feeble he was. (Did Lear kill with a sword? Or, more likely, lacking a weapon, with hands that now weakly clench?) A strong Lear may make a brave, boyish show, as Gielgud did; his note: "Jolly. Stand firm above her body."

The excitement depletes Lear. Returning awareness, stupefaction at awareness, physical and psychic defeat, drain him. Until his final outburst, except for one illumination in his erratic exchanges with Kent, he will brood inwardly, or mourn and keen over Cordelia's body. The words come out one by one, without energy:

> I am old now,
> And these same crosses spoil me (277–278).

The identity question:

> Who are you?
> Mine eyes are not o' th' best: I'll tell you straight (278–279).

Kent's measured language sustains the sight-insight motif in a metaphor of the play's dialectic:

> If fortune brag of two she lov'd and hated,
> One of them we behold (280–281).

Lear concentrates on seeing Kent—Carnovsky's persistent *peering* seemed now almost painful—and finally recognizes him. Granville-Barker advised Gielgud, "... it should clearly be a highly indignant 'How-dare-you-enter-our-presence-after-I-have-banished-you' tone ... and when Kent identifies himself the old gentleman should repeat, rather feebly, the magnificent 'out of my sight' gesture with which ... he banished him." But the text does not suggest this; Lear may briefly welcome Kent, and if the moment is visualized, as sometimes in the theatre, as an intense reunion and communion, an embrace between two old, dying friends, it has a power to arouse empathy that only a few other scenes match.

This is all of Kent's reward; a moment later Lear's attention will fade from him. But Kent, never subtle, wants more, and recalls his services as Caius.* Caius was a good fellow, Lear says, but—all images contaminate now—dead and rotten. The old back-and-forth between these two resumes, the lines interlacing, Lear interjecting, Kent running on. Kent insists he is Caius, Lear will *see that straight*, Kent starts his tale, Lear interrupts to welcome him—the moment of recognition may come here.

Characteristically, Kent loves and hurts: his offense is still honesty, and he is too old to learn. He now reminds Lear of his *difference and decay* (288), that *all's cheerless, dark, and deadly* (290); that Regan

---

*This first textual mention of Kent's identity in disguise suggests that in this play, as elsewhere, Shakespeare may simply have said to the company—perhaps at this point in rehearsals—"Let's call him Caius," having improvised the name; then he may well have told the actors to use the name in the earlier acts, without bothering to write it into his manuscript. This would be one of the advantages of the repertory troupe with a resident playwright.

and Goneril have *foredone themselves, And desperately are dead* (291–292).

Job's comforter; no consolation here. Lear's escape from Kent's attentions, as much as his flight to inwardness, veils his consciousness. How much, Albany and Edgar, interceding between the two, tell:

> *Albany:* He knows not what he says, and vain is it
> That we present us to him.
> *Edgar:* Very bootless (293–294).

Lear is out of touch. Krauss again, as in the shock of the first scene, seemed to be looking at, listening to another world. If Lear does not remain by Cordelia's body mourning, intensely or blankly—Phelps tenderly held her all through, rocking, nursing, and crooning over her—he may move aimlessly: thus Gielgud's note: "Forget Cordelia in passage with Kent . . . Wander about at the back of the stage. Find the body again. The rope around her neck. Crouch by her. Kneel." The dynamic of Lear's mental state shapes the design: so Booth, moving back toward madness, played mindlessly with the rope's end, Mantell gnawed at it. Nevill Coghill believes Lear may even try the rope around his own neck, and so be reminded of the hanging of his *poor fool.* Scofield simply endured his numbing sanity.

Albany has one of the hardest lines of all, at the news of Edmund's death. *That's but a trifle here* (295). Unless said with his characteristic deadly seriousness, it can evoke a laugh in this dark moment. Albany *is* deadly serious here, well meaning—and, in the event, full of alteration and probably self-reproving. He promises all comfort to the unhearing Lear—*this great decay* (297). But he uses the royal we:

> . . . for us, we will resign,
> During the life of this old Majesty,
> To him our absolute power (298–300).

Krauss' Albany handed over the crown to the old king here.

Edgar and Kent are to be well served; Albany speaks, again characteristically, of reward and punishment:

> All friends shall taste
> The wages of their virtue, and all foes
> The cup of their deservings (302–304).

As often, he invites irony. He intends that Lear's resumption of the throne be a kind of rewarding wages for suffering; and the naive spectator may accept this hint of the tonic as a crumb of relief from all that's

cheerless, dark, and deadly. But Albany unintentionally echoes Goneril's meaner, truer prophecy that Lear must *taste his folly* (II, iv, 293),
and now its sour tang starts some convulsion in Lear that startles Albany
into sight, if not insight.

> O! see, see! (304).

Much critical interpretation of *Lear* pivots on the next seven lines,
and indeed almost entirely on the last two. Only there, and in the first
line, ambiguity hovers.

> And my poor fool is hang'd! (305)

does not, because the word *fool* was affectionate, force a choice between
Fool and Cordelia. Nor must Lear be "utterly crazy ... raving" as Empson would have it. More probably the design, as Bradley sensed, involves
a merging of ideas that is implied by the visual as well as verbal imagery:
Lear's tenderness with Cordelia recalls Lear's sheltering of Fool, his
cross-grained love of both. Possibly the visual linkage intended sub-
liminal effect: Gielgud speculated that Cordelia and Fool were probably
much alike because played by the same actor—and Shakespeare's audience knew it. The two are joined by motif as well as character design:
Lear's fool is someone who loves him, stays with him, pities him, suffers
with him—who has been "fooled" into holding on to his downhill
wheel.

If Lear's mind strays, it is not far from center, for the next lines are
as searingly sane as they are uncompromising:

> No, no, no life!
> Why should a dog, a horse, a rat, have life,
> And thou no breath at all? Thou'lt come no more,
> Never, never, never, never, never!
> Pray you, undo this button: thank you, Sir (305–309).

After the echoing *no*'s, Lear may ask his first question out of bewilderment, as Booth did; but more often it emerges in grieving anger. It may
be meant not only for the bystanders, but also for any gods that be—
any powers that made him—for it challenges the whole cosmic system:
what kind of a world, when animals live, and not Cordelia? Implying
that all the world is animal, except Cordelia? That man's dearer life
seems cheaper to the gods than beast's? But any implications are secondary to the personal pain in the design, the felt grief of the suffering
figure, so universal now because it is a prism of plain man, but never so
universal as to blur the individuating design.

Homeliness is in the language: the simple words, the repetitive, keen-
ing rhythms. When Lear finally accepts Cordelia's death, he knows she
is gone forever—no more reunions, he seems to say, on either side of the
grave. The five death-knell *nevers* seal her end, and prepare for his. The
words have been moaned, almost sung, whispered, cried. Simplicity has
seemed essential: Gielgud once tried speaking the *nevers* in a series of
ascending notes to a climax; the effect was powerful, but unsatisfactory;
the actor changed to a simpler, less contrived mode.

The perception the words enforce on Lear, on his worn body, brings
him to the final paroxysm. *Pray you undo this button* may refer to Cordelia's dress; but almost universally it is taken to reflect the constricting
of Lear's throat, a last attack of *this mother*, ironically reverberative of
a child's appeal to a mother. The release from his last garment—symbolically, from life—recalls visually his first divestment, and both visually and verbally the culmination of that undressing before Edgar in the
storm—is there a deep, unspoken impulse to go naked again? go naked, to
death, as he came? His plea is not, as before, promulgated or ordered, but
requested; no king, but agonized man, hurt child, accepts help, and says
humbly *thank you, sir.* Quarto follows with four heartbreaking O's—a
more human equivalent to the howls—and leaves him to die there; Folio
includes the two lines that have been seized upon by "redemptionists"
as casting a warm and hopeful glow over the dark and deadly scene:

> Do you see this? Look on her, look, her lips,
> Look there, look there! (310–311).

What does Lear see? Let the argument over its meaning wait: for the
perception itself, it may be: an ecstatic illusion that Cordelia is alive, that
at last she speaks the words he wants so to hear; a vision of some supernatural aura about her, presumably beatific; even an apparent glimpse of
her spirit, rising toward heaven; or a horror of the ultimate silence that
has stilled her. The facts of the text are that Cordelia is physically dead,
and that all about her—except possibly Lear—see nothing to alleviate a
sense of absolute woe.

The possible modes of Lear's dying, from ecstasy through dread,
must be expressed solely in visual imagery; words fail now. A wide variety of possibilities has been suggested by actors as well as critics: so
Gielgud, dying grandly in joy at his perception of apotheosis in Cordelia; Forrest, frankly hallucinating her reviving, staring vacantly into
space; Carnovsky, shocked to death at the horror of Cordelia's stillness.
But the overt mood is only one expression of the complex of impulses
that energizes Lear in the first scene, and that sustain him until the end.

At last he has *caught* Cordelia; and all that moved him to rest in this final cage with her colors his dying.

Lear's search for identity has been baffled by the multiplicity of selves in his design; now the identities converge, as in his prior crises. King, father, child, lover, man in his many cultural and precultural manifestations: guilt-ridden; shamed; in mental flux; physically worn; angry; touched with love, compassion, self-pity, paranoia—and with transcendence and the root animal inheritance.

Calhern confessed, somewhat guiltily, that he played the scene for its surface grief, to evoke an emotional response from the audience, because he was sure Shakespeare wanted tears. Certainly Shakespeare did; but the subtextual dialectic never stops, Lear's grief is dimensional. Tragedy inheres not merely in Lear's death, and Cordelia's, but in the implications of their past, and of their dying together.

These dominant tonalities may remain ambiguous, as in Scofield's silent death: sitting bolt upright, his eyes looking into the mystery of things, his face a map of his experience and lost hope, he died without moving. More often, Lear's yearnings have gestured with some explicitness. Booth suggested a man afraid, exhausted by suffering, confronting Cordelia at the end with a dreadful terror, as if in fear not only of what was, but what was to come; he died in the grand style of Forrest, standing suddenly erect, in a final spasm as a king—but when he collapsed in death it was to clasp Cordelia in his arms: he had caught her in death. The reminder of kingship is usually muted now, subordinated to the grief of the man—visual in Krauss's death when the crown given him by Albany lay useless in his hand—and in the simplifications of stage business: so Rossi, from an early portrayal of many rhetorical facial and bodily manifestations of *rigor mortis*, complete with death rattle, changed to an easier, quiet death. The physical agony could be spectacular—Mikhoels told how an actor named Zacchoni drew applause when, at the last moment, his beard jerked suddenly, stiffly up, simulating an actual physical death; but the quieter passing could emphasize Lear's release from suffering, the escape from life, as with Macready, who simply sank slowly back. Even here, the webs that paired Lear and Cordelia could be manifested: Irving fainted into death as he was stroking Cordelia's hair; Salvini, after fighting for breath, died swiftly, tranquilly—his weary head sinking down on Cordelia's breast; Gielgud, dying upright, was caught by Albany and Edgar, who lowered him across Cordelia's body.

The bodies are usually engaged at the end. Lear may indeed die bravely, like a bridegroom. Olivier, to the last, kept pumping at Cordelia's heart, holding her close. Mantell wound her arms around his neck, and slowly dropped his head on her breast. Mikhoels, the animal resurgent in him, pulled roughly at her body, uttered wild sounds, as if atavism for a moment might conquer; then, mind returning, shouted out *Why should a dog, a horse, a rat* . . . ; then knew guilt: he perceived that life was revenging itself on him for his blundering with it. Mikhoels felt Lear died of his own accord—he was still breathing, and yet embraced death as one doomed and damned. But first he lay down beside Cordelia, and uttered the love sound—little chuckling laugh—with which he began the play. He reached out for Cordelia's lips, to kiss her; could not; touched her lips with his hand, nodded, and fell back beside her. Carnovsky, shaken by a terrible sigh that signaled his perception that Cordelia was irretrievably dead, unable to speak through straining lips, slowly rested his head on her breast as he died: his comment, "Romeo and Juliet. 'Her kind nursery.' "

Edgar, more assiduous for Lear than he was for Gloster, reacts sharply: *He faints! My Lord, my Lord!* (311) and, as he had asked Gloster (but then with less urgency), *Look up, my Lord!* (312). Kent and Albany know better: there is no more looking up, actual or symbolic. If Lear is still in death throes, Kent wants them finished. With a new sensitivity, perhaps speaking the next lines to himself as well as his master: *Break heart; I prithee, break!* (312.) And he turns on Edgar—in Brook's production fiercely—reviving the wheel-torture image:

> Vex not his ghost: O! let him pass; he hates him
> That would upon the rack of this tough world
> Stretch him out longer (313–315).

Kent brushes off Edgar's *He is gone, indeed* (315), that contrasts with Edgar's cool estimate of Gloster's chances: *Thus might he pass indeed* (IV, vi, 47). Kent then makes his most subtle and penetrating observation in the play, as if suddenly, in these last speeches, with Lear no longer alive to oppose him, he has become free to be thoughtful:

> The wonder is, he hath endur'd so long:
> He but usurp'd his life (316–327).

Usurped: illicitly commandeered Lear's identity, drove out the rightful self, occupied it by force. He did not belong. The image extends the Ixionic: on his wheel, Lear pursued and fled from himself. He is surrounded by the daughters he cursed: curses and daughters have come to rest. In death, Lear may still be staring, open-eyed, at his vision of joy or horror, and then someone gently moves the eyelids down, to end his unseeing.

In the pause, Albany has had time for his characteristic alteration, if not self-reproof. His uncertain mind has been at work, perhaps prompted by his renewed awareness, as he ordered the bodies borne off, of Goneril lying dead before him: he must watch her leave for the last time. But something else works in him, too. He now drops his assumption of absolute power of a moment before, and pleads with the other two to take over for him—and share ruling the kingdom. He is, indeed, full of *abdication*. This may be visual: if Edmund has taken the crown from Lear before imprisoning the old king; if Albany has then relieved Edmund of it; and has then passed it back to Lear—or offered it to Lear —before Lear's death; Albany now finds himself inevitably in possession again. Does he try it on? The burden threatens him. He offers it—in one of the most startlingly dissonant of the scene's reprises of I, i—jointly to Kent and Edgar, as Lear offered it to Cornwall and Albany. To subject the *gor'd* state to a divided crown once more! Kent's weary response may suggest, beyond his expectation of soon following Lear in death— his strings of life may be obviously weakened now—a sense of shock at Albany and his proposal.*

The final lines are clearly, as Folio gives them, Edgar's. The argument that they might be Albany's on the grounds that he ranks the highest has just been undercut by his own refusal to accept that rank. In fact, he does abdicate—as Lear had; he divests himself of the royal *we*—and crown?—that he had so briefly tried on. The weight of the kingdom is thrust on the ambiguous Edgar; and he responds with an ambiguity that is characteristic. He is as the time is—he speaks of time as Edmund did:

> The weight of this sad time we must obey;
> Speak what we feel, not what we ought to say (323–324).

How much in other times has he spoken as he felt? How much as he ought? What kinds of *ought* has shaped his ambivalences—toward Lear in madness, toward his father, toward Edmund? This new king, in abetting the old king's unreason, and in painfully testing Gloster, has played many roles. Does he play one now? He does not resolve uncertainty, rather intensifies it:

> The oldest hath borne most: we that are young
> Shall never see so much, nor live so long (325–326).

*When Kent says, *I have a journey shortly to go*—to follow his master, Lear—is this a Roman thought? Does his hand go to his dagger?

The *we* may signal his prompt assumption of the royal plural, as he puts on the crown; it may too, though, include Albany, whose design of uncertainty perhaps involves—as suggested at the beginning—his presence in the ranks of the young.

Edgar speaks more than an epitaph for a passed generation; he warns of the briefness and insecurity of the young, so many of whom have already died around him. There is even, in this champion of ripeness—was that what he ought to have said?—a hint of his father's embrace of death, a prophecy that recalls his wish for a burst heart: *we*—the royal Edgar?—will not only not *see* (experience and learn) as much, but *our* life shall be short. So dissonance does not cut off with the speech, rather promises to continue; appropriately the language persists, as it began, in tensing words of comparative measure. There is no return to the tonic. The dominant key in sight and sound colors the slow close: on Shakespeare's open stage, the bodies were escorted solemnly out, perhaps to the Folio's dead march; in the modern theatre, lights usually die on the still figures—perhaps kneeling, as in a Japanese Lear—though Brook, as a final accent to grimness, had Edgar drag Edmund's body slowly off; and Jan Bull's Edgar, before leaving the stage, paused for a long, last look up at the heavens. Irving's soldiers slowly lowered their spears. Forrest's *Lear* ended with ominous sounds of storm gathering again. *General woe.*

So oppressive to some critics is the apparently unrelieved darkness of the finale that they must discover in it transcendent illumination: so Bradley's earnest wrestling with the facts of the text to make them fit a "redemptive" pattern. He recognized, honestly, that in the catastrophe, so far from inevitable, and striking down "our reviving hopes," Shakespeare seemed to be saying: " 'Did you think weakness and innocence have any chance here? Were you beginning to dream that? I will show you it is not so.' "

Honestly, too, Bradley confessed what to his worshipful mind seemed almost blasphemy: "I will take my courage in both hands and say boldly"—are critics ever so touching any more?—"that . . . my feelings call for [a] happy ending." Not the gilt image Lamb painted to knock down —of Lear re-throned—but of a quiet domestic bliss. Bradley partly excused himself by saying he felt such an ending would be dramatically right. He was finally "bold" enough, unlike Johnson, to find a way to make the end bearable.

Two ways. First, the catastrophe was softened by Lear's belief that Cordelia lived, enabling him to die—and so an actor must portray him—

as if in ecstatic joy. Second: Cordelia's death becomes only an outward disaster—she is in a sense superior to her world, untouched by her doom, set free of life rather than deprived of it . . . the tragic world is not a final reality, but only part of a larger one; her being, and not what happens to it, is what matters: "the more unmotived, senseless, monstrous, her fate, the more do we feel that it does not concern her."

Both explanations have been supported, and even expanded, by post-Bradleyans, who tend to see *Lear* as a Christian vision, a "sublime morality" (O. J. Campbell). Not only does Lear die ecstatically, but his ecstasy would make a Jacobean audience believe he had, dying, some mysterious insight (Paul Siegel). He dies in spiritual health, no need for tears (Duthie). He dies healed in the spiritual insight Cordelia's death has brought him; patient and resigned, perfected in "ripeness is all" (Virgil Whitaker).

Given these interpretations, the play's actual climax may be seen as at the beginning of Act V, with Lear's *birds in the cage* speech; the later deaths become comparatively unimportant (Ribner, Muir).*

In this Christian system, Cordelia often becomes a kind of holy person. Her death proves there is a just moral order (Whitaker). "The enduring love Cordelia stands for survives" (James Rosier). The dying king stoops over the corpse of Saint Cordelia (Angus McIntosh). Even: She was "hanged as Christ was crucified, so mankind might be saved" (Campbell).

Elton's whole book counters massively the Christian interpretation, notes that at the end Lear fulfills all the criteria of the Renaissance skeptic, who: considers divine providence faulty; denies immortality of the soul; holds man not different from beast; denies—and derides the tradition of—creation *ex nihilo*; attributes to nature what belongs to God. The third and fourth depend on fine arguing, but they are not necessary to Elton's case, supported on page after page of contemporary reference. The argument itself hardly seems necessary, given the intent of the text. The theology of the play—though not its cultural climate—is specifically pre-Christian. Critics uncommitted to a theological point of view generally can find no optimism in the catastrophe, no support from systems of moral belief (Nicholas Brooke). "All we see is an old man dying in unbearable pain" (Northrop Frye). Lear's end is judged as an outgrowth of character design, mainly in terms of his battle with madness: he is not insane, but preoccupied (Josephine Bennett) or greatly

*Charles Lyons suggests, more reasonably, that "the value of the love shared by Lear and Cordelia, her forgiveness and their mutual compassion, transcends the image of the dying Lear who imagines that Cordelia lives."

enfeebled; he dies between extremes of ecstasy and despair, truth and illusion, slips into temporary madness, no mitigation softens his death (J. Stamfer); he dies in a struggle between madness and a need to believe (Sears Jayne), or, in Freudian terms, between his identity as old man facing reality and regressing child needing to believe illusion (Norman Holland); he is irreversibly senile or finally returned to madness (Merchant, Empson).

If Lear's is a world of men, if gods do not intervene—unless to reject—hope does not color it: the play's climate is "terror, darkness, and suffering unmitigated" (S. L. Bethell); pessimistic, amoral, even nihilistic ... (Minas Savas); "all that remains is the earth, empty and bleeding" (Kott); "a gigantic attack on humanity itself" (Webster). The most that can be said, if all is bitterness, is "Bitterness ennobles, bitterness awakens us to a new understanding of life" (Blok).

If Lear dies in the shock of knowing Cordelia dead, the world is wasteland to him; "if he dies in illusion that has no supernatural aura to it, then his final insistence on deception repeats the need to be deceived that dominated him in I, i" (E. D. MacDonald). "Shakespeare's audience might feel relief at his death, but horror at his error [illusion]" (Sylvan Barnet). "This is the fundamental horror of the play—a passion of joy at his false belief," Empson suggests, and indignantly rejects redemption: if Lear were really regenerated, the play would be sickly. John Shaw and J. D. Rosenberg agree: to look for poetic justice in Lear is an outrage to the sense of moral justice and artistic rightness; morally shocking.

The whole case for "illumination" depends on the play's last words. Heilman's very optimistic "redemptive" vision—Keast observed wryly that he makes of the play a "joyful work"—argues: "In the minds of those who survive . . . there is no doubt that justice has been done and that it evidences the working of divine authority." Hardly. This interpretation admirably fits only Tate's ugly refinement—itself a demonstration of what mutilations had to be visited on Lear to make it "redemptive." One might almost say to Heilman, with the atheist, if we knew for certain that a divine authority was supposed to be responsible for all the pain in Lear, then indeed must we be desperate. But Shakespeare does not frighten us with that, as he does not comfort us with the solace of a kind heaven. On his ultimate stage of fools, no one—except possibly Lear dying in illusion—is so foolish as to see any evidence of divinity at work. Kent, himself ready to die, has perceived only torture in Lear's dying. Edgar, who could find miracles in Gloster's misery, sees no sign of the clearest gods now. Albany is even more to the point. Shakespeare seems to have taken trouble to establish that, if any character in the play could be counted on to find evidence of positive divine intervention in *any* shred of action, it is Albany. Now he watches Lear closely—*O, see, see!*— and must note whatever smile or other grimace dies on Lear's face. *Nothing* illuminatory does he see—no saints, no Christs crucified, no mysterious insight, no promise of heaven—only *general woe.*

And why not? Death everywhere, of the "good" as well as the "bad." The killing of a king is one of Shakespeare's favorite themes—but now no stalwart heir, usurper, or foreign successor assures order. The winter king is dead, but no summer haloes the new wearer of the crown, Edgar. When Shakespeare's tragic heroes die, they always leave behind replacements of lesser stature—but perhaps none so doubtful in the role as Edgar. Curious streaks of cruelty and make-believe discolor him; he claims to speak what he feels, and if he is not acting again, what he feels seems to be apprehension and uncertainty. The stage is littered with dead—and particularly dead women. Has anyone observed that in all Shakespeare's major tragedies, no women are left alive to keep life going? In *Lear* this is particularly meaningful—nature's own organs of increase have dried up . . . *no, no, no life.*

All this cannot prevent those who will from sensing exaltation in Lear's final vision of Cordelia's death, or from believing that what Lear has learned was worth the suffering. We perceive what we are prepared to, need to, perceive. The controlling artist may partly determine this, by his conception of the play. And this conception may change. Kozintsev's stage *Lear*, done in the desperate climate of the Leningrad siege during World War II, presented a Lear dying on an ecstatic vision; in Kozintsev's film, made in the troubled peace a generation later, Lear dies bitterly in a world ravaged by war, poverty, and despair.

A reader may more readily imagine the warmer ending, and extrapolate some comfort from it. A naive spectator at the faithfully staged play cannot easily find joy in Lear's finish. Yet if this joy can be sensed —as it sometimes has been—it adds one more dimension of uncertainty, and by that much contributes a further ambiguity to the play's dialectic. The audience, like Lear and Gloster, is this much more moved between extreme passions, joy and grief. If Lear is perceived as dying in ecstasy, when no other character on the stage recognizes this, then true vision can do nothing to light the world's wasteland.

What enjoyment does *Lear* offer, then?
It provides all the hypothetical "pleasures of tragedy": exhileration in the sheer aesthetic beauty of the work, and in the identification with

humanity ultimately tested; shared experience of forbidden behavior without guilt or punishment; vicarious endurance of the limits of human suffering—with the satisfying safety that the suffering *is* vicarious, is in fact happening to others. If this tragedy, too, seems determined, as Montaigne would say Nature seems, to crush man's hubris, "to make men aware of the inanity, vanity, and insignificance of man," it yet deals with undeniably significant men—and is, like Montaigne's own giant work, the awe-demanding product of man.

Beyond this, *Lear* shares with other great tragedy the power to excite the widest range of our repertory of responses. It leaves no part of us alone. The next chapter examines some latent impulses in the play that satisfy deep needs; but let me here summarize briefly its command of thought, sense, and feeling.

The mind is roused by the urgent dialectic of ideas. The conflicting thoughts earn no easy resolution: that good triumphs, or that evil does; for the ideas issue from a world where such qualities as good and evil are not polar, but mingled, where resolutions are no more easily come by than in life. For the Jacobeans, some current uncertainties, tossed back and forth in the play, held special meanings, as we have seen: the role of a king toward his subjects; the responsibility of royalty, nobility, and wealth toward poverty; the relation of gods, stars, fate, nature, and chance to men, of the aged to the young (and vice versa), of the sane to the mad; the anxiety of a nation troubled by an uncertain rule; the dangers of divided government; the ambiguities of succession. The play's attitudes toward these uncertainties never crystallizes; they remain in suspension, as all in *Lear* does, and resist localization. If the play's distance in history could say to the Jacobeans: king-men-fools were like this, its topicality also said: king-men-fools are like this; and its universality insisted: so will they be.

The play's ideas are subordinate to the total aesthetic experience, which builds only secondarily on contemporary political and social relationships, rather primarily on human relationships—including those implicit in any familiar politico-social system, of any time. More centrally still *Lear* draws on the tremendous energy compressed in the *ur*-relationship—the familial. Shakespeare's manipulation of this energy, released here as almost nowhere else in drama, fills out the kings, men, and fools into characters of vast size and impact, that make strenuous demands on our feeling. As long as the characters are not diminished (in the theatre, or the imagination) into symbols or stereotypes of good and bad, of dimensionless saints and devils, if their full polyphonies of mixed qualities are realized, they clamor for us to perceive with some awe, and sharply experience, their complex, unruly, terrible, recognizable passions. For this, Keats kept returning to the "bittersweet fruit" of *Lear*'s

> fierce dispute
> Betwixt damnation and impassioned clay.

Because the clay was—as Keats' was—so impassioned, so driven by the intensest impulses of mortality, it rouses ultimate feelings, from joy to misery, from love to hate, from peace to assault, in subtle combinations as mixed as the play itself.

The senses are stormed: by the sights and sounds of passion, ritual, war, love, humor, grotesquerie, sadism, wounding, dying, by the cruel vagaries of nature and man in turbulence. Stormed, too, by the words, with their inbuilt tensions, their play of conditionals and comparatives, their poetic energies, sometimes wildly loosed in dazzling rhetoric, sometimes tamed in startlingly simple, homely language.

The dark, deadly, grimly comic world of *Lear* evokes so wide and intense a range of responses on so many levels of consciousness because it reflects so many varieties of human possibility, from the transcendent to the animal—so many that it must defeat any attempt to enclose its meaning in limited formulae such as redemption, retribution, endgame, morality, etc. We may find some rest in the assurance that Shakespeare shares our preference for love over hate, honesty over falsehood, loyalty over disloyalty, order over disorder; but we cannot go on to extract morals from his play: that order will triumph, love conquers all, suffering redeems, recompense waits in the next world—unless we invent them. The playwright describes, he does not prescribe. Only a tragic vision as vast as one of his own lines from *Lear* can suggest the whole implication of the play's world for our own: Edgar's

> ... it is,
> And my heart breaks at it (142–143).

The *Lear* Myth

At the heart of the action of *King Lear* lies a fantasy deeply embedded in human consciousness. It is a fantasy that a child readily recognizes, but that grown men generally learn to disguise in the dress of art. The presence of this fantasy in *Lear* helps explain the play's structure, and how an audience can find pleasure in the tragedy it informs.

The basic wish-dream crops up repeatedly in myths and folk tales across the world. There is, to give one example, a Chinese story about a king who, having married his two older daughters to suitable husbands, asks his third and youngest daughter to marry a man with whom she can rule his kingdom. She refuses: a good girl, she wishes to serve as a nun, and attain Buddhahood. The father, furious at not getting his own way, banishes her, and pursues her with his anger until she dies and attains the state of spiritual perfection. Now the father, punished by the gods, is plagued by sickness; and his two sons-in-law plot to poison him and take over the kingdom. But his good youngest daughter, now an immortal, is able to rescue and heal her father.

She gives her left hand and eye to cure the king's left side, and her right hand and eye to cure the king's right side; on her nourishment he becomes well again. The wicked sons are found out and executed, the two older daughters imprisoned; the king now knows which daughter truly loves him, he begs her forgiveness, and she—none the worse for her temporary amputations, since she is immortal—readily grants it.

If we strip away the dress of language and thought in *Lear*, its key fantasy is seen to be similar; and to occur not once, but twice. As in all folk tales of this pattern, there are two main components: First, a father—often seeking the affection of his daughters—rejects the true love of a good child, and mistakenly favors bad ones; the good child at first suffers in silence, while the father is severely punished for his error, and learns to be sorry he was so wrong. Second, the good child saves him from his pain and sorrow; he begs forgiveness, and the good child grants it.

Once we recognize this fantasy, we can easily enough trace it—from the child's point of view—to its source in human experience. It flourishes

329

in infancy, though it does not end there. The child, insatiable for love and self-esteem, insistent on the role of the sole favorite, inevitably makes demands upon a parent that are rejected, because nobody can have —be—everything. The rejection often seems to be accompanied by a favoring of the child's rivals—brothers, sisters, the other parent. The child compensates in fantasy. The most daring dream is the *Oedipus* one. It provides, with little disguise, two satisfactions. The dreamer, wronged by the parent, murders him—though still not intentionally, the daring is limited—and enjoys both the murder and an expiation through suffering. The *Lear* fantasy is more cunning: the parent suffers—dies—because he wrongs the dreamer, who himself may die, or at least endure noble martyrdom: for the suffering and death of the child dreamer is in this context the worst possible punishment for the father. (Freud found that children riven by feelings for—and against—their father often fantasied being beaten by him.) The basic fantasy pattern is easily recognizable: Father wronged me. He'll be sorry. They'll all be sorry. Maybe I'll go away; and someday when he needs me, I'll come back and save him . . . Maybe I'll die . . . Then he'll be sorry.

This is a tenacious fantasy; grown men nurse variants of it, compensating for frustrated lives by dreaming of how their suffering will bring sorrow and retribution to the unappreciative around them. The theme sounds in some religious mythology, and reverberates in fairy tales and folklore. The innocent child-hero is almost always the youngest—for it is when we are youngest, when we have no other weapons to meet rejection, that we begin to arm ourselves with fantasy. The parent's blame —as in the story of Joseph and his brothers—may not be as conspicuous as the siblings', but he is partly responsible for any of the youngest's suffering, and must be sorry. The child may sense abandonment from birth; hence the hero is frequently rejected as an infant; but later returns to punish the abandoning parent. This punitive impulse is as strong in the central fantasy of *Oedipus* as the more familiar Oedipal rivalry; it works less rigorously in a play like Euripides' *Ion*, where the parent is only symbolically killed; and it flowers into warm wish-fulfillments in the kind of ugly-duckling-Cinderella tales where the least and most helpless turn out to be the most beautiful, the most powerful, the wisest, often divine or royal of birth.*

In a *Lear*-like folk tale from India, a king smugly asks his daughters to speak their admiration and love for him: why are they able to live so luxuriously in his palace? The older ones tell him what he wants to hear:

---

*Hence naive spectators wondered, at seeing I, i, if the handsome, underprivileged Edmund would rise to the top.

"Because we are your daughters, O King!" The youngest one says honestly, "We are only what destiny makes us." The angry king banishes her, and orders her to marry the poorest man in the kingdom. No need to worry: the poorest man turns out to be a great monarch, wandering incognito as a holy man, suffering from a mysterious disease. The good, honest daughter manages to cure him, she and her husband establish a rich kingdom, and the unhappy father has to admit that his good daughter was right, and he was not the source of her fortune. Other fathers in these tales get off less easily; there is the African story of a father who was angry at his daughter because she fed her brother when she was not supposed to; he took her to a cannibal village, to be eaten, but when the cannibals heard the whole story they ate him instead. He was sorry.

This generic fantasy seems most satisfying when it is complete with its second part: when, as in *Lear*, the parent who rejects the innocent child not only is made to realize, often through much suffering, how wrong he was, and is very, very sorry, but also is rescued by the child, and begs the child's forgiveness. This has been a common theme in popular drama, fiction, and film; Dickens among others worked variations on it. A handsome primitive example of this kind of retribution occurs in an old Irish tale. A king of Erin, out hunting, meets a stranger, who knocks out three of the king's teeth, and pushes his face in the dirt. The king returns home, and asks his three sons what they would do if they met the stranger. Two of the sons promptly promise great and terrible deeds. We can guess which sons these are. Then the third—the youngest, of course—says simply he will do his best. Honesty never pays in these cases—the father must seem to be immune to the virtues of the true child —so the boy is banished and disinherited. The two older sons go out to seek the stranger, and allow the youngest to go along as their servant. The youngest slays the stranger, and even rescues a beautiful lady. But the mean, tricky older siblings go home with the lady, leaving their brother behind, a captive in a place called the Terrible Valley. (Who has not been imprisoned in a Terrible Valley?) The resourceful boy escapes and returns home just in time to save the lady from marrying an older brother. He gets the lady and half his father's kingdom; the repentant king gets forgiveness—and his three teeth back.

In *King Lear*, the presence of this ur-fantasy is pervasive, in language as well as action. Among the rich, repetitive word clusters that convey so resonantly the play's meaning, none chimes so often, or with as many echoes, as the simple familial one: father, daughter, son, child, babe—as if to emphasize that this tragedy, for all its trappings, concerns the earliest, most essential relationships. The parent-punishment motif makes itself sharply felt from the opening scenes. Gloster's mocking remarks on Edmund's bastardy are an unmistakable invitation to retribution; and Lear's vain choosing among his daughters even more so.

Lear's love auction of his kingdom has been widely criticized as implausible. As I argue earlier, Shakespeare's art transforms the fairy-tale situation into a compelling immediacy of motivated drama; meanwhile the underlying archetypal encounter strengthens the impact of the overt conflict. Below the conscious response to the eventful action is evoked a deep, shared fantasy in which the father-ruler, living with motherless daughters, asks them for expressions of love; he is victimized by the "other"—evil—children, and rejects the true child from whom he most wants love and who is unable to express it to him as he wants it. He drives her off; and suffers. As made by Shakespeare, Lear seems motivated toward a fate of his own choosing, but he is also in the grip of a psychic destiny: the guilty father, and the guilty, offending rival siblings must be punished, while the true child is vindicated in terrible suffering.

Note how this is achieved in *Lear*. Again, from the child point of view, it happens not once, but twice: with Gloster as well as Lear; both fathers and their bad children are made to feel horribly sorry for what they have done. All die; but the bad children worse than die. The fathers discover how bad they are; the fathers come to reject them utterly; they are not true children. One is specifically a bastard. Shakespeare had no puritan shrinking from illegitimacy, as witness Faulconbridge in *King John*; but in *Lear* the bastard turns out to be as fated to be wrong as in a fairy tale; and Lear's evil daughters are accused of illegitimacy by their father, for they, who would pretend to offer him love, must be utterly rejected. This, again, is an archetypal way of punishing siblings in fantasy: in that Irish tale just mentioned, the false older sons turn out to be bastards begot on the queen by a swineherd and a gardener. (What this says about the background mother figure is an interesting question that need not now be considered. But note how often Shakespeare dramatizes the problem of fathers made sorry by their motherless daughters.)

The making-sorry of the parents is the chief aim of the first part of the *Lear* tale, and how sorry indeed they become. The vehicle of their sorrow is again the "other," evil children: who humble them, shame them, drive them out from shelter, leave them helpless, stripped virtually naked, seek to do—and in Gloster's case, indeed do—violence on them. In the parent-punishment fantasy, the dreamer himself—through his paradigm, the true child—never is the agent of punishment, or if he is, it is always by accident or mistake, as in *Oedipus*; he always disguises his revenge impulse by displacing it onto other instruments: fate, chance, or, as in this instance, the sibling villains. So the wicked older sisters and the bastard speak the hateful things that preface the destruction of the father; though what they say is sometimes only true: the younger do indeed rise when the old does fall. In the wicked mouths, these are wicked things to say; and the wicked children achieve the inevitable desposing of the old with wicked acts.

Now the play goes into the second part of the fantasy. When the parents are in deep despair, the good, innocent children suddenly appear from somewhere and help their fathers to perceive the truth about their unjust behaviors. In the subtle "sight" imagery of *Lear*, as the old men learn, out of their blindness—in one case, literal—momentarily to see again, we may perceive a sign of the remarkable kinship of the world's makers of fantasy. It is easy enough to recognize the common "seeing" theme in *Lear* and *Oedipus*; but think too of the metaphor of that ancient Chinese tale, where the good, innocent daughter gives her hands and eyes to nourish her troubled father back to a healthier vision of life.

The agony of Gloster and Lear is accompanied by an interesting reversal of their roles, that grows from the central fantasy. Old fools are indeed babes again; the two old men are reduced to the naked, helpless state of infant dependency. Edgar, watching Lear disintegrate, says, in a line that seems to look two ways, *He childed as I fathered.* Soon Edgar will be leading his father by the hand, caring for him, nursing him, the old man's only stay. Soon Cordelia will be mother and nurse to her *child-changed father.* The old men grieve for the errors they have made in mistaking their true children. Gloster's son comes often into his mind. *Ah, dear son Edgar ... If Edgar live, oh bless him.* Lear wakes from madness to find himself dressed in fresh clothes by his daughter, who gives him a tender kiss—and cannot forbear mentioning that she hopes it will repair the violent harms done him by her two sisters. The old king is now utterly helpless in his beloved daughter's hands.

Freud, originally interpreting the play in terms of dream-wish opposites, saw Lear loving Cordelia most because she represented a mythical mute "third woman"—Death. Hence, also, Lear's ready rejection of her. Lear's carrying her dead, by reversal again, represented his acceptance of death. Later Freud perceived the more likely subtextual impulses to incest; but curiously he never deeply explored the child-parent implications, perhaps because their existence threatened his theory.

Victor Hugo clearly sensed the motivation of the IV, vi reunion between Lear and Cordelia, if not its implications: "The maternity of the daughter for the father ... the most venerable of all maternities ... The old beard against the young breast ... There is no holier spectacle." So the scene is often played: the helpless old man held in the arms of the maid, who nourishes him with her strength. Thus, Henry Irving, as Lear, rested "in the shelter of [Cordelia's] protecting arms. [He] laid his head upon her bosom like a tired child, with a sob of infinite content."*

Lear has at last achieved his dearest wish—to spend his life in *her kind nursery*. He has had to pay a savage price both for what he has wished—to have her love—and for what he has done—rejected her love. Now the foolish, fond old man must beg his daughter's forgiveness; he is as humbled as a father may be.

But humility is not enough for Shakespeare. Mortality must be touched. In the earlier *Leir* play, the king lived on, as he would again in Nahum Tate's "poetically just" revision; and Gloster's prototype lived on in the story from which Shakespeare took his subplot. But these are pale satisfactions. If the full force of the archetypal fantasy is to be evoked, the father must expiate his love for, and his rejection of, the good child to the uttermost limit. So Gloster must die, at the news of how good his rejected son has been to him. Edgar-Oedipus in fact kills his father, but in ambiguous guise: he tells his story too late, and Gloster's *flawed heart* bursts.

Lear's penitence must extend even further. Not only must he undergo his purgatorial punishment, sorrow, and repentence, not only beg for forgiveness and receive it; but now he must live long enough to see his good daughter die. This is the apex of the child's punishment dream: "I'll die, and he'll be sorry"; Lear's ultimate, inevitable punishment is his daughter's dying, which then kills him.

Nothing short of this feast of death could satisfy the rigorous working out of the fantasy by Shakespeare. But note that the dreamer, he for whom the fantasy is created, gets his wish safely. Cordelia, the innocent child, dies and her father is sorry; but Edgar, also the innocent child, survives—though guiltily— the death of his father. So the participant in this fantasy has it both ways: in one guise, he dies and is mourned; in another, he survives the old father in hero fashion to help rule the kingdom. Thus plot and subplot serve complementary, but separate, ends.

I do not mean to suggest that Shakespeare consciously meant *Lear* to be the working out of this dream. But he did choose this story to adapt, and his adaptations are significant: particularly his deliberate doubling of the motif of father punishment, the increase of punishment to the ultimate death. Moreover, and this is perhaps the most important aspect of his artistic handling of the theme, the wronged child-hero recedes in

*So Lear may die with his head on Cordelia's breast.

importance; the emphasis is on the agony of the father for his guilt in siring the children, for his guilty wishes, for his folly—so much so that the focus on his suffering obscures the revenge outline of the play's structure. In Lear's depths—as in Gloster's—lie dark latencies that belong to old men: a *Laius complex*, we may call one, the impulse of the father to destroy his young child-rival; and beyond this—perhaps partly caused by it—the impulse to self-destruction. The reciprocation between child and father identities in Lear—and Gloster—is an important part of the dialectic of the play.

The master poet and playwright was involved in all his characters, searching out their utmost possibilities; at this stage in his own life the role of erring-unloved-father Lear offered him the best means to explore and convey the passions of humanity. The other characters, as I have noted, quickly take on lives of their own; even the innocent child Cordelia has a quality of resistant personality that gives some motivation to the old man's inevitable rejection of her; and the wicked children are endowed with a force and ambition that seems to move them individually to their punishments. All are absorbed into the play's dialectical system. The wronging father is also wronged; he is kind as well as cruel. Lear rises spectacularly beyond the figure of the rejecting parent, and beyond, too, that of the rejected parent—another eternal image. Similarly, the "good," wronged children are also wrong; they inflict pain, as well as suffer it. The "bad" children have some graces. Audiences respond empathetically to both extremes of the roles' polarities. Every important character in the play is designed to release for the audience passions normally repressed in life. In our dreams, we are not only heroes; and that darker part of us that often lurks beyond consciousness finds a way out through the darker language and emotion of all the roles. Lear is only the most powerful focus; and as we grieve for him, we yet participate in and accept his downfall, because fall he must; we are involved in his punishment as well as his hope of escaping it.

This fantasy is not all of *Lear*: the play is too big, it outgrows its pattern as it questions, through a series of intricate and dazzling systems of verbal and visual imagery, the meanings and meaninglessness of dialectic existence. But near the center is this familiar emotional pattern, deepening vastly the experience called *King Lear*.

Lear's Theatre Poetry

Of course *Lear* can be staged. It has been, and will continue to be. Criticism's only sane posture, in fact, is to insist that it must be staged, if the full dimensions of Shakespeare's art are to be perceived sensually as well as cognitively, as the playwright intended.

The staging is not easy. The scenic demands are considerable; the demands on the actor ultimate. Not a single character can be conveniently synthesized into a type: each is designed as a polyphony, to use Mikhoels' word, each is made of mixed and even contradictory qualities. Lear most of all; we have seen that the fissioning of his opposing attributes almost bursts the limits of character possibility. He is all the four streams—and all the tributaries—of characterization we followed: titan king, tough king, mad king, everyman king. These four were only singled out for the convenience of discussion, because they seemed to dominate actors' conceptions: something of all of them—and more—informed such distinguished performances as by Scofield, Devrient, Salvini, Carnovsky, Gielgud. Similarly, the conflicting impulses, ideas, and even physical acts of Lear must, like the play itself, back-forth in tidal flow; to deny the dialectic to the character on the stage—or in criticism—is to congeal the whole mighty ocean of the play. This form, as much as what the play says and does, contributes to its power continuously to arouse.

The temptation to congeal, simplify, fit all into an easily graspable pattern, is great; particularly with the lesser characters. But they too are constellations—Redgrave's word; we have seen how multiple, countering motivations and qualities shape their designs: the best are somewhere discolored, the worst show moldings of dignity and understandable motivation.

To resist closure, to keep the dialectic of the characters—and the play—open-ended, is hard enough for the imagining mind; harder in the theatre where the dynamic designs must be enclosed in physical shapes. But only in the theatre, for the same reason, can the whole be realized. Actors can meet the challenge: can, with their faces and bodies, project the play's ambiguities (as these ambiguities may be intuited by them, or made present to them by scholar-critics). Shakespeare counted on this:

336

hence so much of *Lear's* language is nonverbal, designed for the actor's face and body rather than his tongue. Often, at crucial points, the play's meaning depends on subtextual gesture that may deny, undercut, play against the words. Thus, to recapitulate, Lear's furious angers may issue from a body partly aching for love. The ambivalence of Edgar's curious treatment of Gloster must have, to make sense, nuances of accompanying physical expression. Cordelia's inner resistances are barely indicated in words, are meaningful only in terms of a *persona* projecting them. This of course is why so many arguments flower over these and the other character designs: because so much has to be said without words, and what that is must be intuited. The art of the great actor, as Shakespeare knew, is to say these things superbly, even when, with face and body, as with the words, more than one thing must be said at a time.

What Shakespeare says with faces and bodies—and things—involves a special kind of poetry. Sometimes *Lear's* physical language matches the verbal, as where bodies are wrenched and pierced. Sometimes the physical must say what the words suggest: as when Lear, Fool, Kent, Edgar, Gloster must indicate as a continuing background through Act III the intense cold, the acute bodily discomfort, of heath and hovel. But beyond this, *Lear's* language of gesture has a cumulative symbolic content and texture that command the eye and mind to a special poetic experience as subtle and deeply stirring in its way as the ear-mind's experience of the words (though of course the two complement each other, cannot be separated except for discussion). The whole of this fluid tapestry can be made present only to the seeing eye; the reading mind cannot encompass it. The past pages have traced the artistry of *Lear's* visual imagery; I will summarize here, building on my definition of dramatic poetry:

> an organic structure of verbal symbols, with associated sounds, rich in denotative detail and connotative reverberation and ambiguity, often presented in recurrent, rhythmic patterns and changing perspectives that accumulate and extend the power of the whole to stimulate feeling, thought, and kinesthetic response in its audience.

How does this definition apply to *Lear's* visual imagery (in association with its imagery of sound: the non-verbal poetry of cries, howls, barks, trumpets and other music)? The best way to approach Shakespeare's composition of spectacle is for us to imagine the play as a mime with linked non-verbal sounds. This will enable us to discern, in relief, the poem of Shakespeare's gestures.

For an easy bridge to this imagining, I will concentrate on a single motif in the *Lear* language: the familiar motif of seeing. We have followed the orchestration of the idea through the network of such words as *see, sight, blindness, look, looking glass*, and have sensed the growing reverberative implications for perception, understanding, insight, knowing, and their opposites. These implications converge in Gloster's focal speech

I see it feelingly (150).

On one level, the blind man actually reaches out to Lear, and so sees him in his touch. But Gloster's way of seeing, as well as his words, suggests that he feels he has insight, he understands what is not visible, he does so with his feelings, and he does so very well. A further shadow persists— Gloster does not, even inwardly, really see well. The words say some of this but here as elsewhere words fail in *Lear*; and sight-sound imagery must complete the communication, especially when latent, subconscious impulses must be conveyed.

The scene resonates with visual, as well as verbal, echoes. Shakespeare created a string of "speaking pictures," every line and shape of which said something to the mind. We in this century are learning to demonstrate experimentally what visual artists like Shakespeare have always understood: that the eye thinks, it selects what things or what parts of things it will see, and brings to their interpretation a tremendous store of funded information and preconception. The hieroglyph, the pictograph, in our day the cartoon, more relevantly the Elizabethan emblem are examples of single visual symbolic structures that carry implications far beyond their components. The very components are eloquent. A simple straight line implies one thing; torture the line, and it says something else. Once figures become representational, as in Shakespeare's work they are, they are burdened with social meaning. Some attempts have been made to reduce Shakespeare's speaking pictures to the terms of contemporary emblems; but as an artist he was always breaking and restructuring the familiar. Thus he provided many royal tableaux, but even in the histories they were visually tensed and discolored with ambiguities of character and situation. More: as he shifted perspectives with his startling visual designs, he also used these images—as he used verbal images—in rhythmic and recurrent patterns. The images changed in light, line, color, and shape, their implications and ambiguities widened as the plays progressed. Thus, in our *Lear* mime, the first royal tableau will be refracted in succeeding images that hollow, mock, and grotesquely invert the initial experience.

Let us return to the specific visualized act of seeing. In our life, the act is so central to our way of knowing our world, and particularly the people in it, that any theatre representation is charged with allusion. Shakespeare exploited the act from his very first plays. Even in *Comedy of Errors*, many "see" words and acts help centrally to complicate and solve the puzzle of mistaken identity. In later plays, as deception grows inward, and more inward, words of seeing and insight are more subtly mated and polarized, and associated with visual images that confuse reality and appearance. The "ocular proof" Iago promises is meant to deceive. Macbeth's speech to the knife is loaded with *see* words—he believes the knife is there because he *sees* it—but it is not there.

On the stage, the simple act of looking may be powerfully dramatic. For one character to lock eyes with another, or avoid this, in silence or in speech, may be rich in ambiguity, stir deep responses. No words are needed to convey the potential of an exchange of speaking looks, as—to give an obvious example—between Edmund and Goneril. In a great actor's face the complex of feeling can converge in such singleness of passions as to be frightening; conversely, his fluid face may reveal multiple-layered, struggling impulses. For Lear to look, to see, to try to understand and identify, is peculiarly characteristic; and each seeing adds to the others, extends the implication of the visual imagery.

In the first scene this will become apparent as Lear glances at the other characters while addressing them. Here the playwright is partly, as craftsman, identifying the characters for the audience; but he is also saying something about them, and their relationship to Lear, and he is developing Lear's special way of scrutinizing those he addresses. As we observed, Lear himself has something to say about that later on: in his madness, asked if he is the king, he notes a distinguishing characteristic:

> Ay, every inch a king.
> When I do stare, see how the subject quakes (110–111).

At some level of his consciousness, Lear always tests, with his look, the submission of his subjects. This will be apparent, without words, in the special and different way he *looks* in the first scene at the subservient Gloster, the "fiery" Cornwall, the uncertain Albany, the masked Regan and Goneril, the withdrawn Cordelia. His act of scrutinizing will set off ripples of ambiguity in the recurrent motifs of appearance and reality, of disguise and disclosure, of the success and failure of this primary way of knowing.

In a *Lear* mime, we would observe at once a quality that, we saw, actors of Lear have sometimes accentuated in the play—the mystery of Lear's seeing—by seeming to look at the surrounding court, and all else, with an almost painful intensity, as if indeed Lear's physical capacity to see was strained—as in fact it would fail. Some actors also seemed to look beyond what they saw, as if trying to discern something not present, as if looking into another world. In the first scene, a mime audience would not need Lear's words to know that Lear will believe what he sees; and that what he sees in Goneril and Regan satisfies him. What he sees in Cordelia—however hard he looks—does not satisfy him. Then he makes a negative seeing gesture, often to be repeated—*out of my sight*. He will look elsewhere, cover his eyes, wave away what is present—if he does not like it, he will not see what is there.

On the other hand, he will be seen to communicate with what is not before him. He will look upward toward invisible powers, and seem to command them, as he would command the people around him. Here, he seems indeed to see into a world beyond reason—a vision that will be inverted ironically later.

The visual imagery of Lear's scrutiny of his world is echoed and orchestrated in mime with the disguised figures he encounters: first the banished Kent, whom he examines so closely in I, iv. Shakespeare's design of suspense, we saw, includes the possibility that Lear will recognize this disguised old friend, now called enemy, who must die if discovered: so the scrutiny functions in the action as well as the character. The seeing symbolism partly is extended by Lear's need to assure himself of his own identity, to know he is there. This is central to his confrontations with Oswald, Fool, Goneril. *Who am I sir? Dost thou call me Fool, boy? Does Lear walk thus? Speak thus?* In a mime, we would know, without speech, that Lear is looking for some assurance of who he is. It is himself he is trying to see.

Slowly Lear's way of seeing changes; the rhythm alters. When he banished Cordelia, he looked confidently to unseen powers of night and day to endorse his oath of excommunication. When he calls on the unseen to curse Goneril, he looks with appeal and his eyes are misted now; physically he cannot see so well because of tears (Shakespeare often links *eye* and *tear*), his eyes betray him, he may be seen to threaten them with plucking out; and yet on his face a new seeing is visible, that reflects, *I did her wrong*.

Charged as his glance is with anger and contempt, when he confronts Kent in the stocks, when Gloster servilely keeps him outside the castle door, he yet looks with some insecurity at the approach of Regan, and with even more when Goneril appears. His face reflects many ways of seeing at once because he is designed to experience many feelings at once. He is reduced to glancing helplessly from one to the other daughter as they beat down the number of the knights. And when next he speaks to the unseen powers, he is much less certain, his questing eyes beseech support. Again these organs of his sight cloud with tears; but we see that Lear has nevertheless begun to see reality beneath surfaces.

In the storm, he defies the invisible powers, but also defends himself against them, asks for pity—*you see me here*, he gestures—for what he sees as himself: poor, weak, despised, infirm. Raindrops join teardrops in blurring his sight; and yet a better vision becomes possible to him, the light of it shows on his face, and he kneels to pray. For a moment we see that in this dark night Lear *sees better*.

Then his eyes find Mad Tom, and he slides into madness; and the mime emphasizes a curious, ironic change that happens in his seeing. He sees things no man else sees, but he seems to see them more sharply, more craftily than he ever saw before. The whole base of his knowing, and of ours, as we experience with him, is altered—herein lies much of the power of mad scenes. Lear examines Mad Tom with the same care he gave to the scrutiny of Kent; yet he sees him in a different way. The uncertainties of the rational seeing are replaced by the certainties of the irrational. With this, values are reversed. Where before we saw that Lear saw beauty in robes and furred gowns, he now discovers it in rags and nakedness.

Before, he spoke to invisible powers he saw in space; now, mad, he speaks to invisible hallucinations he sees in space. Handy-dandy—a god or hallucination—is one any more real than the other? And behind this ambiguity lurks another: the eyes that seem to see Edgar, and then Gloster, for what they are not may, on some level, see them for what they are. The line between reason and unreason, we observed, may dissolve in cunning, or accident, or naturally. These uncertainties are latent in the text; they are made visual in Lear's looking, for instance, at Gloster in IV, vi, the face to face searching of the bloody sockets as Gloster peers sightlessly—seeingly—into Lear's eyes. What is it that the empty eyes see that shocks Lear into admitting some awareness of reality?* Silences— those punctuation marks of visual language that are often more powerful than any words or acts in the dramatic art—accent the process of Lear's mad seeing, his staring.

---

*Gloster's own failure to see is painfully visual. He does not, in fact, *see feelingly*. Without eyes, he is seen to be nearly helpless. He cannot tell the identity of his guide, though his happiness depends on it. He cannot know high ground from low, can be led anywhere, deceived anyhow. Edgar, for ambiguous purposes of his own that can only be conveyed by physical imagery, baffles Gloster's attempts to perceive reality through ears and touch. If eyes are no guarantee of seeing, neither is blindness.

Ay, every inch a king.

This is a mock king, a fool king, in a crown of weeds; one subject now, Gloster, may quake before him. When he was a real king, the subjects whom he wanted to quake did not. The stare, now, stirs ironic reverberations of the earlier unavailing look.

The mad king weeps, but the tears do not clear his sight now. Only when the great rage is stilled can he open his eyes in reason again; and then he can hardly believe what he sees. He touches Cordelia's weeping eyes, in an echo of his gesture to Gloster—eyes are for weeping, as well as seeing, whether blind or not. He must try to reestablish a base in knowing, try to see himself again, try to believe the hands he holds up before his eyes are his own.

When Cordelia is dead, he assaults with his eyes—and voice—the heavens themselves; tired eyes now, tired voice, so he must assail the men who do not help him:

> Had I your tongues and eyes, I'd use them so
> That heaven's vault should crack.

The eyes are failing, for sight as well as stare, he can hardly see what to believe, cannot recognize an old friend. A dull sight.

He dies on an ambiguity. He sees something—points—(we don't need the words, *Look there, look there*) and only the visual and subverbal poetry sustains the action now, all else fades away. What Lear sees in Cordelia's face—vision, illusion, joy, horror, or a mixture of all of them—can be known *only* by what his face tells us his eyes see. And somehow, this will be another refraction of the whole preceding, accumulating visual imagery of seeing-knowing.

Seeing involves an act. Some inanimate visual images in the play carry a heavy load of symbolism almost by themselves. One of these is the crown. It is hardly mentioned; and yet it is a centrally significant image in the ironic reversal in which the most powerful are seen to be degraded, robes and furred gowns exchanged for rags, the regal gestures once made with a royal sceptre now parodied by a disheveled madman with a baton of straw. In the complex interweaving of change and loss of garments, where fugitives disguise themselves downward to lower station or divest themselves of opulence while upstarts take on the gorgeous dress and ornaments of higher rank, the crown is a pivotal symbol.

Lear wears it in the first scene. He might continue to wear it as one of the "additions" to a king, and if so, with so much more irony does he carry this ornament charged with authority, now meaningless. More likely he does not wear it again, hunting, or riding in the night toward Regan; he dashes out into the storm, and runs unbonneted. The next reference is to the weedy circlet he will be seen to wear in IV, vi; but there may be other visual allusions to it. To Mikhoels, we observed, the crown's presence was felt most in its absence; after the first scene, when he had let it go, he would reach up, in a habitual gesture, to reassure himself that it was there—and it was not. So Klöpfer, in the trial scene (III, vi), took up a three-legged copper pot, and put it upside down on his head, so that its legs simulated a crown, a simulated power image for simulated authority. The flowered madman's crown, made of plants related to mindsickness, is the primary visual symbol of the irony of surface values. Lear's gestures as he asserts his mad kingship may be exactly the same as those he made in I, i—gestures of magnanimity, authority, power, rage—but now they make only a grotesque charade.

The reappearance and shifting of the real crown can convey the ambiguities of power's meaning. We followed this clearly enough through the play, but a mime would accentuate it. Cordelia may be seen to restore a crown to Lear in IV, vii—she is concentrating on making him feel his royal strength again. He may be seen to wear it in the brief passing over with the army at the beginning of Act V, before he and Cordelia are captured. Then Edmund, their captor, takes it, and tries it—and in this brief gesture makes visual the whole scheme of the king's fall intersecting the bastard's rise to within one planned murder—Albany's—of a kingship. The crown will fit Edmund; but Albany will take it from him, and again a resonant symbolic visual act will be performed: Albany will try to give the crown back to Lear, but now to the true king the piece of metal is as nothing. Albany will momentarily try it himself; but being—in Edmund's Quarto speech—full of abdication and self-reproving, in a ghastly repetition of the first scene—as indeed the whole ending is visually a symbolic reprise of the assembled court at the beginning—Albany will offer to divide the crown between two rulers, Edgar and Kent. Kent will be seen to reject it, perhaps with some shock at Albany's obtuseness; Edgar will accept reluctantly the ultimate symbol of power; in the context of this royal tableau of corpses, he is king of the dead.

None of these kaleidoscopic "speaking pictures" can be taken as moral or philosophical statements. They are poetic images, open ended, reverberant, ambiguous. The crown is seen to be real, and carries real authority; it may also be utterly without value, or dangerous, blinding, subversive. The very power the crown symbolizes is, in its absoluteness, disastrously linked to infantile fantasy: anyone but a child can see that he is not everything. Yet the crown must be worn.

For discussion, I have isolated the developing images of a symbolic act and of a symbolic thing. In fact, they cannot be separated from each other, as they cannot be separated from the interwoven verbal images. Lear's seeing is one aspect of a total character design that reflects one larger design in the play: the necessity and difficulty of seeing to know. Characters strain to see in the dark, in the storm. Again and again they look off to see what mystery, what danger, approaches. No language is needed to convey to us the persistent alarm as to identity: *What's he? Who's there? What are you there?* One of the oldest techniques of the theatre craftsman, to compel the actors—and hence the audience—to look toward an entrance in anticipation or dread, is repeatedly employed in appearances by Edgar, Goneril, Regan, Mad Tom, Gloster, Gentleman. All actors, like Lear, try to look, see, know. What they see may, in a purely visual stroke, defeat their hopes: most obviously, again, Albany, in a prayerful gesture to the gods, begs Cordelia's safety, Lear enters bearing her corpse. Lear may die with his eyes open, unseeing, and someone must close them—a final irony.

Seeing and knowing are never certain in *Lear*, for the play's dialectic insists on ambiguity. Lear's character design, sustained by conflicting and even contradictory qualities, emerges in all its visual manifestations. In a clear light of mime we would see that Lear sees and does not see. He wishes others banished from his sight, and he wishes them by him. When sane, he sometimes looks as if mad; when mad, as if sane. His gestures—as well as his words—would be qualified by what we see him do: when his refusal to see is frustrated—as it invariably is—it is associated with another pervasive visual image: of flight. We saw that men constantly flee pursuit in *Lear*, but he who flees most is Lear himself, who first ordered Kent to fly. A mime would stress how much Lear flees, psychically as well as physically. Lear tries to banish the resistance of others from his sight, but, failing, he always flees confrontation—until finally Cordelia has caught him, and they kneel to each other.

Each repetition of a visual image takes on new meaning in a context that becomes more dense and complex as perspectives accumulate. How Lear kneels in serious prayer refracts the implications of his daughters' initial kneeling to him, of the kneeling of his courtiers, of his mock kneeling to Regan, of Gloster's blind kneeling to him, of his kneeling with Cordelia, of his kneeling over her dead body. So with other symbolic acts, such as putting on or off clothes, weeping, threatening, playing animal, fleeing pursuit, suffering pain, dying.

These images then, and their associated sounds, support an organic structure of symbols rich in denotative detail and connotative reverberation and ambiguity, in rhythmic and recurrent patterns and changing perspectives that accumulate and extend the power of the whole to stimulate feeling, thought, and kinesthetic response in its audience. They can only be known in performance: the mind's eye, imagining Lear's physical action, can never recreate the totality of the visual poetry that the eye's mind, in the theatre, experiences and organizes.

I will be most grateful for reports from readers of any stagings of King Lear—*or, to look forward, of* Macbeth *or* Hamlet—*that illuminate Shakespeare's text.*

MARVIN ROSENBERG
University of California
Berkeley

If more thou dost perceive, let me know more...

Appendix

KING LEAR AND HIS FOOL: A STUDY OF THE CONCEPTION AND
ENACTMENT OF DRAMATIC ROLE IN RELATION TO SELF-CONCEPTION
(Reprinted from *Theatre Journal*, October, 1970.)

by Frank Barron and Marvin Rosenberg
Dr. Barron is a Professor of Psychology at the University of California, Santa Cruz.

This paper describes an approach to the study of role interpretation and
enactment in drama through the use of the technique of personality assessment, including psychological tests and interviews. An application
of the method has previously been reported by Barron.[1] To illustrate the
approach and the methodological problems it generates, we have chosen
to treat in detail the study of two characters whose relationship to one
another in the Shakespearian drama *King Lear* presents a perennially fascinating problem for actors. The solution, in terms of the actual performance, was in this instance considered by audience, critics, and director
an unusually creative one.

A Shakespearian role offers a challenge to an actor that is of special interest to students of behavior; it demands exercise of the actor's talents as
a performer and it also taxes the resources of his personality in a way
that few assumed roles do. In *King Lear*, perhaps Shakespeare's most
subtle work, the actor's capacity to conceptualize, experience, and project a complex, ambiguous character is tested to the limit.

The casting, rehearsal, and production of *King Lear* at the University
of California in Berkeley offered to the authors, through the cooperation
of the director, Professor Robert Goldsby, and his actors, an opportunity to investigate a behavior dynamic that had long interested them:

[1] Frank Barron, "The Generation Gap," *Creativity and Personal Freedom*
(Princeton, 1968), pp. 273–282.

the development and potentialities of a highly complex identity.[2] The problem is related to the process of self-realization in a creative person, as well as to the conceptualization and enactment of a dramatic role in the theatre. (Shakespeare himself, of course, has given us the best-known statement of the "thaumaturgic analogy"—"All the world's a stage.")[3]

All of the major roles in *Lear* were examined in our study, but we have chosen in this report to concentrate on Lear and the Fool. These are the most complex of the play's characters, and they embody an opposition and reciprocation symptomatic of the tragedy's dialectic form. Lear, the great king and father, is at the other extreme from the poor, tolerated Fool. King and Fool exchange bickering and hurt, but they are closest to each other in sympathy, and their identities begin to merge.

We are concerned in this paper mainly with two points: (1) the relationship between the actors' personalities and their capacity to conceptualize these assumed roles; and (2) the process by which the actors realize the characters' potentialities in rehearsal and performance.

METHODOLOGY

The personality assessment method, combining a standardized battery of personality tests with depth interviews, was used in the study, with certain important modifications. The actors who had been chosen to play ten major parts in *King Lear* were first asked, immediately after casting, to participate in an assessment as themselves. Then they were asked to take the same tests as the character they were to play. Some four months later, shortly after the twelfth and final performance of the play, they were asked once again to go through the assessment procedures as the characters. Following this, they were given individual interviews, two to three hours in length, on the process of character creation as they had experienced it in their part in *King Lear*.

The emphasis was thus upon their changing conception of the character as it might relate to their own personalities. In retrospect, it seemed apparent that there were, at least in some cases, changes in the personal-

---

[2] See Marvin Rosenberg, *The Masks of Othello* (Berkeley, 1961) and Frank Barron, *Creative Person and Creative Process* (New York, 1969).

[3] St. Genesius, the patron saint of actors, exemplifies the dangers of using acting for play, for his very life was changed when, in the midst of a satiric impersonation of Christ for the entertainment of the Emperor Tiberius, he suddenly found himself through his own mimicry confronted with a sense that what he played was real, a triumph of empathy for which he eventually paid with his life.

ities of the actors themselves, although no direct information from test scores was available.

The testing procedures which will be considered in this initial report are the Gough Adjective Check List (a list of 300 common personality traits) and the California Psychological Inventory.

RESULTS

Some insight into the process of art and the artist may be discerned in the parallelisms and differences that seem to emerge from a comparison of the tests of Lear and the Fool, the role conceptualizations, and the performances.

A. KING LEAR

1. The Actor as Himself.—The role of King Lear was played by a young man, age 28, a graduate student in Dramatic Art, married and with two young children. In the psychological testing session he appeared reserved, thoughtful, temperate, of serious if not grave demeanor. This impression was heightened by somewhat melancholy eyes deep-set in a bony face. His frame was somewhat spare but muscular, and he was well above average in height. He used relatively few adjectives to describe himself on the Gough Adjective Check List; the most outstanding characteristics he listed, in terms of their singularity for graduate students, were: *awkward, clever, courageous, dreamy, fussy, gloomy, individualistic, irritable, original, painstaking, sensitive, shy, steady, temperamental, thoughtful,* and *touchy.* On the California Psychological Inventory, he made indicative low scores on scales for *Self-acceptance* and *Social Presence,* and he scored quite low also on scales designed to measure *Self-control, Tolerance, Responsibility,* and *Ability to make a Good Impression.* He was also rather low on *Flexibility,* and high on *Femininity.*

2. The Actor's Conceptualization of the Role.—On the Gough Adjective Check List, at time of casting (t-1), the actor described Lear by three clearly different sets of adjectives that together suggested the complexity and ambiguity of the character. He saw Lear as: (1) possessed of considerable energy and aggressiveness (*active, argumentative, arrogant, assertive, blustery, conceited, confident, courageous, forceful, hard-headed, headstrong, individualistic, intolerant, loud, opinionated, self-centered, show-off, sophisticated, stubborn,* and *tough*); (2) somewhat confused, anxious, troubled (*absent-minded, aloof, anxious, confused, dependent, distractible, distrustful, dreamy, fearful, foolish, fussy, high-strung, preoccupied, suggestible,* and *touchy*); (3) a good person withal (*frank, honest, idealistic, insightful, outspoken, serious, warm,* and *wise*). When the actor was asked to submit three adjectives of his own choosing not represented on the Check List, he offered these: *suffering, guilt-ridden, willful.*

On the California Psychological Inventory, the actor at time of casting, taking the test as though he were Lear, earned a profile of scores of which the following were high or low enough to be considered indicative: High—*Self-acceptance, Dominance, Social Presence, Sociability;* Low—*Sense of Well-being, Self-control, Tolerance, Intellectual Efficiency,* and *Socialization.*

It is apparent that the actor's conception of himself and of Lear revealed some similarity: he, like Lear, was low on *Self-control* and *Tolerance*; and among the few adjectives he chose to describe himself, he found almost a third also in the Lear character: *courageous, dreamy, fussy, individualistic, touchy.* The suggestion is that while the actor had, like all his fellow players, to summon to a stage characterization qualities he did not find in himself, he also shared some identity with the character he conceptualized.

He played the role more as man than monarch: he was more Lear than King Lear. In the history of the theatre, many well-known actors, from Garrick on, have similarly emphasized Lear's simpler humanity. This conception shortens the great descent from Kingship to Fool, and more quickly shapes the King-Fool roles toward two-of-a-kind, as happened in this production. Significantly, in the final interview with the Lear actor, after the completion of his quite successful performance, he said that he had not wanted the Lear role and had not intended to try out for it—he had wanted to be the Fool. The director's intuition had found in this actor special qualities that made him so effective a Lear.

So far as statistical results are concerned, i.e., in performance on these standardized tests, the actor played Lear much as he had conceived him originally, and his role-conception did get across clearly to the audience. This is shown by test results following the final performance, also by the results of the tests when taken by a skilled clinical psychologist on the basis of the final performance of the play itself.

On the California Psychological Inventory, the actor after the final performance earned a pattern of scores as King Lear almost identical with the pattern four months earlier. Of the four indicative high points at t-1 [Test 1], three remained highest scores at t-2: *Dominance, Self-acceptance,* and *Sociability.* And of the low scores, five remained lowest at t-2 and in almost the same order: *Sense of Well-being* lowest, followed by *Intellectual Efficiency, Self-control, Tolerance,* and *Socialization.*

As suggested by his extensive adjective checklist, the actor had sensed at the beginning the extreme complexity of the character's dimensions, and the rehearsals were a process of exploring their limits. Critics, or other actors, might well have argued that Lear could be perceived (as this actor perceived him) as high in *Self-acceptance* only at the very beginning of the play; from the mid-point to the end Lear can hardly bear the self that he comes to confront. (This reflects a problem with the test itself: it may only be reliable at given points in a play, since the Shakespearian character is a dynamic one and reflects a series of radically different self-images as it experiences tragedy.) Certainly the Lear of this production, in the last three acts, had—except in his madness—very little self-regard.

The clinician in the audience, taking the test for Lear as projected in the performance, earned indicative high scores on *Dominance, Self-acceptance, Social Presence, Sociability,* and *Psychological-mindedness* (a newcomer), while the indicative low scores were on *Socialization, Self-control, Sense of Well-being,* and *Achievement through Conformance* (also new). The degree of agreement is quite impressive, and indicates a very high amount of validity in the test itself as well as consistency of role interpretation and acting by the actor. (It also shows astuteness of observation on the part of the clinician, of course.)

B. THE FOOL

1. *The Actor as Himself.*—The young man who played the Fool seemed somewhat inclined to play the Fool in real life. Short and sturdy, generous in gesture, he was sometimes whimsical and elliptical—as well as voluble—in his thought and speech. In the Gough test he chose many adjectives for himself that were the same as those he later picked for the Fool: most significantly *foolish,* but also *bitter, charming, cynical, daring, dreamy, egotistical, fickle, hasty, humorous, immature, peculiar, polished, rude, sarcastic, sensitive, sharp-witted, solf-hearted, superstitious, temperamental, unconventional, witty, zany.* On the other hand, he reserved for himself alone: *boastful, cowardly, demanding, flirtatious,*

quarrelsome, self-pitying, unstable, and *weak.* Two of his adjectives for
the Fool matched the other actor's choice of descriptives for Lear:
foolish and *dreamy.*

On the C. P. I., the actor's responses (he wrote on the test, "Only a
fool would answer these questions") earned extremely high scores on
Flexibility, Femininity, and *Self-acceptance.* These jibe quite well with
his manner and attitude in the assessment. He not only manifested a
skipping wit but had a tendency to vanish from testing sessions and to be
elusive in interview through quick changes of subject and esoteric allusions. He earned quite high scores also on *Social Presence* and on *Psychological-mindedness* on the C. P. I., and these traits too were certainly
in evidence.

The actor's very low scores were on *Self-control* and *Good Impression.* Also low enough to be considered indicative were his scores on
Responsibility, Socialization, and *Achievement through Conformance.*

All in all, the actor was, as we have suggested, already familiar with
the role of fool, understanding "fool" in this instance to refer to a deliberate posture not unlike the classical conception of the King's Jester.

2. *The Actor's Conceptualization of the Role.*—On the Adjective
Check List, as observed above, the actor at t-1 described the Fool by
many of the adjectives he had used to describe himself. He sees the Fool
as like himself in his role as a jester, but stronger underneath, more of
a self-determined person.

In taking the C. P. I. as if he were the Fool, the actor earned these indicative high scores: *Social Presence, Flexibility, Psychological-mindedness,* and *Good Impression.* The first three are traits which he represents
as his own, while the fourth is one that he possesses to a notably low
degree. Missing from the high scores in this role-conception compared
with actual self is *Femininity.* He sees the Fool as relatively masculine
(more so than about 80% of men).

The most indicative low scores were on *Responsibility, Sense of Communality with Others, Sense of Well-being, Intellectual Efficiency,* and
Socialization. Three of these (*Re, Wb,* and *So*) are traits in which the
actor himself is also lacking, according to the test. The two exceptions
are *Communality* and *Intellectual Efficiency.*

In summary, there is to begin with a certain fit between the actor's
real-life representation of self and his conception of the Fool. There
are some important differences, however, and these, as we shall see, entered in a significant fashion into the creative process during the period
of rehearsals and in the course of the performances. The differences are

that the actor himself scores quite high on *Femininity* but thinks of the Fool as rather masculine, and he represents himself both as more intellectually efficient and more like other people than he represents the Fool.

The Fool's second C. P. I., at the end of the run, showed significant change. In the first test, the character emerged as rather masculine: in the second, it was being experienced as noticeably feminine (a rise of 20 standard score points, or two standard deviations, on the *Femininity* scale). *Communality* had now risen from 22 to 55, a move through three standard deviations, and *Responsibility* had risen some 30 points. These changes accorded with the actor's style and development in the role. In the early rehearsals, as he felt his way, he played mainly—and masculinely—for the Fool's bite, emphasizing the hardness of the clever verbal assaults. But as the relationship with Lear ripened, tones of plaintiveness and compassion, of a tenderness almost in spite of itself, softened the Fool, made him, in a subtle and moving characterization, poignantly sensitive to Lear's suffering and able to offer an affection that was as close as Lear could then come to the filial love the daughters would not give him.

What remains to be noted here, so far as the C. P. I. evidence is concerned, is that the skilled clinical observer, on the basis of the final performance of the play and taking the C. P. I. now for the Fool as projected, earned highest scores on *Flexibility* and *Femininity* but rather low scores on *Communality* and *Responsibility*. While the actor felt that he was portraying a more responsible Fool, and certainly in human terms of sympathy for a fellow-being in *extremis* he was so, the observer, attempting to empathize with the performance, saw the Fool as being out of touch with ordinary human attitudes and irresponsible socially.

While we must guard against over-interpretation in this instance, since either the actor or the observer in the audience may simply have erred in translating his conception into test responses, the discrepancy is suggestive of an interesting possibility. In terms of the play, the actor was right in *feeling himself* to be more responsible as he remained loyal to the man who needed him so desperately, while to a dispassionate observer the Fool's characteristic appearance of taunting might be taken as a rejection of his social responsibilities, a fact rather than a mask.

Interestingly enough, with the exception of femininity, the picture of the Fool that the actor did convey to the observer was quite consistent with his initial conception of the role, the similarity extending even to the three other most indicative variables. *Socialization, Sense of Wellbeing*, and *Intellectual Efficiency*. What had changed in the interim was the actor's feelings about a character who would behave as the Fool did in relation to Lear. This is an important point and reflects the philosophy of the director of this production. Professor Goldsby's rehearsal process is akin to the creative process itself. Actors and director together explore the implications of the character as they go along; there is no dictation, no rigid preconception; all share responsibility for the final artwork. Here, the director's intuition in making this actor his Fool was confirmed by the evident sympathy that emerged between actor and role, not as the actor originally conceived it, but as he came to know it by living with it.

Most significantly, in terms of the relationship of the two roles, the C. P. I.'s taken by the actors as characters suggested latent resemblances that did not show up in the adjective checklists. Both King and Fool tested low on *Sense of Well-being, Intellectual Efficiency*, and *Socialization*. (Lear was also low on *Self-control* and *Tolerance*, the Fool on *Responsibility* and *Sense of Communality*.) Here the tests seem to confirm the implications of Shakespeare's poetic dialectic: the figure at the top of the royal chain of being shares the alienation and insecurity of the marginal Fool at the other extreme, and can understandably exchange roles with him.

As the rehearsal went on, the relationship between King and Fool became steadily more reciprocal, interdependent; the two often huddled together against the hostility of men and weather, until the troubled Lear began to take on some of the riddling, erratic—and erotic—imagery of the Fool; whereupon the Fool gave way and was seen no more. He "went to bed at noon": and Lear in his madness, played Fool.

Notes

A NOTE ON THE BIBLIOGRAPHY AND REFERENCES

Whenever a specific critic, actor, journal, or other source is mentioned in the text, the reference may be found in these chapter "notes." The reference is either to the entry in the basic bibliography (divided into books and shorter works) that follows, or to the date of a cited periodical.

Descriptions of actors' interpretations are often a compound from many sources, and the separate parts cannot be identified. The references to periodicals, at the end of each section of chapter "notes," indicate the many reports from which I have synthesized stage interpretations. In every case, my personal experience of performances, and my interviews with actors, organizes these reports.

The chapter "notes" to critics and scholars mainly serve to locate those sources, identified in the text, that represent information or points of view significantly in agreement or disagreement with mine. Other references in this section are to relevant discussions of *Lear* that interested readers may want to explore. Separate sections of these "notes" are provided for Fool and Edgar.

Act I, Scene i

Bennett, 149, 151.
Chekhov, 108–9, 121–2, 127–30.
Clarke, n.p.
Crane, 161.
Danby, 32ff.
Drews, 18 (German actors).
Elliott, 251–63.
Elton, 94, 128, 156ff, 216, 339.
Empson, 129.
Fraser, 46.
Frost, 583.

Furness, 451, 450.
German, 10ff.
Granville-Barker, 79, 83.
Hankiss (Scofield).
Heilman (2), 14–5, 45, 53–4, 124ff, 266, 274, 305, 323.
Keast, 113.
Kermode, 89.
Kirschbaum (2), 36.
Knight, G. W. (1), 89.
Kreider, 95, 194–215.

Lear Enters

Prior, 84–92.
Ralli, Vol. 1, 247, 468–83, 543; Vol. 2, 340, 537.
Ribner (2), 18ff, 35, 118–24.
Rosen, 222, 234.
Rosenberg, 1–10 (European actors).
Schoff, 158–70.
Schücking, 17–80.
Sharpe, 226.
Sewell, 83–5.
Sitwell (1), 74.
Skulsky, 6ff.
Smith, 153ff.
Speaight (1), 90–1.
Spurgeon (2), 50.
Stauffer, 85, 209.
Towse, 174–7 (Salvini).
Traversi (2), 45–6.
Victor, 241.
Webster (1), 216–7.
White (1), 115–6.
Whitaker (2), 166–232.
Williamson, A., 53, 133, 194–6.
Williamson, C., 48, 56–8.
Wilson, H., 191.
Winter (1), 177–85 (Booth).
Winter (2), 347 (Booth).
Zingerman, 1–8 (Scofield).

REVIEWS

Academy, 5–6–1876 (Rossi).
Autumn Boer, 1883 (Booth).
Berlin/Preuss, 1934 (Krauss).
Birmingham News, 4–24–1937 (Ayrton).
Birmingham Post, 4–11–1968 (Porter).
Birmingham Post, 4–20–1968 (Porter).
Boston Weekly Transcript, 1–16–1877 (Booth).
Country Life, 4–25–1936 (Ayrton).
Daily Express, 4–11–1968 (Porter).
Daily Mail, 4–11–1968 (Porter).
Daily Telegraph, 2–16–1881 (Booth).
Die Rheinpfalz, 7–6–1957 (Krauss).
Eastern Daily Press, 9–22–71 (West)
Educational Theatre Journal, 10–1967 (Mikhoels).
Era, 5–7–1876 (Rossi).
Evening News, 4–11–1968 (Porter).
Evening Standard, 4–11–1968 (Porter).
Financial Times, 4–16–1968 (Porter).
Financial Times, 8–26–71 (West).

Glasgow Evening Citizen, 10–12–71 (West)
Glasgow Herald, 4–13–1968 (Porter).
Guardian, 4–11–1968 (Porter).
Illustrated London News, 4–24–1858 (C. Kean).
Leamington Spa Courier, 4–19–1968 (Porter).
Listener, 3–1–1963 (Carnovsky).
London News, 11–18–1892 (Irving).
London Times, 7–15–1953 (Redgrave).
London Times, 4–26–1858 (C. Kean).
London Times, 4–8–1963 (Scofield).
Manchester Guardian, 4–20–1950 (Gielgud).
Morning Post, 4–21–1936 (Ayrton).
Neues Wiener Journal, 3–15–1925 (Klöpfer).
New Statesman, 11–16–1962 (Scofield).
New Statesman, 4–19–1968 (Porter).
New York Evening Post, 10–29–1885 (Salvini).
The 19th Century, Vol. 33, No. 191 (Irving).
Observer, 4–18–1858 (C. Kean).
Observer, 4–12–1931 (Gielgud).
Observer, 2–23–1958 (Gielgud).
Pall Mall Gazette, 5–9–1876 (Rossi).
Pall Mall Gazette, 2–18–1881 (Booth).
Plays and Players, 6–1968 (Porter).
Punch, 7–29–1953 (Redgrave).
Putnam's Monthly, 1–1908 (Salvini).
Referee, 6–18–1882 (Rossi).
Royal Leamington Spa Courier, 4–24–1936 (Ayrton).
Saturday Review, 2–19–1881 (Booth).
Saturday Review, 12–8–1962 (Scofield).
Saturday Review, 6–29–1963 (Carnovsky).
Scotsman, 7–20–1950 (Gielgud).
Spectator, 4–17–1936 (Devlin).
Stage and TV Today, 4–18–1968 (Porter).
Stratford-Upon-Avon Herald, 5–3–1968 (Porter).
Sunday Observer, 7–19–1953 (Redgrave).
Sunday Telegraph, 4–7–1968 (Porter).
Sunday Telegraph, 4–14–1968 (Porter).
Sunday Times, 4–25–1858 (C. Kean).
Sunday Times, 7–19–1953 (Redgrave).
Sunday Times, 12–16–1962 (Scofield).
Tablet, 6–29–1968 (Porter).

Toledo Blade, 1-29-1908 (Mantell).
Volkszeitung, #16, III, 1925 (Klöpfer).
Warwick and Worcester, 12-1962 (Scofield).
Washington Post, 4-24-1964 (Scofield).

Wolverhampton Express and Star, 4-11-1968 (Porter).
Wolverhampton Express and Star, 4-13-1968 (Porter).
Miscellaneous unidentified clippings; interviews; personal observation.

Scene

Agate (2), 55.
Alger, 788 (Forrest).
Bablet, 84.
Berg, 181 (Calhern).
Blunden, 17.
Bradley, 198ff.
Brook (interview).
Brown, 144.
Burnim, 141–52.
Carnovsky (interview).
Charlton, 208, 218–21.
Chekhov, 105–9, 121ff.
Clarke, n.p.
Dahl, Norwegian Lear.
Danby, 203.
Day, 231–2.
Downer (1), 432 (Macready).
Drews, 18–24 (German actors).
Elton, 128, 160–3.
Fordham (Gielgud).
French (1), 136–45, 165–75; (2), 523ff.
Frey, 129–34 (Booth and Barrett).
Furness, 440.
Gerould, 212–13 (Mikhoels).
Gielgud (interview).
Goldsby (production).
Granville-Barker, 2–3, 76–7.
Heilman (2), 46, 62, 306.
Hotson, 85.
Jackson, 35–7.
Kermode, 4–5.
Komisarjevsky (Coghill letter).
Kozintsev (letter).
Knight, G. W. (1), 69, 73ff, 129, 192–3.
Lamb, 68–9.
Mack, 21–3 (Macready and E. Kean).
Miller, 245.
Morozov, 39.
Muir, K. (1), xlvi–li.
Nicoll (1), 156.
Norwood, 590–8.
Poel, 178–80.
Pollock, F., 156–7.
Ralli, Vol. I, 543; Vol. II, 340.
Rosenberg, 1–10 (European actors).

Schücking, 518–9.
Shattuck, 211ff (Macready).
Watkins, 231.
Webster (1), 215–20.
Williamson, A., 54, 133, 194ff.
Winter (2), 347 (Booth).

REVIEWS

Birmingham Gazette, 4-21-1936 (Ayrton).
Birmingham Mail, 4-21-1936 (Ayrton).
Birmingham Mail, 7-15-1953 (Redgrave).
Birmingham Mail, 7-28-1955 (Gielgud).
Birmingham News, 4-24-1937 (Ayrton).
Birmingham Post, 4-11-1968 (Scofield).
Birmingham Post, 4-20-1968 (Porter).
Boston Transcript, 2-23-1907 (Antoine).
Boston Transcript, 4-27-1931 (Gielgud).
Catholic Herald, 4-26-1940 (Gielgud).
Cavalcade, 4-25-1936 (Ayrton).
Daily Express, 7-19-1950 (Gielgud).
Daily Express, 7-27-1955 (Gielgud).
Daily Express, 4-11-1968 (Porter).
Daily News, 5-6-1876 (Rossi).
Daily Telegraph, 4-21-1936 (Ayrton).
Daily Telegraph, 7-15-1953 (Redgrave).
Era, 4-25-1858 (C. Kean).
Evening News, 3-3-1884 (Salvini).
Evening Standard, 7-17-1953 (Redgrave).
Financial Times, 4-16-1968 (Porter).
Glasgow Herald, 4-13-1968 (Porter).
Göteborgs Handels Tidning, (June 1929, Hanson).
Guardian, 4-11-1968 (Porter).
Illustrated London News, 4-24-1858 (C. Kean).
Illustrated London News, 2-19-1881 (Booth).
John Bull Illustrated, 4-24-1858 (C. Kean).

Liverpool Daily Post, 7–16–1953 (Redgrave).
London Chronicle, 5–21–1776 (Garrick).
London Examiner, 11–6–1836 (Forrest).
London Examiner, 2–4–1838 (Macready).
London Times, 4–25–1820 (E. Kean).
London Times, 4–26–1858 (C. Kean).
London Times, 4–21–1936 (Ayrton).
London Times, 2–18–1956 (Welles).
London Times, 7–24–1953 (Redgrave).
London Times, 7–15–1953 (Redgrave).
London Times, 4–12–1944 (Wolfit).
London Tribune, 7–24–1953 (Redgrave).
Louisville Times, 5–12–1888 (Booth).
Manchester Guardian, 4–8–1936 (Devlin).
Morning Herald, 4–18–1858 (C. Kean).
Morning Post, 4–25–1920 (E. Kean).
Morning Post, 2–17–1881 (Booth).
Morning Post, 4–21–1936 (Ayrton).
Newsweek, 6–1–1964 (Scofield).
New Yorker, 1–6–1959 (Laughton).
New York Herald Tribune, 1–13–1956 (Welles).
New York Herald Tribune, 12–26–1950 (Gielgud).
New York Herald Tribune, 6–23–1963 (Carnovsky).
New York Times, 6–23–1963 (Carnovsky).
Nottingham Guardian, 7–16–1953 (Redgrave).
New Statesman and Nation, 7–25–1953 (Redgrave).
New Statesman and Nation, 4–20–1940 (Gielgud).
New Statesman and Nation, 4–29–1940 (Gielgud).
Oakland Tribune, 6–23–1963 (Carnovsky).
Observer, 4–18–1858 (C. Kean).

Observer, 1–31–1943 (Wolfit).
Observer, 10–21–1946 (Olivier).
Observer, 4–21–1940 (Gielgud).
Observer, 10–14–1934 (Devlin).
Punch, 8–10–1955 (Gielgud).
Reader, 4–25, 1858 (C. Kean).
Royal Leamington Spa Courier, 4–24–1936 (Ayrton).
Royal Leamington Spa Courier, 7–17–1953 (Redgrave).
Saturday Review, 4–24–1858 (C. Kean).
Scotsman, 7–20–1950 (Gielgud).
South Wales Argus, 4–11–1968 (Porter).
Spectator, 4–25–1931 (Gielgud).
Spectator, 4–17–1936 (Devlin).
Spectator, 9–27–1946 (Olivier).
Stage, 8–18–1955 (Gielgud).
Stage and TV Today, 4–18–1968 (Porter).
Standard, 2–16–1881 (Booth).
Standard, 3–3–1884 (Salvini).
Stratford-upon Avon Herald, 12–2–1955 (Gielgud).
Stratford-upon Avon Herald, 4–24–1936 (Ayrton).
Sunday Observer, 7–17–1953 (Redgrave).
Sunday Observer, 7–19–1953 (Redgrave).
Sunday Telegraph, 4–14–1968 (Porter).
Sunday Times, 1–28–1838 (Macready).
Svenska Dagbladet, 12–14–1906 (Lindberg).
Tablet, 8–22–1953 (Redgrave).
Theatre Arts, 6–1940 (Gielgud).
Time and Tide, 7–29–1940 (Gielgud).
Truth, 8–5–1955 (Gielgud).
Warwickshire Advertiser, 7–17–1953 (Redgrave).
Weekend Review, 4–18–1858 (C. Kean).
Wolverhampton Express and Star, 4–11–1968 (Porter).
Miscellaneous unidentified clippings; interviews; personal observation.

Lear Begins

Abenheimer, 328.
Agate (1), 126.
Alger, 782–3 (Forrest).
Armstrong, 359.
Auden, 126–7.
Bennett, 149–51.
Berg, 180–2 (Calhern).

Block, 500–4.
Blunden, 7.
Boaden (1), 33, 102, 453 (Kemble).
Bradley, 202–3, 225, 255ff.
Bransom, 12–30, 215.
Burckhardt, 35.
Burjan and Lisnevsky (Kistov).

Listener, 3-1-1963 (Scofield).
London Examiner, 2-4-1838 (Macready).
London Times, 3-3-1884 (Salvini).
London Times, 10-16-1845 (Macready).
London Times, 4-8-1936 (Devlin).
London Times, 4-26-1858 (C. Kean).
London Times, 7-15-1953 (Redgrave).
Manchester Guardian, 4-8-1936 (Devlin).
New Statesman and Nation, 4-18-1936 (Devlin).
New Statesman and Nation, 7-29-1950 (Gielgud).
New Statesman and Nation, 7-25-1953 (Redgrave).
Newsweek, 6-1-1964 (Scofield).
New York Herald Tribune, 1-10-1959 (Welles).
New York Herald Tribune, 1-23-1956 (Welles).
New York Times, 6-10-1963 (Carnovsky).
New York Times, 6-23-1963 (Carnovsky).
New York Times, 7-28-1964 (Scofield).
New York Times, 6-25-1965 (Carnovsky).

New York Times, 1-13-1956 (Welles).
Nottingham Evening Post, 10-29-1885 (Salvini).
Pall Mall Gazette, 5-9-1876 (Rossi).
Punch, 7-29-1953 (Redgrave).
Putnam's Monthly, 1-1908 (Salvini).
Saturday Review, 2-19-1881 (Booth).
Saturday Review, 6-29-1963 (Carnovsky).
Saturday Review, 3-8-1884 (Salvini).
Scotsman, 4-11-1884 (Salvini).
Shakespeariana, 11-1883 (Salvini).
Standard, 3-3-1884 (Salvini).
Stratford-upon-Avon Herald, 7-17-1953 (Redgrave).
Sunday Observer, 7-19-1953 (Redgrave).
Sunday Telegraph, 4-14-1968 (Porter).
Sunday Times, 4-25-1858 (C. Kean).
Sunday Times, 12-16-1962 (Scofield).
Sunday Times, 7-19-1953 (Redgrave).
Tatler, 10-29-1946 (Olivier).
Theatre, 12-1-1892 (Irving).
Toledo Blade, 1-29-1908 (Mantell).
Miscellaneous unidentified clippings; interviews; personal observation.

The Family

Abenheimer, 328-9.
Ashley, 26ff (English marriage customs).
Berg, 176ff (Calhern).
Bethell, 58.
Block, 500-507.
Blunden, 14.
Bradley, 198-203, 214, 225, 238-9, 255-6.
Bransom, 8, 16-8, 27, 53, 63, 142, 151, 222.
Burnim, 145 (Garrick).
Campbell, 190ff.
Carnovsky (interview).
Charlton, 190, 221, 227.
Chekhov, 127-34.
Clarke (np).
Clemen, 135-6.
Cobb (performance).
Danby, 115-7, 129-37, 176, 41-3.
Draper (2), 182.
Drews, 20, 25 (German actors).
Dye, 514-6.
Elliott, 251-63.

Elton, 69, 80-1, 116-25, 286, 293-203.
Fletcher, 14.
Fordham (Gielgud).
Furness, 458-61.
German, 10-4.
Gielgud (interview).
Granville-Barker, 17, 21, 46-8, 70-4.
Green (letters).
Greenfield, 281.
Guthrie, 251.
Hawkes, 178-81.
Heilman (1), 34.
Heilman (2), 96-101, 159-66, 174, 183, 247, 258-9, 250-2, 304-5.
Holloway, 80.
Hotson, 90.
Hurstfield, 134 (English marriage customs).
Jaffa, 405-26.
Jayne, 281.
Jorgensen, 85.
Kirsch, 219-20, 233, 280, 300.
Kirschbaum (1), 21-9; (2), 34-49.

Cordelia

Financial Times, 4–16–1968 (Porter).
Glasgow Herald, 4–13–1968 (Porter).
Hereford Times, 4–23–1936 (Ayrton).
Illustrated London News, 2–19–1881
    (Booth).
Illustrated London News, 6–17–1882
    (Rossi).
Illustrated Sporting and Dramatic News,
    2–19–1881 (Booth).
Illustrated Sporting and Dramatic News,
    6–17–1882 (Rossi).
John Bull Illustrated, 2–4–1838 (Mac-
    ready).
John O'London's Weekly, 8–4–1950
    (Gielgud).
Listener, 3–1–1963 (Scofield).
Liverpool Daily Post, 7–16–1953 (Red-
    grave).
London Times, 10–16–1845 (Macready).
London Times, 4–26–1858 (C. Kean).
London Times, 4–8–1936 (Devlin).
London Times, 7–15–1953 (Redgrave).
London Tribune, 7–24–1953 (Red-
    grave).
Manchester Guardian, 4–20–1950 (Giel-
    gud).
Morning Advertiser, 11–5–1836 (For-
    rest).
Morning Post, 4–14–1931 (Gielgud).
New Statesman and Nation, 4–26–1940
    (Gielgud).
New Statesman and Nation, 7–29–1950
    (Gielgud).
New Statesman and Nation, 7–25–1953
    (Redgrave).
New York Times, 6–23–1963 (Carnov-
    sky).
New York Times, 6–25–1965 (Carnov-
    sky).

Nottingham Evening Post, 10–29–1885
    (Salvini).
Nottingham Guardian, 7–16–1953 (Red-
    grave).
Observer, 4–21–1940 (Gielgud).
Observer, 2–23–1958 (Gielgud).
Pall Mall Gazette, 5–9–1876 (Rossi).
Punch, 10–9–1946 (Olivier).
Putnam's Monthly, 1–1908 (Salvini).
Queen, 8–18–1950 (Gielgud).
Reader, 4–24–1858 (C. Kean).
Royal Leamington Spa Courier, 4–24–
    1936 (Ayrton).
Royal Leamington Spa Courier, 7–17–
    1953 (Redgrave).
Saturday Review, 2–19–1881 (Booth).
Scotsman, 11–2–1955 (Gielgud).
Sketch, 8–16–1950 (Gielgud).
Spectator, 11–16–1962 (Scofield).
Stage, 2–19–1881 (Booth).
Stage, 4–18–1940 (Gielgud).
Stage, 7–16–1953 (Redgrave).
Stage, 4–18–1868 (Porter).
Stratford-upon-Avon Herald, 7–21–1950
    (Gielgud).
Stratford-upon-Avon Herald, 7–17–1953
    (Redgrave).
Sun, 1–26–1838 (Macready).
Sunday Telegraph, 4–14–1968 (Porter).
Sunday Times, 12–16–1962 (Scofield).
Svenska Dagbladet, 2–20–1921 (Han-
    son).
Theatre World, 8–1950 (Gielgud).
Time and Tide, 4–20–1940 (Gielgud).
Tribune, 7–28–1950 (Gielgud).
Whitehall Review, 2–17–1881 (Booth).
Wolverhamton Express and Star, 4–11–
    1968 (Porter).
Miscellaneous unidentified clippings; in-
    terviews; personal observation.

Lear and Kent

Block, 500–4.
Carnovsky (interview).
Chekhov, 121, 127.
Danby, 30ff, 115—7, 129ff.
Drews, 5–25 (Klöpfer, Krauss).
Elliott, 251–63.
German, 10, 14.
Gielgud, 122.
Goldsby (production).
Granville-Barker, 142ff.
Heilman (2), 53–4, 183, 266.

Jaffa, 405–26.
Kermode, 4–5.
Kreider, 15–19.
Mikhoels (2), np.
Schoff, 158–70.
Towse, 174–7.

REVIEWS

Glasgow Herald, 4–13–1968 (Porter).
London Times, 7–15–1953 (Redgrave).

New Statesman and Nation, 7–25–1953 (Redgrave).
New York Evening Post, 10–29–1885 (Salvini).

New York Times, 6–25–1965 (Carnovsky).
Toledo Blade, 1–29–1908 (Mantell).
Miscellaneous unidentified clippings.

Daughters

Bell (Hungarian *Lear*).
Hankiss (Hungarian *Lear*).
Milward (Japanese *Lear*).

Spurgeon (1), 49–51.
(For further references to Regan and Goneril, see notes under "The Family.")

Act I, Scene ii

Auden, 248.
Bethell, 57–8.
Boetzkes (letter).
Bradley, 198–9, 240–2.
Bransom, 160.
Charlton, 213–4.
Chekhov, 108–10, 133.
Clemen, 135–6, 145.
Danby, 30–9, 44–51, 115–7, 129ff, 176.
Dye, 514–8.
Elton, 94, 116, 119, 156–61, 124–46, 245–6, 273–5, 284ff.
Empson, 29, 149.
Fraser, 20–6, 46, 102.
Furness, 43, 419.
Garrick, 91–2.
German, 13–4.
Granville-Barker, 17–8, 64–6, 79.
Hankiss (letter).
Heilman (2), 45, 123–6, 141, 236–45, 274.
Howard, interview.
Jayne, 280–4.
Jones, 67–73.
Keast, 113.
Kermode, 4–5.
Kirsch, 204–6, 300.
Kirschbaum (2), 47, 61–6, 189.
Kreider, 28, 36–8, 58–63, 81–5, 98–9, 106, 110, 118–21, 130–2, 138–40, 150–1.
Mack, 58–61, 74–5, 95–6.
Mason, 152.
McIntosh, 54–6.
Morozov, 36, 40.
Muir, E., 14–5.
Murray, interview.
Orwell, 48–9.
Poel, 188.
Prior, 82.
Reimer, 33–42.
Ribner (2), 124.
Skulsky, 9.

Stampfer, 6–7.
Traversi (2), 49–50; (4), 224–7.
Walton, 16.
Whitaker (2), 230–1.
Williamson, C., 197.

REVIEWS

Birmingham Mail, 4–21–1936 (Ayrton).
Evening News, 7–30–1953 (Redgrave).
Evesham Journal, 7–22–1950 (Gielgud).
Financial Times, 4–16–1968 (Porter).
Glasgow Herald, 4–13–1968 (Porter).
John Bull Illustrated, 2–4–1838 (Macready).
Listener, 3–1–1963 (Scofield).
Morning Post, 4–14–1931 (Gielgud).
New Statesman, 10–5–1946 (Olivier).
New Statesman, 4–19–1968 (Porter).
New York Times, 6–10–1963 (Carnovsky).
Nottingham Guardian, 7–16–1953 (Redgrave).
Observer, 4–21–1940 (Gielgud).
Punch, 10–9–1946 (Olivier).
Saturday Review, 9–29–1909 (McKinnell).
Sketch, 10–16–1946 (Olivier).
Spectator, 4–25–1931 (Gielgud).
Stage, 4–18–1940 (Gielgud).
Stage and Television Today, 4–18–1968 (Porter).
Stratford-upon-Avon Herald, 7–21–1950 (Gielgud).
Stratford-upon-Avon Herald, 7–17–1953 (Redgrave).
Time and Tide, 4–20–1940 (Gielgud).
Warwickshire Advertiser, 7–17–1953 (Redgrave).
Miscellaneous unidentified clippings, interviews, personal observation.

Act I, Scene iii

Act I, Scene iv

Winter (3), 342ff (Booth).
Wolfit, 7–8.
Zingerman, 1–10 (Scofield).

REVIEWS

Academy, 5–6–1876 (Rossi).
Academy, 2–19–1881 (Booth).
Albion, 9–16–1865 (C. Kean).
Atlas, 2–3–1838 (Kemble).
Berliner Tageblatt, 12–24–1934 (Krauss).
Birmingham Post, 4–11–1968 (Scofield).
Boston Herald, 1–7–1883 (Salvini).
Boston Weekly Transcript, 1–16–1887 (Booth).
Cambridge News, 8–24–71 (West).
Court Journal, 10–25–1845 (Macready).
Court Journal, 11–3–1845 (Macready).
Daily Mail, 4–11–1968 (Porter).
Daily News, 3–3–1884 (Salvini).
Daily Telegraph, 12–1–1892 (Irving).
Edinburgh Advertiser, 3–24–1825 (E. Kean).
Edinburgh Dramatic Review, 1–19–1823 (Kemble).
Educational Theatre Journal, 10–1967 (Mikhoels).
Era, 2–4–1881 (Booth).
Era, 2–19–1881 (Booth).
Era, 3–8–1884 (Salvini).
Evening News, 4–11–1968 (Porter).
Financial Times, 8–26–71 (West).
Freeman's Journal, 5–5–1845 (Macready).
Glasgow Herald, 4–13–1968 (Porter).
Hereford Times, 4–23–1936 (Ayrton).
Home Journal, 12–2–1888 (Booth).
Illustrated London News, 4–24–1858 (C. Kean).
Illustrated London News, 2–19–1881 (Booth).
Illustrated London News, 11–17–1962 (Scofield).
Illustrated Sporting and Dramatic News, 2–19–1881 (Booth).
John Bull, 1–29–1838 (Macready).
Listener, 3–1–1963 (Scofield).
London Examiner, 2–4–1838 (Macready).
London Figaro, 5–10–1876 (Rossi).
London Times, 3–3–1884 (Salvini).
London Times, 4–26–1858 (C. Kean).
London Times, 3–8–1949 (Wolfit).
London Times, 2–18–1956 (Welles).

London Times, 12–13–1962 (Scofield).
London Tribune, 7–28–1950 (Gielgud).
Morning Herald, 4–19–1858 (C. Kean).
Morning Post, 4–21–1931 (Gielgud).
Morning Post, 11–5–1836 (Forrest).
Morning Post, 4–25–1920 (E. Kean).
Morning Post, 2–17–1881 (Booth).
National Review, 6–13–1964 (Scofield).
New Monthly Magazine, 6–1834 (Macready).
New Statesman and Nation, 4–26–1940 (Gielgud).
New York Evening Post, 12–16–1820 (E. Kean).
New York Herald Tribune, 1–13–1956 (Welles).
New York Herald Tribune, 6–10–1963 (Carnovsky).
New York Times, 6–10–1963 (Carnovsky).
News of the World, 2–20–1881 (Booth).
Nottingham Evening Post, 10–29–1885 (Salvini).
Nottingham Evening Post, 4–11–1968 (Porter).
Overland Monthly, 4–11–1968 (Porter).
Pall Mall Gazette, 5–9–1876 (Rossi).
Pall Mall Gazette, 2–18–1881 (Booth).
Plays and Players, 1–1963 (Scofield).
Punch, 4–22–1936 (Devlin).
Quarterly Review, 6–1826 (Kemble).
Reader, 4–24–1858 (C. Kean).
Referee, 3–2–1884 (Salvini).
Royal Leamington Spa Courier, 4–25–1958 (Gielgud).
Saturday Review, 4–24–1858 (C. Kean).
Saturday Review, 6–29–1963 (Carnovsky).
Scotsman, 11–2–1955 (Gielgud).
Scotsman, 8–23–71 (West).
Spectator, 1–27–1838 (Macready).
Spectator, 10–18–1845 (Macready).
Spectator, 4–25–1931 (Gielgud).
Spectator, 10–30–1953 (Redgrave).
Spectator, 11–16–1962 (Scofield).
Standard, 3–3–1884 (Salvini).
Stratford-upon-Avon Herald, 4–24–1936 (Ayrton).
Sun, 11–5–1836 (Forrest).
Sunday Times, 4–25–1858 (C. Kean).
Sunday Times, 11–11–1962 (Scofield).
Sunday Times, 12–16–1962 (Scofield).
Theatre, 12–1–1892 (Irving).
Theatrical Inquisitor, 4–1820 (E. Kean).

Fool

Mar. 26, 1623. Vol. CXL, number 36, p. 539.
Oct. 11, 1623. Vol. CLII, number 44, p. 94.
Nov. 15, 1623. Vol. CLIV, number 28, p. 110.
Nov. ?, 1623. Vol. CLIV, number 29, p. 111.
Nov. ?, 1623. Vol. CLIV, number 38, p. 113.
June 11, 1627. Vol. LXVI, number 67, p. 212.
July 3, 1635. Vol. CCXCIII, number 24.
May 23, 1638. Vol. CCXC, number 142, p. 448.
British Museum ADD. Mss 5750 F33 (James' order for Archy's cloak).
Stratford Letters, II, p. 154.

REVIEWS

Atlas, 2-3-1838 (Macready).
Berliner Tageblatt, 12-24-1934 (Kraus).
Birmingham Gazette, 7-15-1953 (Redgrave).
Birmingham Gazette, 7-30-1953 (Redgrave).
Birmingham Mail, 7-15-1953 (Redgrave).
Birmingham Mail, 11-24-1942 (Wolfit).
Bolton Evening News, 7-18-1953 (Redgrave).
Court Journal, 10-25-1845 (Macready).
Court Journal, 11-3-1845 (Macready).
Daily Mail, 4-11-1968 (Porter).
Daily Mail, 2-24-1953 (Wolfit).
Daily Mail, 7-16-1953 (Redgrave).
Daily Worker, 7-15-1953 (Redgrave).
Era, 4-25-1858 (C. Kean).
Era, 2-19-1881 (Booth).
Evening News, 3-3-1884 (Salvini).
Evening News, 7-30-1953 (Redgrave).
Evening Standard, 4-5-1944 (Wolfit).
Evening Standard, 7-17-1953 (Redgrave).
Evening Standard, 7-30-1953 (Redgrave).
Hereford Times, 4-23-1936 (Ayrton).
Illustrated London News, 2-19-1881 (Booth).
John Bull Illustrated, 2-4-1838 (Macready).
Liverpool Daily Post, 7-16-1953 (Redgrave).

London Examiner, 1-28-1838 (Macready).
London Examiner, 2-4-1838 (Macready).
London Times, 1-26-1838 (Macready).
London Times, 10-16-1845 (Macready).
London Times, 4-26-1858 (C. Kean).
Manchester Guardian, 4-20-1950 (Gielgud).
Masque, 1946, p. 14 (Olivier).
Morning Chronicle, 4-19-1858 (C. Kean).
Morning Herald, 4-19-1858 (C. Kean).
Morning Post, 1-26-1838 (Macready).
News Chronicle, 7-22-1950 (Gielgud).
New Statesman and Nation, 4-20-1940 (Gielgud).
New Statesman and Nation, 10-5-1946 (Olivier).
New Statesman and Nation, 7-29-1950 (Gielgud).
New Statesman and Nation, 7-25-1953 (Redgrave).
New York Times, 11-17-1878 (Booth).
New York Times, 6-10-1963 (Carnovsky).
New York Times, 1-13-1956 (Welles).
Nottingham Evening Post, 4-11-1968 (Porter).
Nottingham Guardian, 7-16-1953 (Redgrave).
Observer, 2-23-1958 (Gielgud).
Observer, 4-21-1940 (Gielgud).
Overland Monthly, 4-11-1968 (Porter).
Punch, 4-22-1936 (Devlin).
Punch, 10-9-1946 (Olivier).
Punch, 7-29-1953 (Redgrave).
Reynolds Newspaper, 2-20-1881 (Booth).
Royal Leamington Spa Courier, 4-24-1936 (Ayrton).
Saturday Review, 4-24-1858 (C. Kean).
Scotsman, 11-2-1955 (Gielgud).
Shakespeare Newsletter, 12-1958 (Gielgud).
Shakespeare Survey, 1948, p. 98 (Olivier).
Spectator, 1-27-1838 (Macready).
Spectator, 4-25-1931 (Gielgud).
Stratford-upon-Avon Herald, 7-17-1953 (Redgrave).
Sunday Observer, 7-19-1953 (Redgrave).
Sunday Times, 7-19-1953 (Redgrave).

Sunday Times, 1-28-1838 (Macready).
Tablet, 8-22-1953 (Redgrave).
Tatler, 10-29-1946 (Olivier).
Time and Tide, 4-20-1940 (Gielgud).
Theatre, 9-27-1946 (Olivier).

Theatre World, 8-1950 (Gielgud).
Theatrical Journal, 10-31-1840 (Macready).
Warwickshire Advertiser, 7-17-1953 (Redgrave).

Act I, Scene v

Barker, 292 (Olivier).
Carnovsky (interview).
Cobb (performance).
Drews, 21 (German actors).
Elton, 162-3, 272, 320-1.
Empson, 131.
Fordham (Gielgud).
Gielgud (1), 83.
Heilman (2), 72, 191, 267.
James, D. G., 94-6.
Jorgensen, 77, 131.
Maxwell, 144.
Mikhoels (2), np.
Rosenberg, 1-8 (European actors).
Schoff, 167.

Williamson, C., 134, 195-6.

REVIEWS

Academy, 2-19-1881 (Booth).
Illustrated London News, 2-19-1881 (Booth).
Illustrated London News, 11-17-1962 (Scofield).
London Times, 3-8-1949 (Wolfit).
Sunday Times, 11-11-1962 (Scofield).
Sunday Times, 12-16-1962 (Scofield).
Washington Post, 4-24-1962 (Scofield).
Miscellaneous unidentified clippings; interviews; personal observation.

Act II, Scene i

Bransom, 187.
Elton, 95.
Granville-Barker, 83.
Keast, 113-4.
Kirschbaum (2), 61.
Rosenberg, 1-8, 10 (European actors).
Skulsky, 12.

Williamson, C., 136.

REVIEWS

Truth, 2-24-1881 (Booth).
Miscellaneous unidentified clippings; interviews; personal observation.

Act II, Scene ii

Blunden, 14.
Carnovsky (interview).
Danby, 105.
Elton, 197.
Fraser, 14.
Heilman (2), 62, 84, 105, 307.
Gielgud (1), 83.

Williamson, C., 56.

REVIEWS

Listener, 3-1-1963 (Scofield).
New Statesman, 11-16-1962 (Scofield).
Truth, 2-24-1881 (Booth).

Act II, Scene iii

Bradley, 209.
Carnovsky (interview).
Clemen, 144-5.
Elton, 94-5.
Fraser, 14.
Gielgud (1), 83-4.
Heilman (2), 106, 156.
Kozintsev (interview).

Murray (interview).

REVIEWS

Daily Telegraph, 4-11-1968 (Porter).
Glasgow Herald, 4-13-1968 (Porter).
Miscellaneous unidentified clippings; interviews; personal observation.

Edgar

Auden, 212–3.
Bethell, 55–6, 62–3.
Boaden (2), 102, 368.
Bradley, 244–5.
Bransom, 206–8.
Brooke, 77–8.
Burckhardt, 39.
Burnim, 93, 100 (Garrick).
Carnovsky (interview).
Charlton, 212.
Crane, 3.
Danby, 171, 189, 190–1.
Elton, 84–114, 128, 136, 216.
Empson, 140–2, 148, 150.
Fraser, 46.
French (1), 34.
Frost, 580.
Furness, 459–62.
Garrick, 93, 100 (Garrick).
Goldsmith, 98.
Granville-Barker, 67–70.
Hathorn, 65.
Heilman (2), 70, 80–1, 99, 101, 106, 111, 239, 259–61, 302–3, 330.
Howard, interview.
Jones, 59, 71–4.
Kirsch, 246, 280.
Kirschbaum (2), 59–74.
Knight, G. W. (1), 80, 124, 177–82.
Kreider, 6, 9, 14, 17–8, 29.
Mack, 54, 61–3, 67, 70.

Maclean, H., 50–4.
Maxwell, 146–7.
Morozov, 39–40.
Muir, K. (1), xlix, 1.
Muir, K. (2), 39.
Murray (interview).
Myrick, 67.
Poel, 189.
Prior, 189.
Ribner (2), 124, 131, 134.
Skulsky, 9, 12.
Stein, 37, 372.
Traversi (3), 135.
Traversi (4), 206.
Webster (1), 220.
Whitaker (2), 220.
White (1), 115.
Williams, interview.
Williamson, C., 136–7.

REVIEWS

Boston Evening Transcript, 12–3–1884 (Booth).
Boston Evening Transcript, 12–3–1884 (Salvini).
Oakland Tribune, 6–23–1963 (Carnovsky).
Sunday Times, 1–28–1838 (Macready).
Times Literary Supplement, 12–15–1961
Miscellaneous unidentified clippings; interviews; personal observation.

Act II, Scene iv

Agate (2), 54–5.
Alger, 786–8 (Forrest).
Barish and Waingrow, 243–5.
Bennett, 152.
Berg, 177 (Calhern).
Bethell, 55.
Block, 506–9.
Blunden, 7.
Bradley, 209, 220, 250.
Bransom, 55–8, 74, 222.
Burckhart, 40–1.
Byrne, 189–206.
Campbell, 193, 197.
Carnovsky (interview).
Charlton, 220.
Clemen, 140–5.
Danby, 28–30, 178–80.
Day, 232.

Drews, 16, 23–4 (German actors).
Dunn, 330.
Dye, 515–6.
Elton, 190, 198–202, 217, 281, 287, 316–7, 323ff.
Empson, 132–4.
Favorini (Mantell).
Fordham (Gielgud).
French (1), 111–2.
Frye, 252.
Furness, 417, 440–3, 458.
Garrick, 93 (Garrick).
Gerould, 317–9 (Mikhoels).
Gielgud (interview).
Goldsmith, 63–6, 97.
Gould, 144–5 (Elder Booth).
Granville-Barker, 31–3, 79, 121.
Greenfield, 281.

Toledo Blade, 1-18-1883 (Salvini).
Yorkshire Post, 4-14-1931 (Gielgud).

Act III, Scene i

Alger, 788.
Bablet, 187.
Bennett, 144.
Bradley, 207, 216.
Bransom, 82, 189.
Burnim, 129, 148-9 (Garrick).
Campbell, 199.
Charlton, 208.
Clarke (np).
Clemen, 146-7.
Crane, 62.
Day, 232.
Downer (1), 432 (Macready).
Drews, 18-9, 24 (German actors).
Dunn, 329-32.
Elton, 66-7, 198-9, 202-9, 218-9, 261-2, 315.
Empson, 135.
Fansler, 108, 188.
Farjeon, 161.
Fordham (Gielgud).
French (1), 174-5.
Frye, 129-34 (Booth and Barret).
Gielgud (interview).
Goldsby (production).
Goldsmith, 64.
Granville-Barker, 3-8, 20, 22, 273.
Harrison, 121 (Forrest).
Heilman (2), 63, 72, 76, 90.
Holland, 47.
Holloway, 83.
Jennings, 626.
Jorgensen, 126-7, 82-3.
Kirsch, 238.
Kirschbaum (1), 24.
Kirschbaum (2), 40.
Knight, G. W. (1), 73-7, 129-31, 143, 177ff, 192-3.
Knights, 96-8.
Lawrence, 208.
Mason, 156.
Miller, 245.
Morozov, 39.
Muir, K. (1), li.
Nicoll (2), 136-64.
Ribner (2), 125.
Rosenberg, 1-10 (European actors).
Scofield (interview).
Smith, 173.

Squire, 3-5, 121.
Traversi (3), 130.
Watkins, 231.
Webster (1), 218.
Williamson, C., 195.
Winter (3), 218 (Booth).

REVIEWS

Academy, 2-26-1881 (Booth).
Birmingham Gazette, 4-21-1936 (Ayrton).
Birmingham Mail, 7-15-1953 (Redgrave).
Boston Transcript, 4-27-1931 (Gielgud).
Century, 3-1883 (Salvini).
Daily Express, 7-19-1950 (Gielgud).
Daily Mail, 4-11-1968 (Porter).
Daily Telegraph, 4-21-1936 (Ayrton).
Edinburgh Dramatic Review, 4-23-1824 (Vandenhoff).
Educational Theatre Journal, 10-1967 (Mikhoels).
Guardian, 4-11-1968 (Porter).
Illustrated London News, 2-19-1881 (Booth).
Illustrated London News, 4-24-1858 (C. Kean).
Illustrated Sporting and Dramatic News, 2-19-1881 (Booth).
John Bull, 4-24-1858 (C. Kean).
Liverpool Daily Post, 7-16-1953 (Redgrave).
London Examiner, 11-6-1836 (Forrest).
London Times, 4-26-1858 (C. Kean).
London Times, 4-25-1820 (E. Kean).
Manchester Guardian, 4-8-1936 (Devlin).
Morning Herald, 4-19-1858 (C. Kean).
Morning Post, 2-17-1881 (Booth).
Morning Post, 4-25-1820 (E. Kean).
New Statesman and Nation, 7-25-1953 (Redgrave).
New York Times, 6-23-1963 (Carnovsky).
Observer, 4-18-1858 (C. Kean).
Observer, 8-23-1959 (Laughton).
Reader, 4-24-1858 (C. Kean).
Scotsman, 9-26-1946 (Olivier).

Miscellaneous unidentified clippings; interviews; personal observation.

Act III, Scene ii

Literaturen Front, 4-23-1959 (Stamatov).
Literary Gazette, 4-29-1820 (E. Kean).
London Examiner, 11-6-1836 (Forrest).
London Times, 4-25-1820 (E. Kean).
Morning Herald, 4-19-1858 (C. Kean).
Morning Post, 4-25-1820 (E. Kean).
Morning Post, 2-17-1881 (Booth).
Morning Star, 4-13-1968 (Porter).
New Monthly Magazine, 6-1834 (Macready).
New York Herald Tribune, 1-13-1956 (Welles).
New York Times, 6-10-1963 (Carnovsky).
New York Times, 6-23-1963 (Carnovsky).
Observer, 4-18-1858 (C. Kean).

Reader, 4-24-1858 (C. Kean).
Saturday Review, 4-24-1858 (C. Kean).
Scotsman, 2-19-1825 (E. Kean).
Scotsman, 3-24-1825 (E. Kean).
Scotsman, 9-26-1946 (Olivier).
Spectator, 4-25-1931 (Gielgud).
Spectator, 9-27-1946 (Olivier).
The Standard, 2-16-1881 (Booth).
Stratford-upon-Avon Herald, 12-2-1955 (Gielgud).
Sunday Telegraph, 4-14-1968 (Porter).
Tablet, 8-22-1953 (Redgrave).
Theatre Arts, 6-1940 (Gielgud).
Washington Post, 4-24-1964 (Scofield).
Wolverhampton Express and Star, 7-26-1950 (Gielgud).
Miscellaneous unidentified clippings; interviews; personal observation.

Act III, Scene iii

Bennett, 144.
Cobb (performance).
Elton, 282.
Fordham (Gielgud).
Harrison, 122.
Heilman (2), 43, 141-2.
Kirschbaum (1), 24.

Kirschbaum (2), 40.
Ribner (2), 132.

REVIEWS

Academy, 2-19-1881 (Booth).
Interviews; personal observation.

Act III, Scene iv: Part One

Agate (1), 128.
Beckerman, 151.
Bethell, 56-7.
Bradley, 250.
Bransom, 96.
Burjan and Lisnevsky (Kistov).
Byrne, 189-206.
Carnovsky (interview).
Chekhov, 108.
Cobb (performance).
Danby, 185-6.
Elton, 87, 199, 222-5, 281, 288, 330-1.
Empson, 137.
Fordham (Gielgud).
Frye, 220.
Gielgud (interview).
Granville-Barker, 80.
Harrison, 123 (Forrest).
Heilman (2), 74, 99, 110, 142, 145-7, 157.

Jayne, 282.
Jorgensen, 77-82.
Knights, 97-106.
Maxwell, 144-6.
Muir, K. (1), liii, liv.
Murray (interview).
Norwood, 591.
Rosenberg, 10-1 (European actors).
Rosier, 577.
Scofield (interview).
Skulsky, 10.
Taylor, 510.
Whitaker (2), 304-5.

REVIEWS

Boston Evening Transcript, 12-9-1885 (Salvini).
Miscellaneous unidentified clippings; interviews; personal observation.

Madness

Abenheimer, 328.
Agate (1), 200.

Alger, 242-4, 312, 394-6, 789.
Ashton, 532-5.

John Bull Illustrated, 4-24-1858 (C. Kean).
Leamington Spa Courier, 4-19-1968 (Porter).
London Star, 4-25-1820 (E. Kean).
London Times, 4-25-1820 (E. Kean).
London Times, 4-29-1820 (E. Kean).
London Times, 10-16-1845 (Macready).
London Times, 4-24-1858 (C. Kean).
London Times, 4-26-1858 (C. Kean).
London Times, 3-3-1884 (Salvini).
London Times, 9-26-1946 (Olivier).
Louisville Courier Journal, 12-3-1884 (Booth).
Morning Advertiser, 11-5-1836 (Forrest).
Morning Advertiser, 1-18-1883 (Salvini).
Morning Post, 4-25-1820 (E. Kean).
München, 11-1936 (Krauss).
New Statesman and Nation, 4-18-1936 (Devlin).
New York Evening Post, 12-15-1820 (E. Kean).
New York Herald Tribune, 1-13-1956 (Welles).
New York Herald Tribune, 6-10-1963 (Carnovsky).
New York Times, 6-25-1965 (Carnovsky).
Oakland Tribune, 6-23-1963 (Carnovsky).
Observer, 5-7-1876 (Rossi).
Pall Mall Gazette, 5-9-1876 (Rossi).
Pall Mall Gazette, 2-18-1881 (Booth).
Pall Mall Gazette, 3-3-1884 (Salvini).
Punch, 10-9-1946 (Olivier).
Reynolds Newspaper, 4-25-1858 (C. Kean).
Reynolds Newspaper, 2-20-1881 (Booth).
Saturday Review, 4-24-1858 (C. Kean).
Saturday Review, 5-20-1876 (Rossi).
Saturday Review, 3-8-1884 (Salvini).
Saturday Review, 6-29-1963 (Carnovsky).
Saturday Review, 7-29-1963 (Carnovsky).
Sketch, 10-16-1946 (Olivier).
Spectator, 4-25-1931 (Gielgud).
Standard, 3-3-1884 (Salvini).
Sun, 11-5-1836 (Forrest).
Sunday Telegraph, 4-14-1968 (Porter).
Sunday Times, 4-25-1858 (C. Kean).
Sunday Times, 7-23-1950 (Gielgud).
Theatre, 12-1-1883 (Salvini).
Theatrical Journal, 10-4-1845 (Macready).
Toledo Blade, 1-29-1908 (Mantell).
Weekend Review, 4-18-1931 (Gielgud).
Wolverhampton Express and Star, 4-11-1968 (Porter).
Wolverhampton Express and Star, 4-13-1968 (Porter).
Yorkshire Post, 4-14-1931 (Gielgud).
Miscellaneous unidentified clippings; interviews; personal observation.

Act III, Scene iv: Part Two

Act III, Scene v

Act III, Scene vi

Empson, 132, 141.
Fordham (Gielgud).
Garrick, 93 (Garrick).
Gerould, 319–22 (Mikhoels).
Goldsmith, 61.
Granville-Barker, 37–9, 80.
Harrison, 124 (Forrest).
Heilman (2), 59, 77, 94, 149, 196, 221.
Hockey, 391–3.
Kahn, 317, 322–4.
Kiasashivli (letter).
Kirsch, 249.
Kittredge (introduction).
Kreider, 166.
Ljubomirsky (Mikhoels).
Mack, 8, 50.
Maclean, N., 606.
Merchant (1), 122.
Muir, K. (1), xlviii.
Myrick, 69.
Norwood, 595.
Orwell, 49.
Peacock, 155.
Prior, 91.
Righter, 133.
Rosenberg, 5 (European actors).

Sitwell (1), 48–9.
Squire, 208.
Stewart (2), 266–7.
Traversi (3), 138.
Walbrook, 71.
Williamson, C., 196.

REVIEWS

Birmingham Mail, 7-28-1955 (Gielgud).
Daily Mail, 4-11-1968 (Porter).
Educational Theatre Journal, 10-1967 (Mikhoels).
Listener, 3-1-1963 (Scofield).
Morning Advertiser, 7-1-1968 (Porter).
New York Herald, 2-9-1883 (Salvini).
New York Times, 6-23-1963 (Carnovsky).
The Season, 2-11-1871 (Forrest).
Stage, 9-26-1946 (Olivier).
Sunday Times, 1-28-1838 (Macready).
Sunday Times, 7-19-1953 (Redgrave).
Times Literary Supplement, 12-20-1961
Toledo Blade, 1-29-1908 (Mantell).
Miscellaneous unidentified clippings; interviews; personal observation.

Act III, Scene vii

Byrne, 189–206 (Laughton).
Carnovsky (interview).
Cobb (performance).
Clemen, 141.
Dahl (Norwegian *Lear*).
Elton, 223, 288–9, 294.
Furness, 224, 418, 463.
Garrick, 88–9 (Garrick).
Gielgud (interview).
Granville-Barker, 84.
Heilman (2), 15, 48–50, 95, 135, 150, 191, 163, 282, 327.
Hockey, 393.
Kirsch, 255.
Kirschbaum (2), 72.
Mason, 23–48.
Milward (Japanese *Lear*).
Muir, K. (1), li.
Poland, 1970.
Prior, 88.

Rosenberg, 1–10 (European actors).
Scofield (interview).
Traversi (3), 141.
Williamson, C., 197.

REVIEWS

Evening News, 4-14-1931 (Gielgud).
Listener, 3-1-1963 (Scofield).
New Statesman and Nation, 4-20-1940 (Gielgud).
New York Herald Tribune, 1-13-1956 (Welles).
Punch, 7-29-1953 (Redgrave).
Shakespeare Survey, 1948, p. 98 (Olivier).
Stage, 9-26-1946 (Olivier).
Sunday Times, 7-19-1953 (Redgrave).
Miscellaneous unidentified clippings; interviews; personal observation.

Act IV, Scene i

Bethell, 53.
Blunden, 11–2.

Burckhardt, 38.
Carnovsky (interview).

Act IV, Scene v

Bradley, 243, 330.
Gielgud (interview).
Heilman (2), 60, 141, 305.
Kirsch, 271.
Kirschbaum (2), 43.

REVIEWS
Glasgow Herald, 4-13-1968 (Porter).
Interviews; personal observation.

Act IV, Scene vi

Agate (2), 54–5.
Alger, 394, 789.
Bennett, 146–51.
Berg, 176 (Calhern).
Bethell, 59–60, 109.
Blunden, 10.
Bodkin, 139.
Bradley, 207, 516.
Brandes, 46.
Bransom, 117, 119, 125, 129–30, 208, 220.
Brooke, 78–80.
Burckhardt, 43–5.
Burjan and Lisnevsky (Kistov).
Campbell, 205–6.
Carnovsky (interview).
Chekhov, 114–5, 123.
Cibber, II, 31f.
Clemen, 151–2.
Cobb (performance).
Cooke, D., 105.
Crane, 129.
Danby, 34, 125, 170, 192–3.
Downer (1), 432–3 (Macready).
Drews, 2–3, 15 (German actors).
Dye, 516.
Elton, 92–3, 110, 118, 152–3, 163–7, 205, 229, 232–5, 282, 311, 314–5, 317, 320–1.
Empson, 143–6.
Fordham (Gielgud).
French (1), 112–4.
French (2), 527.
Furness, 441, 463.
Garrick, 96–101, 107 (Garrick).
German, 12.
Goddard, 528, 540–1.
Granville-Barker, 39, 42, 75, 84.
Harrison, 125–6.
Hathorn, 57–8.
Heilman (2), 52, 63, 77, 80, 100–3, 111, 155, 158–9, 201, 204, 213, 220–1, 235, 244, 260, 264, 270, 305, 314.
Hockey, 392.
Holland, 295.

Holloway, 87, 93, 96–7, 185.
Hotson, 136–7.
Jayne, 279, 282.
Johnson, *passim*.
Jones, 65–6.
Jorgensen, 90–1, 124–5.
Kahn, 314–38, 416.
Kermode, 4–5.
Kirsch, 268–80.
Kirschbaum (1), 26.
Knight, G. W. (1), 192.
Kott, 100–2, 118.
LeWinter, 373–4.
Mack, 48, 69, 71, 101.
McCloskey, 321–5.
Merchant (1), 123.
Muir, K. (1), xlix, liv, lv.
Murray (interview).
Myrick, 59–60.
Nowottny (1), 184.
Prior, 89.
Ribner (2), 128–9.
Righter, 133.
Rosenberg, 1–8 (European actors).
Schücking, 35, 186.
Scofield (interview).
Sharpe, 226.
Siegel (1), 238.
Simon, 425–6.
Sitwell (1), 78.
Sitwell (2), 50, 55.
Squire, 274.
Sprague (1), 293 (Booth, C. Kean, E. Kean, Macready).
Stein, 375–7.
Traversi (4), 215, 218–20.
Victor, 242.
Walton, 13.
Webster (interview).
Welsford, 267.
Whitaker (2), 220.
Williamson, A., 58, 194.
Wingate, 89.

Act IV, Scene vii

Court Journal, 10-25-1845 (Macready).
Daily Telegraph, 12-1-1892 (Booth).
Daily Telegraph, 4-11-1968 (Porter).
Englishman, 4-30-1820 (E. Kean).
Era, 6-7-1876 (Rossi).
Evening Transcript, 12-3-1884 (Salvini).
Financial Times, 4-16-1968 (Porter).
Illustrated London News, 11-17-1962 (Scofield).
London Figaro, 5-10-1876 (Rossi).
London Times, 10-16-1845 (Macready).
Morning Advertiser, 4-18-1858 (C. Kean).
Morning Herald, 4-19-1858 (C. Kean).
Morning Post, 2-17-1881 (Booth).
New Statesman and Nation, 7-29-1950 (Gielgud).
New York Evening Post, 12-16-1820 (E. Kean).
Nineteenth Century, Vol. 33, no. 191 (Irving).

Observer, 5-7-1876 (Rossi).
Observer, 3-2-1884 (Salvini).
Saturday Review, 4-24-1858 (C. Kean).
Spectator, 10-30-1953 (Wolfit).
Spectator, 12-4-1953 (Redgrave).
Stage, 7-16-1953 (Redgrave).
Standard, 5-18-1876 (Rossi).
Standard, 3-3-1884 (Salvini).
Stratford-upon-Avon Herald, 7-17-1953 (Redgrave).
Sun, 11-4-1836 (Forrest).
Sun, 11-5-1836 (Forrest).
Sunday Times, 4-25-1858 (C. Kean).
Tablet, 8-22-1953 (Redgrave).
Theatrical Journal, 10-31-1840 (Macready).
Toledo Blade, 1-29-1908 (Mantell).
Vanity Fair, 2-19-1881 (Booth).
Washington Post, 4-24-1964 (Scofield).
Whitehall Review, 2-17-1881 (Booth).
Miscellaneous unidentified clippings; interviews; personal observation.

Act V, Scene i

Bransom, 155-7.
Greg, 34.
Heilman (2), 80, 248.
Kahn, 323.

Kirschbaum (1), 26-7.
Kirschbaum (2), 44-5.
Personal observation; interviews.

Act V, Scene ii

Brooke, 82.
Elton, 99-107, 332-3.
Empson, 147.
French (1), 34.
Heilman (2), 112, 128.

Jones, 64.
Kirschbaum (2), 45.
Roumania
Squire, 66.
Personal observation; interviews.

Act V, Scene iii

Agate, 126-8.
Alger, 311, 396, 790.
Barnet, 81-82.
Bell, 241.
Bennett, 154-5.
Berg, 153, 177 (Calhern).
Bethell, 6off.
Blunden, 16.
Bradley, 204, 205, 217, 232-4, 241-3, 246-60.
Brandes, 458-9.
Bransom, 162-3, 168, 175-9.
Brooke, 72-8, 82-6.
Burckhardt, 47-50.
Burnim, 149 (Garrick).

Campbell, O. J., 94ff.
Carnovsky (interview).
Chambers, 40-1.
Charlton, 212.
Chekhov, 107-8, 124.
Clemen, 152.
Coghill, letter.
Coleman, 261.
Colorado Festival (see bibliography).
Danby, 195.
Day, 232-3.
Drews, 3, 4, (German actors).
Duthie (introduction).
Dye, 517.

Wilson, H., 201–4.
Wingate, 89.

REVIEWS

Academy, 5–6–1876 (Rossi).
Atlas, 2–3–1838 (Macready).
Birmingham Post, 4–21–1936 (Ayrton).
Birmingham Post, 4–11–1968 (Scofield).
Century, 3–1883 (Salvini).
Daily News, 3–3–1884 (Salvini).
Daily Telegraph, 2–16–1881 (Booth).
Daily Telegraph, 12–1–1892 (Booth).
Daily Telegraph, 7–15–1953 (Redgrave).
Dramatic Censor, Vol. 1, 361.
Educational Theatre Journal, 10–1967 (Mikhoels).
Era, 5–7–1876 (Rossi).
Globe, 11–8–1836 (Forrest).
Home Journal, 12–2–1888 (Booth).
Illustrated London News, 2–19–1881 (Booth).
Illustrated London News, 11–17–1962 (Scofield).
John Bull Illustrated, 1–29–1838 (C. Kean).
John Bull Illustrated, 4–24–1858 (Macready).
Leamington Spa Courier, 4–19–1968 (Porter).
Listener, 3–1–1963 (Scofield).
Literaturen Front, 4–23–1959 (Stamatov and Trandafilov).
London Examiner, 2–4–1838 (Macready).
London News, 11–18–1892 (Irving).
London Times, 10–16–1845 (Macready).
London Times, 4–21–1936 (Ayrton).
Louisville Times, 5–12–1888 (Booth).
Monthly Mirror, 4–1802 (Kemble).
Morning Star, 4–13–1968 (Porter).
Morning Post, 4–25–1820 (E. Kean).
Morning Post, 5–5–1876 (Rossi).
Morning Post, 2–17–1881 (Booth).
National Review, 3–3–1947 (Wolfit).
National Review, 6–13–1964 (Scofield).
New Monthly Magazine, 6–1834 (Macready).
News of the World, 2–20–1881 (Booth).
New Statesman and Nation, 4–20–1940 (Gielgud).
New Statesman and Nation, 10–5–1946 (Olivier).
New Statesman and Nation, 7–25–1953 (Redgrave).

Newsweek, 6–1–1964 (Scofield).
Nottingham Evening Post, 10–29–1885 (Salvini).
Nottingham Evening Post, 4–11–1968 (Porter).
Nottingham Guardian, 7–16–1953 (Redgrave).
Pall Mall Gazette, 2–18–1881 (Booth).
Plays and Players, 1–1963 (Scofield).
Punch, 7–29–1953 (Redgrave).
Putnam's Monthly, 1–1908 (Salvini).
Reynolds Newspaper, 2–20–1881 (Booth).
Royal Leamington Spa Courier, 7–17–1953 (Redgrave).
Saturday Review, 9–29–1909 (McKinnell).
Saturday Review, 1–28–1956 (Welles).
Saturday Review, 6–29–1963 (Carnovsky).
Scotsman, 3–24–1825 (E. Kean).
Shakespeare Newsletter, 10–5–1951.
Shakespeare Newsletter, 11–5–1954.
Shakespeare Newsletter, 12–1958 (Gielgud).
Sketch, 10–16–1946 (Olivier).
Spectator, 1–27–1838 (Macready).
Spectator, 10–18–1845 (Macready).
Spectator, 4–25–1931 (Gielgud).
Spectator, 12–4–1953 (Redgrave).
Spirit of the Times, 1–13–1877 (Booth).
Standard, 2–16–1881 (Booth).
Standard, 3–3–1884 (Salvini).
Sun, 11–5–1836 (Forrest).
Sun, 1–26–1838 (Macready).
Sunday Times, 5–25–1834 (Macready).
Svenska Dagbladet, 3–20–1967 (Mantzius).
Tablet, 8–22–1953 (Redgrave).
Tablet, 6–29–1968 (Porter).
Theatre, 12–1–1883 (Salvini).
Theatrical Journal, 10–31–1840 (Macready).
Time and Tide, 7–29–1940 (Gielgud).
Uppsala Nya Tidning (1929 *Lear* in Sweden).
Vanity Fair, 2–19–1881 (Booth).
Wolverhampton Express and Star, 4–11–1968 (Porter).
Warwickshire and Worcester, 12–1962 (Scofield).
Miscellaneous unidentified clippings; interviews; personal observation.

The *Lear* Myth

(References to the folk-tale cousins of
   Lear may be found in the following:)

Beckwith
Bloomhill
Callaway
Cross
Dracott
Espinosa
Freud
Gayton
Graves

Hunt
Jacottet
Jobes
McKay
Neogi
Propp
Rappoport
Rooth
Stack
Thompson (1), (2)
Werner

Bibliography

BOOKS

Agate, James (1), *Brief Chronicles*, London, 1943.
———— (2), *The Contemporary Theatre, 1944 and 1945*, London, 1946.
———— (3), *The English Dramatic Critics, An Anthology, 1660–1932*, London, 1932.
Alger, William R., *Life of Edwin Forrest*, Vol. I, New York, 1877.
Alpers, Paul, "*King Lear* and the Sight Pattern," in *Defense of Reading*, New York, 1963.
Archer, William, *William Charles Macready*, London, 1890.
Armstrong, Archy, *Archy's Dream*, in *The Old Book Collector's Miscellany*, Vol. III, London, 1873.
Armstrong, Edward, *The Emperor Charles V*, London, 1902.
Ashley, Maurice P., *The Stuarts in Love*, London, 1963.
Ashwell, Lena, *Reflections from Shakespeare*, London, 1926.
Auden, Wystan H., *The Dyer's Hand and Other Essays*, New York, 1932.
Ausubel, Nathan, ed., *A Treasury of Jewish Folklore*, New York, 1957.
Bab, Julius (1), *Das Theatre der Gegenwart*, Berlin, 1928.
———— (2), *Shakespeare Wesen und Werke*, Berlin, 1925.
Bablet, Dennis, *Edward Gordon Craig*, trans. by Daphne Woodward, London, 1966.
Barker, Arthur, *A Shakespeare Commentary*, New York, 1938.
Basedow, Herbert, *The Australian Aborigines*, Adelaide, 1925.
Barker, Felix, *The Oliviers*, New York, 1953.
Barnay, Ludwig, *Über Theater und Anderes*, Berlin, 1913.
Bates, Daisy, *The Passing of the Aborigines*, London, 1944.
Beckerman, Bernard, *Shakespeare at the Globe*, New York, 1962.
Beckwith, Martha, *Hawaiian Mythology*, New Haven, Conn., 1940.
Benson, G. C., *Mainly Players*, London, 1926.
Bethell, S. L., *Shakespeare and the Popular Dramatic Tradition*, Durham, N. C., 1946.
Bloom, Alan D., *Shakespeare's Politics*, New York, 1964.
Bloomhill, Greta, *The Sacred Drum*, Cape Town, 1960.
Blunden, Edmund, *Shakespeare's Significances*, London, 1929.
Boaden, James, *Memoirs of Mrs. Siddons*, London, 1893.

Bodkin, Maud, *Studies of Type Images*, London, 1951.
Bonheim, Helmut, ed., *The King Lear Perplex*, San Francisco, 1960.
Bradbrook, M. C., *Elizabethan Stage Conditions*, Cambridge (England), 1932.
Bradley, A. C., *Shakespearian Tragedy*, London, 1956.
Brandes, George, *William Shakespeare*, New York, 1936.
Bransom, J. S. H., *The Tragedy of King Lear*, Oxford, 1934.
Brink, Bernhard T., *Five Lectures on Shakespeare*, London, 1895.
Brown, John Russell, *Shakespeare's Plays in Performance*, London, 1966.
Burjan, B. and I. Lisnevsky, *Portrait of an Actor* (Kistov), Moscow, n. d.
Burnim, K. A., *David Garrick, Director*, Pittsburg, 1961.
Busby, Olive Mary, *Studies in the Development of the Fool in Elizabethan Drama*, New York, 1923.
Bush, Geoffrey, *Shakespeare and the Natural Condition*, Cambridge (USA), 1956.
Calhoun, Eleanor, *Pleasures and Palaces*, New York, 1915.
Callaway, Henry, *Nursery Tales, Traditions, and Histories of the Zulus*, Vol. I., London, 1868.
Campbell, Lily B., *Shakespeare's Tragic Heroes*, New York, 1952.
Campbell, Thomas, *Life of Mrs. Siddons*, London, 1839.
Camus, Albert, *The Myth of Sisyphus*, New York, 1961.
Cavell, Stanley, *Must We Mean What We Say*, New York, 1969, 267–353.
Chambers, E. K., *The Medieval Stage*, Oxford, 1903.
Chambers, R. W., *King Lear*, Glasgow, 1940.
Chapman, John Jay, *A Glance Toward Shakespeare*, Boston, 1922.
Charlton, H. B., *Shakespearian Tragedy*, Cambridge (England), 1952.
Chekhov, Michael, *To the Actor*, New York, 1953.
Cibber, Theophilus, *Two Dissertations on the Theatres*, London, 1956.
Clarke, Mary, *Shakespeare at the Old Vic*, London, 1958.
Clapp, Henry Austin, *Reminiscences of a Dramatic Critic*, Cambridge (Mass.), 1902.
Clemen, Wolfgang, *The Development of Shakespeare's Imagery*, London, 1951.
Coffin, Robert P.T., *The Dukes of Buckingham*, New York, 1931.
Cokes, Blanche, *Shakespeare's Four Giants*, Rindge (New Hampshire), 1957.
Coleman, John (1), *Fifty Years of an Actor's Life*, Vol. 1, London, 1904.
Coleman, John (2), *Players and Playwrights I Have Known*, London, 1888.
Coleridge, Henry Nelson, ed., *The Literary Remains of S. T. Coleridge*, Vol. 11, London, 1836.
Cooke, Dutton, *Nights at the Play*, London, 1883.
Cooke, William, ed., *Memoirs of Charles Macklin*, London, 1804.
Cox, Marian R., *Cinderella*, London, 1893.
Crane, Milton, *Shakespeare's Prose*, Chicago, 1951.
Cross, Tom Peete, and Clark Harris Slover, ed., *Ancient Irish Tales*, New York, 1936.
Curtin, Jeremiah, *Hero-Tales of Ireland*, London, 1894.
Danby, John, *Shakespeare's Doctrine of Nature*, London, 1949.
Davies, Thomas (1), *Dramatic Miscellanies*, Vol. II, London, 1783.
Davies, Thomas, ed. (2), *Memoirs of the Life of David Garrick, esq.*, London, 1808.

Day, M. C. and J. C. Trewin, *Shakespeare Memorial Theatre*, London, 1932.
Dent, Alan, *Preludes and Studies*, London, 1942.
Disher, M. Willson, *Clowns and Pantomimes*, London, 1923.
Doran, John, *History of Court Fools*, London, 1858.
Douce, Frances, *Illustrations of Shakespeare and of Ancient Manners: with Dissertations on the Clowns and Fools of Shakespeare* . . . , London, 1907, 2 vols.
Downer, Alan, (1) *The Eminent Tragedian*, Cambridge (USA), 1966.
Doyle, Francis Hastings, *Lectures on Poetry*, London, 1877.
Dracott, Alice Elizabeth, *Simla Village Tales*, London, 1906.
The Dramatic Censor, I, ed. by F. Gentleman, London, 1770.
The Dramatic Censor, IV, ed. by F. Gentleman, London, 1801.
Draper, John W., *The Humors and Shakespeare's Characters*, Durham, N. C., 1945.
Drews, Wolfgang, *Konig Lear auf der Deutsch Buhne bis zur Gegenwart*, Berlin, 1932.
Duthie, George Ian, ed., *King Lear*, Cambridge (England), 1960.
Elton, W. R., *King Lear and the Gods*, San Marino, Calif., 1967.
Empson, William, *Structure of Complex Words*, London, 1951.
Erasmus, Desiderius, *In Praise of Folly*, Princeton, 1941.
Espinosa, Auralio, *Cuentos Populares espanoles*, 3 vols., 2nd ed., Madrid, 1946–7.
Evans, E. P., *Criminal Prosecution and Capital Punishment of Animals*, London, 1906.
Fansler, Harriott Ely, *The Evolution of Technic in Elizabethan Tragedy*, Chicago, 1914.
Farjeon, Herbert, *The Shakespearean Scene*, London, 1949.
Faucit, Helen, *On Some of Shakespeare's Female Characters*, London, 1888.
Felver, Charles S., *Robert Armin, Shakespeare's Fool*, Kent State University Bulletin, January 1961.
Findlater, Richard, *Michael Redgrave: Actor*, London, 1956.
Fitzgerald, P., *The Life of David Garrick*, London, 1808.
Flatter, Richard, *Shakespeare's Producing Hand*, New York, 1948.
Foote, Jesse, *The Life of Arthur Murphy, esq.*, London, 1811.
Fraser, R. A., *Shakespeare's Poetics in Relation to King Lear*, London, 1962.
Frazer, Sir James, *The Golden Bough*, London, 1911–1915.
Frye, Roland, *Shakespeare and Christian Doctrine*, Princeton, N. J., 1963.
Frye, Northrop, *Fools of Time*, Toronto, 1969.
Furness, Horace H., ed., *A New Variorium Edition of Shakespeare: King Lear*, Philadelphia, 1880.
Gardner, Helen, *King Lear*, London, 1967.
Gayton, A. H. and Stanley Newman, *Yokuts and Western Mono Myths*, Berkeley, 1940.
Gielgud, John, *Stage Directions*, London, 1963.
Gildon, Charles, *The Life of Betterton*, London, 1710.
Gittings, Robert, *The Living Shakespeare*, London, 1960.
Goddard, Harold, *The Meaning of Shakespeare*, Chicago, 1951.
Goldsmith, Robert, *Wise Fools in Shakespeare*, East Lansing, Mich., 1955.
Gould, Thomas, *The Tragedian*, New York, 1968.

Granville-Barker, Harley, *Prefaces to Shakespeare*, series 1, London, 1963.
Graves, Robert, *The Greek Myths*, New York, 1957.
Green, Mrs. Everett, *Life and Letters of Elizabeth of Bohemia*.
Greg, Walter W., *The Variants in the First Quarto of King Lear*, London, 1940.
Gregor, J., *Meister Deutsch er Schauspielkunst*, Berlin, 1939.
Guthrie, Tyrone, introduction to *Shakespeare's Ten Great Plays*, New York, 1962.
Harbage, Alfred (1), *Conceptions of Shakespeare*, Cambridge (Mass.), 1966.
Harbage, Alfred (2), *Shakespeare and the Rival Traditions*, New York, 1952.
Harrison, Gabriel, *Edwin Forrest: the Actor and the Man*, New York, 1889.
Hawkins, Frederick W., *The Life of Edmund Kean*, Vol. II, London, 1869.
Heilman, Robert (2), *This Great Stage: Image and Structure in King Lear*, New Orleans, 1948.
Heraud, John A., *Shakespeare, His Inner Life*, London, 1865.
Hill, John, *The Actor*, London, 1755.
Hillebrand, Harold N., *Edmund Kean*, New York, 1933.
Hogan, G. B., *Shakespeare in the Theatre, 1710–1800*, London, 1957.
Holland, Norman, *Psychoanalysis and Shakespeare*, New York, 1964.
Holloway, John, *The Story of the Night*, Lincoln, Neb., 1961.
Hotson, Leslie, *Shakespeare's Motley*, London, 1952.
Houtchens, L. and Carolyn Washburn, eds., *Leigh Hunt's Dramatic Criticism, 1808–1831*, New York, 1949.
Howe, P. P., ed., *The Complete Works of William Hazlitt*, London, 1930.
Howitt, A. W., *The Native Tribes of Southeast Australia*, London, 1904.
Hudson, H. N., *Lectures on Shakespeare*, New York, 1848.
Hugo, Victor, *William Shakespeare*, Paris, 1864.
Hunt, Martha, trans. and ed., *Grimm's Household Tales with the Author's Notes*, 2 vols., London, 1915.
Hurstfield, Joel, *The Queen's Ward*, Cambridge (England), 1958.
Irving, Henry, *A Book of Remarkable Criminals*, London, 1918.
Jacobsohn, Siegfried, *Max Reinhardt*, Berlin, n. d.
Jacottet, Edward, ed., *The Treasury of Ba-Suto Lore*, Vol. I, London, 1908.
Jacox, Francis, *Shakespeare's Diversions*, New York, 1875.
James, D. G., *The Dream of Learning*, Oxford, 1951.
James, Henry, *The Scenic Art*, New Brunswick, 1948.
Jobes, Gertrude, *Dictionary of Mythology, Folklore, and Symbols*, New York, 1961.
Johnson, Samuel, *Johnson on Shakespeare*, by Walter Raleigh, ed., London, 1952.
Jorgensen, Paul, *Lear's Self-Discovery*, Berkeley, 1967.
Joseph, B. L., *Elizabethan Acting*, London, 1951.
Kaiser, Walter, *Praisers of Folly—Erasmus, Rabelais, Shakespeare*, Cambridge (Mass.), 1963.
Kahrl, G. M., ed., *Letters of David Garrick*, Vols. I and II, Cambridge (Mass.), 1963.
Keast, W. R., ed., *Critics and Criticism*, Chicago, 1952.
Kemble, Frances (1), *Journal*, Vol. II, Philadelphia, 1835.
Kemble, Frances (2), *Records of Later Life*, Vol. III, London, 1882.

Kirsch, James, *Shakespeare's Royal Self*, New York, 1966.
Kirschbaum, Leo, *Characters and Characterization in Shakespeare*, Detroit, 1962.
Kittredge, George L., ed., *The Tragedy of King Lear by William Shakespeare*, Boston, 1940.
Knight, G. Wilson (3), *The Imperial Theme*, London, 1961.
Knight, G. Wilson (1), *Principles of Shakespearean Production*, London, 1949.
Knight, G. Wilson (2), *The Wheel of Fire*, London, 1954.
Knight, Joseph, *Theatrical Notes*, London, 1893.
Knights, L. C., *Some Shakespearean Themes*, London, 1959.
Kökeritz, Helge, *Shakespeare's Pronunciation*, New Haven, Conn., 1953.
Kott, Jan, *Shakespeare Our Contemporary*, New York, 1964.
Kozintsev, Grigori, *Shakespeare: Time and Conscience*, New York, 1966.
Krauss, Werner, *Das Schauspiel meines Lebens*, Berlin, 1939.
Kreider, Paul, *Repetition in Shakespeare's Plays*, Princeton, N. J., 1941.
Lamb, Charles, *The Works of Charles Lamb*, Vol. IV, ed. by Edward Moxon, London, 1850.
Lawrence, W. J., *Pre-Restoration Stage Studies*, Cambridge (England), 1927.
Legg, J. Wickham, ed., *The Coronation Order of King James I*, London, 1902.
Levi-Strauss, Claude, *The Raw and the Cooked*, New York, 1969.
Lewes, George Henry, *On Actors and the Art of Acting*, New York, 1878.
LeWinter, Oswald, ed., *Shakespeare in Europe*, New York, 1963.
Lewis, Wyndam, *The Lion and the Fox*, London, 1927.
Mack, Maynard, *King Lear in Our Time*, Berkeley, 1965.
MacKenzie, Agnes M., *The Women in Shakespeare's Plays*, London, 1924.
Mantzius, Karl, *A History of Theatrical Art*, London, 1903–21.
Marston, John W., *Our Recent Actors*, London, 1888.
Martin, Theodore, *Helena Faucit*, London, 1900.
Masefield, John, *William Shakespeare*, New York, 1911.
Maskell, William, *Monumenta Ritualia Ecclesiae Anglicanae*, 3 vols, 2nd edition, Oxford, 1882.
Matthews, Honor, M. V., *Character and Symbol in Shakespeare's Plays*, Cambridge (England), 1962.
McCurdy, Harold Grier, *The Personality of Shakespeare*, New Haven, Conn., 1953.
McKay, John G., *More West Highland Tales*, London, 1940.
Mikhoels, Solomon, *Essays, Speeches, and Articles*, Moscow, 1960.
Morley, H., *The Journal of a London Playgoer*, London, 1866.
Muir, Edwin, *The Politics of King Lear*, Glasgow, 1947.
Muir, Kenneth, ed., *King Lear*, London, 1964.
Murdock, James, *The Stage*, Philadelphia, 1880.
Murray, James A. H., ed., *The New English Dictionary on Historical Principles* (cover title: *The Oxford English Dictionary*), Oxford, 1884–1928.
Murry, John Middleton, *Shakespeare*, London, 1936.
Murphy, Arthur (1), *Gray's Inn Journal*, Vol. II, London, 1756.
Murphy, Arthur (2), *The Life of Garrick*, London, 1801.
Neogi, Dwijendra Nath, *Sacred Tales of India*, London, 1916.
Nicoll, Allardyce (3), *Shakespeare*, London, 1952.

Nicoll, Allardyce, *Stuart Masques and the Renaissance Stage*, New York, 1938.

Nicoll, Allardyce (1), *Studies in Shakespeare*, London, 1927.

Niklaus, Thelma, *Harlequin Phoenix*, London, 1956.

Noskowki, W., *Tygodnik Illustrowany* (in Polish, on Ladnowski), Warsaw, 1879.

Nowottny, Winifred (i), *Language Poets Use*, London, 1962.

Odell, George (1), *Annals of the New York Stage*, New York, 1927–1949.

Odell, George (2), *Shakespeare from Betterton to Irving*, New York, 1963.

O'Keefe, John, *Recollections*, London, 1826.

Ornstein, Robert, *The Moral Vision of Jacobean Tragedy*, Madison, Wis., 1960.

Ovid, *Metamorphoses*, trans. by John Clarke, London, 1790.

Peacock, Ronald, *The Poet in the Theatre*, New York, 1946.

Phelps, W. May and Forbes-Robertson, John, *The Life and Lifework of Samuel Phelps*, London, 1886.

Poel, William, *Shakespeare in the Theatre*, London, 1913.

Poel, William (2), *Monthly Letters*, London, 1929.

Polgar, Alfred, *Auswahl*, Rowohlt, 1968.

Pollock, Frederick, ed., *Macready's Reminiscences and Diaries*, New York, 1874.

Pollock, W. H., *Impressions of Henry Irving*, London, 1908.

Prior, Moody, *The Language of Tragedy*, New York, 1947.

Proctor, B.W., *The Life of Edmund Kean*, Vol. II, London, 1835.

Propp, Vladimir, *Morphology of the Folk-tale*, Indiana, 1958.

Public Records Office (see notes for Fool, after notes for I, iv).

Purdom, C. B., ed., *The Swan Shakespeare*, New York, 1930.

Quiller-Couch, Arthur T., *Shakespeare's Workmanship*, London, 1918.

Rabkin, Norman, *Shakespeare and the Common Understanding*, New York, 1967.

Raleigh, Walter, *Shakespeare*, London, 1907.

Ralli, Augustus, *A History of Shakespearean Criticism*, 2 vols., London, 1932.

Rappoport, Angelo S., *The Folklore of the Jews*, London, 1937.

Redgrave, Michael, *The Actor's Ways and Means*, London, 1953.

Rees, J., *The Life of E. Forrest*, Philadelphia, 1874.

Ribner, Irving (2), *Patterns in Shakespearean Tragedy*, London, 1960.

Righter, Anne, *Shakespeare and the Idea of the Play*, New York, 1963.

Robertson, J. M., *Shakespeare and Chapman*, London, 1917.

Robinson, Henry Crabb, *Diary*, London, 1869.

Rosen, William, *Shakespeare and the Craft of Tragedy*, Cambridge (Mass.), 1960.

Rooth, Anna B., *Cinderella Legend*, Lund, 1951.

Rothe, Hans, *Max Reinhardt*, Berlin, 1930.

Rushworth, John, *Historical Collections*, London, 1721.

Schlegel, A. W., *Lectures on Dramatic Art*, trans, by J. Black.

Schücking, Levin, *Character Problems in Shakespeare's Plays*, London, 1922.

Seccombe, Thomas and Allen, J. W., *The Age of Shakespeare*, New York, 1909.

Sewall, Richard B., *The Vision of Tragedy*, New Haven, Conn., 1959.

Sewell, Arthur, *Characters and Society in Shakespeare*, Oxford, 1951.
Shakespeare Allusion Book, 1591–1700, London, 1932.
Sharpe, Ella Freeman, *Collected Papers on Psychoanalysis*, London, 1950.
Shattuck, Charles H., ed., *William Charles Macready's King John*, Urbana, Ill., 1962.
Siegel, Paul N. (3), *Shakespearean Tragedy and the Elizabethan Compromise*, New York, 1957.
Sillard, Robert M., *Barry Sullivan and His Contemporaries*, London, 1901.
Sitwell, Edith (1), *A Notebook on William Shakespeare*, London, 1962.
Speaight, Robert (1), *Nature in Shakespearean Tragedy*, London, 1955.
Speaight, Robert (2), *William Poel and the Elizabethan Revival*, London, 1954.
Spencer, Theodore, *Shakespeare and the Nature of Man*, New York, 1949.
Spevack, Marvin (2), *A Complete and Systematic Concordance to the Works of Shakespeare*, Vol. III, Hildesheim, Germany, 1960.
Spauling, K. J., *The Philosophy of Shakespeare*, Oxford, 1953.
Sprague, Arthur Colby (1), *Shakespeare and the Actors*, Cambridge (Mass.), 1944.
Sprague, Arthur Colby, *Shakespearian Players and Performances*, Cambridge (Mass.), 1953.
Spurgeon, Caroline, F. E. (1), *Keats' Shakespeare*, London, 1928.
Spurgeon, Caroline F. E. (2), *Shakespeare's Imagery and What It Tells Us*, New York, 1936.
Squire, John, *Shakespeare as a Dramatist*, London, 1935.
Stael-Holstein, Anne, *Germany*, Vol. II, New York, 1859.
Stauffer, Donald A., *Shakespeare's World of Images*, New York, 1949.
Stebbins, Emma, *Charlotte Cushman*, Boston, 1879.
Sternfeld, F. W., *Music in Shakespearean Tragedy*, London, 1963.
Stewart, J. I. M. (1), *Character and Motive in Shakespeare*, New York, 1949.
Stoll, Elmer Edgar, *Art and Artifice in Shakespeare: A Study in Dramatic Contrast and Illusion*, New York, 1933.
Stuart, Donald C., *The Development of Dramatic Art*, New York, 1928.
Swain, Barbara, *Fools and Folly During the Renaissance*, New York, 1932.
Swinburne, A. C. (2), *A Study of Shakespeare*, London, 1895.
Swinburne, A. C. (3), *Three Plays of Shakespeare*, London, 1909.
Terry, Ellen A. (1), *Four Lectures on Shakespeare*, London, 1932.
Terry, Ellen A. (2), *The Story of My Life*, London, 1908.
Thompson, Stith (1), *Motif-index to Folk Literature*, Bloomington, Ind., 1932–1936.
Thompson, Stith and Balys, Jonas (2), *The Oral Tales of India*, Bloomington, Ind., 1958.
Tietze-Conrat, Erica, *Dwarfs and Jesters in Art*, London, 1957.
Tillyard, E. M. W., *Elizabethan World Picture*, London, 1958.
Tolstoy, Leo, *Recollections and Essays by Leo Tolstoy*, London, 1937.
Towse, John Ranken, *Sixty Years of the Theatre*, New York, 1916.
Toynbee, William, ed., *The Diaries of William Charles Macready, 1833–1851*, New York, 1912.
Traversi, D. A. (1), *An Approach to Shakespeare*, New York, 1956.
Trevor-Roper, H. R., *Archbishop Laud 1573–1645*, London, 1940.

Trewin, J. C. (1), *Mr. Macready*, London, 1955.
Trewin, J. C. (2), *Shakespeare on the English Stage, 1900–1964*, London, 1964.
Ulrici, Hermann, *Shakespeare's Dramatic Art*, London, 1876.
Vandenhoff, George, *Leaves from an Actor's Notebook*, New York, 1860.
Van Gyseghem, Andre, *Theatre in Soviet Russia*, London, 1943.
Vaughan, C. E., *Types of Tragic Drama*, London, 1908.
Victor, Benjamin, *Original Letters, Dramatic Pieces, and Poems*, London, 1776.
Walbrook, H. M., *Nights at the Play*, London, 1883.
Waller, A. R. and Grove, Arnold, ed., *Collected Works of William Hazlitt*, London, 1903.
Watkins, Ronald, *On Producing Shakespeare*, New York, 1950.
Webster, Margaret (1), *Shakespeare Today*, London, 1957.
Webster, Margaret (2), *Shakespeare Without Tears*, London, 1942.
Weldon, Sir Anthony, *The Court and Character of King James*, London, 1817.
Welsford, Enid, *The Fool: His Social and Literary History*, New York, 1936.
Wendell, Barrett, *William Shakespeare: a Study in Elizabethan Literature*, New York, 1901.
Werner, E. T. C., *Myths and Legends of China*, London, 1922.
Whitaker, Virgil K. (1), *The Mirror Up to Nature*, San Marino, Calif., 1965.
Whitaker, Virgil, K. (2), *Shakespeare's Use of Learning*, Los Angeles, 1953.
White, Richard G. (2), *Studies in Shakespeare*, Boston, 1887.
Williamson, Audrey, *Old Vic Drama*, Vol. I, New York, 1949.
Wilson, Harold S., *On the Design of Shakespearean Tragedy*, Toronto, 1957.
Wingate, Charles E., *Shakespeare's Heroes on the Stage*, New York, 1896.
Winstanley, Lillian, *Hamlet and the Scottish Succession*, Cambridge (Engl.), 1921.
Winter, William (1), *The Life and Art on Edwin Booth*, London, 1894.
Winter, William (2), *Shadows of the Stage*, London, 1896.
Winter, William (3), *Shakespeare on the Stage*, series 2, New York, 1915.
Wolfit, Donald, introduction to *King Lear*, New York, 1956.
Zandvoort, R. W., *King Lear and the Scholars and Critics*, Antwerp, 1956.
Zarian, Rouben (1), *Shakespeare Acted by Adamyan*, Yerevan, 1964.
Zarian, Rouben (2), *Shakespeare and the Armenians*, Yerevan, 1969.

ARTICLES AND ESSAYS

Periodical Abbreviations

APSR	American Political Science Review
BuR	Bucknell Review
CE	College English
CEA	CEA Critic
CQ	Cambridge Quarterly
ELH	Journal of English Literary History
ELN	English Language Notes
ES	English Studies
ETJ	Educational Theatre Journal

Expl	Explicator
Hud R	Hudson Review
JEGP	Journal of English and Germanic Philology
MinnR	Minnesota Review
MLQ	Modern Language Quarterly
MLR	Modern Language Review
N&Q	Notes and Queries
NMQ	New Mexico Quarterly
PQ	Philological Quarterly
QQ	Queen's Quarterly
QR	Quarterly Review
REL	Review of English Literature
RES	Review of English Studies
RenP	Renaissance Papers
SEL	Studies in English Literature, 1500–1900.
ShN	Shakespeare Newsletter
ShS	Shakespeare Survey
SP	Studies in Philology
SQ	Shakespeare Quarterly
TDR	The Drama Review (formerly Tulane Drama Review)
ThS	Theatre Survey
XUS	Xavier University Studies

Abenheimer, Karl M., "On Narcissism—including an Analysis of Shakespeare's *King Lear*," *British Journal of Medical Psychology*, XX: 3, 322–9.

Anikst, Alexander, "Kozintsev and his *King Lear*," *Moscow News*, No. 2, 1971.

Arms, G. W., et. al., "Shakespeare's *King Lear*, v. iii," Explicator, III: 3.

Ashton, J. W., "The Wrath of King Lear," *JEGP*, XXXI, 530–6.

Banu, George, "First Echoes of 'Lear'," *Contemporanul* 11–6–70. Trans. by Gabriel Plesea.

Barish, Jonas A. and Waingrow, Marshall, "Service in *King Lear*," *SQ*, IX:3, 347–55.

Barnay, Ludwig (1), "Der Narr in König Lear," *Erinnerungen*, I, Berlin, 1903, 216–7.

Barnet, Sylvan, "Some Limitations to a Christian Approach to Shakespeare," *ELH*, XXII, 81–92.

Bennett, Josephine Waters, "The Storm Within: the Madness of Lear," *SQ*, XIII:2, 137–55.

Berkovsky, N., "*King Lear* at the Bolshoy Dramatic Theatre," essay published in Russia in 1941.

Block, Edward A., "*King Lear*: a Study in Balanced and Shifting Sympathies," *SQ*, X:4, 499–512.

Blok, Alexander, "Shakespeare's *King Lear*: a Speech to the Actors," Russian trans. by Daniel Gerould, ETJ, XIX, 370–5.

Boaden, James (1), "The Life of J. P. Kemble," *QR*, XXXIV, 197–248.

Boyadzhiev, G., "His Majesty Shakespeare's Servants" (in Russian), *Sovetskaya Kultura*, 9 April 1964.

Brooke, Nicholas, "The Ending of *King Lear*" in *Shakespeare 1564-1964*, ed. by E. A. Bloom, Providence, R. I., 1964.

Burckhardt, Sigurd, "*King Lear*: the Quality of Nothing," *MinnR*, II:1, 33-50.

Byrne, M. St. Clare, "*King Lear* at Stratford-on-Avon, 1959," *SQ*, XI:2, 189-206.

Camden, C. (1), "An Absurdity in King Lear," *Philological Quarterly*, XI:4, 408-9.

Camden, C. (2), "Suffocation of the Mother: Lear's Physical Symptoms," *Modern Language Notes*, 63:390-3.

Campbell, O. J., "The Salvation of Lear," *ELH*, XV:2, 93-109.

Chapman, J. A., "*King Lear*," *Nineteenth Century*, August 1947, 95-100.

Chwalewik, Witold, "Royal Shakespeare Company in Warsaw," *Stolica*, XV, 7.

Clarke, George Herbert, "The Catastrophe in *King Lear*," *QQ*, XLI, 369-82.

Clay, James H., "A New Theory of Tragedy: a Description and Evaluation," *ETJ*, VIII, 295-305.

Copeau, Jacques, "*King Lear* at the Theatre Antoine," trans. by Bernard Dukore and Daniel Gerould, *ETJ*, XIX, 376-81.

Craig, Hardin, "The Ethics of *King Lear*," *PQ*, IV:2, 97-109.

Cummins, Thomas J., "In Search of Goneril's Mew," *CEA*, XXXI:1, 4-5.

Cutts, John P., "Lear's Learned Theban," *SQ*, XIV:4, 477-81.

Darby, Robert H., "Astrology in Shakespeare's *Lear*," *ES*, XX, 250-7.

DeMendonca, Barbara H. C., "The Influence of *Gorboduc* on *King Lear*," *ShS*, XIII, 41-8.

Doran, Madeleine, "Reviews: *King Lear*," *SQ*, XII:4, 456.

Dove, John, and Gamble, Peter, "Our Darker Purpose," *Neuphilologische Mitteilungen*, LXX: 2, 306-18.

Downer, Alan, (2) "The Making of a Great Actor—William Charles Macready," *Theatre Annual*, 1949.

Draper, John W. (2), "The Occasion of *King Lear*," *SP*, XXXIV, 180-5.

Draper, John W. (3), "The Old Age of King Lear," *JEGP*, XXXIX, 527-40.

Dunn, Katherine E., "The Storm in *King Lear*," *SQ*, III:4, 329-33.

Dye, Harriet, "Appearance-Reality in *Lear*," *CE*, XXV:7, 514-8.

Dzyubinskaya, O., "*King Lear* at Kiev" (in Russian), *Shakspirovski Sbornik*, 1961, #2, 282-6.

Ehrenzweig, Anton, "The Creative Surrender," *American Imago*, 193-210.

Elliott, G. R., "Initial Contrast in *Lear*," *JEGP*, LVIII, 251-63.

Farren, W., "On the Madness of Lear," *London Magazine*, X, 79-84.

Finci, Eli, "Monumental Inner Life," *Politika*, 6 March 1964 (Brook's production in Yugoslavia).

Fleissner, Robert F. (1), "King Lear's Love-Test: a Latin Derivation," *N&Q*, XV, 143-4.

Fleissner, Robert F. (2), "The 'Nothing' Element in *King Lear*," *SQ*, XIII:1, 69-70.

Fleming, P., "King Lear at the New Theatre," *Spectator*, 1946.

French, Carolyn F. (2), "Shakespeare's 'Folly': *King Lear*," *SQ*, X:4, 523-9.

Freud, Sigmund, "A Child Is Being Beaten," *Sexuality and the Psychology of Love*, ed. Philip Rieff, New York, 1963, 107-32.

Frey, Albert R., "The Booth and Barrett *King Lear*," *Shakespeariana*, V:51, 129-39.

Frost, William, "Shakespeare's Rituals and the Opening of *King Lear*," *HudR*, X:4, 577-85.

German, Sharon K., "The Upward Passage in King Lear," *Ball State Teachers College Forum*, Autumn 1964, 10-15.

Gerould, Daniel, "Literary Values in Theatrical Performances: *King Lear* on Stage,"*ETJ*, XIX:3, 311-22.

Gold, Charles H., "A Variant Reading on *King Lear*," *N&Q*, VIII:4, 141-2.

Golovashenko, J., "Lear Recovers his Vision" (in Russian), *Teatralnaya-zhyzn*, XII, 29-31.

Got, Jerzy, "Polish Actors in Shakespearean Roles (1739-1939)," *Poland's Homage to Shakespeare*, Warsaw, 1965.

Greenfield, Thelma N., "The Clothing Motif in *King Lear*," *SQ*, III:3, 281-6.

Griffin, Alice, "Shakespeare Through the Camera's Eye, 1953-1954," *SQ*, VI:1, 63-6.

Grodzicki, August, "The Royal Shakespeare Company in Warsaw" (in Polish), *Zycie Warszawy*, 1964, #16.

Hales, J. W., "*King Lear*," *Fortnightly Review*, XXIII, 84-102.

Hathorn, Richard, "Lear's Equations," *Centennial Review*, Winter 1960, 51-69.

Hawkes, Terence, "Love in *King Lear*," *RES*, ns, X, 178-81.

Hawkins, Frederick W., "*Lear* on the Stage," *English Illustrated Magazine*, X, 157-65.

Heilman, Robert (1), "Manliness in the Tragedies: Dramatic Variations," *Shakespeare 1564-1964*, ed. by E. A. Bloom, Providence, R. I., 1964.

Heilman, Robert (3), " 'Twere Best Not Know Myself: Othello, Lear, Macbeth," *Shakespeare 400*, ed. by James G. McManaway, New York, 1964.

Heilman, Robert B. (4), "Unity of King Lear," *Sewanee Review*, LVI, 58-68.

Hockey, Dorothy C., "The Trial Pattern in *King Lear*," *SQ*, X:3, 389-95.

Hoepfner, Theodore C., " 'We that are young,' " *N&Q*, I:3, 110.

Hubler, Edward, "Shakespeare at Princeton," *SQ*, XII:4, 445.

Irving, Henry (2), "My Four Favorite Parts," *The Forum*, XVI, 34-5.

Isham, Gyles, "The Prototype of King Lear and His Daughters," *N&Q*, I:4, 150-1.

Jackson, Esther, M., "*King Lear*: the Grammar of Tragedy," *SQ*, XVII:1, 25-40.

Jaffa, Harry V., "The Limits of Politics: an Interpretation of King Lear, Act I, Scene 1," *APSR*, LI, 405-27.

Jayne, Sears, "Charity in *King Lear*," *SQ*, XV:4, 277ff.

Jenkins, Raymond, "The Socratic Imperative and *King Lear*," *RenP*, 1963, 85-93.

Jennings, H. J., "Famous Lears," *Gentleman's Magazine*, December 1892, 624-32.

Jones, James L., "*King Lear* and the Metaphysics of Thunder," *XUS*, III:2, 51-80.

Kahn, Sholom, "Enter Lear Mad," *SQ*, VIII:3, 311-29.

Kalashnikov, Y., "*King Lear* at the Theatre of the Moscow Soviet" (in Russian), *Shekspirovski Sbornik*, 1961, #2, 281-2.

Kermode, Frank, *"Lear* at Lincoln Center," *New York Review of Books*, 25 June 1964.

Kirschbaum, Leo (1), "Albany." *ShS*, XIII, 20–9.

Kirschbaum, Leo (3), "Shakespeare's 'Good and Bad,'" *Review of English Studies*, XXI, 136–42.

Landstone, Charles, "Four Lears," *ShS*, I, 98–102.

Lash, Kenneth, "Captain Ahab and King Lear," *NMQ*, Winter 1949, 439–45.

Law, Robert (1), "Holinshed's Lear Story and Shakespeare's," *Studies in Philology*, XLVII:1, 42–50.

Law, Robert Alger (2), *"King Lear:* Warning or Prophecy?" *SQ*, X:1, 114–5.

"Lear's Psychic Abyss," *ShN*, XIX:2, 20.

Levidov, Michael, "Thought and Passion" (in Russian), *Literatarny Critik*, 1935 (on Mikhoels).

Literaturen Front 16 (in Bulgarian, on actors G. Stamatov & V. Trandafilov), 23 April 1959.

Litovsky, O., *"King Lear* at Goset," *Sovetskaye iskusstvo*, 17 February 1935.

Lloyd, Roger, "The Rack of this Tough World," *QR*, October 1947, 530–40.

Lyons, Charles, "The Folly of Love in King Lear," *Revue Des Langues Vivantes Tijdschrift Voor Levende*, XXXIV, 115.

Maclean, Hugh, "Disguise in *King Lear:* Kent and Edgar," *SQ*, XI:1, 49–54.

Maclean, Norman, "Episode, Scene, Speech, and Word: the Madness of Lear," *Critics and Criticism*, ed. by W. R. Keast, Chicago, 1952, 94–114.

Maeterlinck, Maurice, *"King Lear* in Paris," *Fortnightly Review*, LXXVII, 189–94.

Major, John H., "Shakespeare's *King Lear*, IV, ii, 62," *Expl.*, XVII, 13.

Maretzkaya, M., "Talk with Peter Brook" (in Russian), *Ogoniek*, XVII, 29.

Markov, P., "Shakespeare on the Moscow Stage" (in Russian), *Pravda*, 8 April 1964.

Marks, Carol, "Speak What We Feel: the End of *King Lear*," *ELN*, V, 163–71.

Marowitz, Charles, *"King Lear* Log," *TDR*, VIII: 2, 103–21.

Mason, H. A., *"King Lear:* the Central Stream," *CQ*, II:1, 23–40.

Maulnier, Thierry, "Du Roi Lear a Thyeste," *Le Revue de Paris*, LXXIV:4, 130–3.

Maxwell, James C., "The Techniques of Invocation in *King Lear*," *MLR*, XLV, 142–7.

McClosky, John C., "The Emotive Use of Animal Imagery in *King Lear*," *SQ*, XIII:3, 321–5.

McIntosh, Angus, *"King Lear*, Act I, Scene 1, A Stylistic Note," *RES*, XIV: 53, 54–6.

McNeir, Waldo (1), "The Last Lines of *King Lear*, V, iii, 320–7," *ELN*. XII, 183–9.

McNeir, Waldo (2), "The Role of Edmund in *King Lear*," *SEL*, VII, 187–216.

Meagher, John C., *"King Lear*, I, iv: Exit an Attendant," *N&Q*, ns, XII:3, 97–8.

Merchant, W. Moelwyn (1), "Lawyer and Actor: Process of Law in Elizabethan Drama," *English Studies Today*, 3rd series, ed. by G. I. Duthie, Edinburgh, 1964.

Merchant, W. Moelwyn (2), "Shakespeare's Theology," *REL*, October 1964, 72–88.

Merchant, W. Moelwyn (3), "Francis Hayman's Illustrations of Shakespeare," *SQ*, IX:2, 141–7 (Garrick).

Messerer, A., "Paul Scofield and *King Lear*" (in Russian), *Sovetskaya kultura*, 2 April 1964.

Mikhoels, Solomon (2), "My Work on Shakespeare's *King Lear*," essay published in Russia in 1936.

Mikhoels, Solomon (3), "The King and the Fool," *Literaturny Leningrad*, 1936, 4.

Miller, Edwin, "Shakespeare in the Grand Style," *SQ*, I:4, 243–6.

Morris, Ivor, "Cordelia and Lear," *SQ*, VIII:2, 141–58.

Muir, Kenneth (2), "Madness in *King Lear*," *ShS*, XIII, 33–40.

Myrick, Kenneth, "Christian Pessimism in *King Lear*," *Shakespeare 1564–1964*, ed. by E. A. Bloom, Providence, R. I., 1964.

Naydakova, V., "In the Vastness of Zabaykal'e," *Teatralnaya*, XXII, 19.

Norwood, Gilbert, "A Twisted Masterpiece," *Continental Review*, CXXVII, 590–8.

Nowottny, Winifred (2), "Some Aspects of the Style of *King Lear*," *ShS*, XIII, 49–57.

"On Staging Shakespeare," *The New Hungarian Quarterly*, Spring 1964.

Orwell, George, "Lear, Tolstoy, and the Fool," *Polemic*, VII, 2–17.

Parkinson, Richard H., "Shakespeare's Revision of the Lear Story and the Structure of *King Lear*," *PQ*, XXII:4, 315–29.

Pauncz, Arpad (1), "The Concept of Adult Libido and the Lear Complex," *American Journal of Psychotherapy*, V:2, 187–95.

Pauncz, Arpad (2), "Psychopathology of Shakespeare's King Lear," *American Imago*, IX, 57–78.

Platt, Anthony M. and Bernard L. Diamond, "The Origins and Development of the 'Wild Beast' Concept of Mental Illness and its Relation to Theories of Criminal Responsibility," *Journal of the History of Behavioral Sciences*, I:4, 355–67.

Reimer, Andrew, "*King Lear* and the Egocentric Universe," *Balcony*, Winter 1966, 33–42.

Ribner, Irving (1), "The Gods are Just: a Reading of *King Lear*," *TDR*, II, 34–54.

Ribner, Irving (3), "Shakespeare and Legendary History: Lear and *Cymbeline*," *SQ*, VII:1, 47–52.

Rosenberg, John D., "King Lear and his Comforters," *Essays in Criticism*, XVI, 135–46.

Rosenberg, Marvin, "*King Lear* in Germany, France and Italy," *ThS*, IX:1, 1–10.

Rosier, James L., "The Lex Aeterna and *King Lear*," *JEGP*, LIII, 574–80.

Rusche, Harry, "Edmund's Conception and Nativity in *King Lear*," *SQ*, XX:2, 161–4.

Salter, K. W., "*Lear* and the Morality Tradition," *N&Q*, ns, XXI:3, 109–10.

Salvini, Tommaso, "Impression of Shakespeare's *King Lear*," *Century Magazine*, XXVII, 563–6.

Săvulescu, Monica, "Rehearsal at the National," *Teatrul*, 9 (September 1970), trans. by Gabriel Pleşea.

Savas, Minas, "*King Lear* as a Play of Divine Justice," *CE*, XXVII, 560ff.

Schoff, Francis G., "King Lear: Moral Example or Tragic Protagonist," *SQ*, XIII:2, 157–72.

Scofield, Paul, "The Mortal Nature," *The Sunday Times*, 24 April 1966.

Selenic, Slobodan, "Greatness and Simplicity," *Borba*, 7 March 1964, 7 (Brook's production in Belgrade).

Senart, Philippe, "Le Roi Lear," *La Revue des Deux Mondes*, 15 July 1967, 281–2.

Seronsky, Cecil C., discussion of use of "Apollo" in Kent's banishment, *Expl.*, XVII, 21.

Shaw, John "*King Lear*: the Final Lines," *Essays in Criticism*, XVI, 261–7.

Siegel, Paul (1), "Adversity and the Miracle of Love in *King Lear*," *SQ*, VI:3, 325–6.

Siegel, Paul (2), "Willy Loman and King Lear," *CE*, XVII:6, 343.

Simon, John, "Theatre Chronicle," *HudR*, XVII, 421–30.

Sitwell, Edith (2), "*King Lear*," *Atlantic Monthly*, CLXXXV:5, 57–62.

Skulsky, Harold, "*King Lear* and the Meaning of Chaos," *SQ*, XVII:1, 3–17.

Smith, Roland, "*King Lear* and the Merlin Tradition," *MLQ*, VII, 153–74.

Snider, D. J., "Shakespeare's Tragedies: *King Lear*," *Western Magazine*, I, 230ff.

Soens, A. L., "*King Lear*, III, iv, 62–5: a Fencing Pun and Staging," *ELN*, VI, 19–24.

Solodonikov, A., "At the Performance of the Shakespeare Theatre" (in Russian), *Literaturnaya gazeta*, 9 April 1964.

Spencer, Benjamin T., "*King Lear*: a Prophetic Tragedy," *CE*, V, 302–8.

Speaight, Robert (3), "The Actability of King Lear," *Drama Survey*, II, 1.

Spevack, Marvin (1), discussion of "feelingly," *Expl.*, XVI, 4.

Stack, Elliot, "The Outcast Child," *The Folklore Journal*, IV, 308–49.

Stampfer, J., "The Catharsis of *King Lear*," *ShS*, XIII, 1–10.

Stein, Walter, "Tragedy and the Absurd," *Dublin Review*, CCXXXIII, 363–82.

Stevenson, Warren, "Albany as Archetype in *King Lear*," *MLQ*, XXVI, 257–63.

Stewart, J. I. M. (2), "The Blinding of Gloster," *RES*, XXI:84, 264–70.

Stockholder, Katherine, "The Multiple Genres of *King Lear*: Breaking the Archetypes," *BuR*, XVI:1, 40–63.

Stone, George W., Jr., "Garrick's Production of *King Lear*," *SP*, XLV, 89–103.

Stone, Lawrence, "Marriage Among English Nobility," *Comparative Studies in Society and History*," III, 198–9.

Sutherland, W. O. S., "Polonius, Hamlet, and Lear in Aaron Hill's Prompter," *SP*, XLIX, 605–18.

Swinburne, A. C. (1), "King Lear," *Harper's Monthly Magazine*, CVI:631, 1–8.

Szyfman, Arnold, "*King Lear* on the Stage: a Producer's Reflections," *ShS*, XIII, 69–71.

Taylor, E. M. M., "Lear's Philosopher," *SQ*, VI:3, 364–5.

Taylor, Warren, "Lear and the Lost Self," *CE*, XXV:7, 509–14.

Thaler, Alvin, "The Gods and God in *King Lear*," *RenP*, 1955, 32–9.

Traversi, D. A., (2), "*King Lear* (I)," *Scrutiny*, XIX:1, 43–64.

Traversi, D. A. (3), "*King Lear* (II)," *Scrutiny*, XIX:2, 126–42.

Traversi, D. A. (4), "*King Lear* (Conclusion)," *Scrutiny*, XIX:3, 206–30.

Tree, Maud Holt, "Herbert and I," *Herbert Beerbohm Tree*, ed. by Max Beerbohm, London, 1924.

"A Variant Reading in *King Lear*," *N&Q*, CCVI:8, 141–2.

Vickers, Brian, "*King Lear* and Renaissance Paradoxes," *MLR*, LXIII, 305–14.

Vitale, Geoffrey, "Cordelia's Death and the Problem of Succession," *N&Q*, XV, 141–3.

Volk, Petar, "Eternity of Human Existence," *Knjizevne Novine*, 20 March 1964, 6–7 (Brooke's production).

Wadsworth, Frank W., "'Sound and Fury'–*King Lear* on Television," *Quarterly of Film, Radio, and TV*, Spring 1954, 254–68.

Walton, J. L., "Lear's Last Speech," *ShS*, XIII, 11–19.

Weidhorn, Manfred, "Lear's Schoolmasters," *SQ*, XIII:3, 305–45.

West, Robert H., "Sex and Pessimism in *King Lear*," *SQ*, XI:1, 55–60.

Willeford, William, *The Fool and his Scepter*, Evanston, 1969.

Williams, George W. (1), "The Poetry of the Storm in *King Lear*," *SQ*, II:1, 57–71.

Williamson, Colin, comment on McIntosh's "*King Lear*, Act I, scene i, a Stylistic Note," *RES*, XIV:53, 56–8.

White, Richard Grant (1), "*King Lear*," *Atlantic Monthly*, XLVI, 114–9.

Winslow, Forbes, "Madness as Portrayed by Shakespeare," *Arena*, XV, 414–24.

Wrigley, E. A., "Family Limitation," *Economic History Review*, 2nd series, XIX, 86–9.

Wyatt, Euphemia Van Rensselaer, "Ripeness is All: a Study of *King Lear*," *Drama Critique*, VII, 2–8.

Zingerman, B., "Shakespeare's Theatre in Moscow" (in Russian), *Teatra*, VIII, 122–8.

Zuskin, V., on his interpretation of the Fool, *Sovetskoye iskusstvo*, 11 February 1955.

UNPUBLISHED WORKS

Anikst, Alexander, letter, March 1971.

Badel, Alan, interview, M. Rosenberg, April 1971.

Bell, Mary, letters, 1969–1971.

Berg, David, "Twentieth Century Lears," unpublished master's thesis, University of Utah, 1952.

Blom, Anita, interview, Nigel Rollison, April 1971.

Boetzkes, Manfred, letters (on German Lears), 1968–1970.

Greg Boyd, Kent Odell, Paul Oertel, report on Colorado Shakespeare Festival, 1971.

Carnovsky, Maurice, interview and performance notes, M. Rosenberg, June 1966.

Cobb, Lee J., notes on performance, Anne Marie Corbett, December 1968.
Coghill, Nevill, letters, 1968–71.
Dahl, Ingrid, report on 1971 Norwegian *Lear*, April 1971.
Favorini, Attilio, "Robert Mantell's *King Lear*," read to the American Educational Theatre Association, August 1971.
Fordham, Hallam, "Gielgud as Lear," unpublished manuscript at Shakespeare Centre, Stratford.
Freeman, Walter, personal discussion of madness, M. Rosenberg, September 1969.
French, Carolyn S. (1), "King Lear: Poem or Play?", unpublished doctoral dissertation, Stanford University, 1958.
Gielgud, John (2), interview, M. Rosenberg, May 1966.
Goldsby, Robert (director), rehearsal and performance notes, M. Rosenberg, Winter 1963–4.
Got, Jerzy, letters on Polish Lears, 1968 and 1970.
Hankiss, Elemer, letters about Peter Brook's production in Hungary, and native Hungarian productions, January 1967, April 1968, June 1969.
Hodek, Brett, letters on Czech *Lears*, 1971.
Howard, Alan, interview (role of Edgar in Porter's *King Lear*), M. Rosenberg, September 1968.
Kiasashivli, Nico, letters on Russian Lears, March 1969, June 1969.
Komarova, Valentina, letters on Russian *Lears*, 1970.
Komisarjevsky, Theodore (director), production notes by Nevill Coghill.
Kozintsev, Grigori (2), letters, April 1968, May 1968, September 1968, October 1968, December 1969, April 1971. Interview, September 1970, August, 1971.
Levidova, Inna, letters on Russian *Lears*, 1970, 1971.
MacDonald, E. D., "Lear's Regression," unpublished essay.
MacGowran, Jack, interview, December 1970.
Milward, S.J., Peter, report on Japanese *Lear* (1967), April 1971.
Mincoff, M., letters on Bulgarian *Lears*, 1971
Minotis, Alexis, letter, March 1971.
Murray, Brian, interview (role of Edgar in Peter Brook's production) Edgar Reynolds, January 1968.
Pleşea, Gabriel, letter on Romanian *Lears*, 1971.
Porter, Eric, interview, M. Rosenberg, September 1968.
Rollison, Nigel, letters on Swedish *Lears*, 1971.
Schrixx, W., letter on Belgian Lears, February 1971.
Scofield, Paul, interview, M. Rosenberg, August 1967.
Svoboda, Josef, interview.
Webster, Margaret (3), interview, M. Rosenberg, Spring 1966.
Williams, Michael, interview (role of Fool in Porter's *King Lear*), M. Rosenberg, September 1968.
Wolfit, Donald, interview, M. Rosenberg, August 1967.

"KING LEAR" PROMPTBOOKS CONSULTED

Bridges-Adams, W., Stratford-upon-Avon, 1932, Shakespeare Centre Library (Randle Ayrton).

Carnovsky, Maurice, personal promptbook.
Colman, George, London (Covent Garden), 1768, Shakespeare Centre Library.
Creswell, Peter, Stratford-upon-Avon, 1943, Shakespeare Centre Library (Abraham Sofaer).
Creswick, Newcastle-on-Tyne, 1873, Shakespeare Centre Library.
Devine, George, London (Palace), 1955, Shakespeare Centre Library (John Gielgud).
Devine, George, Stratford-upon-Avon, 1953, Shakespeare Centre Library (Michael Redgrave).
Forrest, Edwin, promptbook by George Becks, New York Public Library.
Forrest, Edwin, a promptbook revised to match Forrest's version, Folger: Lear, 8.
Gielgud, John, London (Old Vic), 1940, Folger Shakespeare Library.
Gielgud, John, Stratford-upon-Avon, 1950, Shakespeare Centre Library.
Kean, Charles, souvenir promptbook by T. W. Edmonds, 1859, Folger: Lear, 11.
Kean, Edmund, London (Drury Lane), 1820, London Museum.
Kemble, John Philip, London (Covent Garden), 1809, Harvard Theatre Collection.
Kemble, John Philip, London (Drury Lane), 1795, Garrick Club.
Komisarjevsky, Theodore, Stratford-upon-Avon, 1936, Shakespeare Centre Library (Ayrton).
Macready, William C., London (Covent Garden), 1838, Victoria and Albert, Forster Library.
Macready, William C., London (Haymarket), 1851, Folger.
Macready, William C., transcription of original, Folger.
McCullough, John, New York (Booth's), 1877, Harvard Theatre Collection.
Phelps, Samuel, London (Sadler's Wells), 1845, Folger.
Phelps, Samuel, London (Sadler's Wells), 1855, Shakespeare Centre Library.
Phelps, Samuel, London (Sadler Wells, Drury Lane), 1860–66, Folger.
Roberts, James B., imitation of Charles Kean staging, Folger.
Roberts, James B., New York (Burton's), 1858, Folger.
Shaw, Glen Byam, Stratford-upon-Avon, 1959, Shakespeare Centre Library (Charles Laughton).
Vezin, Hermann, promptbook by G. Johnson Franmpton, Folger.

BIBLIOGRAPHY OF INDIVIDUAL ACTORS

(Actors are American or British, unless otherwise noted. Where actors are not well-known, or are infrequently referred to, plays are listed by country or by location in England or America.)
ANSCHÜTZ, Heinrich, 1785–1865 (German)
    Drews, Wolfgang, König Lear auf der deutschen bühne bis zur Gegenwart
    Rosenberg, Marvin, "King Lear in Germany, France and Italy"
ANTOINE, André, 1858–1943 (French)
    Boston Transcript, 23 February 1907
    Le Figaro, 6 December 1904

Fortnightly Review, 1 February 1905
La France de Demain, 8 December 1904
Le Gauloise, 6 December 1904
L'Intransigeant, 6 December 1904
Journal de Débats, 7 December 1904
Le Monde Illustré, 10 December 1904
AYRTON, Randle, 1869–1940
    Day, M. C., and J. C. Trewin, *Shakespeare Memorial Theatre*
    French, Carolyn S., *"King Lear*: Poem or Play?"
    Promptbooks
    Birmingham Gazette, 21 April 1936
    Birmingham Mail, 9 June 1931, 21 April 1936
    Birmingham News, 24 April 1937
    Birmingham Post, 21 April 1936
    Boston Transcript, 27 April 1931
    Cavalcade, 25 April 1936
    Country Life, 25 April 1936
    Daily Telegraph, 21 April 1936
    Hereford Times, 23 April 1936
    London Times, 21 April 1936
    Morning Advertiser, 5 December 1959
    Morning Post, 14 April 1931, 21 April 1936, 25 April 1936
    Royal Leamington Spa Courier, 24 April 1936
    Sheffield Telegraph, 21 April 1936
    Stratford-upon-Avon Herald, 21 August 1931, 24 April 1936, 26 April 1936
BARNAY, Ludwig, 1842–1924 (German)
    Barnay, Ludwig, "Der Narr in König Lear"
    ———, *Über Theater und Anderes*
    Winter, William, *Shakespeare on the Stage*
    Boetzkes, letters
BARRY, Spranger, 1719–1777
    Cooke, William, ed., *Memoirs of Charles Macklin*
    Victor, Benjamin, *Original Letters, Dramatic Pieces and Poems*
BASSERMANN, Albert, 1867–1952 (German)
    Bab, Julius, "Reinhardt und Shakespeare"
    Drews, Wolfgang, *König Lear auf der deutschen Bühne bis zur Gegenwart*
    Berliner Tageblatt, 2 February 1914
    Preussische Jahrbücher, CLV, 365–370
    Letters, Boetzkes
BELGIUM, Antwerp, 1969. Director, Walter Tillemans
    De Nieuwe, 24 January 1969
    De Nieuwe Gazet, 20 January 1969
    De Standaard, 20 January 1969
    De Nieuwe Roterdamse Currant, 26 February 1969
    Schrixx, W., letter, February 1971
BOOTH, Barton, 1681–1733
    Miscellaneous references
BOOTH, Edwin, 1821–1883
    Pollock, W. H., *Impressions of Henry Irving*

Sprague, Arthur Colby, *Shakespearian Players and Performances*
Towse, John Rankin, *Sixty Years of the Theatre*
Wingate, Charles E., *Shakespeare's Heroes on the Stage*
Winter, William, *The Life and Art of Edwin Booth*
————, *Shakespeare on the Stage*
Wyatt, Euphemia Van Rensseler, "Ripeness is All: a Study of *King Lear*"
Academy, 19 February 1881, 26 February 1881
Athenaeum, 19 February 1881
Autumn Boer, 1883
Bell's Life in London, 19 February 1881
Boston Evening Transcript, 3 December 1884
Boston Transcript, 8 November 1883, December 1886
Boston Weekly Transcript, 16 January 1877
Daily Telegraph, 16 February 1881, 1 December 1892
Era, 4 February 1881, 19 February 1881
Home Journal, 2 December 1888
Illustrated London News, 19 February 1881
Illustrated Sporting and Dramatic News, 19 February 1881
London Times, 21 February 1881
Louisville Courier Journal, 3 December 1884
Louisville Times, 12 May 1888
Morning Post, 17 February 1881
News of the World, 20 February 1881
New York Times, 27 January 1878, 17 November 1878
Pall Mall Gazette, 18 February 1881
Reynolds Newspaper, 20 February 1881
St. James Gazette, 17 February 1881
Saturday Review, 19 February 1881
Spirit of the Times, 13 January 1877
Stage, 19 February 1881
Standard, 16 February 1881
Truth, 24 February 1881
Vanity Fair, 19 February 1881
Whitehall Review, 19 February 1881, 17 February 1881
Miscellaneous clippings, unidentified
BOOTH, Junius Brutus, 1821–1883
Gould, Thomas, *The Tragedian*
CALHERN, Louis, 1895–1956
Berg, David, *Twentieth Century Lears*
French, Carolyn S., *King Lear: Poem or Play?*
Wyatt, Euphemia Van Rensseler, "Ripeness is All: a Study of *King Lear*"
New Yorker, 6 January 1951, 20 January 1951
New York Times, 31 December 1950
Shakespeare Newsletter, October 1951
Miscellaneous clippings, unidentified
CARNOVSKY, Maurice, b. 1898
Carnovsky, Maurice, performance notes and interview
Promptbook
Christian Science Monitor, 12 June 1963

Hartford Times, 10 June 1963
Listener, 1 March 1963
Montreal Star, n. d .
New Britain Herald, n. d.
New York Herald Tribune, 9 June 1963, 10 June 1963, 23 June 1963
New York Times, 10 June 1963, 23 June 1963, 29 June 1963, 28 July 1963,
  25 June 1965
Oakland Tribune, 23 June 1963
Saturday Review, 29 June, 1963, 29 July 1963
Theatre Arts No. 8, 1963
Westport, Connecticut, *Town Crier*, n. d.
Worcester Gazette, n. d.
Miscellaneous clippings, unidentified
COBB, Lee J. b. 1911
  Cobb, Lee J., performance notes
  New Yorker, 14 November 1968
  New York Times, 12 November 1968, 17 November 1968
  Time, 15 November 1968
  Village Voice, 14 November 1968
  Colorado Shakespeare Festival, 1971. Personal reports by Greg Boyd, Kent
    Odell, Paul Oertel
CRESWICK, William, 1813–1888
  Promptbook
DEVLIN, William, b. 1911
  Agate, James, *Brief Chronicles*
  Berg, David, *Twentieth Century Lears*
  Granville-Barker, Harley, *Prefaces to Shakespeare*
  Landstone, Charles, "Four Lears"
  Miller, Edwin, "Shakespeare in the Grand Style"
  William, Audrey, *Old Vic Drama*
  London Times, 8 April 1936
  Manchester Guardian 8 April 1936
  New Statesman and Nation, 18 April 1936
  Observer, 14 October 1934
  Punch, 22 April 1936
  Saturday Review, 18 April 1936
  Spectator, 17 April 1936
  Variety, 1 March 1950
  Miscellaneous clippings, unidentified
DEVRIENT, Ludwig, 1784–1832 (German)
  Drews, Wolfgang, *König Lear auf der deutschen Bühne bis zur Gegenwart*
  Furness, Horace H., ed., *A New Variorum Edition of Shakespeare: King
    Lear*
  Mantzius, Karl, *History of Theatrical Art*
  Letters, Boetzkes
DULLIN, Charles, 1885–1949 (French)
  Action, 20 April 1945
  Arts, 13 April 1945, 20 April 1945
  L'Aurore, 1 May 1945

Carrefour, 28 April 1945
La Dépêche de Paris, 11 April 1945
L'Hebdomadiare du Temps Present, 11 May 1945
Le Monde, 13 April 1945
Le Monde Illustré, 5 May 1945
Les Nouvelles Littéraires Artistiques et Scientifiques, 19 April 1945
Le Populaire, 15 April 1945.
DUNN, James C
  Production at Los Gatos, California, Summer 1969
  Performance notes, interviews
FLECK, Ferdinand, 1757–1801 (German)
  Drews, Wolfgang, *König Lear auf der deutschen Bühne bis zur Gegenwart*
FORREST, Edwin, 1806–1872
  Alger, William R., *Life of Edwin Forrest*
  Harrison, Gabriel, *Edwin Forrest: the Actor and the Man*
  Promptbooks
  Rees, J., *The Life of Forrest*
  Sprague, Arthur Colby, *Shakespeare and the Actors*
  Toynbee, William, ed., *The Diaries of William Charles Macready*
  Wingate, Charles E., *Shakespeare's Heroes on the Stage*
  Atlas, 6 November 1836
  Commercial, 7 December 1869
  Edinburgh Weekly Chronicle, 14 February 1846, 21 February 1846
  Freeman's Journal, 5 May 1845, 7 May 1845
  Globe, 5 November 1836, 8 November 1836
  John Bull, 20 November 1836
  London Examiner, 6 November 1836
  London Times, 5 November 1836
  Manchester Guardian, 14 January 1837
  Morning Advertiser, 5 November 1836
  Morning Herald, 5 November 1836
  Morning Post, 5 November 1836
  Observer, 6 November 1836
  Season, 11 February 1871
  Standard, 5 November 1836
  Sun, 4 November 1836, 5 November, 1836
  Sunday Mercury, 5 November 1836
  Miscellaneous clippings, unidentified
GARRICK, David, 1717–1779
  Boaden, James, ed., *Memoirs of Mrs. Siddons*
  Brown, J. R., *Shakespeare's Plays in Performance*
  Burnim, Kalman, *David Garrick, Director*
  Cooke, William, ed., *Memoirs of Charles Macklin*
  Davies, Thomas, *Dramatic Miscellanies*
  Fitzgerald, P., *The Life of David Garrick*
  Garrick, David, "An Essay on Acting"; *Letters*
  Gildon, Charles, *The Life of Betterton*
  Harrison, Gabriel, *Edwin Forrest: the Actor and the Man*
  Mack, Maynard, *King Lear in Our Time*

Mantzius, Karl, *History of Theatrical Art*
Merchant, W. Moelwyn, "Francis Hayman's Illustrations of Shakespeare"
Murphy, Arthur, *The Life of Garrick*
Sprague, Arthur Colby, *Shakespeare and the Actors*
————, *Shakespearian Players and Performances*
Stone, George W., Jr., "Garrick's Production of *King Lear*"
Victor, Benjamin, *Original Letters, Dramatic Pieces and Poems*
Winter, William, *Shadows of the Stage*
Dramatic Censor, Vol. I, 373
London Chronicle, 21 May 1776.
Monthly Mirror, February 1802
Prompter, 7 October 1735
Theatrical Monitor, 24 October 1767
Theatrical Review (1772) I, 218
Unidentified clippings
GERMANY, Frankfurt, March 1970
  Frankfurter, 11 March 1970
GIELGUD, Sir John, b. 1904
  Agate, James, *Brief Chronicles*
  Dent, Alan, *Preludes to Shakespeare*
  Farjeon, Herbert, *The Shakespearean Scene*
  Fordham, Hallam, *Gielgud as Lear*
  Gielgud, *Stage Directions*
  Granville-Barker, Harley, *Prefaces to Shakespeare*
  Interview
  Jackson, Esther M., "*King Lear*: the Grammar of Tragedy"
  Promptbooks
  Trewin, J. C., *Shakespeare on the English Stage*
  Williamson, Audrey, *Old Vic Drama*
  Art News, December 1955
  Birmingham Gazette, 19 July 1950
  Birmingham Mail, 28 July 1955
  Boston Transcript, 27 April 1931
  Catholic Herald, 26 April 1940, 22 October 1940
  Christian Science Monitor, 6 August 1955
  Daily Dispatch, 14 April 1931
  Daily Express, 19 July 1950, 27 July 1955
  Daily Mail, 14 April 1931, 15 July 1955
  Daily Sketch, 14 April 1931
  Daily Telegraph, 14 April 1931, 19 July 1950, 27 July 1955
  Drama Magazine, Winter 1955
  Evening News, 14 April 1931
  Evesham Journal, 22 July 1950
  Glasgow Herald, 2 November 1950
  Illustrated London News, 2 August 1950
  John O'London's Weekly, 4 August 1950
  London Star, 14 April 1931, 27 July 1955
  London Times, 14 April 1931, 20 July 1950, 27 July 1955, 26 April 1958
  Manchester Guardian, 14 April 1931, 20 April 1940, 27 July 1955

Melbourne Age, 10 November 1955
Morning Post, 14 April 1931, 21 April 1931
News and Nation, April 1940
News Chronicle, 22 July 1950, 29 July 1955
New Statesman and Nation, 25 April 1931, 20 April 1940, 27 April 1940, 29 July 1950
New York Herald Tribune, 26 December 1950
Observer, 12 April 1931, 19 April 1931, 10 May 1931, 21 April 1940, 23 July 1950, 20 August, 1950, 31 July 1955, 31 August 1955, 23 February 1958
New York Times, 28 April 1940
Punch, 10 August 1955
The Queen, 18 August 1950
Royal Leamington Spa Courier, 24 April 1958
Saturday Review, 23 April 1931
Scotsman, 20 July 1950, 2 November 1955
Shakespeare Newsletter, November 1955, September 1958, December 1958
Sketch, 16 August 1950
Spectator, 25 April 1931
Stage, 18 April 1940, 20 July 1950, 18 August 1955
Statesman, 2 November 1955
Stratford-upon-Avon Herald, 21 July 1950, 2 December 1955
Sunday Times, 19 April 1931, 23 July 1950
Theatre Arts, June 1940
Theatre World, August 1950
Time and Tide, 20 April 1940, 29 July 1940
Times Literary Supplement, 30 November 1955
Tribune (London), 28 July 1950
Truth, 5 August 1955
Weekend Review, 18 April 1931
Wolverhampton Express and Star, 26 July 1950
Yorkshire Post, 14 April 1931
Miscellaneous unidentified clippings
IRVING, HENRY, 1838–1905
  Agate, James, *Brief Chronicles*
  Irving, Henry, "My Four Favorite Parts"
  Mack, Maynard, *King Lear in Our Time*
  Mantzius, Karl, *A History of Theatrical Art*
  Sprague, Arthur Colby, *Shakespeare and the Actors*
  Winter, William, *Shakespeare on the Stage*
  Academy, 19 November 1892
  Athenaeum, n. d.
  Daily Chronicle, 11 November 1892
  Daily Graphic, 11 November 1892
  Daily News, 11 November 1892
  Daily Telegraph, 11 November 1892, 1 December 1892
  The Eastern and Western Review, n. d.
  The Evening News, 11 November 1892
  The Gentlewoman, 19 November 1892
  Gloucester Journal, n.d.

Hearth and Home, 17 November 1892
The Hospital, 19 November 1892
Illustrated London News, 19 November 1892
L'Independence, n.d.
Le Journal des Debats (Augustine Filon), n. d.
The Lady's Pictorial, 10 November 1892
Licensed Victualler's Gazette, 18 November 1892
Liverpool Daily Post, 14 November 1892
London Figaro, 19 November 1892
London News, 18 November 1892, 19 November 1892, 3 December, 1892
London Star, 12 November 1892
London Times, 11 November 1892
Magazine Journal, 19 November 1892
Morning Post, 11 November 1892
Newcastle Daily Journal, 12 November 1892
The New Review, n. d.
19th Century, XXXIII: 191
Pall Mall Gazette, 11 November 1892
The Period, 28 November 1892
Sala's Journal, 19 November 1892
Saturday Review, 19 November 1892
Sheffield Independent, n.d.
Standard, 11 November 1892
Sunday Sun (Newcastle-on-Tyne), n. d.
The Theatre, 1 December 1892
Unidentified clippings
JAPAN, Tokyo, December 1967
     Directed by Tsunedri Fukuda, with Hiroshi Akutugawa as Lear. Reported
     by Peter Milward, S. J.
KEAN, Charles, 1811–1868
     Mantzius, Karl, *A History of Theatrical Art*
     Pollock, Frederick, *Macready's Reminiscences and Diaries*
     Sprague, Arthur Colby, *Shakespeare and the Actors*
     ————, *Shakespearian Players and Performances*
     Winter, William, *Shakespeare on the Stage*
     Albion, 16 September 1865
     Atlas, 24 April 1858
     Era, 25 April 1858
     Illustrated London News, 24 April 1858, 26 April 1858
     John Bull, 24 April 1858
     London Times, 26 April 1858, 24 April 1858
     Morning Advertiser, 18 April 1858
     Morning Chronicle, 19 April 1858
     Morning Herald, 18 April 1858, 19 April 1858
     Observer, 18 April 1858
     Reader, 24 April 1858
     Reynolds Newspaper, 25 April 1858
     Saturday Review, 24 April 1858
     Spectator, 2 April 1858

Sunday Times, 25 April 1858
Weekend Review, 18 April 1858
KEAN, Edmund, 1787–1833
Furness, Horace H., *A New Variorum Edition of Shakespeare: King Lear*
Hawkins, F. W., *The Life of Edmund Kean*
Hillebrand, Harold N., *Edmund Kean*
Houtchens, L., and Washburn, Carolyn, *Leigh Hunt's Dramatic Criticism*
Jennings, H. J., "Famous Lears"
Pollock, Frederick W., ed., *Macready's Reminiscences and Diaries*
Promptbook
Sprague, Arthur Colby, *Shakespeare and the Actors*
Williamson, Audrey, *Old Vic Drama*
Wingate, Charles, *Shakespeare's Heroes on the Stage*
Winter, William, *Shakespeare on the Stage*
Atlas, 3 February 1838
The Drama, May 1821
Edinburgh Advertiser, 24 March 1825, 31 March 1825
Englishman, 30 April 1820
Globe, 25 April 1820
Literary Gazette, 29 April 1820, 15 February 1823
London Examiner, 23 April 1820
London Times, 25 April 1820, 29 April 1820
London Star, 25 April 1820
Morning Chronicle, 25 April 1820
Morning Post, 25 April 1820
National Gazette, 10 February 1821
New Monthly Magazine, 1 February 1821
New Times, 11 February 1823, 11 November 1928
New York Evening Post, 15 December 1820, 16 December 1820
Observer, 30 April 1820
St. James Chronicle, 25 April 1820
Scotsman, 29 February 1825, 24 March 1825.
Sun, 25 April 1820
Theatrical Inquisitor and Monthly Mirror, April 1820
KEMBLE, Charles, 1775–1854
Boaden, James, ed., *Memoirs of Mrs. Siddons*
Mantzius, Karl, *History of Theatrical Art*
Promptbooks
Atlas, 3 February 1838
Edinburgh Dramatic Review, 19 January 1823
Examiner, 22 May 1808
Monthly Mirror, January 1801, April 1802, May 1808, June 1808, April 1810
Morning Post, 19 May 1808
Quarterly Review, June 1826
KISTOV, A. F., 1903–1960 (Russian)
Burjan, B., and I. Lisnevsky, *Portrait of an Actor*
KLÖPFER, Eugen, 1886–1950 (German)
Drews, Wolfgang, *König Lear auf der deutschen Bühne bis zur Gegenwart*

Neue Freie Presse, 15 March 1825
Neues Wiener Journal, 15 March 1925
Der Morgen, 16 March 1925
Volkszeitung, March 1825
Letters, Boetzkes
KOZINTSEV, Grigori, b. 1905 (Russian)
    Anikst, Alexander, "Kozintsev and his *King Lear*", *Moscow News*, No. 2,
      1971.
    Berkovsky
    Kozintsev, Grigori, letters, interviews, performance notes (filmed *Lear*).
    ————, *Shakespeare, Time and Conscience*
    Letters, Levidova
KRAUSS, Werner, 1884–1959 (German)
    Drews, Wolfgang, *König Lear auf der deutschen Bühne bis zur Gegenwart*
    Krauss, Werner, *Das Schauspiel meines Lebens*
    Berlin/Preuss, 1934
    Berliner Tageblatt, 24 December 1934
    Der Kurier, 28 December 1956
    Der Tag, 24 June 1950
    Die Rheinpfalz, 6 July 1957
    Die Welt, Essen, 31 December 1956
    Hamburger Freie Presse, 27 June 1930
    Hamburger Echo, 24 September 1951
    Herforder Anzeiger, 29 December 1956
    Münchner Merkur, 3 January 1957
    Mühlheimer Zeitung, 21 December 1956
    München, November 1936
    Oberhausen, 28 December 1956
    Rhein-Echo, 23 June 1950
    Rheinische Post, 24 December 1956
    Völkischer Beobachter, 25–26 December 1934
LADNOWSKY, Boleslaw, 1841–1911 (Polish)
    Got, Jerzy, "Polish Actors in Shakespearean Roles (1739–1939)"
    Got, letters
    Noskowski, W., *Tygodnik Illustrowany*
    See also POLAND
LAUGHTON, Charles, 1899–1962
    Byrne, M. St. Clare, "*King Lear* at Stratford-on-Avon"
    Mack, Maynard, *King Lear in Our Time*
    Promptbooks
    Birmingham Evening Dispatch, 19 August 1959
    Birmingham Mail, 19 August 1959
    Birmingham Post, 19 August 1959, 31 August 1959
    Birmingham Weekly Post, 21 August 1959
    Bolton Evening News, 19 August 1959
    Bradford Telegraph and Argus, 5 September 1959
    Coventry Standard, 21 August 1959
    Daily Express, 19 August 1959
    Daily Mail 19 August 1959

Daily Telegraph, 19 August 1959
Financial Times, 19 August 1959
Guardian, 20 August 1959
Illustrated London News, 29 August 1959
Leamington Spa Courier, 21 August 1959
Liverpool Daily Post, 19 August 1959
London Evening Standard, 19 August 1959
London Star, 19 August 1959
London Times, 19 August 1959
London Tribune, 28 August 1959
Manchester Evening Chronicle, 19 August 1959
Manchester Guardian, 19 August 1959, 20 August 1959
News Chronicle, 19 August 1959
New Statesman, 22 August 1959
Nottingham Guardian Journal, 19 August 1959
Observer, 23 August 1959
Oxford Times, 21 August 1959
Plays and Players, October 1959
Punch, 26 August 1959
The Queen, 15 September 1959
Scotsman, 21 August 1959
South Wales Argus, 20 August 1959
Spectator, 18 August 1959, 20 August 1959
Stage and TV Today, 20 August 1959
Sunday Dispatch, 23 August 1959
Sunday Express, 23 August 1959
Tablet, 7 November 1959
Tatler, 2 September 1959
Theatre World, September 1959
Time, 31 August 1959
Western Evening Herald, 28 August 1959
Western Independent, 23 August 1959
Miscellaneous unidentified clippings
MACREADY, William Charles, 1783–1873
Agate, James, *Brief Chronicles*
————, *English Dramatic Critics*
Archer, William, *William Charles Macready*
Coleman, John, *Players and Playwrights I Have Known*
Downer, Alan, "The Making of a Great Actor—William Charles Macready"
————, *The Eminent Tragedian*
Kemble, Frances, *Records of Later Life*
Lewes, George Henry, *On Actors and the Art of Acting*
Mack, Maynard, *King Lear in Our Time*
Mantzius, Karl, *History of Theatrical Art*
Marston, John W., *Our Recent Actors*
Odell, George, *Shakespeare from Betterton to Irving*
Pollock, Frederick W., *Macready's Reminscences and Diaries*
Promptbooks

Sprague, Arthur Colby, *Shakespeare and the Actors*
————, *Shakespearian Players and Performances*
Trewin, J. C., *Mr. Macready*
Wingate, Charles, *Shakespeare's Heroes on the Stage*
Winter, William, *Shakespeare on the Stage*
The Age, 25 May 1834, 28 January 1838
Albion, 24 May 1834
Athenaeum, 31 May 1834, 9 February 1839
Atlas, 3 February 1838
Court Journal, 25 October 1845, 3 November 1845
Echo, May 1834
Freeman's Journal, 5 May 1845
Globe, 24 May 1834
John Bull, 29 January 1838, 4 February 1838
London Examiner, 8 June 1834, 28 January 1838, 4 February 1838, 25
    October 1845
London Times, 24 May 1834, 26 January 1838, 16 October 1845
Morning Herald, 24 May 1834, 26 January 1838
Morning Post, 24 May 1834, 26 January 1838
Naval and Military Gazette, 31 May 1834
New Monthly Magazine, June 1834
Observer, 19 October 1845
Satirist, 1 June 1834, 14 June 1834, 28 January 1838, 26 October 1845
Spectator, 27 January 1838, 18 October 1845
Sun, 26 January 1838
Sunday Mercury, 26 January 1838
Sunday Times, 25 May 1834, 28 January 1838
Temple Bar, July 1873
Theatrical Journal, 31 October 1840, 4 October 1845
MANTELL, Robert B., 1854–1927
    Attilio Favorini, "Robert Mantell's *King Lear*"
    Winter, William, *Shakespeare on the Stage*
    Toledo Blade, 29 January 1908
McCULLOUGH, John, 1832–1885
    Promptbook
    Towse, John Rankin, *Sixty Years in the Theatre*
    Winter, William, *Shakespeare on the stage*
    Miscellaneous clippings, unidentified
McKINNELL, Norman, 1870–1936
    Berg, David, *Twentieth Century Lears*
    Walbrook, H. M., *Nights at the Play*
    Saturday Review, 18 February 1909, 29 September 1909
MIKHOELS, Solomon, 1890–1948 (Russian)
    Gerould, Daniel, "Literary Values in Theatrical Performances of *King
        Lear* on Stage"
    Kozintsev, interview
    Levidov, Michael, "Thought and Passion"
    Litovsky, O., "King Lear at Goset"
    Lijubomirsky, O., essay on Mikhoels

Mikhoels, Solomon, *Essays, Speeches and Articles*
———, "The King and the Fool"
———, "My Work on Shakespeare's *King Lear*"
Morozov, Mikhail, *Shakespeare on the Soviet Stage*
Nels, S., *Shakespeare on the Soviet Stage*
Van Gyseghem, Andre, *Theatre in Soviet Russia*
Jewish Daily Post, 1 April 1935
London *Times*, 10 September 1935
Time and Tide, 21 September 1935
NORWAY, Norwegian National Theatre, Spring, 1971.
   Directed by Jan Bull. Reports by Ingrid Dahl
OLIVIER, Sir Laurence, b. 1907
   Barker, Felix, *The Oliviers*
   Knight, G. Wilson, *Principles of Shakespearean Production*
   Trewin, J. C., *Shakespeare on the English Stage 1900–1964*
   Williamson, Audrey, *Old Vic Drama*
   Arts, 6 December 1946
   Carrefour, 5 December 1946
   Daily Express, 25 September 1946, 24 February 1953
   Daily Telegraph, 25 September 1946
   Evening News, 25 September 1946, 24 February 1953
   Le Figaro, 27 November 1946
   London Times, 26 September 1946
   Manchester Guardian, September 1946
   Masque, 1946, p. 14
   Le Monde, 28 November 1946
   New Statesman and Nation, 5 October 1946
   New York Times, 25 September 1946
   Les Nouvelles Littéraires Artistiques et Scientifiques, 5 December 1946
   Observer, 23 September 1946, 21 October 1953, 29 August 1950, 1 March
      1953
   Le Populaire, 28 November 1946
   Punch, 9 October 1946
   The Queen, 16 October 1946
   Scotsman, 26 September 1946
   Shakespeare Newsletter, 5 October 1951
   Shakespeare Survey, 1948, p. 98
   Sketch, 16 October 1946
   Spectator, 27 September 1946
   Stage, 26 September 1946
   Sunday Times, 29 September 1946
   Tatler, 9 October 1946, 29 October 1946
   The Theatre, 27 September 1946
   Theatre Arts, December 1946
PHELPS, Samuel, 1804–1878
   Morley, H., *The Journal of a London Playgoer*
   Phelps, W. May and Forbes-Robertson, John, *The Life and Lifework of
      Samuel Phelps*
   Promptbooks

Sprague, Arthur Colby, *Shakespeare and the Actors*
————, *Shakespearian Players and Performances*
Wingate, Charles, *Shakespeare's Heroes on the Stage*
Winter, William, *Shakespeare on the Stage*
Athenaeum, 1 April 1848
Court Journal, 8 November 1845
Miscellaneous clippings, unidentified
POLAND Warsaw, Warsawa Teatr Polski, March 1962
Nowa Kultura
Trybuna Ludu
Zycie Warszawy
Got, Jerzy, letter
POLAND, Warsaw, January 1970
Teatr, 1970, No. 5
Got, Jerzy, letter
PORTER, Eric Richard, b. 1928 Stratford-upon-Avon, Summer 1968, Trevor
Nunn, director
Porter, Eric, interview (Lear)
Williams, Michael, interview (Fool)
Howard, Alan, interview (Edgar)
Birmingham Mail, 14 April 1968
Birmingham Post, 14 April 1968, 20 April 1968, 11 April 1968
Daily Express, 11 April 1968
Daily Mail, 11 April 1968
Daily Telegraph, 11 April 1968
Evening News, 11 April 1968
Evening Standard, 11 April 1968
Financial Times, 16 April 1968
Glasgow Herald, 13 April 1968
Guardian, 11 April 1968
Illustrated London News, 27 April 1968
Leamington Spa Courier, 19 April 1968
London Times, 11 April 1968
Morning Advertiser, 7 July 1968
Morning Star, 13 April 1968
New Statesman and Nation, 19 April 1968
Nottingham Evening Post, 11 April 1968
Overland Monthly, 11 April 1968
Oxford Mail, 11 April 1968
Plays and Players, June 1968
Punch, 24 April 1968
South Wales Argus, 11 April 1968
Spectator, 19 April 1968
Stage, 18 April 1968
Stage and TV Today, 18 April 1968
Stratford-upon-Avon Herald, 3 May 1968
Sunday Observer, 18 April 1968
Sunday Telegraph, 7 April 1968, 14 April 1968
Sunday Times, 14 April 1968

Tablet, 29 June 1968
Woverhampton Express and Star, 11 April 1968, 13 April 1968
PRUCHA, Jaroslav, 1893–1963 (Czechoslavakian)
  Divadlo, IX, 1958
  Hodek, Brett, letter
REDGRAVE, Michael, b. 1908
  Webster, Margaret, *Shakespeare Today*
  Promptbook
  Birmingham Gazette, 15 July 1953, 30 July 1953
  Birmingham Mail, 15 July 1953, 17 July 1953
  Birmingham Post, 29 July 1953, 14 September 1953, 22 September 1953, 9
    October 1953
  Bolton Evening News, 18 July 1953
  Coventry Evening Telegraph, 19 July 1953
  Coventry Standard, 17 July 1953
  Daily Mail, 15 July 1953, 16 July 1953
  Daily Telegraph, 15 July 1953, 17 July 1953
  Daily Worker, 15 July 1953
  Evening News, 30 July 1953
  Evening Standard, 17 July 1953, 30 July 1953
  Gloucester Journal, 15 August 1953
  Liverpool Daily Post, 16 July 1953
  London Times, 15 July 1953, 24 July 1953
  London Tribune, 24 July 1953
  Manchester Guardian, 16 July 1953
  New Statesman and Nation, 25 July 1953
  Nottingham Guardian, 16 July 1953
  Punch, 29 July 1953
  Royal Leamington Spa Courier, 17 July 1953
  Saturday Review, 26 September 1961
  Solihull and Warwick County News, 18 July 1953
  Spectator, 19 September 1953, 4 December 1953, 30 October 1953
  Stage, 16 July 1953
  Stratford-upon-Avon Herald, 17 July 1953
  Sunday Observer, 17 July 1953, 19 July 1953
  Sunday Times, 19 July 1953
  Tablet, 22 August 1953
  Time and Tide, 25 July 1953, 22 August 1953
  Warwickshire Advertiser, 17 July 1953
ROSSI, Ernesto, 1829–1896
  Knight, Joseph, *Theatrical Notes*
  Poel, William, *Shakespeare in the Theatre*
  Wingate, Charles, *Shakespeare's Heroes on the Stage*
  Winter, William, *Shakespeare on the Stage*
  Academy, 6 May 1876, 16 May 1876
  Athenaeum, 17 June 1882, 13 May 1876, 15 May 1876
  Daily News, 6 May 1876, 13 June 1882
  Daily Telegraph, 5 May 1876
  Era, 5 May 1876, 7 May 1876, 17 June 1882

Illustrated London News, 17 June 1882
Illustrated Sporting and Dramatic News, 15 May 1876, 17 June 1882
London Figaro, 10 May 1876
Morning Post, 5 May 1876
Observer, 7 May 1876
Pall Mall Gazette, 9 May 1876
Referee, 18 June 1882
Saturday Review, 20 May 1876
Standard, 18 May 1876
ROUMANIA Bucharest, November 1970
Contemporanul, 6 November 1970
Letter, Michael Bogdan
Letter, Gabriel Pleşea
SALVINI, Tommaso, 1829–1915 (Italian)
Chapman, J. J., *A Glance Toward Shakespeare*
Furness, Horace H., *A New Variorum Edition of Shakespeare: King Lear*
James, Henry, *The Scenic Art*
Sprague, Arthur Colby, *Shakespeare and the Actors*
Towse, John Rankin, *Sixty Years of the Theatre*
Wingate, Charles, *Shakespeare's Heroes on the Stage*
Winter, William, *Shadows of the Stage*
————, *Shakespeare on the Stage*
Athenaeum, 8 March 1884
Boston Evening Transcript, 13 January 1883, 3 December 1884, 9 December 1885, 2 September 1887
Boston Herald, 7 January 1883
Boston Weekly Transcript, 16 January 1887
Century, March 1883, February 1884
Critic, 17 February 1883
Daily News, 3 March 1884
Daily Telegraph, 3 March 1884, 1 December 1892
Edinburgh Evening News, 11 April 1884
Era, 8 March 1884
Evening News, 3 March 1884
Globe, 3 March 1884
Illustrated London News, 15 March 1884
Illustrated Sporting and Dramatic News, 8 March 1884
Ladies Pictorial, 8 March 1884
London Figaro, 8 March 1884
London Times, 3 March 1884
Morning Advertiser, 18 January 1883
Morning Post, 3 March 1884
New York Evening Post, 29 October 1885
New York Herald, 9 February 1883
New York Times, 9 February 1883, 22 February 1883, 17 December 1883, 29 October 1885, 9 February 1886
Nottingham Evening Post, 29 October 1885
Observer, 2 March 1884
Pall Mall Gazette, 3 March 1884

Putnam's Monthly, January 1908
Referee, 2 March 1884
Saturday Review, 8 March 1884
Scotsman, 11 April 1884
Shakespeariana, November 1883
Standard, 3 March 1884
Theatre, 1 December 1883, 1 December 1892
Times Philadelphia, 18 January 1883
Toledo Blade, 18 January 1883
Vanity Fair, 8 March 1884
Washington Post, 29 November 1885
The World, 5 March 1884
SCHILDKRAUT, Rudolf, 1862–1930 (German)
    Drews, Wolfgang, *König Lear auf der deutschen Bühne bis zur Gegenwart*
    Shakespeare-Jahrbuch, XLV, 260–1
    Berliner Tageblatt, 2 February 1914
    Preussische Jahrbücher, 1908
SCHROEDER, Friedrich Ludwig, 1744–1816 (German)
    Drews, Wolfgang, *König Lear auf der deutschen Bühne bis zur Gegenwart*
    Stael-Holstein, Anne, *Germany*
SCOFIELD, Paul, b. 1922 (Peter Brook, director)
    Hankiss, Elemer, letter
    Kermode, Frank, "Lear at Lincoln Center"
    MacGowran, Jack, interview
    Merchant, W. Moelwyn, "Shakespeare's Theology"
    Murray, Brian, interview
    Scofield, Paul, interview
    Zingerman, B., "Shakespeare's Theatre in Moscow"
    America, 20 June 1964
    Arts, 8 May 1963
    Birmingham Post, 7 November 1962, 11 April 1968
    Borba, 7 March 1964
    Daily Mail, 7 November 1962
    Daily News, 19 May 1964
    Guardian, 20 December 1962
    Illustrated London News, 17 November 1962
    Journal American, 19 May 1964
    Listener, 1 March 1963
    London Times, 13 December 1962, 8 April 1963
    The Nation, 26 January 1963
    National Review, 13 June 1964
    New Statesman, 16 November 1962, 21 December 1962
    Newsweek, 1 January 1964, 1 June 1964
    New York Herald Tribune, 19 May 1964
    New York Post, 19 May 1964
    New York Times, 17 May 1964, 19 May 1964, 28 July 1964
    New York World Telegram, 19 May 1964
    Observer, 11 November 1962, 16 December 1962
    Oxford Mail, 7 November 1962

Plays and Players, January 1963
Politika, 6 March 1964
Punch, October 1964
The Queen, 27 January 1962
Reporter, 14 March 1963
Saturday Review, 8 December 1962, 23 May 1964
Scene, 15 November 1962
Shakespeare Quarterly, Autumn 1961
South Wales Evening Argus, 6 November 1962
Spectator, 16 November 1962
Stage, 16 April 1964
Stage and TV Today, 20 December 1962
Stratford-upon-Avon Herald, 23 November 1962
Sunday Telegraph, 11 November 1962
Sunday Times, 16 December 1962, 11 November 1962
Theatre Arts, December 1962, January 1963
Theatrical World, December 1962
Theatrical Journal, October 1967
Washington Post, 24 April 1964
SOFAER, Abraham, b. 1896
  Landstone, Charles, "Four Lears"
  Promptbook
  Birmingham Post, 3 May 1943
  Stratford-upon-Avon Herald, 7 May 1943
SONNENTHAL, Adolf, 1834–1909 (German)
  Drews, Wolfgang, *König Lear auf der deutschen Bühne bis zur Gegenwart*
  Letter, Boetzkes
STAMATOV, Georgi, 1893–1965 (Bulgarian)
  Literaturen Front, 23 April 1959
  Letter, Mincoff
SWEDEN
  Letters, Nigel Rollison
  August Lindberg, 1946–1916. Actor and director, December 1906
    Svenska Dagbladet
    Dagens Nyheter
    Stockholms Dagblad
  Karl Mantzius, Stockholm, 1907
    Svenska Dagbladet, 20, 25 March 1907
  Lars Hanson, 1886–1965, Stockholm, February–March 1921, directed by
    Per Lindberg
    Göteborgs-Posten
    Svenska Dagbladet
  Lars Hanson, 6 December 1929, directed by Per Lindberg
    Svenska Dagbladet
    Göteborgs Handels Tidning
    Aftonbladet
    F. D. P.
    N. D.A.
    Dagens Nyheter

Sydsvenska Dagbladet
Göteborgs-Posten
Uppsala Nya Tidning
Rune Turesson, b. 1921, Gothenburg, April 1970, directed by Ingve Nord-
vall
Aftonbladet
Göteborg Handels Tidning
Svenska Dagbladet
Expressen
Dagens Nyheter
Jan-Olof Strandberg, b. 1926, Uppsala, January 1971, directed by Anita
Blom
Uppsala Nya Tidning
Personal interview with Anita Blom by Nigel Rollison
TRANDAFILOV, Vladimir, b. 1891 (Bulgarian)
Literaturen Front, 23 April 1959
Letter, Mincoff
VANDENHOFF, George, 1790–1861
Edinburgh Dramatic Review, April 1824
WELLES, Orson, b. 1915
Wadsworth, Frank W., " 'Sound and Fury'–*King Lear* in Television"
Commonweal, February 1963
Journal American, 13 January 1956
London Times, 18 February 1956
New York Herald Tribune, 10 January 1956, 13 January 1956, 23 January
1956
New York Times, 13 January 1956
Saturday Review, 21 January 1956, 28 January 1956
WEST, Timothy, b. 1934 (Edinburgh Festival, 1971)
Birmingham Post, 29 August 1971
Cambridge News, 24 August, 2 November 1971
Daily Telegraph, 26 August 1971
Eastern Evening News (Norwich), 22 September 1971
Edinburgh Evening News, 24 August 1971
Financial Times, 26 August 1971
Glasgow Evening Citizen, 12 October 1971
Glasgow Herald, 28 August 1971
New Statesman, 23 September 1971
Scotsman, 23 August, 25 August, 28 August, 13 October 1971
The Stage, 26 August 1971
Yorkshire Post, 31 August, 17 September 1971
WOLFIT, Sir Donald, 1902–1968
Interview
Agate, James, *The Contemporary Theatre*, 1944 and 1945
Trewin, J. C., *Shakespeare on the English Stage*
Wolfit, Donald, *Introduction to King Lear*
Birmingham Gazette, 24 November 1942, 27 January 1943, 11 September
1945

Birmingham Mail, 24 November 1942, 11 September 1945, 23 September
   1947
Birmingham Post, 24 September 1942, 11 September 1945
Daily Express, 24 February 1953
Daily Mail, 24 February 1953
Evening Dispatch, 11 September 1945
Evening News, 24 February 1953
Evening Standard, 5 April 1944
London Times, 26 January 1943, 12 April 1944, 8 March 1949
Manchester Evening News, 6 October 1942
National Review, 3 March 1947
Observer, 13 January 1943
Punch, 3 February 1943
Spectator, 30 October 1953
Stage, 26 February 1953
ZAKARIADZE, Serge Alexandrovic, 1909–1971 (Russian)
   Letters, Kiasashivli

Index